D1765124

E UNIVE
NCHE

WITHDRAWN FROM
THE LIBRARY

UNIVERSITY OF
WINCHESTER

KA 0430773 9

EVIDENTIAL UNCERTAINTY IN CAUSATION IN NEGLIGENCE

This book undertakes an analysis of academic and judicial responses to the problem of evidential uncertainty in causation in negligence. It seeks to bring clarity to what has become a notoriously complex area by adopting a clear approach to the function of the doctrine of causation within a corrective justice-based account of negligence liability. It first explores basic causal models and issues of proof, including the role of statistical and epidemiological evidence, in order to isolate the problem of evidential uncertainty more precisely. Application of Richard Wright's NESS test to a range of English case law shows it to be more comprehensive than the 'but for' test that currently dominates, thereby reducing the need to resort to additional tests, such as the *Wardlaw* test of material contribution to harm, the scope and meaning of which are uncertain. The book builds on this foundation to explore the solution to a range of problems of evidential uncertainty, focusing on the *Fairchild* principle and the idea of risk as damage, as well as the notion of loss of a chance in medical negligence which is often seen as analogous with 'increase in risk', in an attempt to bring coherence to this area of the law.

Volume 15 in the series Hart Studies in Private Law

Evidential Uncertainty in Causation in Negligence

Gemma Turton

·HART·
PUBLISHING

OXFORD AND PORTLAND, OREGON

2016

UNIVERSITY OF WINCHESTER
LIBRARY

Published in the United Kingdom by Hart Publishing Ltd
16C Worcester Place, Oxford, OX1 2JW
Telephone: +44 (0)1865 517530
Fax: +44 (0)1865 510710
E-mail: mail@hartpub.co.uk
Website: http://www.hartpub.co.uk

Published in North America (US and Canada) by
Hart Publishing
c/o International Specialized Book Services
920 NE 58th Avenue, Suite 300
Portland, OR 97213-3786
USA
Tel: +1 503 287 3093 or toll-free: (1) 800 944 6190
Fax: +1 503 280 8832
E-mail: orders@isbs.com
Website: http://www.isbs.com

© Gemma Turton 2016

Gemma Turton has asserted her right under the Copyright, Designs and Patents Act 1988, to be
identified as the author of this work.

Hart Publishing is an imprint of Bloomsbury Publishing plc.

All rights reserved. No part of this publication may be reproduced, stored in a retrieval system,
or transmitted, in any form or by any means, without the prior permission of Hart Publishing,
or as expressly permitted by law or under the terms agreed with the appropriate reprographic
rights organisation. Enquiries concerning reproduction which may not be covered by
the above should be addressed to Hart Publishing Ltd at the address above.

British Library Cataloguing in Publication Data
Data Available

Library of Congress Cataloging-in-Publication Data

Names: Turton, Gemma, author.

Title: Evidential uncertainty in causation in negligence / Gemma Turton.

Description: Oxford ; Portland, Oregon : Hart Publishing Ltd, 2016. | Series: Hart studies
in private law ; volume 15 | Based on author's thesis (doctoral—University of
Birmingham, 2013) issued under title: A critical analysis of the current approach
of the courts and academics to the problem of evidential uncertainty in causation
in tort law. | Includes bibliographical references and index.

Identifiers: LCCN 2015049497 (print) | LCCN 2015049637 (ebook) |
ISBN 9781849467049 (hardback : alk. paper) | ISBN 9781509900336 (Epub)

Subjects: LCSH: Proximate cause (Law) | Proximate cause (Law)—England. |
Wright, Richard W. (Law professor)

Classification: LCC K940.T87 2016 (print) | LCC K940 (ebook) | DDC 346.03/2—dc23

LC record available at http://lccn.loc.gov/2015049497

ISBN: 978-1-84946-704-9

Typeset by Compuscript Ltd, Shannon
Printed and bound in Great Britain by
CPI Group (UK) Ltd, Croydon CR0 4YY

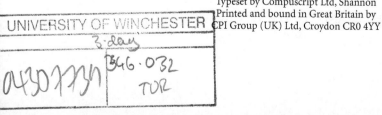
UNIVERSITY OF WINCHESTER
3-day
04307734 346.032
TUR

ACKNOWLEDGEMENTS

As a final year undergraduate studying tort law in 2003–4, the *Fairchild* decision was recent and controversial and it ignited my interest in causation, although I had little sense at the time of the full impact it would have on the law of negligence or on my academic career. My tort law lecturer was Sarah Green, and I am thankful to her for encouraging my interest. Since then the law on causation has continued to develop rapidly so while the writing of this book has sometimes felt like a potentially never-ending task, it has remained intellectually stimulating and a fascinating subject.

This book started life as my doctoral thesis and I owe a huge debt of gratitude to my supervisor, Claire McIvor, for all her help and support throughout both the writing of my thesis and its development into this book. She has been as much of a mentor and indeed friend to me as she has supervisor, and I am grateful.

Thanks are also due to my examiners, Donal Nolan and Ken Oliphant, whose thought-provoking questions have helped shape the development of this book and made its arguments more robust.

I am grateful to the University of Birmingham for giving me the postgraduate teaching assistantship that made my PhD financially possible, and to the University of Leicester for giving me a period of study leave during which I was able to complete my thesis. I have been fortunate to present papers on aspects of this research, which helped shape my ideas, and particular thanks are due to seminar organisers at the universities of Birmingham, Leicester and Oxford. I would like to thank James Lee, John Hartshorne, Jose Miola, Tracey Elliott and Alex Broadbent, for reading sections of this book and giving me invaluable feedback. Further thanks go to the production team at Hart Publishing, and in particular Bill Asquith, for their support in bringing the book to fruition.

A number of my friends have been incredibly supportive (and patient), especially Martin George, Laura Stack, Sophie Boyron, Sally Kyd, Troy Lavers and Carla Crifo. I owe great thanks to my parents for their encouragement. Most of all, I would like to thank my sister, Samantha, for her support throughout the years; without her this would not have been possible and I dedicate the book to her.

CONTENTS

Introduction

It has been said that '[t]o insist on a causal connection between conduct ensures that in general we impose liability only on those who, by intervening in the world, have changed the course of events for the worse'.[1] The factual causation requirement is therefore an essential ingredient of negligence liability, yet in recent years the approaches of courts and academics to the doctrine of causation have become increasingly complicated and confused. The landscape of causation in negligence is now characterised by tests and exceptional approaches whose meaning and scope are unclear. The primary aim of this work is to identify a coherent legal response to a number of the evidential problems that underlie these exceptional approaches.

In order to identify a coherent solution to problems of evidentiary uncertainty it will first be necessary to situate the issue within the broader context of causation in negligence more generally. This will involve addressing both the nature and function of the tort of negligence as well as the role played by causation within that tort. The work will therefore begin by outlining the theoretical framework underpinning negligence liability. In chapter one, it will be argued that negligence is best understood in terms of corrective justice-based interpersonal responsibility because this provides an account of negligence that prioritises coherence and morality in the law. Accounts of corrective justice vary, so this chapter outlines a preferred account. Indeed a recurring theme in this work is that a significant source of the confusion surrounding causation is that terminology is not used consistently and those inconsistencies are not always acknowledged, so since this work subscribes to corrective justice it is essential to indicate what 'corrective justice' is taken to mean. The analysis of causation in this book, of course, pursues an approach based in corrective justice; but, whether you subscribe to that approach or not, the remainder of the book has value regardless.

Chapter two then turns to the concept of causation and the demands that the law places on a test for causation. Since causation is pivotal to interpersonal responsibility it is important that the legal approach to causation is premised on a philosophically sound account of the concept of causation. In this chapter it will be argued that Wright's NESS test more accurately translates the philosophical account of causation into a workable test than the but-for test that currently

---

[1] Tony Honoré, *Responsibility and Fault* (Hart Publishing, 1999) 120.

dominates judicial approaches to causation. In the majority of negligence cases where causation is relatively straightforward, the NESS test is no more complicated to apply than the but-for test, but in the small number of cases where the causal problem is more complex the NESS test is able to identify causes where the but-for test fails.

It will be demonstrated that, under NESS, it is essential to define the damage that forms the gist of the negligence action, and that the causal problem will vary depending on whether the harmful outcome is 'divisible', ie dose-related, or 'indivisible' ('all-or-nothing'). Chapter two will also evaluate the *Wardlaw* test of 'material contribution to harm'.[2] It is currently unclear when and why this test applies, and therefore it is unclear whether it is an exception to the but-for test and/or to the causation requirement. Using the NESS analysis it will be shown that the *Wardlaw* test seems to address a wide range of causal problems: where damage is divisible it equates to an application of the but-for test to a portion of the harm, where damage is indivisible it is often an exception to the but-for test but not an exception to the causation requirement. In these circumstances the *Wardlaw* test compensates for the conceptual inadequacies of the but-for test. This has important consequences for the approach to evidentiary uncertainty. The NESS test will enable us to see that cases where the *Wardlaw* test is applied are not really problematic, nor are they exceptional. Since the *Wardlaw* test is not exceptional, it cannot be used as a stepping-stone towards the adoption of exceptional solutions to problems of evidential uncertainty as happened in *McGhee*.

Having addressed the conceptual aspects of causation in chapter two, the remaining chapters turn towards evidential problems. Chapter three addresses general issues of proof of causation and seeks to reconcile legal and scientific approaches and standards of proof. The aim is to enable courts to make full use of the evidence available before considering resorting to exceptional approaches. This chapter therefore considers how evidence can be used to satisfy an orthodox test for causation, and begins by examining what the balance of probabilities standard of proof actually entails. Problems of proof arise in particular in cases involving injuries or diseases whose aetiology is not well understood since resort must then be made to scientific evidence that is explicitly probabilistic in nature. On the one hand there is a perception that scientific standards of proof are higher than the civil law standard and a consequent concern, expressed by Lord Phillips in *Sienkiewicz*, that scientific experts may not be particularly helpful to a court where there is scientific uncertainty.[3] At the same time there is judicial scepticism concerning some scientific disciplines, most notably epidemiology. In this chapter, epidemiology is used as a lens through which to view some broad points about the interaction of law and science, as well as narrower points that are specific to negligence and epidemiology. It also examines the emerging 'doubles the risk' test that is increasingly applied to probabilistic evidence.

---

[2] *Bonnington Castings v Wardlaw* [1956] AC 613 (HL).
[3] *Sienkiewicz v Greif* [2011] UKSC 10, [2011] 2 AC 229, [9].

Chapter four considers the so-called 'loss of a chance' argument that was raised by the claimants in *Hotson*[4] and in *Gregg*.[5] These claims arose in the context of medical negligence resulting in a delay in the diagnosis and treatment of patients who were already unwell. Since the patients' prospects were poor at the time of the negligence, they faced difficulty in proving that the negligent delay in diagnosis had caused them to suffer physical harm. Instead they sought to redefine the damage forming the gist of the action as the loss of a chance of avoiding physical harm. Although this argument centres on the definition of the relevant damage, its inclusion in this work is important for a number of reasons. The claimant's attempt to redefine the damage was motivated because of difficulties of proving a causal link between the negligence and the physical harm, and one of the recurring issues addressed in this work is the relationship between the doctrines of damage and causation. It is also essential to understand and evaluate the loss of a chance argument because 'loss of a chance of avoiding harm' is often considered to be the equivalent of 'a material increase in the risk of harm' which is contained in the *McGhee/Fairchild* exception in cases of evidential uncertainty.

In chapter five, the discussion turns to an analysis of the approaches taken by courts and academics to the problem of the 'evidentiary gap' that arose in *McGhee* and in *Fairchild*, drawing together the themes running through the previous chapters. It begins by evaluating the evidence relating to the diseases in *McGhee* and in *Fairchild* in order to understand more precisely what the 'evidentiary gap' consists of. The NESS account of causation developed in chapter two enables the 'evidentiary gap' to be defined with greater clarity than under the but-for test. The chapter then engages with the *McGhee/Fairchild* test of 'material increase in the risk of harm' as a test of sufficient causal connection.

One interpretation of *McGhee* is that the Court had simply taken a 'robust' view of the available evidence, drawing an inference that the negligence had materially contributed to the harm from the fact that it had materially increased the risk of that harm. It will be argued that the nature of the evidentiary gap means that it is simply not possible to draw a rational inference of causation, so this interpretation rests on a fiction.

Following *Fairchild*, the Court in *Barker* apportioned liability according to the defendant's contribution to the total risk to which the claimant was exposed, and Lord Hoffmann rationalised this on the basis that because the claimant was only able to prove that the defendant had materially increased the risk of harm, it was the risk of harm rather than the harm itself that constituted the gist of the negligence action.[6] Chapter five analyses the notion of risk in order to determine whether risk can, and did, form the gist of the negligence action in that case. Ultimately it will be argued that if risk exposure was the damage forming the gist of the action, the damage requirement would be subsumed into the breach inquiry

---

[4] *Hotson v East Berkshire Health Authority* [1987] AC 750 (HL).

[5] *Gregg v Scott* [2005] UKHL 2, [2005] 2 AC 176.

[6] *Barker v Corus (UK) plc* [2006] UKHL 20, [2006] 2 AC 572, [35] (Lord Hoffmann).

which asks whether the defendant exposed the claimant to an unreasonable risk of harm. This means that liability would be based solely on the careless conduct of the defendant so liability would be based on a retributive form of justice rather than on corrective justice.

Concluding that a causal link between the negligence and the physical harm cannot be proved in cases involving an evidentiary gap, the chapter will finally consider the arguments that liability should nonetheless be imposed because of policy arguments relating to the perceived need to compensate the victims of mesothelioma. This section will draw on the exposition of the theoretical foundations of negligence from chapter one in order to evaluate the policy concerns and arguments as to the 'demands of justice'.

Therefore while this work takes the analysis of the responses to evidential uncertainty as its ultimate objective, its contribution to the study of causation extends beyond that problem. It seeks to enhance the understanding of the basic tests of causation and to add clarity to the relationship between the causation requirement and the other negligence doctrines, especially the notions of damage and quantification. The arguments that are made in relation to evidentiary uncertainty are part of an overarching vision of negligence liability and the place of causation within negligence law, so it makes insights into evidentiary problems that might otherwise be lost, and gives these arguments a much stronger foundation. Much of the confusion surrounding causation arises from courts and academics discussing problems of causation too much in isolation and without giving sufficient weight to the theoretical and doctrinal framework of the negligence enquiry. This work seeks to show that while causation is a complex field, it need not be confusing.

1

Theoretical and Doctrinal Framework

The law on causation in negligence is in a confused state and the objective of this work is to adopt an approach to causation that is not only internally coherent but that also maintains a coherent relationship with negligence law as a whole. It is therefore essential to have a clear understanding of the theoretical basis of the tort of negligence. In light of the concern for coherence this work subscribes to a corrective justice-based theory which, it is argued, provides coherence that cannot be achieved by instrumentalist theories of negligence. When exceptional approaches to causation are proposed they are often based on functionalist arguments such as the need to compensate the claimant or to achieve an economically efficient solution. It will be argued that since such theories cannot provide a coherent basis for negligence it is inappropriate to invoke them in difficult cases of causation.

The purpose of the first part of this chapter is, therefore, to set out the corrective justice-based theory that underpins this approach to causation in negligence. Since accounts of corrective justice vary, the aim is to identify the key features and requirements of corrective justice, and the place that causation occupies within it. It will be argued that corrective justice provides the most appropriate theoretical justification for the tort of negligence because the bipolar structure of the negligence action reflects the bipolarity of corrective justice and prevents the attainment of instrumentalist conceptions which are distributive, and therefore multi-polar, in nature. As such the interpersonal morality encapsulated by corrective justice ought to be reflected in the interpersonal responsibility enforced through negligence. However, the strict formalism that is characteristic of Weinrib's approach to corrective justice is arguably divorced from the practical and realistic need to take account of how liability decisions impact on wider society.[1] It would be inappropriate to insist on giving effect to interpersonal responsibility through negligence liability where this would have disproportionately adverse effects on community welfare. As Robertson explains, '[i]n the absence of adequate justification on the basis of [corrective] justice considerations, a duty cannot be imposed in the public interest, however strong the community welfare justifications'. But, as he adds, 'a duty can be denied in the public interest, however strongly considerations of [corrective] justice favour the recognition of a duty'.[2]

---

[1] Peter Cane, 'Tort Law as Regulation' (2002) 31 *Common Law World Review* 305, 310.
[2] Andrew Robertson, 'On the Function of the Law of Negligence' (2013) 33 *Oxford Journal of Legal Studies* 31, 36.

The second source of strain that is placed on the doctrine of causation in exceptional cases is that the causation requirement is used to address issues that are not really causal and ought to be addressed by the other negligence doctrines. The chapter will therefore consider how the theory of corrective justice is translated into concrete legal rules through the various doctrines of the tort of negligence. It will be seen that factual causation plays a vital but limited role in corrective justice-based liability, and that it is important to reflect this in the legal rules relating to causation. Most importantly, non-causal issues relating to the concept of responsibility must be addressed through the other doctrines. Isolating the role of causation within responsibility in this way will help to clarify the causal issues in particular cases. Chapter two will turn to the question of 'what causation is', but first this chapter is concerned with identifying what causation 'is not', in other words with identifying those aspects of responsibility that are not causal and showing how they are addressed by the other doctrines.

I. The Theoretical Basis of Negligence

It is important to note at the outset that the focus is on the tort of negligence so it is beyond the scope of this work to address the theoretical foundations of tort law or private law more generally. This section sets out to signal why corrective justice is the preferred foundation for negligence law and the place of distributive or consequentialist concerns.

A. Prioritising Coherence

Interpretive legal theories are often evaluated against the four criteria enumerated by Smith: fit, transparency, coherence and morality.[3] Indeed, it has been said that '[a]lthough "interpretivism" is sometimes treated as a particular camp within private law scholarship, Stephen Smith's statement of interpretive legal theory describes what is really an orthodox and widely followed approach to legal analysis'.[4] It should therefore be uncontroversial to refer to these criteria to assess the theories encountered in this chapter. Robertson has helpfully summarised them as follows:

> Those four limbs are: *fit* (the extent to which the theory is consistent with the outcomes of cases and possibly also the accepted rules of the given body of law), *coherence* (the extent to which the theory reveals an intelligible order in the given body of law and allows it and related bodies of law to be understood as a unified system), *transparency*

[3] Stephen A Smith, *Contract Theory* (Clarendon Press, 2004) 7–32.
[4] Andrew Robertson, 'Rights, Pluralism and the Duty of Care' in Donal Nolan and Andrew Robertson (eds), *Rights and Private Law* (Hart Publishing, 2011) 438.

(the extent to which the theory is consistent with the explanation given by lawmakers, which in the case of interpreting the common law means the explanations given by judges in the cases), and *morality* ('how the law might be thought to be justified even if it is not justified').[5]

Robertson continues to explain how these criteria are used:

> The two most significant points of difference between scholars in the application of the interpretive method relate to the weight to be attributed to each of the four elements and the kinds of normative criteria that occupy the place of 'morality' in the framework ... Different explanations will score better on different elements. A scholar must therefore make a choice as to which of the criteria should be weighted more heavily.[6]

The reason for preferring corrective justice over pluralist theories is that coherence ought to be prioritised and, as a monistic theory, corrective justice scores highly for coherence whereas pluralist approaches are necessarily weak in this respect. Furthermore it will be argued that a monistic theory based on an instrumentalist goal such as economic efficiency is also lacking in coherence and moral force. As Wright has explained, coherence is important because without it the law would be indeterminate:

> [W]hen in a particular situation two or more of the pluralistic norms conflict—which usually will be the case—the theory will be normatively, descriptively and analytically arbitrary and indeterminate in terms of specifying which competing norm(s) should predominate, unless there is some foundational norm that can resolve conflicts between the competing subnorms. Yet if such a foundational norm exists, the theory at its deepest level is monistic rather than pluralistic.[7]

Given that coherence is valued to such an extent, it is important to understand more precisely what coherence entails. Wright continues:

> This is not to say that any single norm, no matter how fundamental, can explain and justify *every* aspect of the law in general, or any particular area of law ... But a successful normative and descriptive theory of law should at least be able coherently to explain and justify the principal features of the existing law.[8]

Beever, whose corrective justice-based approach to negligence prioritises coherence, draws on Smith's work to identify two senses in which a theory can be described as coherent: weak coherence requires the law to be non-contradictory, strong coherence requires that the law 'can be understood as a unified system, perhaps under a single principle'.[9] This, he explains, rules out the notion of 'limited rationality' whereby one negligence doctrine such as duty of care could be based on one principle, and another negligence doctrine such as standard of care

---

[5] ibid 437–38. Referring to Smith, *Contract Theory* (n 3).

[6] ibid 438.

[7] Richard Wright, 'Right, Justice, and Tort Law' in David G Owen (ed), *Philosophical Foundations of Tort Law* (Oxford University Press, 1995) 160.

[8] ibid.

[9] Allan Beever, *Rediscovering the Law of Negligence* (Hart Publishing, 2009) 22.

could be based on a contradictory principle. Although each doctrine may display coherence within itself, the incompatibility of the underlying principles of each doctrine would prevent the tort of negligence from being coherent in either the strong or weak senses outlined above. This is important to the scope of this work which seeks to understand causation itself but does not treat causation in isolation from the rest of negligence law. Beever further argues that not only should the doctrines be compatible, ie display weak coherence, it is desirable that they should be based on a single unifying principle, ie strongly coherent:

> Because unity leads to greater coherence, and hence to a theory possessing greater explanatory power, other things being equal, a theory that provides a unified explanation of the law in the sense elucidated is preferable to one that does not. Unity may not be mandatory, but it is attractive.[10]

This work approaches causation from the basis of the Kantian-Aristotelian theory of corrective justice since it provides a strongly coherent account of negligence. The focus of this section of the chapter is to illustrate briefly what the theory consists of in order to provide a framework for evaluating exceptional approaches to causation. Later sections will then consider the implementation of this theory through the negligence system and through the doctrines of negligence law.

B. Corrective and Distributive Justice

Corrective and distributive justice were originally elaborated by Aristotle in the *Nicomachean Ethics*,[11] and the dominant corrective justice-based account of private law has been developed by Weinrib.[12] Aristotle's account is largely formalistic, addressing the different structures and forms of justice, and this formalism highlights the impossibility of achieving distributive justice through the bipolar structure of negligence law. Weinrib goes beyond formalistic arguments and explains that the correlative structure of corrective justice requires a similarly correlative account of wrongdoing. As such, the demands of corrective justice are reflected not only in the structure of the negligence action but ought also to be reflected in the rules of negligence law.

As Gardner explains, 'Norms of justice are moral norms of a distinctive type. They are norms for tackling *allocative* moral questions, questions about who is to get how much of what'.[13] Distributive justice is societal and addresses the

---

[10] ibid 23–24.

[11] Sarah Broadie and Christopher Rowe, *Aristotle: Nicomachean Ethics: Translation, Introduction and Commentary* (Oxford University Press, 2002). For ease of reference, citations will be made to chapter and line numbers from Aristotle's original text rather than to pages of this particular translation.

[12] Ernest Weinrib, *The Idea of Private Law* (Harvard University Press, 1995); *Corrective Justice* (Oxford University Press, 2012).

[13] John Gardner, 'What is Tort Law For? Part 1: The Place of Corrective Justice' (2011) 30 *Law and Philosophy* 1, 6.

distribution of goods among the members of a community according to merit but it does not entail any particular criterion of merit:

> [E]verybody agrees that what is just in distributions must accord with some kind of merit, but everybody is not talking about the same kind of merit: for democrats merit lies in being born a free person, for oligarchs in wealth or, for some of them, in noble descent, for aristocrats in excellence.[14]

Distributive justice is a multi-polar form of justice wherein limited resources are shared among members of a community according to a particular measure of merit. Distributive justice is not, therefore, an appeal to what the man on the Underground might consider fair.[15] It is a comparative exercise, so is closer in nature to Lord Hoffmann's concern in *White* 'to preserve the general perception of the law as system of rules which is fair *between one citizen and another*' (emphasis added),[16] although 'fairness' is inevitably still dependent on what criteria of distribution is prioritised.

In contrast, corrective justice is interpersonal and concerns the meaning of 'having one's share' in an interaction between two individuals. There is a corrective injustice when one person causes a wrongful loss to another and corrective justice requires the wrongdoer to repair that loss. The parties are regarded as being equal before their interaction, so corrective justice is achieved by repairing the wrongful loss that is caused. As Weinrib has explained, 'The parties do not have the same quantity of holdings, but they are equal as the owners of whatever they do have'.[17] The pre-transaction equality is an abstract equality of right to be free from injury, so the extent of the injury inflicted on another represents the extent to which the wrongdoer has taken more than she should. As Gordley has explained:

> By voluntarily harming the plaintiff, [the defendant] has chosen to use the plaintiff's resources for his own ends. The pre-existing equality that corrective justice seeks to restore is a state in which each party achieves his own goals out of his own resources.[18]

In practical terms the correction is made by requiring the injurer to repair the victim's loss and this is achieved through compensation because, as Aristotle explains, currency 'acts like a measure, making things commensurable'.[19]

In summary, the key features of corrective justice are that it addresses justice in interactions so it is bipolar, the two parties are treated as equal before the interaction which gives rise to a correlative gain and loss and necessitates a correction which is also correlative, ie the injustice can only be corrected by requiring the wrongdoer to repair the victim's loss. As a form of justice it correlates with the bipolar form of negligence liability, whereas distributive justice is multi-polar

---

[14] Broadie and Rowe, *Aristotle: Nicomachean Ethics* (n 11) V.3 1131a25-30.
[15] cf *White v Chief Constable of South Yorkshire* [1999] 2 AC 455 (HL), 495 (Lord Steyn).
[16] ibid 511.
[17] Ernest Weinrib, 'Corrective Justice' (1992) 77 *Iowa Law Review* 403, 408.
[18] James Gordley, 'Tort Law in the Aristotelian Tradition' in Owen (ed), *Philosophical Foundations of Tort Law* (n 7) 138.
[19] Broadie and Rowe (n 11) V.5 1133b16.

since it addresses justice across a community and thus requires a broad institution to implement the correct distribution across the community.[20]

C. The Moral Basis of Corrective Justice: Aristotelian Corrective Justice and Kantian Right

It is vital to understand that corrective justice is not merely a procedural require-ment; it is not 'an empty formalist shell'.[21] Beever argues:

> According to corrective justice theory, while corrective justice tells us how the injustice should be corrected, it must also be true that the injustice itself is interpersonal. That is, the structure of corrective justice must be reflected in the nature of the wrongdoing to which corrective justice responds.[22]

This means that corrective justice cannot accommodate an account of wrongdo-ing that is distributive, such as aggregate social welfare. Posner has proposed such an approach, arguing that corrective justice dictates form but not substance so the concept of wrongdoing must be sought outside Aristotle's corrective justice and can be based on aggregate social welfare.[23] The formalist reading of correc-tive justice shows, however, that this would lead to incoherence because liability would be based on a distributive premise. Strong coherence requires that the prin-ciple of corrective justice is reflected not only in the structure but also in the rules of negligence liability. England has explained, 'it has to be remembered that even from a strictly formalist conception, the difference in the formal structures implies

---

[20] It is important to signal these key features because not all 'corrective justice' theories of negligence actually reflect these characteristics. One of the primary problems for Coleman's 'annulment' theory was that it was not based on correlativity, and this led to him abandoning it in favour of a 'mixed conception' of corrective justice which also incorporates a relational approach. Coleman identified his annulment theory as being one of corrective justice because, for him, corrective justice required the annulment of wrongful gains and losses. The interpersonal character of corrective justice was not reflected, however, in Coleman's account where the victim's claim for compensation was based on wrongful loss and the imposition of liability on the defendant was based on wrongful gain, so the grounds of recovery were conceptually distinct from the grounds of liability. This violated the correla-tive character of corrective justice where the grounds of recovery are the same as the grounds of liability i.e. the loss and gain derive their 'wrongful' character from the same source. In his 'mixed conception' he incorporates a relational approach, explaining that the relational conception of 'wrong' explains why the wrongdoer and nobody else has a duty to repair the loss. His work will not be addressed in depth, however, because his approach is still not based on a single overarching principle as required for strong coherence since he takes a relational approach to explain the wrong, and an annulment approach to explain the loss. Jules Coleman, 'Corrective Justice and Wrongful Gain' (1982) 11 *Journal of Legal Studies* 421; Jules Coleman, 'The Mixed Conception of Corrective Justice' (1992) 77 *Iowa Law Review* 427.
[21] Wright, 'Right, Justice and Tort Law' (n 7) 170. Wright also criticises the 'formalist evisceration' of corrective justice: Richard Wright, 'Substantive Corrective Justice' (1992) 77 *Iowa Law Review* 625, 710.
[22] Allan Beever, 'Corrective Justice and Personal Responsibility in Tort Law' (2008) *Oxford Journal of Legal Studies* 475, 477.
[23] Richard Posner, 'The Concept of Corrective Justice in Recent Theories of Tort Law' (1981) 10 *Journal of Legal Studies* 187, 191–201.

some important consequences for the substances. Form and substance become linked through the idea of coherence'.[24] In contrast, Kantian Right, espoused by academics such as Weinrib and Wright, provides an understanding of wrongdoing that conforms to the requirement of correlativity. As Weinrib states, 'the Kantian interpretation fits readily into, and provides content for, corrective justice'.[25] Although the ideas of Aristotelian corrective justice and Kantian Right are not explicitly articulated by courts, 'they are implicit in [private law] as a coherent justificatory enterprise, in that they provide its unifying structure and its normative idea'.[26] Kantian Right thus provides the moral theory, or normative idea, underlying negligence.

Kant's theory belongs in the tradition of natural right and is based on the idea of free will. Free will, or freedom, is a characteristic possessed by every rational being and gives every rational being absolute and equal moral worth:

> [M]an regarded as a person, that is, as the subject of a morally practical reason, is exalted above any price; for as a person (*homo noumenon*) he is not to be valued merely as a means to the ends of others or even to his own ends, but as an end in himself, that is, he possesses a *dignity* (an absolute inner worth) by which he exacts *respect* for himself from all other rational beings in the world. He can measure himself with every other being of this kind and value himself on a footing of equality with them.[27]

Respect for the absolute and equal moral worth of everyone gives rise to the 'categorical imperative': 'act only according to that maxim by which you can, at the same time, will that it should become a universal law'.[28] This is similar to, but wider than, the Golden Rule that you should treat others as you wish to be treated yourself:

> It is morally wrong under the categorical imperative to fail to respect the absolute moral worth of anyone, including yourself, as a self-legislating rational being, regardless of whether you would allow others to treat you without proper respect.[29]

Whereas the Golden Rule allows you to treat others badly if you would be happy to be similarly treated yourself, the categorical imperative does not allow this because it demands respect for one's own moral worth. As Wright explains, '[t]he idea of freedom does not imply completely unrestricted self-determination, but rather self-legislation: self-determination according with universal law'.[30]

---

[24] Izhak Englard, *Corrective and Distributive Justice: From Aristotle to Modern Times* (Oxford University Press, 2009) 194.

[25] Weinrib, *The Idea of Private Law* (n 12) 19.

[26] ibid 19.

[27] Immanuel Kant, *The Metaphysics of Morals* (Mary Gregor trans, 1991) (1797) cited in Wright (n 7) 162.

[28] Kant, *Foundations of the Metaphysics of Morals* (trans Lewis White Beck) (Bobbs-Merrill Education Publishing, 1969) 44.

[29] Wright (n 7) 162–63.

[30] ibid 162.

This concept of equality, which is clearly distinct from quantitative assessments, clarifies the correlativity of the gain and loss in corrective justice:

> The relevant loss is the damage suffered by the plaintiff as a result of the defendant's failure to give him equal consideration … The defendant's gain is that he did not carry the burden of appropriate precautions as he implicated the plaintiff into the web of his own projects. And the notion of equality against which these gains and losses are measured is the Kantian prohibition against self-preference in action.[31]

Kantian Right has important implications for corrective justice because it provides an account of equality which is divorced from any assessment of the relative merits of the parties according to a criterion of merit, as well as being independent of the relative holdings of the parties prior to their interaction.

It therefore illuminates some of the features of corrective justice. In terms of wrongdoing, Wright says:

> Unlike distributive justice, corrective justice does not use interpersonal comparisons or rankings to implement a relative or proportional equality among the parties to the interaction … this means that all comparative criteria for determining unjust gains and losses in corrective justice—including utilitarian, efficiency, and all other aggregative criteria—are excluded from consideration. This is a powerful substantive implication from Aristotle's account.[32]

So Aristotelian corrective justice and Kantian Right together imply not only the form of the correction but also the nature of wrongdoing at its core.

D. Incoherence of Consequentialist Theories

Since corrective justice provides a coherent account of the form of negligence law and of the wrongdoing at its core, it is preferred over consequentialist accounts which are distributive in nature so cannot be achieved through the bipolar structure of a negligence action. Moreover, pluralist consequentialist theories, such as the idea that negligence pursues the twin goals of compensation of victims and deterrence of wrongdoers, suffer from 'a surfeit of reasons and norms,'[33] which pose artificial limits on one another. This means that if negligence doctrines, including exceptional approaches to causation, are developed in pursuit of consequentialist goals the law of negligence will become incoherent. Subsequent criticism of negligence law for being ineffective or inefficient as a system of compensation or deterrence stems from the fact that these are distributive goals so are necessarily precluded from being effectively achieved through the structure of negligence.

---

[31] Ernest Weinrib, 'Toward a Moral Theory of Negligence Law' (1983) 2 *Law & Philosophy* 37, 53.
[32] Wright, 'Substantive Corrective Justice' (n 21) 700–01.
[33] Wright, 'Right, Justice, and Tort Law' (n 7) 160.

Wright explains that compensation and deterrence cannot provide a sound basis for negligence law because 'compensation and deterrence of all losses is normatively insupportable, descriptively implausible, and analytically impossible'.[34] He goes on to explain that it is normatively insupportable because there is 'no plausible moral argument for requiring others to compensate every person for every loss no matter how it occurred'.[35] It is also impossible because compensation does not eradicate loss but shifts the loss to others, and because it is neither possible nor desirable to deter all risky conduct. The bipolar structure of negligence liability prevents each goal from being fully attained:

> The fundamental reason why these criteria are inconsistent with tort law's correlative structure is that there is no reason to limit the search for the deepest pocket, or the best loss-spreader, or the cheapest cost-avoider, to the two parties to the tort claim—the harm-doer and the harm-sufferer.[36]

Additionally the different distributive criteria impose artificial limits on one another:

> When juxtaposed within the tort relationship, compensation and deterrence are mutually truncating. What limits compensation is not the boundary to which its justificatory authority entitles it, but the competing presence of deterrence in the same legal relationship. Thus, tort law compensates victims only when damages serve the purpose of deterrence. In the same way, tort law artificially restricts deterrence by tying deterrence not to what is needed to deter wrongdoers, but to what is needed to compensate victims. In this mixing of justifications, neither goal occupies the entire area to which it applies. Accordingly, neither in fact functions as a justification.[37]

Perry objects that compensation and deterrence could be combined in a way that is not mutually truncating in a system such as compulsory first-party insurance where compensation would be achieved through insurance payouts and deterrence would be achieved through the setting of premium levels.[38] It is clear, however, that this example is premised on a different institutional structure, insurance, where a harm-sufferer would be compensated independently of the insurance premium imposed on the harm-doer. The structure is distributive and matched to the distributive functions it seeks to achieve. So although Perry may be right to assert that compensation and deterrence can be combined in a way that is not mutually truncating, it remains the case that this cannot be achieved through the negligence system which links the harm-sufferer to the harm-doer in a bipolar relationship.

This means that criticisms targeted at the inefficiency of negligence law as a system of compensation and/or deterrence ought to be directed at the normative

---

[34] ibid 159.

[35] ibid 159.

[36] Peter Cane, 'Distributive Justice and Tort Law' [2001] *New Zealand Law Review* 401, 419.

[37] Ernest Weinrib, 'The Jurisprudence of Legal Formalism' (1993) 16 *Harvard Journal of Law & Public Policy* 583, 587.

[38] Stephen R Perry, 'Professor Weinrib's Formalism: The Not-So-Empty Sepulchre' (1993) 16 *Harvard Journal of Law & Public Policy* 597, 614.

question of whether there ought to be a system of negligence liability. The significance of this choice is thrown into sharp relief by the concerns raised by Atiyah who made an important attack on negligence law as a system of compensation in *The Damages Lottery*. The need for financial support clearly extends beyond those injured by others' wrongdoing to those suffering due to an accident or natural causes. As a system for compensation based on need, the negligence system is obviously unjust:

> Of all the disabled or handicapped people in society about ten percent suffer from birth defects, about another ten percent have been injured in accidents, and the remaining eighty percent are suffering from illnesses and conditions of natural origin. Of the total number, only about one and a half percent apparently obtain any damages at all. How is this tiny group selected for preferential treatment?[39]

But this is a *distributive* injustice because it is giving preferential treatment to people injured through someone else's wrongdoing in a distributive model where the criterion of merit is need. The assertion is therefore that the negligence system introduces a second, unjustified criterion of merit according a special status to injury caused by wrongdoing and this has resulted in an unjust distribution of goods. Arguably Atiyah is criticising negligence unfairly because a system that takes the form of corrective justice cannot be expected to achieve distributive justice. Atiyah's criticism is more serious though, because he argues that the rules of negligence law have been 'stretched' by the courts in order to promote compensation.[40] In other words, the courts treat negligence law as a means of achieving compensation so they are adapting the legal rules to try to achieve compensation in more cases.

As an interpretive theory, Atiyah's explanation of negligence as a system of compensation is therefore based more strongly on 'fit' and 'transparency'. As he sees it, the courts reason in terms of promoting compensation and have shaped the law to compensate more victims of harm. And the logical conclusion at which he arrives, given that compensation is a distributive model, is that the negligence system should be abandoned in favour of a fairer compensatory system. It is important that negligence law adheres to principles of corrective justice to avoid this claim. Weinrib warns that 'a functionalist might regard causation as an indirect way of achieving market deterrence or some other extrinsic goal, an internal account treats causation as causation, that is, as a concept that represents the unidirectional sequence from action to effect'.[41] Coherence will be lost if the courts 'stretch' the concept of causation in order to promote compensation and deterrence.

It is important to note that proponents of corrective justice theories of negligence such as Weinrib and Beever do not generally claim that their theories are

---

[39] Patrick S Atiyah, *The Damages Lottery* (Hart Publishing, 1997) 143–44.
[40] ibid 32–95.
[41] Weinrib, *The Idea of Private Law* (n 12) 11–12.

normative in the sense that the law has to have a system of corrective justice-based responsibility.[42] Instead Beever characterises it as a political choice, arguing that:

> In deciding whether to implement a compensation scheme … to replace tort law, it is necessary to decide whether the political concerns that support the scheme are sufficient to outweigh the values that the scheme would undermine, including corrective justice.[43]

Their theories are interpretive and therefore compatible with claims that the law of negligence could be abandoned and replaced with distributive systems of compensation (such as no-fault compensation or insurance) and of deterrence (such as fines or insurance premiums). Weinrib explains:

> To take a modern example, the legal regime of personal injuries can be organized either correctively or distributively. Correctively, my striking you is a tort committed by me against you, and my payment to you of damages will restore the equality disturbed by my wrong. Distributively, the same incident activates a compensation scheme that shifts resources among members of a pool of contributors and recipients in accordance with a distributive criterion. From the standpoint of Aristotle's analysis, nothing about a personal injury as such consigns it to the domain of a particular form of justice. The differentiation between the corrective and distributive justice lies not in the different subject matters to which they apply, but in the differently structured operation that each performs on a subject matter available to both.[44]

Their theories do, however, have normative force in that since there *is* a legal system of negligence liability, in other words a bipolar system where the victim is compensated by the person whose wrongdoing caused his loss, then the system *ought* to conform to corrective justice.[45] Cane explains, 'it seems clear that Weinrib's theory is meant to have normative force to the extent that in his view, if a society chooses to organize some aspect of its life in accordance with the demands of corrective justice, it should do so consistently'.[46] Since the negligence system takes the form of corrective justice then the content of the legal rules that flesh it out must also reflect corrective justice, otherwise the system will become incoherent and unjustifiable.

It is therefore clear that Atiyah and Weinrib's positions can be reconciled since both insist on the impossibility of achieving distributive justice through a corrective justice structure. The difference lies in where they proceed from this basis: Weinrib argues that the law should be matched to the structure, so the rules of negligence law ought to reflect corrective justice; Atiyah argues that the structure should be matched to the law's objective, so negligence law ought to be replaced with a fairer compensation scheme. The problem with Atiyah's analysis is that it fails to measure negligence law in its own terms.

---

[42] Beever, 'Corrective Justice and Personal Responsibility' (n 22) 498–99.

[43] ibid 499.

[44] Weinrib, 'Corrective Justice' (n 17) 415.

[45] Beever, 'Corrective Justice and Personal Responsibility' (n 22) 498–99.

[46] Peter Cane, 'Corrective Justice and Correlativity in Private Law' (1996) 16 *Oxford Journal of Legal Studies* 471, 471–72. Referring to Weinrib, *The Idea of Private Law* (n 12) 228.

It is one thing to acknowledge, as the next section will, that negligence liability has compensatory and deterrent effects, but it is another thing to say that it has compensatory and deterrent goals and to measure its success against those goals. As a system of compensation or deterrence it has been shown that negligence will necessarily be a failure because the goals are mutually truncating and incompatible with the correlative structure of the negligence action.

E. Moving Beyond Formalism to the Legal System—Combining Kantian Right and Societal Morality

Corrective justice has been shown to be more than just an 'empty formalist shell'; it does not simply proscribe distributive goals but actually prescribes ideas about wrongdoing based on the Kantian conception of absolute and equal moral worth of rational beings. However, Weinrib's formalist conception, in particular his assertion that 'the purpose of private law is simply to be private law',[47] has been criticised for being too rigid in its formalism and divorced from the realities of the legal system. In the recent High Court decision in *Heneghan v Manchester Dry Docks*, extending the *Fairchild* exception to a case of lung cancer, Jay J said 'the disadvantage of strict adherence to logic and principle is that frank injustice may arise in certain types of case, and therefore the common law constantly strains at the leash of the intellectually pure approach'.[48] This is an important criticism because, as already seen, coherence is not the only quality that is desirable in a justificatory theory.[49] The practical implementation of corrective justice through the negligence system has effects that extend beyond the parties to society more generally so whilst issues of societal morality cannot be the driving force behind negligence law they must be taken into account. While it is clear that a pluralist account cannot provide the premise of negligence law it will be argued that acknowledging, as Cane does, that the law has distributive effects does not entail reconceptualising the law as an instrument of distributive justice.

Cane distinguishes between treating consequences as the goals of tort law and acknowledging them as the effects of tort law:

> The fact that private law is not instrumental or distributional in its explicit purposive orientation does not mean that it does not have instrumental and distributional *effects* ... To the extent that the traditional view denies that private law has instrumental and distributive effects, it is wrong. But it would be wrong to think that the common law leopard has changed (or could—or is likely to—change) its responsibility spots for instrumentalist and distributional stripes.[50]

---

[47] Weinrib, *The Idea of Private Law* (n 12) 21.
[48] *Heneghan v Manchester Dry Docks Ltd* [2014] EWHC 4190 (QB) [50].
[49] See text to n 3.
[50] Cane, 'Tort Law as Regulation' (n 1) 330.

This is an important distinction because it emphasises that while consequentialist theories cannot provide the premise of negligence law, it might be appropriate to limit the implementation of corrective justice where the demands of social welfare are particularly convincing.

Weinrib's account of corrective justice is known for its purism, yet as Morgan has noted it has been criticised as being 'so demanding that no actual legal system has ever lived up to it'.[51] Cane explains in more detail that Weinrib's focus on coherence neglects other aspects of interpretive legal theory:

> An important feature of Weinrib's 'formalistic' approach is that it is concerned with 'the law in the books', and it ignores 'the law in action'—in other words, it focuses on tort *law* at the expense of what is commonly called 'the tort *system*'. As an account of the internal normative structure of tort law, Weinrib's idea of correlativity of rights and obligations (decoupled from Kantian right) seems to me to be essentially correct. On the other hand, it paints a distorted picture of the way tort law operates in practice.[52]

This tension can be illuminated by returning to Smith's four criteria against which to measure interpretive legal theories: fit, transparency, coherence and morality.[53] Weinrib's account of corrective justice scores highly in terms of coherence, but it must be remembered that Weinrib's account is not entirely an interpretive one. As discussed above, Weinrib's account is normative insofar as he argues that *if* we choose to implement a system of private law then the rules of private law *ought* to conform to corrective justice. This means that it does not claim to be perfect in terms of fit and transparency. But it is important to find a balance between the normative force of the coherence of corrective justice, and the practical force of the reality of the operation of the negligence system. This reality is that liability decisions do have redistributive effects beyond the parties which may generally be considered desirable, but not at the extreme. It will be argued that the territory on which such a balance can be sought is the remaining criterion in Smith's four: morality.

The focus so far has been on an individualistic morality inherent in Kantian Right, the function of which, Cane says, 'is to protect and promote the value of human autonomy rather than other human values such as community and solidarity'.[54] Yet, as he argues elsewhere, it would be morally wrong to ignore the wider social consequences of our actions:

> All tort liability is based on some notion of personal responsibility. The fact that matters of social value are taken into account in tort law does not alter this; it is simply an outworking of the straightforward moral principle that a man's responsibilities are partly a function of the fact that man is a social being.[55]

---

[51] Jonathan Morgan, 'Tort, Insurance and Incoherence' 67 (2004) *Modern Law Review* 384, 395 referring to arguments of Ken Kress, 'Coherence and Formalism' (1993) 16 *Harvard Journal of Law & Public Policy* 639.

[52] Cane, 'Tort Law as Regulation' (n 1) 310.

[53] See text to n 3.

[54] Peter Cane, 'Rights in Private Law' in Nolan and Robertson (eds), *Rights and Private Law* (n 4) 56.

[55] Peter Cane, 'Justice and Justifications for Tort Liability' (1982) 2 *Oxford Journal of Legal Studies* 30, 62.

So whilst coherence should be prioritised, this should not be at the expense of morality. This concern will be revisited in the context of loss of a chance claims in medical negligence. Patient autonomy is a dominant principle in medical law but it has been criticised for prioritising the individual over the wider society and 'relational autonomy' is increasingly invoked to emphasise the duties that the individual owes to others.[56] For example, a patient cannot insist on receiving particular treatment that is not offered within the framework of NHS resources; indeed, she cannot insist on any treatment that is not clinically indicated.[57] Although Weinrib contends that distributive and corrective justice cannot be integrated into 'any overarching form',[58] it will be argued that it is wrong to ignore societal morality completely, especially once we acknowledge that the practical operation of the negligence system does have effects that extend beyond the parties to the case. Whilst the focus on autonomy is consistent with the concept of Kantian Right which dovetails with corrective justice this it is too extreme and fails to reflect man's regard for society. At some point respect for the moral worth of the individual crosses a line to become so extreme that it disproportionately impacts on the collective interests of the other members of a society.

It could be argued that Cane is simply observing that people interact on a societal level as well as on an individual level and that this is the equivalent of Aristotle's explanation that there are two forms of justice to correspond to these two forms of interaction. But Cane is making the important point that a person does not draw a clear, distinct line between her interactions with individuals and with the community, or rather, she does not make an absolute distinction between her reasons for acting in the two different contexts. Beever identifies four different 'spheres of morality': personal, interpersonal, societal and international.

> Personal morality asks how an individual should behave in order to be a good person. Interpersonal morality considers interactions between one individual and another. The focus here is on how persons should conduct themselves vis-à-vis one another as two individuals rather than as isolated individuals or as members of a collective. The third sphere is societal. The concern here is how to govern society and how to regulate the behaviour of individuals for the common good. The final sphere is the international. This sphere considers the impact of our actions on everyone, whether they belong to our political community or not, or the impact of our state on other states.[59]

For Beever, negligence liability is based on corrective justice so it reflects interpersonal morality.[60] As such, interpersonal morality is reflected in key features of negligence law, for example the objective standard of care arises because negligence

[56] Charles Foster, *Choosing Life, Choosing Death: The Tyranny of Autonomy in Medical Ethics and Law* (Hart Publishing, 2009) 14.

[57] *R (on the application of Burke) v General Medical Council* [2005] EWCA Civ 1003, [2005] 3 WLR 1132 (CA).

[58] Weinrib, 'The Jurisprudence of Legal Formalism' (n 37) 589.

[59] Beever, *Rediscovering* (n 9) 42.

[60] ibid 44.

is a form of interpersonal morality rather than personal so it does not matter in negligence whether there was subjective blameworthiness.[61] Thinking of morality as operating in different spheres can therefore help to understand the different concerns relevant to each. But it would seem strange to think that these spheres of morality actually operate in isolation from one another. Personal morality informs interpersonal morality; its equivalent in the Kantian approach is virtue which informs Right through the shared concept of conformity with universal law. There should be a similar exchange of ideas between societal and interpersonal morality.

This is an important limit to the coherence of corrective justice when it is implemented through the practices of negligence law, and it risks appearing indeterminate and therefore blurring the line between showing an awareness for avoiding extreme redistributive effects of liability and actually adopting redistribution as a goal of liability. Yet the reality is that a theory of negligence is measured not only in terms of coherence but also in terms of morality, fit and transparency. While fit and transparency may be descriptive, both coherence and morality have prescriptive force and the effort should be made to combine them. The account of negligence set out in this work is still based on corrective justice but takes a view of interpersonal responsibility that combines autonomous and societal moral values. It is a moral account that is premised on the absolute and equal moral worth of beings, but which shows an awareness that individual liability decisions can sometimes effect an extreme change to the distributive pattern. Whilst consequentialist accounts are distributive and thus cannot provide a coherent basis for negligence we cannot ignore the effects that liability has and should remember that a person, as a societal being, will draw the line somewhere and say that her individual needs should not be prioritised over the needs of others when the effects become too significant. So while social welfare considerations cannot ground liability, exceptionally they may limit it.[62]

A final clarification is needed in relation to terminology. It is important to refer to this corrective justice-based approach as reflecting 'interpersonal responsibility'. Morgan has referred to the principles of 'individual responsibility and corrective justice' as distinct from collective responsibility, and Cane has said that 'tort law is a set of rules and principles of personal responsibility'.[63] Beever equates personal responsibility with personal morality which, as explained above, is distinct from interpersonal morality and responsibility. He explains that personal responsibility would be undermined by liability insurance because it is not the defendant personally who compensates the claimant, whereas corrective justice requires only that the defendant see to it that the claimant is compensated and 'does not imply any moral claim about the defendant per se'.[64] Although 'interpersonal responsibility' is a more cumbersome expression than 'personal responsibility' it will be used to avoid ambiguity when referring to corrective justice-based liability.

---

[61] Beever, 'Corrective Justice and Personal Responsibility' (n 22) 491.
[62] Robertson, 'On the Function of the Law of Negligence' (n 2).
[63] Cane, 'Distributive Justice' (n 36) 403.
[64] Beever (n 22) 494.

F. The Place of Causation in Corrective Justice-Based Interpersonal Responsibility

Causation has been largely unmentioned up until this point because the focus has been on the theoretical foundations of negligence generally rather than on the theory of causation. Causation is a central feature of corrective justice-based interpersonal responsibility since it is the causal relationship that connects the claimant and defendant as parties to an interaction. As a conception of responsibility, however, causal responsibility is not synonymous with interpersonal responsibility, so causation occupies a vital but limited role which must be supplemented by ideas about wrongdoing and wrongful loss.

Causation is central to corrective justice because corrective justice concerns justice in interactions and without causation there is no transaction between the parties to the interaction as Weinrib explains:

> The requirement of factual causation establishes the indispensable nexus between the parties by relating their rights to a transaction in which one has directly impinged upon the other. Tort law does not typically pursue wrongful conduct in the abstract. It concerns itself with such conduct only when it materializes in harm to a given person so that compensation can flow from a particular tortfeasor to his particular victim.[65]

The causation requirement in negligence is therefore crucial. The causation requirement is sometimes criticised as posing an artificial barrier to achieving compensation, for example, faced with difficulty establishing causation in *Chester v Afshar*, Lord Hope objected that:

> A duty was owed, the duty was breached and an injury was suffered that lay within the scope of the duty. Yet the patient to whom the duty was owed is left without a remedy.[66]

Yet this is the nature of corrective justice. Corrective justice is not concerned with punishing wrongdoing and it is not primarily concerned with compensating loss. Corrective justice is concerned with wrongdoing that results in loss. The causation requirement has been criticised as introducing an element of 'moral luck' into negligence liability.[67] Howarth suggests it is 'a kind of privilege for defendants, a privilege that allows defendants to escape liability because of coincidences for which they can take no credit'.[68] Concerns about the morally arbitrary nature of the causation requirement focus on the claimant and defendant as separate entities but, as Beever contends:

> The focus of the law, and the focus of corrective justice that motivates the law, is on the claimant and the defendant taken as a unit ... Moreover, the law is interested in the

---

[65] Weinrib, 'Toward a Moral Theory (n 31) 38.

[66] *Chester v Afshar* [2004] UKHL 41, [2005] 1 AC 134, [73] (Lord Hope).

[67] David Howarth, 'Many Duties of Care—or a Duty of Care? Notes from the Underground' (2006) 26 *Oxford Journal of Legal Studies* 449, 461. See also Jeremy Waldron, 'Moments of Carelessness and Massive Loss' in Owen (n 7) 388.

[68] Howarth, 'Many Duties of Care—or a Duty of Care?' (n 67) 461.

defendant only if the defendant violated a right in the claimant. Hence, causation is not morally arbitrary but is internal to corrective justice. We are not looking for a defendant who should pay money to someone and a claimant who should receive compensation from someone. Rather, we are looking for a defendant who should pay because he violated the claimant's rights and a claimant who should receive because his rights were violated by the defendant.[69]

Weinrib notes, however, that causation alone is not a sufficient basis for liability within a corrective justice-based system. Causes can be traced back endlessly, so the law requires some theory to identify the kinds of causes that are considered relevant,[70] and to place a limit on how far back to trace them:

> Because any cause is as much a cause as the one that precedes or follows, causation itself does not identify the sequence's particular starting point.[71]

This is achieved through the remaining negligence doctrines, damage and breach of duty in particular, that frame the causation inquiry. In corrective justice a person is not responsible for all loss that they cause, only for wrongful loss. Causation thus provides the essential link between the parties so it is the starting point for being able to find interpersonal responsibility but its role is limited because it cannot explain where interpersonal responsibility for outcomes ends. It is the concept of wrongdoing that provides the dividing line between those losses that are wrongful and those that are not, and this must be addressed through the remaining negligence doctrines other than causation.

II. The Doctrinal Framework

Having outlined the view of negligence as a corrective justice-based system, ie a system premised on interpersonal responsibility and a conception of morality that takes seriously the intrinsic moral worth of people, and having seen the place of causation within interpersonal responsibility, it is important to turn to the question of how this is translated into practice through the doctrines of negligence law. Coherence 'signifies a mode of intelligibility that is internal to the relationship between the parts of an integrated whole',[72] such that '[t]he negligence concepts form an ensemble that brackets and articulates a single normative sequence'.[73] Since causation has a vital yet limited role within interpersonal responsibility it is essential that this is reflected in the negligence doctrines and, as explained in the introduction to this chapter, there is a danger that where causation is a problem it is thought of as determinative of liability. The other doctrines must play their part

---

[69] Beever, *Rediscovering* (n 9) 414.
[70] Ernest Weinrib, 'Causation and Wrongdoing' (1987) 63 *Chicago-Kent Law Review* 407, 417.
[71] ibid 418.
[72] Weinrib, *The Idea of Private Law* (n 12) 14.
[73] Weinrib, 'The Jurisprudence of Legal Formalism' (n 37) 593.

in defining the contours of liability so the objective of this section is not a detailed exposition of each element of negligence, but to signal how causation is related to the other negligence doctrines and to illuminate their role in determining liability.

A. Identifying Issues of Interpersonal Responsibility in the Duty of Care

The function of the duty of care concept is much debated. Weinrib has lamented the disintegration of the duty concept which he regards as an essential element of the negligence inquiry.[74] Coherence requires that the negligence doctrines come together to form an integrated whole and a virtue of Beever's corrective justice-based approach to negligence is that it seeks to achieve this:

> [T]he 'principled approach' ... treats the stages of the negligence enquiry as forming a unified investigation. This investigation is an enquiry into whether the unreasonable risk created by the defendant (standard of care) was an unreasonable risk of injury to the claimant (the duty of care) and an unreasonable risk of the injury that the claimant suffered (remoteness).[75]

Treating the negligence doctrines as forming a 'unified investigation' reflects Weinrib's concern, noted above, that the negligence doctrines 'articulate a single normative sequence'.[76]

In contrast, Nolan argues that the 'duty of care' is not really a duty to take care but merely an obligation not to injure. He argues that, in fact, the duty of care concept 'has served to obscure what Allan Beever terms the "rights base" of the law of negligence, and has encouraged precisely the kind of open-ended policy reasoning which advocates of a rights-based conception of negligence law so strongly deprecate'.[77] He advocates the 'deconstruction of duty', suggesting that issues currently addressed under the heading of duty of care actually encompass a variety of concerns that could, and should, be addressed within the other negligence doctrines.[78]

Although this work subscribes to a corrective justice-based account of negligence and therefore accepts that the duty of care occupies an important place within the negligence enquiry, this is not incompatible with accepting Nolan's argument that some issues that are currently addressed under the duty heading ought properly to be addressed within other negligence doctrines. For example, Nolan highlights the misuse of the duty of care to determine the quantum of damages in wrongful conception cases where liability itself is 'not in doubt'.[79] The claimant in

---

[74] Ernest Weinrib, 'The Disintegration of Duty' in Stuart Madden (ed), *Exploring Tort Law* (Cambridge University Press, 2005).
[75] Beever, *Rediscovering* (n 9) 115.
[76] Weinrib, 'The Jurisprudence of Legal Formalism' (n 37) 593.
[77] Donal Nolan, 'Deconstructing the Duty of Care' (2013) 129 *Law Quarterly Review* 559, 564.
[78] ibid 568–73.
[79] ibid 572.

McFarlane v Tayside was unable to recover the cost of bringing up a healthy child. While the defendant doctor was held to owe the claimant a duty of care in respect of the personal injury constituted by the unwanted pregnancy itself, Lord Slynn and Lord Hope considered that the duty of care did not extend to the 'pure economic loss' constituted by the cost of raising the child.[80] Nolan argues that Lord Clyde in *McFarlane*, and Lord Millett in both *McFarlane* and another unwanted pregnancy case *Rees v Darlington*,[81] were right to conclude that this was not really a question of the doctor's duty of care but a question of the extent of the losses recoverable.[82] This is correct, and issues of damage should be squarely addressed as such. We have seen a similar blurring of arguments in respect of claims for loss of a chance of a better medical outcome which have arisen in response to difficulties of proof of factual causation but effectively seek to reformulate the damage forming the gist of the negligence action which is considered in chapter four. One of the advantages that Nolan attributes to the deconstruction of the duty of care is that it would 'allow similar issues which currently arise at different stages of the negligence enquiry to be dealt with alongside each other, thereby promoting consistency and facilitating the drawing of appropriate analogies'.[83] He also explains that 'using an overarching notional duty concept to soak up so many of the issues of law raised by negligence litigation inevitably tends to mean that other important questions are under-analysed',[84] so the deconstruction of duty would 'pave the way for fuller consideration of the important question of what does and does not amount to damage for the purposes of a negligence action'.[85] This highlights the need to draw clear boundaries between the various negligence doctrines. Questions of damage and the extent of loss that is recoverable should be addressed as such, and not be integrated into questions of duty and causation.

A detailed defence of the duty doctrine is beyond the scope of this work, but arguably greater conceptual clarity can be achieved without committing to abandoning the duty of care. As previously noted, the negligence doctrines should articulate a single normative sequence, so issues of interpersonal responsibility identified at the duty stage of the inquiry may be taken into account in the application of the remaining negligence doctrines. Corrective justice is a moral theory so it implies an idealist approach to duty as a meaningful duty to take care since this takes seriously the moral worth of people. In contrast, in a 'cynical' view of duty, McBride explains that

> [t]he law of negligence would no longer purport to guide people's behaviour ... Instead, the law of negligence would simply attach costs to certain forms of behaviour and leave it up to individual citizens to decide whether or not to participate in those forms of behaviour.[86]

---

[80] *McFarlane v Tayside Health Board* [2000] 2 AC 59, 75–76 (Lord Slynn), 97 (Lord Hope).
[81] *Rees v Darlington Memorial Hospital NHS Trust* [2003] UKHL 52, [2004] 1 AC 309.
[82] Nolan, 'Deconstructing' (n 77) 572–73.
[83] ibid 578.
[84] ibid 579.
[85] ibid 579.
[86] Nicholas J McBride, 'Duties of Care—do they Really Exist?' (2004) 24 *Oxford Journal of Legal Studies* 417, 424.

This cynical view is incompatible with Kantian Right since it treats the claimant (and potential claimants) merely as a commodity or as a cost to be entered into an equation.

McBride goes on to argue that the duty is the 'central organizing concept around which the whole of the law of negligence revolves' in an idealist account:

> After all, an idealist would say, a claimant will only be entitled to sue a defendant in negligence if: (1) the defendant owed her a *duty of care*; (2) the defendant breached that *duty of care*; (3) the breach of that *duty of care* caused her to suffer some kind of loss; and (4) the loss suffered by the claimant as a result of the defendant's breach was the kind of loss which the *duty of care* breached by the defendant was imposed on him in order to avoid.[87]

Logically, therefore, duty must be analysed before the other doctrines. This is important because the arguments raised at the duty stage focus on the relationship between the parties, so they bring to the foreground the considerations of interpersonal responsibility in that particular relationship. Where problems arise in the remaining doctrines, and a solution is sought that forms part of a coherent approach to negligence, then we must go back to the issues of interpersonal responsibility identified at the duty stage and carry them through into the solution to the problem. This work advocates the conceptual separation supported by Nolan whilst maintaining that the duty concept, with its focus on the relationship between the parties, can usefully identify issues of interpersonal responsibility that might shape the subsequent approach to issues such as damage.

B. Distinguishing Damage, Causation and Quantification

A claimant must have suffered an actionable form of damage in order to bring a successful negligence action; damage is said to form the gist of the action. But the question of what constitutes actionable damage is often overlooked for the simple reason that in most cases a claimant will have suffered clearly observable physical damage to his person or property. The definition of damage is inextricably linked to the causation inquiry as Stapleton insists:

> It cannot be over-emphasised that the formulation of the 'damage' forming the gist of the action *defines* the causation question. Logically one can only deal with causation after one knows what the damage forming the gist of the action is.[88]

Both damage and causation are then closely related to the later question of quantification of the claimant's loss, or the question of damages. One theme that will recur in this work is that the three concepts of damage, causation and quantification, though related, must remain analytically distinct. This is especially important

---

[87] ibid 423–24.
[88] Jane Stapleton, 'The Gist of Negligence: Part 2 The Relationship Between "Damage" and Causation' (1988) 104 *Law Quarterly Review* 389, 393.

where claimants have attempted to overcome difficulties of proof of causation by reconceptualising the damage as the loss of a chance of a better outcome, or an increase in the risk of harm.[89] This section prepares the groundwork by briefly explaining the concept of damage before outlining its relationship to causation and quantification so that the basic issues are understood in advance of the more detailed analysis in later chapters.[90]

As explained, corrective justice concerns wrongful loss in interactions. The question of whether a loss is wrongful depends partly on whether it was caused by wrongdoing, and also on whether it is legally recognised as constituting damage. Property damage, some personal injury, and financial loss are recognised forms of damage (although with regard to purely financial loss, the circumstances in which one is owed a duty of care are much more limited). Conditions such as anxiety and grief that fall short of medically recognised psychiatric illness are not actionable.[91] Similarly, not all physical illness will constitute damage: it was held in *Rothwell* that although asymptomatic pleural plaques are a medically recognised condition they do not constitute damage in negligence.[92] In *Rothwell*, Lord Hoffmann held that damage 'is an abstract concept of being worse off, physically or economically, so that compensation is an appropriate remedy. It does not mean simply a change in physical condition'.[93] This definition is not adequate, however, since because 'not all forms of being worse off count as damage' and 'in some cases the claimant may be better off, not worse off, as a result of the defendant's negligence, but this will make no difference'.[94] Nolan is led to conclude that 'it is impossible to define damage for the purposes of a negligence action without falling into circularity'.[95] Most of the cases on causation addressed in this work involve recognised forms of damage, but the damage concept will be developed in more detail in chapters four and five in respect of attempts to reformulate the damage as the loss of a chance of a better outcome or the risk of harm.

The term 'damage' is also used to connote different types of conclusion by different writers. Nolan differentiates between 'damage' and 'damages', so that damage focuses on whether the claimant's harm is *ever* actionable, while 'damages' addresses 'the harms in respect of which recovery is permitted once the cause

---

[89] eg *Hotson v East Berkshire Health Authority* [1987] AC 750, 3 WLR 232 (HL); *Gregg v Scott* [2005] UKHL 2, 2 AC 176; *Barker v Corus* [2006] UKHL 20, 2 WLR 1027. These attempts to reformulate the damage form the focus of chs 4 and 5.

[90] Ch 4 addresses loss of a chance and ch 5, which addresses the evidentiary gap, considers a range of responses including reformulating actionable damage as the risk of harm rather than the physical outcome.

[91] *Hinz v Berry* [1970] 2 QB 40 (CA); *Rothwell v Chemical and Insulating Co Ltd* [2007] UKHL 39, [2008] 1 AC 281.

[92] *Rothwell* (n 91).

[93] ibid [7] (Lord Hoffmann).

[94] Donal Nolan, 'Damage in the English Law of Negligence' (2013) 4 *Journal of European Tort Law* 259, 265.

[95] ibid 265.

of action has been established'.[96] Stapleton differentiates between the claimant's injury and the question of whether the injury represents damage:

> It is a defining and well-known principle of the approach the law of torts takes to the assessment of compensatory damages that it should not make a claimant better off than he would have been had he not been the victim of tortious conduct. A convenient way of expressing this 'no better off' principle is that the injury must represent 'damage' relative to the benchmark of where the victim would have been absent tortious conduct.[97]

In this account, labelling the claimant's injury as 'damage' expresses a conclusion that all the elements of the negligence inquiry have been satisfied in respect of the injury, whereas in Nolan's account 'damage' is identified at the outset as the focus for the negligence inquiry. It is in the latter sense that damage is used here: the claimant's damage is identified at the outset, the factual causation question then asks whether the defendant's negligence was a cause of that damage, and at the quantification stage the court will assess the loss flowing from that damage. A key aspect of defining the claimant's damage at the outset of the negligence enquiry, which will be addressed in greater detail in chapter two, is to distinguish between 'divisible' and 'indivisible' damage. These terms are not used consistently amongst academics. The appropriate definition will be discussed in detail in that chapter, but broadly speaking damage is said to be divisible if it is dose-related whereas indivisible damage is 'all or nothing'.

The quantification stage of the enquiry asks whether the claimant is any worse off than she would have been without the defendant's negligence. If the defendant's negligence caused damage but this did not result in any loss compared to the claimant's pre-tort position then there is no recovery. In *Performance Cars v Abraham*,[98] the claimant's car had been damaged in a collision due to the defendant's negligence. Among the damage caused to the car was damage to the front wing which, due to the nature of the paint, necessitated the re-spraying of the whole lower part of the car. However, in a previous collision the rear wing had been damaged which also necessitated the re-spraying of the whole lower part of the vehicle. Although the claimant had obtained judgment against the party responsible for the first accident, the judgment had not been satisfied and he sought to recover the cost from the defendant responsible for the second collision. The Court of Appeal held that although the defendant had caused physical damage to the front wing of the car, the cost of re-spraying the lower part could not be recovered from the defendant because the pre-tort state of the car was that the lower part already needed re-spraying. In other words, the defendant was a cause of physical damage to the car but at the valuation stage it was found that the physical damage had not caused the claimant to be any worse off. This is not a question of causation—it is clear that the defendant's negligence was a factual cause of the physical damage—but with respect to the portion of the loss associated with

---

[96] ibid 262.

[97] Jane Stapleton, 'Unnecessary Causes' (2013) 129 *Law Quarterly Review* 39, 54–5.

[98] *Performance Cars v Abraham* [1962] 1 QB 33 (CA).

the physical damage the value is zero because the car already needed re-spraying before the physical damage occurred.

At the quantification stage courts must also determine what course the claimant's life would otherwise have taken and whether other factors would have led to her incurring similar loss in the future anyway. This can be illustrated through *Smith v Leech Brain*.[99] In this case the defendant's negligence caused the claimant to suffer a burn on his lip which triggered a pre-cancerous condition and led to his eventual death. As a matter of factual causation there was no doubt that the defendant's negligence had caused the claimant to suffer the harm at that particular time. But in quantifying the value of the loss caused by the defendant, the Court made a reduction in damages to account for the fact that the claimant had a pre-cancerous condition so was likely to have died prematurely anyway. This issue will be revisited in chapter four since it is apt to be confused with claims for proportionate recovery for loss of a chance of a better outcome. Under the 'vicissitudes of life' principle, courts ordinarily must reduce the value of damages to take account of the likelihood that the claimant would have suffered similar loss at some stage in his life, and where there is information specific to the claimant allowing them to personalise this calculation then they will do so. This 'reduction' in damages does not reflect any doubt that the defendant's negligence was a cause of the claimant's loss, but reflects the attempt to value that loss as accurately as possible by calculating how likely it was that the claimant would have suffered similar misfortune at some stage in his life because of independent events.[100]

The question of what course the claimant's life would have taken, and how far the defendant's responsibility extends, is informed by factual causation but it is also a qualitative inquiry that involves evaluating the extent of the loss that is 'wrongful'. This is apparent in the contrast between the solutions in *Jobling v Associated Dairies*[101] and *Baker v Willoughby*.[102] In terms of the causal processes, *Jobling* and the American case of *Dillon v Twin State Gas*,[103] seem closer to *Smith v Leech Brain* than *Baker* does. In *Jobling* the defendant caused the claimant a back injury which reduced his earning capacity but before reaching the Court the claimant suffered a naturally occurring back illness which would have prevented him from working anyway. Although the negligence did not trigger this underlying condition, as had been the case in *Smith*, the Court was still able to accurately calculate the vicissitudes of life for this claimant by the time of trial. Likewise in *Dillon*, as the claimant was falling to his death he was electrocuted due to the defendant's negligence. It was known that at the time of the negligence he already had a (significantly) reduced life expectancy. In contrast, in *Baker* the claimant's leg was damaged by the defendant's negligence, reducing his earning capacity, but by

---

[99] *Smith v Leech Brain & Co* [1962] 2 QB 405 (QBD).
[100] Jane Stapleton, 'The Gist of Negligence' (n 88) 398.
[101] *Jobling v Associated Dairies Ltd* [1982] AC 794 (HL).
[102] *Baker v Willoughby* [1970] AC 467 (HL).
[103] *Dillon v Twin State Gas & Electric Co*, 85 NH 449, 169 A 111 (1932).

the date of trial he had been shot in that leg by robbers and the leg was amputated. The defendant was held liable to compensate the claimant for the loss of earnings flowing from the damaged leg, even after the date of the shooting. This issue of quantification reflects the Court's qualitative assessment of the extent to which the claimant's loss was wrongful, with the concern in *Baker* that the claimant had been exposed to two careless acts and his claim should not be allowed to 'fall between two stools'.[104] The robbery could have been construed as a 'vicissitude of life' and damages reduced accordingly, but this would amount to declaring that the claimant's loss was no longer a wrongful loss simply because it would have been caused by the second wrong even if it had not been caused by the defendant.[105]

Stevens is critical of accounts of causation that address the question of whether the claimant was worse off under the separate heading of quantification, arguing that 'the diligent reader is entitled to feel slightly let down, as this is just the "but for" test reintroduced under another name'.[106] It is important, however, that we first identify whether the negligence was a cause of the damage, and then ask separately whether the claimant would have suffered the same losses flowing from that damage. If the defendant's negligence was not a cause of the damage then she cannot be held liable in respect of that damage within a corrective justice-based system of negligence. If her negligence was a cause of the damage then we must ask the separate question of whether the losses flowing from it can properly be considered 'wrongful losses' and that is a normative question best addressed within a doctrine that is openly evaluative in nature. If the same loss would have been caused by another defendant's negligence then the claimant will recover, but if it would have been caused by natural events or non-negligent acts then the claimant will not recover. This is not a question of causation, but of the appropriate extent of liability within negligence.

An alternative approach to causation has been proposed by Green whose 'necessary breach analysis' reverses the order in which these questions are approached, asking first whether it is 'more likely than not that *a* defendant's breach of duty changed the normal course of events so that damage (including constituent parts of larger damage) occurred which would not otherwise have done so when it did', then asking of each defendant individually 'was the effect of *this* defendant's breach operative when the damage occurred?'.[107] One of the main reasons she provides for preferring this approach is that:

> Establishing causation is rarely straightforward, speedy and inexpensive. There is more to be said, therefore, for a means of streamlining the process sooner rather than later, so

---

[104] *Baker v Willoughby* [1969] 2 WLR 489 (CA), 483 (Harman LJ).

[105] See also Sarah Green, *Causation in Negligence* (Hart Publishing, 2015) 41: ''others' breaches of duty are not "vicissitudes of life" for this purpose and do not, therefore, count as part of any claimant's "normal course of events"'.

[106] Robert Stevens, *Torts and Rights* (Oxford University Press, 2007) 144.

[107] Green, *Causation in Negligence* (n 105) 4.

that resources are not consumed by causal investigations which turn out ultimately to have no legal relevance.[108]

However, it is surely open to a court to address the quantification question as a preliminary issue based on presumed facts if it seems likely that the claimant would have suffered the same losses through non-negligent causes. Additionally, as she recognises, in some cases the answer to her first question will require the same input of resources. In cases where proof of causation is not straightforward, the first question will be as complex to answer as the second.

C. Framing the Causation Question: Breach of Duty

Just as the definition of damage is inextricably linked to the causation question, so is the framing of the breach of duty since it must be established that the defendant's negligence in particular, rather than the defendant's conduct in general, was a cause of the damage suffered. Stapleton has illustrated this through her analysis of the decision in *McWilliams v Arrol*.[109] The claimant fell to his death from scaffolding and the defendant employer was negligent in failing to provide a safety harness. To prove that failure to provide a harness was a cause of the death, it is necessary to prove that the victim would have worn a harness if it had been provided, and the claimant was unable to prove this. If, however, reasonable care required not only the provision of safety harnesses but also instating a surveillance system to ensure that safety equipment was used, then this breach of duty would be a cause of his death.[110] This has important consequences for the solution to the evidentiary gap problem that arose in *McGhee* where both the innocent and negligent sources of the harmful agent were attributable to the defendant, and this will be discussed in chapter five.

III. Conclusion

This chapter has shown that it is important not only for the doctrine of causation to be internally intelligible but also for it to form part of an overarching approach to the tort of negligence that is itself coherent. Aristotelian corrective justice and Kantian Right, it was argued, provide a coherent theoretical foundation that is not only formal but also implies a moral account of wrongdoing that expresses interpersonal responsibility. The various negligence doctrines should come together to give effect to this corrective justice-based interpersonal responsibility and

[108] ibid 16.

[109] *McWilliams v Sir William Arrol Co Ltd* [1962] 1 WLR 295 (HL).

[110] Jane Stapleton, 'Cause in Fact and the Scope of Liability for Consequences' (2003) 119 *Law Quarterly Review* 388, 391–92.

'articulate a single normative sequence'. Causation is an essential element of inter-personal responsibility because it is the causal relationship between the wrong-doing and the loss that joins the defendant and claimant in an interaction that has resulted in a 'wrongful loss'. However, causation also has a limited role and the evaluative elements of responsibility must be addressed through the remaining negligence doctrines. These doctrines also help frame the causation question because they identify the loss and the wrongdoing between which the causal relationship is sought. The remainder of this work focuses squarely on causation, drawing on the overview of negligence in this chapter to guide the analysis of causal problems.

2

Identifying the Proper Function
of Causation

As established in chapter one, causation is central to interpersonal responsibility, but the law relating to causation is currently in a state of confusion. This confusion extends not only to the exceptional approaches to causation, but characterises the standard approaches as well. This chapter will attempt to undo the confusion by adopting a clear approach to understanding the causal problems as well as their solutions. The starting point to developing any test for causation must be an accurate understanding of what purpose the doctrine of causation has in negligence. It will be argued here that the concept of causation in law is narrower and more precise than the use made of the term 'cause' in everyday language because, as Stapleton has explained, causation can be understood in a wide range of senses, from involvement, to explanation, to blame.[1] Moreover, as Wright, building on the work of Hart and Honoré, argues, philosophy provides the law with a robust account of causation that ought to form the basis of any legal test.[2] By understanding the philosophical account of causation developed by Hume and Mill, we can visualise and better understand the causal problems that come before the courts. This will enable the law to distinguish between those cases that are straightforward, and those that are actually problematic. Negligence law does, however, put its understanding of causation to a specific purpose, namely establishing a causal link between a particular instance of negligence and a particular harmful outcome.[3] A certain level of pragmatism must therefore be allowed in order to avoid becoming distracted by details that affect philosophers and scientists. Effectively, we all use a shared concept of causation, derived from philosophy, but we must retain a clear vision of what demands the law places on a test of causation.

The philosophical account of causation is best reflected by Richard Wright's NESS test rather than the but-for test that currently dominates.[4] The but-for test is

---

[1] Jane Stapleton, 'Choosing what we Mean by "Causation" in the Law' (2008) 73 *Modern Law Review* 433, 438.
[2] Richard Wright, 'Causation in Tort Law' (1985) 73 *California Law Review* 1735, 1774–1812.
[3] Richard Wright, 'The NESS Account of Natural Causation: A Response to Criticisms' in Richard Goldberg (ed), *Perspectives on Causation* (Hart Publishing, 2011) 290–91.
[4] Wright, 'Causation' (n 2); Richard Wright, 'Causation, Responsibility, Risk, Probability, Naked Statistics, and Proof: Pruning the Bramble Bush by Clarifying the Concepts' (1987) 73 *Iowa Law Review* 1001; Wright, 'The NESS Account' (n 3). Wright builds on the idea of a 'causally relevant factor' first developed by Hart and Honoré, *Causation in the Law* (Clarendon Press, 1959).

mismatched with the predominant philosophical account of what causation is and this means that the use of the but-for test has created apparent problems that do not, in reality, exist. The legal solutions to these problems, particularly the 'material contribution to harm' test,[5] have created more difficulties than they have solved. The reasons for this are twofold. First, because causation is approached from the paradigmatic mind-set of the but-for test which is not an accurate reflection of the meaning of causation, we are unable to conceptualise the problems that exist. This has contributed to the second difficulty regarding the emergence of a vocabulary of causation-specific terminology: divisibility of disease, cumulative causes, alternative causes. These terms are technical so they ought to have a technical meaning but the difficulties of conceptualising the causal problems to which they relate mean that they do not have any agreed meaning. They are used to mean different things by different people, thus exacerbating the confusion. By beginning again from the most basic causal problems and explaining them through the conceptual framework of the NESS test, many of these problems can be avoided. This chapter seeks to show that the NESS test is both accessible and, as a more robust test, helps us to articulate and resolve causal problems more clearly.

This chapter will therefore begin by asking how the legal concept of causation relates to causation in the fields of everyday language, and philosophy and science. After explaining the philosophical account of causation, it addresses the question of how best to translate this into a legal test. Both the but-for test and the NESS test will be applied to a range of theoretical problem scenarios to illustrate how the NESS test is able to solve problems that the but-for test cannot. Finally, the NESS test will be applied to existing case law to show how it allows us to reconceptualise the problems and to understand the specific terminology.

Part I: Identifying the Function of Causation in Negligence

I. The Demands on Causation

Before it is possible to say what qualities are required from a test for causation, we must understand what is actually meant by 'causation'. More importantly, we need to know what we, as lawyers, mean by causation. What role does it fulfil in the negligence inquiry, and does it have a special 'legal' definition? In the previous chapter it was shown that causation has a pivotal yet limited place in corrective justice, and the two strands of the current section will unpack what this implies for the doctrine of causation within the negligence inquiry. First, causation has

---

[5] *Bonnington Castings v Wardlaw* [1956] AC 613 (HL).

a limited role in attributions of responsibility so as Wright argues, in comparison with the use of the word 'causation' in everyday language, there is a technical legal meaning.[6] 'Causation' in everyday language is used flexibly to mean different things in different circumstances. In contrast, the law requires greater consistency and precision in the definition of causation. The factual causation element of negligence is concerned with causation in a purely factual sense, what Hart and Honoré call being a 'causally relevant condition',[7] or Stapleton calls 'involvement'.[8] The second part of this section addresses the point that causation is essential to interpersonal responsibility meaning that the doctrine of causation must be conceptually robust. As argued first by Hart and Honoré, and subsequently by Wright, the most complete account of factual causation can be found in the philosophy of Hume and Mill, and this should inform the legal doctrine of factual causation.

A. The Limited Role of Causation in Negligence

It has been suggested that the doctrine of causation should reflect the ordinary person's use of the word; for example, in *McGhee v National Coal Board*, Lord Reid said 'it has often been said that the legal concept of causation is not based on logic or philosophy. It is based in the practical way in which the ordinary man's mind works in the everyday affairs of life'.[9] Indeed the seminal work of Hart and Honoré on causation sought to explain causation by reference to the way it is used in ordinary language.[10] Wright has shown, however, that in everyday language 'cause' is often shorthand for 'the cause' rather than 'a cause':

> The phrase 'a cause' usually refers to causation per se—the fact of being one of many contributing conditions. The phrase 'the cause' generally is used to denote which of the many contributing conditions is legally or morally responsible ... 'The cause' is merely an elliptical way of saying 'the (most significant for our purposes) cause'.[11]

In other words the ordinary person uses the word 'cause' to express a conclusion about responsibility or blame rather than limiting herself to observing a purely factual relationship of cause and effect. In comparison, the legal notion of factual causation is a technical concept since it refers to 'a cause' so care must be taken to separate the fact of causation from any attribution of responsibility that may be considered to flow from it.

---

[6] Indeed Wright suggests that although Hart and Honoré's philosophical account of causation was 'a major advance in the analysis of causation in both law and philosophy' it was 'overshadowed and distorted by their primary emphasis on elaborating supposedly factual 'common sense' principles for treating only some causally relevant factors as causes, so that, initially, it received minimal attention in the legal literature'. See Wright, 'The NESS Account' (n 3) 288.

[7] Hart and Honoré, *Causation in the Law* (2nd edn, Oxford, Clarendon Press, 1985) lvi, lxiv.

[8] Stapleton, 'Choosing' (n 1) 438.

[9] *McGhee v National Coal Board* [1972] 3 All ER 1008 (HL), 1011.

[10] Hart and Honoré, *Causation in the Law* (n 7).

[11] Wright, 'Pruning' (n 4) 1012.

A relatively straightforward example illustrates the distinction Wright draws.[12] When a lit match is dropped and a fire results, the ordinary person might identify the dropping of the match as the cause. It is, however, only 'a cause', along with the presence of oxygen and flammable material. If a fire occurred during a particular manufacturing process that required the absence of oxygen, then common sense is to call the introduction of oxygen the cause of the fire. If a sofa does not meet safety standards concerning flammability then we might say that this, not the dropping of a match onto it, is the cause of the fire. In each of these scenarios 'the cause' is selected because it is the factor that is abnormal in the circumstances and, as Mackie has argued, '[w]hat is normal may depend upon man-made norms'.[13] The identification of 'the cause' depends upon the purpose of the inquiry and the circumstances of the event. When the ordinary person determines the cause of an event, such as a fire, she goes through two stages, the first factual and the second evaluative. The second of these stages is to pick out the particular factor that was unusual or blameworthy in the circumstances, which in the case of the fire above could be the match or the presence of oxygen or the flammability of the material depending on the circumstances. But first, although she did not necessarily consciously articulate it, she was aware that the conditions that must come together for a fire to start are oxygen, flammable material and a source of ignition. Each of these conditions is 'a cause' of a fire because they must each be present, but the ordinary person tends only to identify one as 'the cause', and which one she chooses will vary depending on the particular circumstances. As a test of factual causation it is therefore inappropriate for the law to rely on the ordinary person's use of the word causation because the ordinary person makes an evaluative judgement without first articulating the factual judgement on which it is based.

The distinction between 'a cause' and 'the (responsible) cause' broadly corresponds to the division between factual and legal causation in negligence. Factual causation addresses causation in the objective sense of being 'a cause' while legal causation is an evaluative question of the appropriate extent of liability. Hart and Honoré, however, identified three issues and it is important to understand which of these are causal and which are evaluative. These three issues are: causally relevant condition, causal connection and remoteness of damage.[14] The identification of 'causally relevant conditions' is the factual question of the historical involvement of the negligence in the occurrence of the harm.[15] This is what Wright referred to above as being 'a cause'. The second question of 'causal connection' identifies which of the causally relevant conditions actually are, in Hart and Honoré's terminology, causes and which are just conditions.[16] It was in making the distinction between causes and conditions that Hart and Honoré turned to the

---

[12] This example is used by Hart and Honoré (n 7) 11.
[13] John L Mackie, *The Cement of the Universe: A Study of Causation* (Clarendon Press, 1974) 119.
[14] Hart and Honoré (n 7) xlvii.
[15] ibid lvi, lxiv.
[16] ibid 33.

use of the word 'cause' in everyday language. They argued that the ordinary person identifies something as a cause rather than a condition if it is non-coincidental, is free and deliberate human action or if it is something abnormal. Finally, the third issue considers whether the harm was too remote a consequence of the defendant's conduct. This, Hart and Honoré conceded, is a policy-based decision as to the appropriate scope of liability.[17] In essence they identified the first stage as factual, the second as being based on principle and the third as based on policy.

For them, the first two issues are truly causal and the final issue is non-causal. This conclusion was probably driven by Hart and Honoré's aim of countering the Legal Realists' criticisms that causation is not neutral but is policy-driven.[18] Hart and Honoré's work is important, among other reasons, for having shown that the task of identifying 'the cause' from among everything that could be called 'a cause' is not driven purely by policy but also by principle. However although the identification of causal connection is based on principle it is still an evaluative process and as such it ought not to be considered part of factual causation.

As Stapleton has highlighted, when Hart and Honoré address 'causally relevant condition' they say that 'a cause is basically like an element in a recipe' but when they discuss 'causal connection' they say that 'a cause is ... an intervention in the existing or expected course of events'.[19] To say that both of these inquiries are causal would create confusion whenever the word 'cause' is used as to which of these senses is intended. Stapleton explains, '[n]ot only are there two distinct underlying enquiries, one historical and one purposive, but the disputes to which they give rise are of a fundamentally different nature'.[20] Glanville Williams explained that Hart and Honoré's contention that '"it is the plain man's notions of causation (and not the philosopher's or the scientist's) with which the law is concerned" ... may be partly true of the legal notion of proximity, but it is not true of the lawyer's use of the notion of but-for causation'.[21] The first stage of identifying 'causally relevant conditions' is the factual aspect of causation which identifies the defendant's negligence as *a cause* and it is from this that Wright later developed the NESS account of causation. It is for this stage that the label of 'factual causation' ought to be reserved.[22] The later stages of causal connection and remoteness are both evaluative and address the question of whether the defendant can be considered *the cause* and should be grouped together under the rubric of 'legal causation'.

---

[17] ibid 305–07.

[18] Wright, 'Causation' (n 2) 1739.

[19] Hart and Honoré (n 7) 31 and 29. See Jane Stapleton, 'Unpacking "Causation"' in Peter Cane and John Gardner (eds), *Relating to Responsibility: Essays in Honour of Tony Honoré on his 80th birthday* (Hart Publishing, 2001) 159.

[20] Stapleton, 'Unpacking "Causation"' (n 19) 159.

[21] Glanville Williams, 'Causation in the Law' [1961] *Cambridge Law Journal* 62, 65.

[22] Stapleton has argued that since 'legal causation' is evaluative and not truly a question of causation it should be relabelled 'scope of liability for consequences' to avoid confusion ('Cause-in-Fact and the Scope of Liability for Consequences' (2003) 119 *Law Quarterly Review* 388). Analysis of this proposal is outside the scope of this work, what matters is that the doctrine of 'factual causation' has been defined.

Stapleton has highlighted an advantage of limiting the doctrine of causation to the purely factual question of involvement:

> This would then require us to locate the normative controversies about their different degrees of *responsibility* for the death under analytical labels such as 'duty', 'breach', … and so on. The great attraction of this approach is that under these analytical labels, unlike the label of 'causation', it has traditionally been unacceptable merely to assert a conclusion on the basis of 'intuition' or 'common sense'.[23]

So although the notion of a causally relevant condition is very inclusive when viewed in isolation, causation alone is not determinative of liability and the other doctrines enable the law to narrow liability from causal responsibility to interpersonal responsibility.

B. The Robustness of the Philosophical Account

The NESS test for factual causation that was developed by Wright, building on the work of Hart and Honoré on causally relevant conditions, is based on the dominant philosophical account of causation. This is David Hume's regularity account of causation and counterfactual analysis, later modified by John Stuart Mill.

Lord Hoffmann has questioned why academics insist on strict factual causation and say that if a court holds something that 'did not qualify as "cause in fact" as nevertheless satisfying its causal requirements, then it should be regarded as deeming something to be a cause when it was not *really* a cause'.[24] He argues:

> It is this concept of something having to be *really* a cause according to criteria lying outside the law which puzzles lawyers. On what basis are academic writers entitled to say that judges should take into account a philosophically privileged form of causation which satisfies criteria not required by the law?[25]

However, given that causation is essential to corrective justice it is important that the concept of causation adopted in law reflects the natural relation. It is the task of philosophers of causation to understand and explain this, rather than it being a legal creation or fiction. The confused state of the law on causation, in particular the lack of clarity concerning the meaning and scope of the legal test of 'material contribution to harm', shows what happens when courts develop causal requirements that are not firmly rooted in a philosophically sound account of causation. As Moore explains:

> [C]orrective-justice … demands a robustly metaphysical interpretation of cause. For legal liability tracks moral responsibility on this view, and moral responsibility is for those harms we *cause*. 'Cause' has to mean what we mean when we assign moral responsibility

---

[23] Stapleton, 'Choosing' (n 1) 446.
[24] Lord Hoffmann, 'Causation' in Goldberg (ed), *Perspectives on Causation* (n 3) 5.
[25] ibid.

for some harm, and what we mean in morality is to name a causal relation that is natural and *not* of the law's creation.[26]

Seeking an explanation from philosophy has been called 'philosophically naïve' by Broadbent who accuses Richard Wright of 'underestimat[ing] how difficult it is to provide a satisfactory account of causation itself'.[27] As Fumerton and Kress have also observed, '[p]hilosophers have labored long and hard on the question of how to analyze causation, with a striking lack of success'.[28] Furthermore, in the absence of a 'fully adequate universal test for factual causation', Broadbent asserts that there can be no such thing as 'factual causation' and that it will always be determined by the law.[29] Stapleton notes, for example, that for some philosophers an omission cannot constitute a cause while the law will readily identify omissions as causal.[30] What is sought, then, is an account of causation that is philosophically robust but also meets the law's needs. Pragmatism is required in law because the need to reach concrete decisions precludes waiting for philosophical accord. Miller explains, '[p]oliticians are not philosophers; they cannot wait for certainty before, for example, banning a drug which appears to have a harmful side-effect. Certainty will be similarly absent in evidence presented in any civil action taken by those so harmed'.[31] While there do remain points of philosophical debate about the meaning of causation, there is a dominant account and it is preferable for the law to adopt this account rather than seeking a distinct definition.

II. Causation in the Philosophy of Hume and Mill

To understand what it means to be a cause Hart and Honoré, and subsequently Wright, turned to the dominant philosophical account of causation provided by Hume and Mill.

A. Hume: Contiguity, Priority, Constant Conjunction and Necessity

According to Hume's account of causation the qualities that can be observed in the relationship between causes and effects are contiguity, succession, and constant

---

[26] Michael S Moore, *Causation and Responsibility: An Essay in Law, Morals, and Metaphysics* (Oxford University Press, 2009) 95.

[27] Alex Broadbent, 'Fact and Law in the Causal Inquiry' (2009) 15 *Legal Theory* 173, 176.

[28] Richard Fumerton and Ken Kress, 'Causation and the Law: Preemption, Lawful Sufficiency, and Causal Sufficiency' (2001) 64 *Law and Contemporary Problems* 83, 102.

[29] Broadbent, 'Fact and Law in the Causal Inquiry' (n 27) 178.

[30] Jane Stapleton, 'An "Extended But-For" Test for the Causal Relation' (2015) 35 *Oxford Journal of Legal Studies* 697.

[31] Chris Miller, 'Causation in Personal Injury: Legal or Epidemiological Common Sense?' (2006) 26 *Legal Studies* 544, 547.

conjunction. These observations form the regularity account of causation. They can be illustrated with an example provided by Hume:

> Here is a billiard-ball lying on the table, and another ball moving towards it with rapidity. They strike; and the ball, which was formerly at rest, now acquires a motion ... There was no interval betwixt the shock and the motion. *Contiguity* in time and place is therefore a requisite circumstance to the operation of all causes. 'Tis evident likewise, that the motion, which was the cause, is prior to the motion, which was the effect. *Priority* in time, is therefore another requisite circumstance in every cause. But this is not all. Let us try any other balls of the same kind in a like situation, and we shall always find, that the impulse of the one produces motion in the other. Here, therefore, is a *third* circumstance, *viz.* that of a *constant conjunction* betwixt the cause and effect. Every object like the cause, produces always some object like the effect.[32]

Hume then went on to consider the question of whether there is a relationship of necessity between cause and effect, and this is where the novelty of his account lay as Wright explains:

> Hume revolutionized philosophic thinking on causation when he insisted that, contrary to the then-popular belief, singular causal judgments are not based on direct perception of causal qualities or forces inherent in objects or events: no such quality or force has ever been identified. Instead, causal judgments are based on the belief that a certain succession of events instantiates one or more causal laws.[33]

In other words, we observe that necessity is what distinguishes a causal relationship but it does not exist as a quality internal to objects. So for any relationship of objects displaying contiguity, succession and constant conjunction, the element that distinguishes the causal from the non-causal is necessity. This introduces the element of counterfactual analysis in causation that allows us to test whether a factor that satisfies the regularity account is actually a cause. For example, an 'epiphenomenon' displays contiguity, succession and constant conjunction but does not cause the outcome: if *c* is an epiphenomenon of the causal history of *e* it is 'a more or less inefficacious effect of some genuine cause of *e*'.[34] An illustration of this is the needle on a barometer dropping before a storm. The drop in pressure *c*, first causes the barometer needle to fall *effect e*, and then causes a storm *effect f*: '*c* causes first *e* and then *f*, but *e* does not cause *f*'.[35] If the barometer is broken and the needle does not fall this does not affect the fact that the drop in the pressure has occurred so *effect f*, the storm, will still occur.

The necessity requirement explains an aspect of the House of Lords' decision in *Rothwell v Chemical and Insulating Co Ltd*[36] concerning claims for pleural plaques.

---

[32] David Hume, *An Abstract of a Treatise of Human Nature*, ed John Maynard Keynes and Piero Sraffa (Cambridge University Press, 1938) 11f.

[33] Wright, 'Pruning' (n 4) 1019.

[34] David Lewis, 'Causation' (1973) 70 *Journal* of Philosophy 556, 557.

[35] ibid 566.

[36] *Rothwell v Chemical and Insulating Co Ltd and another, Topping v Benchtown Ltd (formerly Jones Bros Preston Ltd), Johnston v NEI International Combustion Ltd, Grieves v F T Everard & Sons Ltd and another* [2007] UKHL 39, [2008] 1 AC 281.

Among other heads of damages, the claimants were unable to recover for the increased risk of contracting asbestos-related illness because pleural plaques do not increase this risk. Pleural plaques will often be observed prior to the development of other asbestos-related illness; however, they do not increase the risk of such illness but merely signal that the patient is at an increased risk of contracting an illness because he has inhaled asbestos dust. It is the quality of necessity that differentiates asbestos dust as causative of certain cancers from pleural plaques as non-causative but merely indicative of the risk. Pleural plaques are, in effect, a human equivalent of the needle on a barometer dropping before a storm.

In summary, causation thus consists of three empirical elements: contiguity, succession and constant conjunction; and a non-empirical element: belief in necessary connection.[37] Despite its non-empirical character, Hart and Honoré have observed that necessity has entered modern thinking in an altered form having 'changed its psychological form for a logical one'.[38]

B. Mill: The Addition of 'Plurality' and 'Complexity'

Hume, however, still largely wrote about 'an object' or 'an event' as cause and effect, so of a cause having a single effect, and an effect having a single cause. Mill subsequently made two crucial modifications to Hume's account of causation, recognising the 'plurality of causes' and the 'complexity of causes'.[39]

i. Complexity of Causes

The complexity of causes means that an occurrence does not have a single object or event as its cause, but the cause is the sum total of a set of positive and negative conditions. Drawing on the scenario used by Hume above, the causal law concerning the movement of the billiard ball did not just contain the event of being struck by the other ball, but of being struck by a ball 'of the same kind in a like situation'. Being struck by a smaller ball, at a different speed, or on a different surface, may not lead to the same result. So an event is caused by the coming together of a set of conditions. Wright explains:

> A fully specified causal law or generalization would state an invariable connection between the cause and the consequence: given the actual existence of the fully specified set of antecedent conditions, the consequence must follow.[40]

Each of the conditions that makes up the complete set has an equal status. Each is equally deserving of being called a cause, because in the absence of any of them

---

[37] Tom L Beauchamp and Alexander Rosenberg, *Hume and the Problem of Causation* (Oxford University Press, 1981) 4.

[38] Hart and Honoré (n 7) 14.

[39] Hart and Honoré (n 7) 19. Writing about Mill, *System of Logic*.

[40] Wright, 'Causation' (n 2) 1789.

the outcome would not have occurred: 'it is in fact related to the effect in precisely the same way as the other constituents of the set'.[41] The idea that every factor that makes up the set is equally deserving of the label 'cause' is a situation Mackie describes as being 'symmetrical with respect to all the factors'.[42] Causation, in Honoré's words, provides a 'recipe' for the set of conditions that are together sufficient to produce a given result.[43]

As noted at the start of this chapter,[44] the causal inquiry in negligence is focused on the question of whether the negligence was a cause of the damage, so it is unnecessary to provide the whole 'recipe'. This does not prevent the legal concept of causation from being based on the philosophical account since it is possible to remain faithful to Mill's explanation of causation whilst on a practical level being content to only partially populate the sufficient set that instantiates the causal law in question as Wright explains:

> In the typical singular causal statement, the causal assertion includes, explicitly or implicitly, only a few of the antecedent conditions but nevertheless asserts that they were only part of an incompletely specified (and incompletely understood or known) set of actual conditions that was sufficient for the occurrence of the consequence.[45]

Beever criticises this position, arguing that it means that 'the law's understanding of causation is looser than science's' and that this is inconsistent with the requirement that 'the lawyer's conception of causation must be philosophical and scientific for it to be a conception of causation'.[46] Beever provides an example of a barn that has burnt down because the defendant placed his rick of hay against it which caught on fire. He says that science would require not just the presence of the rick of hay, but all the other conditions making up the sufficiency of the set for the causal law, such as the dryness of the hay, sufficient heat, the barn being made of flammable material, the presence of oxygen etc. In contrast, Wright would say that these conditions are not relevant in law, because the law is satisfied to say that the rick of hay was one antecedent condition which was part of an incompletely specified set. This leads Beever to believe that Wright is saying that the legal concept of causation is different to the scientific concept of causation. To support this argument he says that the other constituents of the set are not irrelevant because the court would not be likely to conclude that the rick of hay caused the destruction of the barn if the rick was soaking wet, or the hay did not ignite, or the barn was made of concrete.[47] Whilst Beever is right to say that the court would reach a

---

[41] Hart and Honoré (n 7) 21.

[42] Mackie, *The Cement of the Universe* (n 13) 34.

[43] Tony Honoré, 'Necessary and Sufficient Conditions in Tort Law' in David G Owen (ed), *Philosophical Foundations of Tort Law* (Oxford University Press, 1995) 375.

[44] See text to n 11.

[45] Wright, 'Causation' (n 2) 1789.

[46] Allan Beever, 'Cause-in-fact: Two Steps Out of the Mire' (2001) 51 *University of Toronto Law Journal* 327, 344.

[47] ibid 344.

different conclusion about causation if it knew that any of these other conditions were present, this does not mean that it adopts a different, unscientific and unphilosophical concept of causation if it does not list all of the conditions. The underlying concept of causation is the same as the philosophical or scientific one, but the court's purpose is not to discover every element of the causal set. Instead the court's objective is to determine simply whether one specific candidate condition, the defendant's negligence, in fact belonged to the set. The court therefore relies on the information presented to it, so if the defendant establishes that counter-conditions, such as the rick being soaking wet, were present, then the court will add these into the causal set. But if no such conditions are presented, then as a practical measure the court is justified in being satisfied that the rick was a cause of the destruction of the claimant's barn, particularly when we remember that a court need only be persuaded on the balance of probabilities that it was a cause. The concept of causation does not change, but pragmatism (and the evidential standard) leads the law to be satisfied to address only those candidate conditions that are presented to it.

ii. Plurality of Causes

In addition to causes being 'complex', they are also 'plural': there is not just one set of conditions that is capable of causing the outcome; instead, there are a number of different possible sets, each of which is capable of causing the same outcome. So, for example, a billiard ball may move because it is struck by another ball, or because the table is tilted or because air is blown at it etc. In summary, a single outcome is caused by a set of conditions rather than having a single cause, and various different sets of conditions can exist that are all capable of causing the same single outcome.

In this account necessity is still essential as the quality that distinguishes causally relevant antecedents:

> [O]ne must be careful when constructing a causal law or generalization to distinguish the causally relevant antecedent conditions from the causally irrelevant antecedent conditions. This differentiation is necessary to insure that the set of jointly sufficient antecedent conditions includes only those that are indeed invariably connected with the consequence. Thus, the antecedent conditions must be restricted to those that are *necessary* for the sufficiency of the set.[48]

Necessity has been confined to a smaller role because for a given effect it is not *necessary* for it to be preceded by a particular cause since there exist a number of possible sets capable of causing the effect. So although each condition is necessary for the sufficiency of a particular set, each particular set can only be described as 'sufficient' to bring about the effect.

---

[48] Wright, 'Causation' (n 2) 1790.

Hart and Honoré noted a philosophical objection to the idea of plurality of causes in the argument that there may exist an equal plurality of effects but we fail to differentiate effects with the same precision that we apply to causes: the 'apparent plurality of causes is due to our failure or inability to analyse the effects with the same particularity as the causes'.[49] So if we were able to particularise any single effect sufficiently we would see that it only has one possible cause. This is similar to saying that we must be more precise than simply saying a person died and, for example, specify that she died from a heart attack, or from poisoning. It is simply saying that we need to continue this process of precision in our description of the event until we have as many effects as we have causes.

They noted that this philosophical objection is not universally accepted, but argued that whether or not it is well-founded, 'the lawyer, the historian, and the plain man accept the doctrine that an event of a given kind may be produced by different causes'.[50] That the doctrine of plurality of causes is accepted can be illustrated by close consideration, for example, of the cause of a heart attack. A heart attack occurs because part of the heart muscle dies when it is starved of oxygen, usually because of a blockage in a coronary artery. Such blockages can occur for a multitude of reasons with risk factors including smoking, high blood pressure, lack of exercise and poor diet.[51] Rather than attempting to analyse the effect, the heart attack, in ever more detail, the ordinary person accepts that the effect has a plurality of possible causal sets, each containing one of the many possible combinations of these, and other, risk factors. Hart and Honoré's pragmatism is justifiable on the basis that if we did not accept plurality of causes then we would never accept any causal law as being true, and never be able to make causal judgements. Causal conclusions in law cannot wait until the moment when, indeed if, science advances to a point where effects can be adequately particularised. In other words, this is one point where pragmatism is necessary since the law cannot wait for philosophy and science to become settled.[52]

Part II: Tests for Causation

So far this chapter has identified the demands that negligence places on the doctrine of causation, and the philosophical account of the concept of causation. It is now possible to build on these foundations to analyse the possible tests for causation. It will be argued that the NESS test should be adopted instead of the but-for test because it reflects the concept of causation more accurately. While the but-for test has the attraction of apparent simplicity compared to the NESS test,

---

[49] Hart and Honoré (n 7) 20.
[50] ibid 20.
[51] www.nhs.uk/Conditions/Heart-attack/Pages/Causes.aspx
[52] See text to n 31.

it only functions correctly in straightforward cases, and in those cases the NESS test operates just as simply. In the more complex cases of over-determined causation, the but-for test fails because it is not an accurate test of causation, so courts have developed exceptions whose scope and meaning are unclear. In contrast, the NESS test is able to cope with these more complex cases, and because it accurately reflects the concept of causation it enables us to visualise the causal problems and solutions without resorting to exceptional tests.

I. Complexity and Plurality of Causes as Necessary and Sufficient Conditions

The philosophical account of causation described above established the following qualities as characteristics of causes: contiguity of cause and effect, priority in time and constant conjunction. In addition, necessity is the quality that distinguishes causal factors from non-causal factors. Moreover, causes are complex: an outcome is the result of a set of conditions coming together; and plural: multiple possible sets can each bring about the same outcome. The NESS test will be shown to be preferable to the but-for test on a theoretical level because it more accurately reflects these qualities.

There are different degrees to which a single factor, such as a defendant's negligence, might be thought sufficient or necessary for the occurrence of the harm. These are explained by Wright:

> In descending order of stringency, a strict-necessity test requires that Q be necessary for the occurrence of R whenever R occurs; a less stringent, strong-necessity test requires only that Q have been necessary for the occurrence of R on the particular occasion, considering the circumstances that existed on the particular occasion; and the least stringent, weak-necessity test requires only that Q have been a necessary element of some set of actual conditions that was sufficient for the occurrence of R ... A strict sufficiency test requires that Q be sufficient by itself for the occurrence of R; a less stringent, strong-sufficiency test requires only that Q be a necessary element of some set of existing conditions that was sufficient for the occurrence of R ...; and the least stringent, weak-sufficiency test 'requires' only that Q be a part of some set of existing conditions that was sufficient for the occurrence of R.[53]

Some of these types of test can easily be discarded because they clearly do not reflect the characteristics of causes. Strict necessity would mean that a particular effect only ever has one possible cause, but this is precluded by the notion of plurality of causes. Similarly, strict sufficiency, the idea that one single factor can be sufficient to bring about an effect, is precluded since causes are 'complex'. Weak sufficiency does not incorporate the vital characteristic of necessity to any

---

[53] Wright, 'Pruning' (n 4) 1020.

UNIVERSITY OF WINCHESTER LIBRARY

degree so it is unable to determine whether a factor was a cause. The remaining possibilities are strong necessity and weak necessity (or its equivalent, strong sufficiency). The but-for test asks whether a factor was necessary for the occurrence of harm on the particular occasion so it is a test of strong necessity. The NESS test does not require the factor to have been necessary for the harm on the particular occasion, but allows for the possibility that more than one sufficient set of factors may have existed on the particular occasion. As long as the factor was necessary for the sufficiency of one of the sets that actually occurred on the particular occasion then it was a cause. The NESS test therefore corresponds to weak necessity.[54] Although the but-for test acknowledges the plurality of causes insofar as it recognises that a variety of different sets *could* potentially cause a particular outcome, it does not take the notion of plurality to its logical conclusion because it assumes that each potential set only ever occurs singularly.[55] The NESS test recognises that more than one set may *actually* occur simultaneously. Practical examples will show that this complete incorporation of plurality is correct.

A. But-For and NESS in Simple Cases

The but-for test is illustrated clearly by the case of *Barnett v Chelsea and Kensington Hospital Management Committee*[56] where the claimant's husband became ill after drinking a cup of tea. He went to hospital where the staff were negligent in their failure to examine and treat him, instead sending him home with advice to see his GP the next day. The victim died from arsenic poisoning in his tea but despite the negligence of the hospital staff his claim failed at the causation stage because but-for their negligence he would still have died. Given the time that had elapsed between drinking the tea and arriving at hospital, the time it would have taken to examine and diagnose the illness and begin treatment, the treatment would have failed to save him. In the circumstances, including the stage of advancement of the poisoning, the doctor's negligence was not necessary for the outcome, it made no difference. Herein lies the appeal of the but-for test, it answers the question 'did the defendant's act make a difference?'.[57] Yet it is widely recognised that the but-for test is of limited use because as well as excluding irrelevant conditions 'it can also exclude others that are relevant'[58] in cases where

---

[54] ibid 1021.

[55] Mackie's INUS test ('insufficient but necessary part of an unnecessary but sufficient set' test) incorporates the plurality of causes since it recognises that a particular sufficient set of conditions need not be necessary for the outcome. See Mackie (n 13). For any particular instance of causation, however, it only recognises the occurrence of one sufficient set which, as Wright explains, converts the INUS account into the *sine qua non* ('but-for') account. See Wright, 'The NESS Account' (n 3) 288. Since it is applied in the same way as the but-for test it will not be analysed separately.

[56] *Barnett v Chelsea and Kensington Hospital Management Committee* [1968] 2 WLR 422 (QBD).

[57] Moore, *Causation and Responsibility* (n 26) 84.

[58] Honoré, 'Necessary and Sufficient Conditions in Tort Law' (n 43) 363–64.

an outcome is 'over-determined' as in the classic double-hit hunters scenario discussed in the next section.

The NESS test was developed by Richard Wright in response to the weaknesses of the but-for test and built upon ideas initially developed by Hart and Honoré in *Causation in the Law*. In this account of causation something is a cause if it was a Necessary Element of a Sufficient Set:

> *a particular condition was a cause of (condition contributing to) a specific consequence if and only if it was a necessary element of a set of antecedent actual conditions that was sufficient for the occurrence of the consequence.* (Note that the phrase 'a set' permits a plurality of sufficient sets.).[59]

The first part of this is uncontroversial; since causes are 'complex' any outcome is caused by the coming together of a set of conditions which are together sufficient to cause it. The novelty of the NESS test is that it fully incorporates plurality, so while in most instances one particular outcome will only have been preceded by one of these possible sets, the NESS test recognises that multiple sets may actually occur.

Where only one set actually occurs the NESS test would not complicate the way the law currently works. For example in *Barnett* there are many ways that the claimant's husband's death could have been caused but only one, poisoning with arsenic, actually occurred. The doctor's negligence was not necessary for the sufficiency of the set of conditions that actually occurred because the treatment would still have been too late even if the doctor had examined the patient. In these straightforward cases the NESS test would effectively collapse into the but-for test; the but-for test is shorthand for the NESS test where there is only one set of conditions. This makes it clear that widespread adoption of the NESS test would not have the effect of complicating cases generally which should allay possible fears that adopting the NESS test would lead to increased litigation.

A sufficient set could, of course, be infinite in the sense that it would extend backwards to include all prior factors leading up to the event in question including, for example, the defendant's conception and birth. This same concern also afflicts the but-for test since the defendant's birth is a but-for condition of her eventually going on to act negligently. Miller explains that:

> Rather than ponder with incredulity the infinite web of contingency that has made the present what it is rather than what it might have been, we assume the existence of boundaries, within space and time, within which we can effectively confine our causal discourse.[60]

Since the causation question in negligence is not open-ended but is focused on whether the defendant's negligence was a cause of the claimant's damage, the breach of duty inquiry forms such a boundary. Although an infinite number of people's failure to prevent the harm could be included in a sufficient set for that

---

[59] Wright, 'Causation' (n 2) 1790.
[60] Chris Miller, 'NESS for Beginners' in Goldberg (n 3) 333.

harm, the duty and breach doctrines limit the search to those who breached a legal duty to take positive steps to prevent the harm.

It has been suggested that Wright's NESS test could also identify spurious true statements about the world as being NESSs which are not actually causal. Fumerton and Kress claim that in Wright's NESS test a factor such as the colour of a person's shirt could become a necessary element of a sufficient set of conditions for a fire. We know that the set of conditions for a fire is fuel, oxygen and ignition. The fact that I am wearing a blue shirt is not a NESS of the fire. Fumerton and Kress then ask us to imagine a complex state of affairs where 'either I did not wear a blue shirt or there was a fire'. If we combine this with the fact that I was wearing a blue shirt then we have the statements: 'I was wearing a blue shirt' *and* 'if I did not wear a blue shirt there was not a fire'. Working backwards from our knowledge that there was a fire, the wearing of a blue shirt becomes a necessary condition for it. In this case, they say, 'clearly, something has gone wrong'.[61] Wright has shown that it is not the NESS test that goes wrong, but Fumerton and Kress's misinterpretation of the test, since this possibility is excluded by the requirement that the set is *actually occurring*. His test is not simply that of a 'necessary element of a sufficient set' but a 'necessary element of an actually occurring sufficient set'. In the above example it is not possible for both 'I wore a blue shirt' and 'I did not wear a blue shirt' to *actually* occur.[62] Thus, if we remember that NESS is shorthand for 'a necessary element of an actually occurring sufficient set' then NESS remains accurate and simple to apply.

Returning to the but-for test, since strong necessity (but-for) is more stringent, a factor that is strongly necessary will also satisfy a test of weak-necessity. But the reverse is not true—a factor that fails the test of strong-necessity may still be a cause because causation only requires weak-necessity. The but-for test can tell us that something *was* a cause, it is 'a test of inclusion',[63] but it cannot accurately tell us whether something *was not* a cause. As Honoré has said:

> No one will deny that the but-for test has in many instances a heuristic value: it often provides a quick way of testing the existence of causal connection. However, it is another matter whether it is part of the *meaning* of 'causally relevant condition' or 'cause'.[64]

The but-for test fails to deal adequately with more complex causal problems because it does not accurately correspond to the characteristics of causation identified by Hume and Mill. So the fact that we are often able to rely on the but-for test should not be allowed to mislead into the belief that it is the best test to use. As Wright argues, 'the substitute must give way to the more accurate and comprehensive concept when the situation is more subtle and complex'.[65]

---

[61] Fumerton and Kress, 'Causation and the Law' (n 28) 95.
[62] Wright, 'The NESS Account' (n 3) 295.
[63] Wright, 'Pruning' (n 4) 1022.
[64] Honoré (n 43) 367.
[65] Wright, 'Causation' (n 2) 1792.

B. Over-determined Causation

'Over-determination' means that there seem to be too many causes. Where this takes the form of 'duplication' two or more possible causes occur at the same time, and in 'pre-emption' the possible causes occur one after the other.[66]

i. But-For, NESS and Pre-Emption

Pre-emption describes a scenario where two acts could each have been sufficient to cause the harm, but one occurs before the other so the second one never gets to run its course. This is illustrated by the classic desert traveller scenario: *A* puts poison in the water keg of a desert traveller which is sufficient to kill her if she drinks it but before she drinks the water, *B* empties the keg, and the traveller dies of thirst. The but-for test leads to the conclusion that neither act was a cause of the traveller's death: if she had not died of thirst she would have died from poisoning and *vice versa*. Effectively, the but-for test 'produces the absurd result that the plaintiff's injury was uncaused'.[67]

It has been suggested that the but-for test would identify *B* as the cause of the desert traveller's death if the outcome was described more precisely as 'death when and as it happened', ie death through dehydration at that particular moment. This tactic of 'detailing the injury', Wright argues, is 'nothing more than proof by tautology' because '[t]he factors believed to be causally relevant ... are incorporated into the description of the manner of occurrence of the injury ..., and they are then demonstrated to be causally relevant because we cannot construct that precise description without them'.[68] It is therefore clear that the but-for test cannot cope adequately with pre-emptive causation.

The legal solution to this absurd outcome would be to impose liability on one or both parties despite the failure to satisfy the legal test for causation. Such a solution is driven by the instinctive knowledge that the death cannot be 'uncaused', one or both parties must be responsible for the death despite the difficulty of establishing

---

[66] Hart and Honoré used different labels to describe the forms of over-determined causation, stating that 'an event may be causally over-determined either because two conditions each sufficient though not necessary in the circumstances for its occurrence are present together (additional causes) or because they are so related that if one had not been present the other would have been (alternative causes)' (Hart and Honoré (n 7) xl). Wright's terminology of 'duplication' and 'pre-emption' is adopted here for two reasons. First, given the emphasis on the importance of clear use of technical terminology, it is preferable to avoid the term 'alternative causes' which is sometimes used with a different meaning in the case law as a contrast with 'cumulative causes'. Secondly, Wright's account benefits from greater analytical clarity on this point because, as he observed, 'Hart and Honoré also submerged and sometimes confused the critical distinction between duplicative and pre-emptive causation by constructing an overlapping typology of overdetermined cases', so they did not always maintain a clear distinction between the two forms of over-determination (Wright, 'The NESS Account' (n 3) 287).

[67] Beever, 'Cause-in-fact' (n 46) 331.

[68] Wright, 'Causation' (n 2) 1778.

a causal link. Thus reliance on the but-for test effectively turns the legal solution to pre-emption into a value judgement as to responsibility. But, as Hamer has argued, 'the over-determination problem is one of fact and philosophy rather than value and policy'.[69] This is also an unnecessarily complicated 'solution' because there is not really a 'problem' regarding the existence of a causal link and this can be seen by explaining and applying the NESS test.

In contrast to the but-for test, the NESS test asks whether the negligence was a 'necessary element of a set of antecedent *actual* conditions that was sufficient for the occurrence of the consequence' (emphasis added).[70] In the desert traveller scenario, by poisoning the water flask A created the *potential* for a set to occur that would be sufficient to bring about the traveller's death. However, for the set of conditions to be complete, in other words for it *actually* to be sufficient, the traveller must drink the water containing the poison. Until she drinks the poison there is not an *actually occurring* set of conditions sufficient to cause her death that contains A's act of adding poison to the water. Since B then emptied the water (and therefore also the poison) the traveller never actually drank the poison. This means that A's act was prevented from becoming part of an *actually occurring* set of conditions that were together sufficient to cause the death, so A is not a cause of the harm.[71] A set of conditions jointly sufficient to cause the death now exists containing just B's act of emptying the flask. This set of conditions runs its course so it is an *actually occurring* set, so B is a cause.

This has an appearance of similarity with the 'detailing the injury' tactic that was dismissed above, but there is a subtle yet significant difference in emphasis. The effect of detailing the injury is to incorporate certain conditions into the description of the outcome, and then to undertake a retrospective inquiry to locate those factors. The emphasis in applying the NESS test is more prospective, working through the events that occurred until a sufficient set actually occurs. As Wright explains, 'the focus in the analysis of factual causation is (or should be) not on what might have happened if things had been different, but rather on what actually did happen and why'.[72]

ii. But-For, NESS and Duplication

The plurality of causes means that one outcome could be caused by a variety of sufficient sets and usually only one of these sets will actually have occurred, but over-determination in the form of duplication arises when more than one sufficient set of conditions actually occurs. Duplication, in its simplest form, is

---

[69] David Hamer, 'Chance would be a Fine Thing': Proof of Causation and Quantum in an Unpredictable World' (1999) 23 *Melbourne University Law Review* 557, 571.

[70] Wright, 'Causation' (n 2) 1790.

[71] See ibid 1795.

[72] Richard Wright, 'Acts and Omissions as Positive and Negative Causes' in Jason W Neyers, Erika Chamberlain and Stephen GA Pitel (eds), *Emerging Issues in Tort Law* (Hart Publishing, 2007) 296.

illustrated by the classic 'double-hit hunters' example: Hunter *A* fires her gun and the bullet hits a walker. The walker dies and the bullet was sufficient to cause her death. In the ordinary course of events, Hunter *A* would be considered to have caused the death because her bullet was sufficient to result in the death. However, Hunter *A*'s bullet was 'duplicated' by Hunter *B* simultaneously firing her gun and also hitting the walker with a bullet that was sufficient to cause the death.

If we apply the but-for test to determine whether Hunter *A* was a cause of the walker's death then the answer is 'no'. But-for Hunter *A*'s shot, the walker would still have died because Hunter *B*'s bullet was sufficient to kill her, so Hunter *A* made no difference to the outcome and was not a cause of the death. Likewise, but-for Hunter *B*'s shot, the walker would still have been killed by Hunter *A* so Hunter *B* made no difference to the outcome and is not a cause. Once again, the but-for test 'produces the absurd result that the plaintiff's injury was uncaused'.[73]

In contrast, the NESS test fully incorporates the plurality of causes and asks whether the negligence was necessary for the sufficiency of *a* sufficient set that actually occurred.[74] It therefore allows for the existence of more than one actually occurring set. If we subtract Hunter *B*'s shot we are left with a set of conditions containing Hunter *A*'s shot, along with wind speed and direction, the walker's presence, the walker still being alive etc., that are sufficient to cause the walker's death, and Hunter *A*'s shot is necessary for this set to be sufficient. Likewise if we subtract Hunter *A*'s shot we are left with a set of conditions containing Hunter *B*'s shot that is sufficient to cause the walker's death and Hunter *B*'s shot is necessary for the sufficiency of this set. The plurality of causes, as identified by Mill, means that there are also many other possible sets that would hypothetically have been sufficient to cause the walker's death had they occurred at that moment, for example a tree toppling onto her, but none of these other sets *actually* occurred. However, the fact that two sufficient sets independently and simultaneously have *actually* occurred does not prevent either set from being a cause. Usually only one set will actually occur, but on the rare occasion that two sets *actually* occur then both are causes.

Whereas the but-for test told us that Hunter *A made no difference to the outcome* because the walker would have died anyway so Hunter *A* is not a cause, the NESS test tells us that in order for the walker's death to have been prevented Hunter *A*'s shot *would have to be absent* so Hunter *A* is a cause, and that Hunter *B*'s shot would also have to be absent so Hunter *B* is also a cause.[75] This is a subtle yet significant shift in emphasis and one which better reflects the reality that given the plurality of causes it is possible, albeit rare, for two or more causes independently to occur at the same time.

Naturally, more complex causal problems exist, and these will be addressed in due course, but so far it is clear that the NESS test, rather than the but-for test,

---

[73] Beever (n 46) 331.
[74] See text to n 70.
[75] Stapleton, 'Choosing' (n 1) 438.

accurately reflects and tests the qualities that were shown by Hume and Mill to characterise causes. The NESS test has therefore been described as 'a real contribution to legal analysis. It provides an extremely helpful way of conceptualizing the nature of causal problems, and it offers a rational process for identifying causes in over-determined cause cases'.[76] This means that on a theoretical level it would be preferable to adopt the NESS test. It represents a slight shift in emphasis from the but-for test which treats as a cause 'something in the absence of which harm would not have come about', to calling a cause 'something such that in the prevailing conditions harm comes about' under the NESS test.[77] This may seem subtle but it is very significant because it accurately translates the meaning of causation and the characteristics of causes into a workable test. In practice, the NESS test will frequently collapse into the but-for test because most cases involve straightforward causal models, but NESS is to be preferred because it is able to tackle complex issues of causation in a way that the but-for test cannot. This choice is 'not governed by policy considerations, but rather by how well each test corresponds with our intuitive concept of causation' based on the philosophical explanation of causation.[78]

II. Overcoming Potential Problems with NESS

The final section of this chapter will use the NESS test to overcome some common legal problems that are currently addressed using the *Wardlaw* test of 'material contribution to harm',[79] but first the penultimate section addresses some potential problems with the NESS test.

The problem with the *Wardlaw* test is that it is not clear how exceptional it is; it may be an exception to the but-for test that compensates for the conceptual inadequacies of that test, or it may involve a relaxation of the causation requirement itself. This problem arises because it is unclear precisely what causal problem is addressed by the test. The NESS test would similarly face potential problems in more complex cases if causation were analysed in isolation from the negligence inquiry. This section therefore uses the damage doctrine to incorporate a more nuanced idea of 'outcome' into Wright's NESS test. In the final section it will then be seen that the NESS test allows us a level of conceptual clarity that is absent in the *Wardlaw* test.

Wright has explained that duplicated causation can take a more complex form than that encapsulated in the double-hit hunters scenario. The double-hit hunters scenario involves 'symmetrical duplication': causation is duplicated since the

---

[76] David A Fischer, 'Insufficient Causes' (2005) 94 *Kentucky Law Journal* 277, 281.
[77] Honoré (n 43) 385.
[78] Wright, 'Pruning' (n 4) 1020.
[79] *Bonnington Castings v Wardlaw* (n 5).

two shots are simultaneous, and this duplication is symmetrical in the sense that since each shot (as part of a set of conditions) is sufficient for the walker's death independently of the other. In a case of 'asymmetrical duplication' there is still duplication in that there is simultaneous exposure to the harmful substance in excess of the required threshold for harm, but it is 'asymmetrical' in that each exposure is not independently sufficient. To borrow an example from Stapleton, where a group of company directors vote unanimously to market a product that harms customers and only a majority vote is required, there is duplication in that the number of votes exceeds the number required for harm, and this duplication is 'asymmetrical' in that no single vote is independently sufficient for harm but must be combined with others.[80] Wright explains that the NESS test can be used to address asymmetrical duplication, but his application of the NESS test seems to be so inclusive that it risks becoming useless as a functioning test for causation in negligence. It is important, however, to apply the NESS test within the context of the negligence inquiry, and defining the damage precisely at the outset shows that asymmetrical duplication is actually a very limited causal problem. In this limited problem, the NESS test is very inclusive but is also accurate. Again it is important to remember that causation is not determinative of liability; causation is a factual relation so the contours of the test for it cannot be driven by the perceived fairness of the outcome. The limits of liability must be addressed by other doctrines, and here there are issues relating to quantification and to the effects of joint and several liability.

A. Defining Key Causal Terms

A distinction is drawn in negligence cases between so-called 'divisible' and 'indivisible' damage. This terminology broadly corresponds to the scientific terminology of 'stochastic' or 'non-stochastic' disease. An indivisible, or stochastic, disease is an 'all-or-nothing' phenomenon:

> There is almost always a clear distinction between people who have the disorder and those who do not. The disease can differ in its severity from one case to another, but the factors that determine its severity are in general quite different from those that determine whether or not it occurs at all.[81]

In contrast, non-stochastic diseases 'occur in a continuum of severity with no clear distinction between cases and non-cases' although '[d]octors may adopt a

---

[80] Jane Stapleton, 'Reflections on Common Sense Causation in Australia' in Simone Degeling, James Edelman and James Goudkamp (eds), *Torts in Commercial Law* (Thomson Reuters Australia, 2011) 350, drawing on the 'Lederspray' case: Bundesgerichtshof (German Federal Court of Justice), 37 BGHSt 106, 6 July 1990 reported in (1990) BGH NJW 2650.

[81] David Coggon and Anthony Newman Taylor, 'Causation and Attribution of Disease in Personal Injury Cases: a Scientific Perspective' [2009] *Journal of Personal Injury Law* 12, 13.

dichotomous case definition to facilitate the practical management of patients'.[82] In other words, the disease gradually worsens and at a particular level of severity it is deemed to exist although 'the chosen threshold is to some extent arbitrary'.[83] Divisible disease is therefore dose-related and each exposure to the causal agent makes the illness more severe. For example, in *Thompson v Smiths Shiprepairers*,[84] the claimant's loss of hearing was divisible because it gradually worsened with exposure to noise. Similarly, the claimant's pneumoconiosis in *Cartledge v E Jopling*,[85] and the claimant's asbestosis in *Holtby v Brigham & Cowan*[86] were divisible diseases because they became more severe the more the claimant inhaled silica dust or asbestos respectively.

As Coggan and Taylor explain, the term 'stochastic' means relating to chance, so the probability of suffering a stochastic disease depends on exposure to risk factors. This means that although it is not possible to state whether an individual will develop a particular disease, it is possible to say how their probability of developing the disease is affected by particular factors. So

> the potency of a cause can be quantified in terms of the 'relative risk' that it carries for the disease … For example, smoking 20 cigarettes per day for 40 years might increase the risk of lung cancer 15-fold in comparison with a non-smoker—a relative risk of 15.[87]

In contrast, because non-stochastic diseases gradually develop in severity, we cannot sensibly talk about the probability of developing the disease and instead 'the potency of a cause is most meaningfully quantified by its average impact on the severity of a disease'.[88] The term 'divisible' is effectively a lay term to describe the relationship between the disease and its causes in non-stochastic diseases where each exposure to the harmful agent makes the disease worse.

It is important to note that describing the outcome as divisible is not the same as describing the exposure to sources or triggers of the harmful outcome as 'divisible' or 'cumulative'.[89] If the exposures are 'divisible' in the sense that there were a number of exposures, simultaneous or spread over a period of time, the damage may still be indivisible if it occurs once a particular threshold has passed but does not continue to increase in severity with the increase in dose.[90]

---

[82] ibid.

[83] ibid.

[84] *Thompson v Smiths Shiprepairers (North Shields) Ltd* [1984] QB 405 (QBD).

[85] *Cartledge v E Jopling & Sons Ltd* [1963] AC 758 (HL).

[86] *Holtby v Brigham & Cowan (Hull) Ltd* [2000] 3 All ER 421 (CA).

[87] Coggon and Taylor, 'Causation and Attribution of Disease' (n 81) 14.

[88] ibid.

[89] See also *Sienkiewicz v Greif (UK) Ltd* [2011] UKSC 10, [2011] 2 WLR 523, [12]–[14] (Lord Phillips)

[90] This will be revisited in relation to terminology used to describe *Wardlaw* since some commentators use the terms alternative and cumulative to signal that the exposures are divisible/indivisible, others use these terms to signal divisibility of damage.

B. Applying NESS to Indivisible Damage: The Problem of Asymmetrical Duplication

To illustrate asymmetrical duplication, Wright considers a river pollution scenario where five units of pollution were necessary and sufficient for the injury that followed, and each of seven defendants discharged one unit of pollution.[91] He explains two details in a footnote. First, he 'assume[s] that the injury was not accelerated or aggravated by the extra units of pollution. If it was, causal contribution would be even clearer'.[92] Second, he assumes

> that the units of pollution arrived simultaneously at the site of the injury. Obviously, if five units arrived before the other two and produced the injury before the other two arrived, the first five units were causes of the injury and the last two were not. Their potential effects were pre-empted by the effects of the first five.[93]

Where these criteria are met the NESS test, as will be explained later, considers each unit to be a cause. These details, however, are immensely significant in understanding the causal problem so they should not be confined to a footnote. The facts must be addressed in more detail before addressing the application of the NESS test to them.

First of all, it is essential to identify whether the injury was aggravated by the extra units of pollution. If each unit aggravated the injury, ie made it more severe, then the damage occurs along a continuum of severity and is 'divisible'.[94] As explained in chapter one, Stapleton insists:

> It cannot be over-emphasised that the formulation of the 'damage' forming the gist of the action *defines* the causation question. Logically one can only deal with causation after one knows what the damage forming the gist of the action is.[95]

It is essential to identify the damage at the outset, and to determine whether it is divisible or indivisible. If the damage is divisible then each unit of pollution causes a portion of the damage. So where the damage is divisible, the duplication

---

[91] Wright, 'Causation' (n 2) 1793. If this seems somewhat abstract, Stapleton provides an alternative example based on the 'Lederspray' decision of the German Federal Supreme Court 37 BGHSt 106, 6 July 1990 where a group of company directors each voted in favour of marketing a product that was extremely toxic and its use resulted in the death of a number of consumers. Although the vote was unanimous, only a majority was required under the company's voting rules. As in the fish example, the damage is indivisible, the votes are effective simultaneously, a threshold number of votes is required, and no single vote is independently necessary or sufficient. See Stapleton, 'Unnecessary Causes' (2013) 129 *Law Quarterly Review* 39, 43.

[92] ibid.

[93] ibid.

[94] If it was 'accelerated' then the damage is actually still indivisible, this point will be revisited later in relation to indivisible damage.

[95] Jane Stapleton, 'The Gist of Negligence: Part 2 The Relationship Between 'Damage' and Causation' (1988) 104 *Law Quarterly Review* 389, 393.

problem simply does not arise because each unit causes the damage to be more severe.[96] (This does not mean that proof of causation in divisible damage cases is entirely unproblematic, indeed it will be analysed in more depth later, it just means that where the damage is divisible we do not face a problem of duplication.)

It should also be noted that the problem of asymmetrical duplication, as the name implies, is unique to duplication rather than pre-emption, as Wright commented in his footnote. If the units of pollution were added consecutively rather than simultaneously then those units that were added after the harm occurred (the death of the fish) would be pre-empted from becoming causes. They could never form part of a causally sufficient set that *actually* occurred.

In practical terms this means that the problem of asymmetrical duplication is confined to limited circumstances. It only arises where the damage is indivisible and is caused once a threshold of exposure is met, and various sources of the harmful agent combine to form an indecipherable mass so that they operate simultaneously.

i. The Solution to Asymmetrical Duplication

In the river pollution example of asymmetrical duplication, application of the but-for test would lead to the conclusion that none of the individual units was a cause of the injury in the sense of strong necessity because the remaining six units would still have caused it. The but-for test once again suggests that the injury was 'uncaused'.

Yet the solution under the NESS test is not as simple as it was in the double-hit hunters scenario. In that scenario, the duplication was symmetrical because each shot was independently sufficient to cause the injury. To avoid the injury, each shot would have to have been absent. But where the duplication is asymmetrical as in this river pollution scenario, each unit is not independently sufficient, so we cannot say of any individual unit that it must be absent if the injury is to be avoided. Since no individual unit is either strongly necessary (a but-for cause) or independently sufficient (symmetrical duplication) its presence or absence seems to be irrelevant to the outcome. Yet the same could be said of each of the seven units, returning us to a position where the harm seems to be mysteriously 'uncaused', and logically we know that this is not true. However, Wright explains that this is not because of a weakness in the NESS test; it is because the NESS test is being misapplied. If the NESS test is applied correctly, each unit is still a cause of the injury:

> [E]ach defendant's one unit was necessary for the sufficiency of *a* set of actual antecedent conditions that included only four of the other units, and the sufficiency of this particular set of actual antecedent conditions was not affected by the existence of two additional duplicative units.[97]

---

[96] Martin Hogg, 'Developing Causal Doctrine' in Goldberg (n 3) 42.
[97] Wright, 'Causation' (n 2) 1793.

This is because of the plurality of causes whereby there can be more than one sufficient set for any outcome, and it is possible for more than one set *actually* to occur. Where the exposures operate simultaneously overlapping sets occur. As noted in an earlier section, the philosophical account of causation involves strong sufficiency (or its equivalent, weak necessity) so it does not require *independent* sufficiency. Instead of asking whether a particular unit would have to be absent for the harm to be avoided (strong necessity), the correct question is whether *the set* containing that unit would have to be absent for the harm to be avoided (weak necessity). The situation appears complicated. However, this is only because the two sets are not independently sufficient so there is an overlap between sets.

Wright continues to explain that this conclusion is logically the same whether each of the seven units was contributed by a different individual, or whether one person contributed five units and another contributed two units.[98] Since the units combine in an indecipherable mass the causal status of a unit of pollution is not dependent on whether the remaining units were contributed by one person or by many people. The two units contributed by the second person are still 'necessary for the sufficiency of a set of actual antecedent conditions that included only three of the first defendant's five units, a set whose sufficiency was not affected by the existence of two additional duplicative units also provided by the first defendant'.[99] The fact that the two sources occur at the same time, and combine to form an indecipherable whole, makes this disaggregation of the five-unit contribution into its component units logically possible: if we are able notionally to disaggregate the defendant's contribution from the other contribution then logically we can also notionally disaggregate the units of the other contribution.

Wright thus argues that the same causal situation exists whether the harmful agent is one that would normally be thought of as existing in 'units' or not, so if two or more fires merge to destroy a building, each is a cause of the destruction even if it would have been insufficient on its own, and even if one of the other fires alone would have been sufficient. The second fire 'was necessary for the sufficiency of a set of actual antecedent conditions which included another fire ... that was "*at least* large enough to be sufficient for the injury if it merged with a fire the size of the second fire"'.[100] It will be argued below that in principle Wright is correct to assert that disaggregation is appropriate even when the harmful agent is something such as fire that would not normally be thought of as existing in units. However the practical example that he uses to support this assertion is inappropriate because the harm in cases of fire may be divisible so it should not be used to support an argument concerning an indivisible harm.[101]

---

[98] Richard Wright, 'Once More into the Bramble Bush: Duty, Causal Contribution, and the Extent of Legal Responsibility' (2001) 54 *Vanderbilt Law Review* 1071, 1106.

[99] Wright, 'Causation' (n 2) 1793.

[100] ibid 1793.

[101] eg if two fires combine to damage a house it may be the case that one fire would have damaged one room, the second fire another room so the damage would be divisible, but if a person was trapped and killed by the fire their death would be an indivisible damage.

Wright has since come to question this 'at least enough' formulation, describing it as 'overly demanding'.[102] This description is surprising given that his 'at least enough' formulation seems to make the NESS test very inclusive because in cases of duplication it allows any contribution, which is neither strongly necessary nor independently sufficient, to be labelled as a cause by constructing a set containing that contribution and just enough of the other contributions. He explains:

> My initial elaborations of the NESS account were overly demanding. I incorporated the weak-necessity requirement in the definition of singular instances of causation. As I have previously stated, this it too restrictive. The weak-necessity requirement is sufficiently incorporated in a properly formulated causal law, which contains in its antecedent only those abstract conditions the instantiation of which is necessary for the sufficiency of the set of conditions that is sufficient for the immediate instantiation of its consequent. When analysing singular instances of causation, an actual condition *c* was a cause of an actual condition *e* if and only if *c* was a part of (rather than being necessary for) the instantiation of one of the abstract conditions in the completely instantiated antecedent of a causal law, the consequent of which was instantiated by *e* immediately after the complete instantiation of its antecedent, or (as is more often the case) if *c* is connected to *e* through a sequence of such instantiations of causal laws. This formulation of the requirement for a NESS condition is more straightforward and simpler to apply than my initial formulations, which requires 'at least so much' descriptions of actual conditions in some situations in order to (validly) treat other conditions as NESS conditions.[103]

This is unconvincing. Without more, a test that asks where the defendant's negligence was 'a part of the instantiation of one of the abstract conditions in the completely instantiated antecedent of a causal law, the consequent of which was instantiated by the claimant's damage immediately after the complete instantiation of its antecedent or through a sequence of such instantiations of causal laws' is simply not practical to apply. This also seems like a looser approach to causation where the NESS test allows us to understand whether a condition is capable of being a cause but does not allow us to determine whether it actually was a cause on a particular occasion because 'being a part of the instantiation of one of the abstract conditions' does not clearly allow us to differentiate between duplicative and pre-emptive exposures. This would mean that it has little or no value as a legal test where the law requires a causal link to exist between the particular defendant's negligence and the particular claimant's loss.

In this new approach, a factor is a cause if there is a causal law wherein it is a necessary element of a sufficient set for that outcome, *and* on the particular occasion it was a part of a necessary element of an actually occurring sufficient set. Technically then, this still does not let us identify pre-empted factors as causes, but in cases involving a single harmful substance the emphasis is lost. The substance itself remains a necessary element of an actually occurring sufficient set, so the process of eliminating those sources that arrived after the harm has already

---

[102] Wright, 'The NESS Account' (n 3) 291.
[103] ibid.

occurred seems to take place at the 'a part of' stage of the test and this is too vague. The 'at least enough' formulation may be clunky but this is preferable to risking over-inclusiveness in the practical application of the test.

Wright's new test is effectively the same as the second stage of Stapleton's 'extended but-for' test which states that 'a specified factor is a cause of the existence of a particular phenomenon (as that phenomenon is individuated by the law) only if, but for that factor alone, (i) the phenomenon would not exist or (ii) an actual contribution to an element of the positive requirements for the existence of the phenomenon would not exist'.[104] The second limb of the extended but-for test is designed to capture contributions to positive conditions rather than to omissions, although such contributions can take the form of omissions. It effectively requires us to identify a sufficient set of conditions and then to ask, as Wright proposes above, whether the negligence was a part of one of those conditions. The problem with both Stapleton and Wright's formulations is that we need to have a sense of what we mean by being 'a part of' or making 'an actual contribution to' an element of the positive requirements for the existence of the phenomenon before we can say whether the negligence satisfies this test. This is achieved by providing examples and relying on us to recognise an 'actual contribution' when we see it. The value of Wright's original approach is that it relies less on intuition and shows us the reasoning process that we need to go through to identify causes. It is essential to retain the emphasis on the *actual occurrence* of the sufficient set in order to be clear that this does not capture pre-emptive causation.

Wright's previous 'at least enough' formulation is appropriate in cases of asymmetrical duplication because asymmetrical duplication only arises where the sources of the harmful agent are factually combined into an indecipherable mass. Since the units are physically combined together their effects overlap so we are able to construct overlapping sufficient sets of units containing A's unit and 'just enough' of the other units, or B's unit and 'just enough' of the other units. It is impossible to say that five particular units had an effect and the remaining units had no effect because they were all present together and all operated at the same time—they formed an indecipherable whole so the effects of each unit are similarly indecipherable.

The 'at least enough' formulation would be unnecessary and inappropriate in other scenarios that do not involve indivisible damage and sources of the harmful agent combining in an indecipherable mass. If only five units of pollution are added to the water, one by A and four by B, then each unit was necessary for the sufficiency of the set, so A's unit was a cause of the harm occurring. This is a simple scenario like *Barnett* because only one sufficient set has actually occurred so there is no duplication. If A added five units and B simultaneously added five units then the scenario is equivalent to the double-hit hunters case of symmetrical

---

[104] Jane Stapleton, 'An "Extended But-For" Test for the Causal Relation' (2015) 35 *Oxford Journal of Legal Studies* 697, 713.

duplication so both *A* and *B* would be labelled as causes on the NESS test because they are independently sufficient. If *A* added five units and *B* later added five units then *A*'s units may pre-empt *B*'s units from being causes so there is no duplication. Likewise, if a total of seven units were added one after the other then the first five units may pre-empt the final two units from becoming causes. There is no danger of the 'at least enough' formulation being so expansive that it included cases of pre-emption because the NESS test correctly requires the unit to be necessary for a sufficient set of conditions that *actually occurred*. One ingredient in any sufficient set must be the condition that 'the damage has not already occurred'. It is impossible to construct a sufficient set containing some of *A*'s units and some of *B*'s in a pre-emptive situation like this, because as soon as *A*'s five units have caused the damage we lose the requisite 'the damage has not already occurred' condition in relation to any of *B*'s units.

The NESS test is very inclusive here, for example if one litre of pollution was sufficient to cause the injury and *A* added a teaspoon (five millilitres) of pollution while other parties added pollution up to a level of several litres, then the NESS test still leads to the conclusion that *A*'s teaspoon of pollution was a cause of the damage. Yet it is important to remember that this problem of asymmetrical duplication only arises when (i) the harm is indivisible and (ii) the defendant contributes a source of a harmful agent that combines with other sources to form an indecipherable mass so that they operate simultaneously. It is also important to remember that causation is only one element of legal liability. Although liability would be joint and several, the defendant can seek contribution from the other responsible tortfeasors. Additionally, a defendant is not liable in negligence if her causal contribution was *de minimis*,[105] reflecting the idea that interpersonal responsibility is narrower than causal responsibility so a defendant will not be liable merely because she was a cause of the harm.

ii. *Indivisible Damage: The Question of Apportionment*

In chapter one we saw that corrective justice-based interpersonal responsibility is narrower than causal responsibility because it only corrects *wrongful* loss, so it is open to negligence law to hold a defendant liable for less than she caused. This raises the question of whether some kind of apportionment would be appropriate in cases of indivisible damage despite the fact that, as we have seen, each cause is a cause of the whole of the damage. In England, where two or more defendants are liable for the same damage, liability is joint and several. In contrast, all Australian jurisdictions have introduced proportionate liability provisions, although these are limited to cases of property damage and economic loss, meaning that joint

---

[105] *Bonnington Castings v Wardlaw* (n 5).

and several liability continues to apply in cases of personal injury.[106] As Barker and Steele explain:

> The idea that we can precisely judge relative causal contributions to an injury that is indivisible is seemingly oxymoronic and it may be that the process here is one of assessing relative contributions to risk, rather than injury.[107]

Since the defendant has not caused a distinct portion of the damage, the justification for apportionment of liability for indivisible damage lies outside the realm of causation. It cannot be based on causal contribution and instead is based on contribution to risk and/or comparative fault.

Proportionate liability for indivisible damage cannot be equated with the apportionment exercise that takes place between the claimant and defendant in cases of contributory negligence since, as Barker and Steele explain, they 'distribute different things':

> The familiar system of joint and several liability, combined with comparative [contributory] negligence doctrine and contribution between defendants, divides two *different* cakes. One cake is shared between plaintiff and defendants according to the plaintiff's relative fault and responsibility. There is a plaintiff's share and defendant's share. This is the (rather unpalatable) 'loss' cake: the defendant takes on a share of the loss in the form of liability; the plaintiff bears no liability, but takes on the financial burden of the rest of the loss. These portions of responsibility for the loss are dispensed by comparative [contributory] negligence doctrine. *Joint and several liability* and *contribution* are concerned with a different cake. That is the liability cake. The plaintiff is not involved with the liability cake.[108]

This explains the solution in *Fitzgerald v Lane* where two defendants, acting independently, were found to have caused the indivisible injury (partial tetraplegia) suffered by the claimant who was also a cause of his own injury through contributory negligence.[109] The Court correctly reduced damages by 50 per cent for the claimant's contributory negligence but held the defendants jointly and severally liable for the remaining 50 per cent. Given that a defendant who is a cause of indivisible damage is a cause of the whole of that damage, joint and several liability is appropriate and, as Barker and Steele argue, 'the choice of proportionate liability is exactly that—a non-principled, primarily political choice between different interests'.[110]

The quantification question is particularly pertinent where a defendant is held liable in respect of indivisible damage that was causally over-determined since it raises normative questions about the extent to which the loss can be characterised as wrongful given that the claimant would have suffered loss without

---

[106] See Kit Barker and Jenny Steele, 'Drifting Towards Proportionate Liability: Ethics and Pragmatics' (2015) 74 *Cambridge Law Journal* 49.
[107] ibid 67.
[108] ibid 68.
[109] *Fitzgerald v Lane* [1989] AC 328 (HL).
[110] Barker and Steele (n 106) 76.

the defendant's negligence. Beever draws our attention to the decision in *Corey v Havener*.[111] In cases of symmetrical duplication by two negligent defendants, joint and several liability will continue to apply; for example, in *Corey v Havener* two defendants riding motorcycles each created a noise that frightened the claimant's horse, causing him to lose control and suffer personal injury, and the noise from each defendant alone was sufficient to cause the injury. In that case, both defendants were found liable but, Beever says, if there had been one defendant and the other source of noise was lightning, the defendant would escape liability. It is important to recognise that this is a normative decision to characterise the loss as wrongful or not. Both cases involve (symmetrical) duplication, so the defendant is a cause of the whole loss in both scenarios. Beever argues that the defendant in the second scenario is still liable to compensate the claimant because her negligence was a cause of the damage, but since the claimant is not any worse off than she would have been without the negligence no loss flows from the damage, so liability would only be for nominal damages. In contrast in the first scenario, he suggests, the claimant ought to be compensated for the personal injury. If defendant *A* had not acted negligently, the claimant would still have suffered the same injury at defendant *B*'s hands, but the claimant would also have been able to recover compensation from defendant *B* in respect of that loss and is now unable to because causation was duplicated by defendant *A*, so the claimant is still left worse off by the same amount. This, he says, does not amount to reconceptualising the damage in such cases as the loss of the right to sue, but merely recognises that this is the value of the loss caused by the interference with the claimant's right to bodily integrity due to the practical consequence that the claimant cannot sue the other defendant.[112] This argument seems circular since it would apply with equal force to each defendant, at which point the fact that the claimant *can* recover from each of the defendants undermines the basis of the argument. Instead it seems that the law makes a choice to aggregate the defendants to say that this claimant has suffered a wrongful loss since all the causes were negligent while the claimant whose injury was also caused by lightning has not suffered wrongful loss. This does not obviously sit comfortably with principles of corrective justice whose focus is on the interaction of the individual claimant and defendant. It is consistent with corrective justice, however, since the defendant's *liability* has been established as an individual. When it comes to quantifying the loss, negligence law will look to natural events that reduce the value of the loss since natural events have the potential to affect the claimant and defendant equally throughout their lives, but it will not look to other defendants' negligence as a way of reducing this defendant's burden since those negligent acts affect only the claimant.

This section has addressed asymmetrical duplication which, along with symmetrical duplication, only arises in cases of indivisible damage. The next section

---

[111] Allan Beever, *Rediscovering the Tort of Negligence* (Hart Publishing, 2007) 432, discussing *Corey v Havener* 65 NE 69 (Mass SJC 1902).
[112] ibid 436.

looks at divisible damage to address the potential problems that could arise with the NESS test there.

C. Applying NESS to Divisible Damage

Divisible damage can be explained through a variation on the river pollution example. This time, instead of saying that an indivisible injury occurs at a level of five units of pollution, divisible disease is the equivalent of a situation where each unit of pollution will kill, for example, 10 fish. If A adds one unit of pollution and B adds three units of pollution, then in total there will be four units of pollution so 40 fish will die. The death of 40 fish could be the outcome to which we apply the NESS test. In order for the set of factors to be sufficient to kill 40 fish there must be four units of pollution so each unit was necessary for the sufficiency of the set. This would mean that A and B were both a cause of the outcome.

This does not seem to be the best way to understand the outcome. A corrective justice-based system of negligence liability is focused on interactions between individuals. Even though a claimant might be seeking compensation for her total loss, if this total loss consists of a number of smaller losses each of which is attributable to a different individual wrongdoer, then there have been a number of individual interactions. An individual wrongdoer is only responsible for loss that she caused, and has no moral responsibility for entirely separate loss caused by a separate wrongdoer. So in the pollution example of divisible damage A's one unit constituted a set that caused 10 fish to die, and B's three units constituted a separate set that was sufficient to cause 30 fish to die. The presence of A's unit and B's units are in no way related to each other, they have occurred independently, so their respective harms should also be treated independently. This is clearer in the following scenario: A shoots a walker and hits her arm, B shoots the walker and hits her leg. The shots were independent and the harms are independent. A caused the loss of the arm, B caused the loss of the leg. These examples seem potentially different because in the shooting scenario the causes remain separate and the effects are visibly separate too. In contrast, in the river scenario the causes cannot be separated once in the water and the effects are not visibly different. Although this means that A's unit of pollution cannot be tied to 10 specifically identified fish, this is a difficulty of proof and does not change the underlying causal model which is one where A has only caused the death of 10 fish. This is important because in corrective justice-based interpersonal responsibility a person can only be morally responsible for an outcome if she was a cause of that outcome, so it would be wrong to impose moral responsibility on A for fish deaths that were caused by B.

The aetiology of divisible diseases is not always straightforward because there is not always a linear correlation between the potency of the cause and the severity of the disease. This is known as 'effect modification' but this is not an insurmountable challenge. Effect modification describes the phenomenon whereby a particular causal factor becomes more potent when combined with another causal factor and affects both divisible and indivisible diseases.[113] For example if smoking carries X relative risk of lung cancer, and exposure to asbestos carries Y relative risk of lung cancer, the relative risk of lung cancer in a smoker who has been exposed to asbestos is not necessarily simply $X+Y$, but may be higher because the interaction between smoking and asbestos may be an 'effect modifier'. Similarly, in non-stochastic (divisible) diseases where the disease occurs along a continuum of severity, repeated exposure to one harmful agent, or exposure to that agent in combination with another harmful agent may increase the severity exponentially rather than incrementally. To return to the example of river pollution, say each unit of pollutant A would kill five fish, and each unit of pollutant B would kill five fish, but a combination of a unit each of pollutant A and B would kill 15 fish. The harm can still be divided into five dead fish for which A's pollutant forms a NESS set, five dead fish for which B's pollutant forms a NESS set, and five more dead fish for which the NESS set comprises both A and B's pollutants.

Coggan and Taylor explain that the task of apportionment remains 'relatively straightforward' even in cases involving effect modification. This can be illustrated by considering the apportionment that the Court achieved in the case of *Rahman v Arearose Ltd*.[114] In this case, the Court undertook a detailed analysis of the various psychiatric harms suffered by the claimant and determined which were causally attributable to the negligence of the first defendant alone, the second defendant alone, and to both defendants' negligence together. The Court was thus able to apportion liability for each head of damages based on causal responsibility, with joint and several liability operating only in respect of the damage caused by both defendants' negligence. Although the decision in *Rahman* has been criticised by Weir since in his view psychiatric illness is 'aetiologically indiscerptible' and 'there is no scientific basis for any such attribution of causality',[115] it does illustrate that, where the expert evidence shows it to be appropriate, courts are able to apportion damage relatively simply.

This solution might be criticised for entailing an element of moral luck in whether the damage is divisible or indivisible, which is further accentuated in cases of synergistic divisible damage where the defendant has no knowledge that another exposure is interacting with hers to make the damage more severe. However moral luck is inherent in corrective justice-based negligence liability which is not concerned with the degree of wrongdoing by the defendant but with the wrongful loss that is caused to the claimant. As Green explains:

> We are all potential claimants, but we are also all potential defendants; what makes us winner also makes us losers. So, every time we act negligently but cause no harm, we

---

[113] Coggan and Taylor (n 81) 14.

[114] *Rahman v Arearose Ltd* [2001] QB 351 (CA).

[115] Tony Weir, 'The Maddening Effect of Consecutive Torts' (2001) 60 *Cambridge Law Journal* 237, 238. See also Janet Smith, 'Causation—the Search for Principle' [2009] *Journal of Personal Injury Law* 101, 103.

chalk up a credit to the account we must draw upon when our sub-standard behaviour leads to loss.[116]

i. Calculating Apportionment of Divisible Damage

In *Holtby v Brigham*, the defendant employer was held liable for 75 per cent of the claimant's damages, yet was only responsible for 50 per cent of the exposure to asbestos.[117] This section considers how that figure might be justified and identifies a range of factors to be taken into account when calculating apportionment.

Since apportionment is a causal issue, in that the defendant was a cause of only a portion of the total damage suffered, then the only factor relevant in apportioning damages is identifying the extent of the damage that was caused by the defendant. This means that broader considerations of fairness do not have a place, at least within a corrective justice-based account of negligence liability. In *Rahman v Arearose*, the Court of Appeal correctly stated that 'the judge was wrong to temper his conclusions as to the respective "causative potency" of each defendant's tort by a separate and free-standing reliance on the extent of the first defendant's blameworthiness'.[118] The task for the court is to quantify what portion of the damage the defendant caused through her negligence; it is not merely a matter, as the appeal tribunal in *Thaine v LSE* suggested, that 'it accords with our sense of what fairness dictates'.[119]

The Court of Appeal in *Holtby* found that a broad brush approach to apportionment was appropriate. Similarly in *Allen v British Rail* the Court of Appeal held that:

> The amount of evidence which should be called to enable a judge to make a just apportionment must be proportionate to the amount at stake and the uncertainties which are inherent in making any award of damages for personal injury.[120]

The Court in *Thompson* said that a broad brush approach was justified on the basis that 'the whole exercise of assessing damages is shot through with imprecision. Even the measurements of the plaintiffs' hearing loss contain a substantial margin of error'.[121] Given the imprecision of assessment of damages, little was to be gained by seeking precision in the apportionment of those damages. Mustill J later explained that whilst it might be appropriate to apply a fraction or percentage reduction in cases where 'the disability proceeds by clearly identifiable stages', it 'may be misleading in a case such as the present, as it gives to the calculations a spurious air of accuracy'.[122]

---

[116] Sarah Green, *Causation in Negligence* (Hart Publishing, 2015) 92.
[117] *Holtby* (n 86).
[118] *Rahman* (n 114) [25] (Law LJ).
[119] *Thaine v LSE* (Employment Appeal Tribunal) [2010] ICR 1422, [23].
[120] *Allen v British Rail Engineering Ltd* [2001] EWCA Civ 242, [20].
[121] *Thompson* (n 84) 443 (Mustill J).
[122] ibid 450 (Mustill J).

The Court of Appeal in *Holtby* noted that in awarding 75 per cent of the damages the trial judge had 'erred on the side of generosity to the claimant',[123] but ultimately found that was open to him to make such a finding. Stuart-Smith LJ explained, however, that 'it might be said that the judge should have made the defendants liable only to 50 per cent. If the other employers had been before the Court, then subject to exposure which ought to be considered *de minimis*, I think this is what he would have done'.[124] If, as it appears, the decision to award 75 per cent of damages was motivated by sympathy for the claimant rather than being based solely on causal considerations, then the calculation was inappropriate since the defendant was held liable for damage that he had not caused.

However, the Court in *Thompson* had also noted that normal principles of calculation of damages should apply, so for example each defendant should be liable not only for the symptoms immediately flowing from the portion of the disease she caused, but also for those that will occur in the future as a result of that portion of the disease.[125] This is a standard aspect of the calculation of damages; for example, if the defendant damages the claimant's knee, and as a result of that injury she will develop osteoarthritis in the future, the defendant must compensate this future damage.[126] In a case where there is exposure by successive employers, the task of identifying the damage immediately caused by employer *A* as well as damage that would/would likely be suffered in the future as a result of employer *A*'s negligence is complicated by the fact that there has also been subsequent damage caused by employer *B*. It will surely prove difficult to separate those symptoms that were caused by employer *B* from those that were made likely by employer *A*. As noted above, there are two issues at stake: first identifying the portion of the damage that the defendant caused through her negligence, then quantifying the loss flowing from that damage. This may go some way to explaining why the Court in *Holtby* only reduced damages by 25 per cent where the defendant was responsible for only 50 per cent of the exposure—weighting damages towards earlier periods of employment may broadly seek to allocate the claimant's future losses to this defendant, although this should have been explained if it was the case.

In cases of divisible damage, the defendant's negligence is a cause of a portion of the damage, and since there is a single sufficient set for each portion, the NESS test effectively collapses into the but-for test in respect of each portion of damage. In cases of indivisible damage, the NESS test is able to function whether there is a single sufficient set (in which case the but-for test can also be used as shorthand for NESS), or pre-emption, or symmetrical or asymmetrical duplication. By incorporating a clear definition of damage, the NESS test is able to address a range of scenarios without recourse to any exceptional tests. The discussion so far has, however, centred on minimalistic hypothetical examples and if the NESS test

---

[123] *Holtby* (n 86) [25] (Stuart-Smith LJ) and [29] (Clarke LJ).
[124] ibid [25].
[125] *Thompson* (n 84) 438.
[126] See *Hotson v Fitzgerald and others* [1985] 1 WLR 1036 (QBD), 1045.

is to gain traction it must bring clarity in practice. The next section will apply the NESS test to decided cases to illustrate how its adoption would help overcome the problems associated with the *Wardlaw* test of material contribution to harm.

Part III: Using NESS to Overcome Common Problems with Exceptional Legal Tests

In negligence law the but-for test is supplemented with the *Wardlaw* test of 'material contribution to harm',[127] so it is often said that the claimant must prove that the defendant's negligence 'caused or materially contributed to' the damage.[128] It is unclear in the case law and academic literature whether the *Wardlaw* test is an application of the but-for test or an exception to it. If it is an exception to the but-for test it is further unclear whether it is an exception to the factual causation requirement, or whether it is a test of factual causation that compensates for the conceptual inadequacy of the but-for test. This has led Honoré to criticise it as an 'indefinite, if not indeterminate' notion which is 'purely pragmatic and leaves the theoretical problem untouched'.[129] This uncertainty, concerning just how exceptional the *Wardlaw* test is, has been important in the development of the law since the *Wardlaw* test was used as a kind of stepping stone between the but-for test and the *McGhee/Fairchild* test of 'material contribution to the risk of harm'.[130] The uncertainty is most significant because it is unclear what causal problem is addressed by the test so its scope of application and its effects are ill-defined.[131]

A lot of ink has been spilt attempting to define the notion of a 'material contribution to harm' as well as its status as a test of causation, yet this has resulted in more confusion rather than less. Attempts to understand it will necessarily be fraught with confusion if approached from the framework of the but-for test; since the but-for test is conceptually inadequate it is simply unhelpful to ask whether a 'material contribution to harm' is an exception to, or an application of,

---

[127] *Wardlaw* (n 5).

[128] ibid 620. Note that this phrase pre-dates the decision in *Wardlaw* but this is the leading case on the test of material contribution to harm.

[129] Honoré (n 43) 364.

[130] The *McGhee/Fairchild* test is the subject of ch 5.

[131] See *Jones v Secretary of State for Energy and Climate Change* [2012] EWHC 2936 (QB), [2012] All ER 271, [6.47]–[6.49]. It is worth noting that this is not identical to the American concept of a 'substantial factor' since that seems to apply only to cases of symmetrical duplication (see David W Robertson, 'Causation in the *Restatement (Third) of Torts*: Three Arguable Mistakes' (2009) 33 *Wake Forest Law Review* 1007, 1018). This means that the 'substantial factor' solution addresses the double-hit hunters problem of duplicative causation but it is not clear that it would apply in a case such as *Wardlaw* which involved a build-up of the harmful substance in unknown quantities. The scope of the 'substantial factor' test is unclear because it has not been scrutinised in technical detail, instead 'difficult puzzles … have been simply handed over to the jury' (Stephen Bailey, 'Causation in Negligence: What is a Material Contribution?' (2010) 30 *Legal Studies* 167, 169). Caution must therefore be exercised in referring to American scholarship on the practical implementation of the NESS test.

the but-for test. The conceptual inadequacy of the but-for test means that it needs to be supplemented with another test if negligence law is to test factual causation accurately, but by taking the but-for test as our frame of reference we are unable to articulate the appropriate limits of such a test. The previous section has demonstrated how the NESS test applies to a range of theoretical cases that cannot properly be addressed by the but-for test. The NESS test will not receive a warm welcome, however, unless it is simple to apply in practice, so in this chapter the analysis will focus on the application of the NESS test to cases where the *Wardlaw* test has previously been applied. Through this NESS lens it will be possible to understand why the but-for test is inadequate in those cases, and how they ought properly to be resolved. It will be suggested that it is preferable simply to use the NESS test in those cases rather than to use the *Wardlaw* test which can only be understood properly by drawing on the NESS analysis and which risks adding to confusion by introducing its own vocabulary surrounding 'contribution'.

This section begins by presenting the facts and decision in *Wardlaw* and identifying the sources of confusion in that case and its subsequent applications. The NESS test is then applied to cases where courts have applied the *Wardlaw* test, eliminating the need for any exceptional tests.

I. The Current State of the *Wardlaw* Test

A. The Facts of *Bonnington Castings v Wardlaw*

The claimant in this case was exposed to silica dust in the air at work coming from two sources. The majority of the dust, the 'innocent' dust, was produced by the hammer operated by the claimant and it was not possible to fit a dust extraction plant there. This was therefore a non-negligent source of silica dust in that it was unavoidable. The remainder, the 'guilty' dust, was present due to the negligence of the defendant in failing to provide adequate extraction at the swing grinders in the workshop. The claimant inhaled this silica dust in the air at work and developed pneumoconiosis, a disease of the lungs.

As Bailey has explained, the decision of the House of Lords cannot be fully understood without presenting the previous decisions and the point of appeal.[132] At first instance the Lord Ordinary had found that failure to provide respirators was a cause of the disease, which suggests that all the dust was considered 'guilty' at first instance. On appeal, the defendant argued that only the dust from the swing grinders was a result of negligence, and that the claimant had failed to establish causation in respect of this source of dust since the dust from the innocent source was far greater in quantity so was the 'most probable' cause of the disease. The Court of Session did not reach the question of whether the negligence concerned

---

[132] Bailey, 'Causation in Negligence: What is a Material Contribution?' (n 131).

only the dust from the swing grinders, and disposed of the case on the point of causation.[133] It held that exceptionally the onus of proof lay on the defendant to prove that the dust from the swing grinders could not have been a cause of the disease, and the defendant had failed to prove this. The issues to be decided in the House of Lords were therefore, first, whether the Court of Session had been correct to reverse the onus of proof, and, second, if the onus of proof lay on the defendant, whether he could discharge this by proving that the innocent dust was the most probable cause because it was the far greater source of dust.

The House of Lords held that the onus of proof was not reversed; it remained the task of the claimant to prove that the negligence had caused or materially contributed to the damage. On the facts, both sources had 'materially contributed' to the injury. The guilty dust had made a 'material', that is more than *de minimis*, contribution to the illness. Lord Reid explained that the medical evidence was that pneumoconiosis is caused by 'a gradual accumulation in the lungs of minute particles of silica inhaled over a period of years'.[134] He continued:

> That means, I think, that the disease is caused by the whole of the noxious material inhaled and, if that material comes from two sources, it cannot be wholly attributed to material from one source or the other. I am in agreement with much of the Lord President's opinion in this case, but I cannot agree that the question is: which was the most probable source of the respondent's disease, the dust from the pneumatic hammers or the dust from the swing grinders? It appears to me that the source of his disease was the dust from both sources, and the real question is whether the dust from the swing grinders materially contributed to the disease. What is a material contribution must be a question of degree. A contribution which comes within the exception *de minimis non curat lex* is not material, but I think that any contribution which does not fall within that exception must be material. I do not see how there can be something too large to come within the de minimis principle but yet too small to be material.[135]

Lord Keith noted also that the defendant's argument was based on the lack of evidence to show the precise proportions of dust coming from each source.[136]

Part of the problem with understanding the scope of the test of material contribution to harm is that the decision in *Wardlaw* has acquired significance beyond the specific points of appeal that it actually addressed. The objective of the appeal was to determine whether the onus of proof was reversed, and whether the defendant could prove the absence of a causal link by showing that the innocent source was the 'most probable' cause. It was the reversing of the onus of proof by the Court of Session that was the unusual and unorthodox approach. By contrast, there was nothing controversial about holding that the claimant should prove that the negligence 'caused or materially contributed to' the disease. The claimant argued that 'inhalation of the dust was the cause of the disease. If [the defendants] were shown

---

[133] *Bonnington Castings Ltd v Wardlaw* 1955 SC 320 (Court of Session, Inner House).
[134] *Wardlaw* (n 5) 621 (Lord Reid).
[135] ibid 621 (Lord Reid).
[136] ibid 626.

negligently to have contributed a part of the dust which was not negligible, [the claimant's] case was proved'.[137] As Bailey has observed, '[n]o authorities were cited for this proposition and there was no suggestion that it was regarded as novel'.[138] This means that little attention was paid to the exact boundary between proof that the negligence 'caused' and proof that it 'materially contributed to' the disease, so the definitions and scope of application have been gleaned through subsequent analysis of the case and its application in later decisions. Consequently, factual aspects of the case such as the 'cumulative' exposure to dust, the divisibility of the disease, the lack of precise evidence as to the proportions of 'guilty' and 'innocent' dust, as well the absence of apportionment in the case, have been relied upon as determining the scope of the test of material contribution to harm.

II. Defining Damage: Divisibility of Damage or Divisibility of Trigger?

A. Divisibility of Damage in *Wardlaw*

It is unclear from *Wardlaw* and subsequent cases what significance the divisibility of damage has for the applicability of the test of material contribution to harm. Divisible damage, as previously seen, is damage that is dose-related in its severity while indivisible damage is 'all or nothing'. The Court in *Wardlaw* did not determine whether the claimant's disease was divisible. It was called a 'disease of gradual incidence' which suggests it is divisible, but Lord Keith also said that without the negligent dust the claimant 'would not have developed pneumoconiosis when he did and might not have developed it at all',[139] which is compatible with it being indivisible.

Pneumoconiosis has since been held to be divisible,[140] so Hogg has suggested that *Wardlaw*

> settled the point that, for a defender to have caused a pursuer's injury, it is not necessary that the defender was the sole cause of the injury, but merely that, but-for the defender's conduct, the injury would not have occurred to the same extent.[141]

Yet it has also been noted that where damage is divisible and the defendant has only caused a portion of the total loss there should be an apportionment of damages. The absence of apportionment in *Wardlaw* has led some to suggest that the disease was treated as though it were indivisible, so the divisibility of the disease is

---

[137] ibid 617.
[138] Bailey (n 131) 172.
[139] *Wardlaw* (n 5) 626.
[140] *Nicholson v Atlas Steel Foundry & Engineering Co Ltd* [1957] 1 WLR 613.
[141] Martin Hogg, 'Causation and Apportionment of Damages in Cases of Divisible Injury' (2008) 12 *Edinburgh Law Review* 99, 99.

not the *reason* for the application of the test. Thus Smith LJ (extra-judicially) has said 'material contribution to harm' was a modification of the but-for test.[142] In her view, the disease in *Wardlaw* was treated as indivisible but today it would be treated as divisible and apportioned. When the damages are apportioned it shows that the negligence was a but-for cause of a portion of loss. The absence of apportionment in *Wardlaw* could be taken as an indication that the but-for test was not satisfied in that case.[143] In *Sienkiewicz*, Lord Phillips concluded that the *Wardlaw* test applies to both divisible and indivisible damage so long as the exposures operate 'cumulatively and simultaneously'.[144]

Bailey notes, however, that damages had been assessed at first instance on the basis that provision of respirators would have prevented the claimant inhaling dust from both sources, so if damages were to be apportioned later the case would have to have been remitted to the Court of Session to consider evidence as to the appropriate measure of damages. It may have been the case that the state of the evidence would not have permitted such an assessment, and it 'presumably would not have been worth it in terms of cost'.[145] This means that the case 'cannot be read as holding that ... the harm must as a matter of law be regarded as indivisible'.[146]

B. Divisibility of Exposures to Harmful Agent

The second source of confusion for determining the scope of the material contribution to harm test is the common failure to distinguish between the divisibility of damage and the 'divisible' or 'cumulative' nature of the trigger. In *Wardlaw*, Lord Reid observed that the disease was caused by 'the whole of the noxious material inhaled'.[147] Lord Keith also noted that the negligent exposure was continuous over a long period of time and that 'it was the atmosphere inhaled by the pursuer that caused his illness and it is impossible ... to resolve the components of that atmosphere into particles caused by the fault of the defenders and particles not caused by the fault of the defenders, as if they were separate and independent factors in his illness'.[148] This has been taken as suggesting that the test of material contribution to harm applies where the exposure to the harmful agent is 'cumulative' rather than 'alternative'.

This confusion has been exacerbated by the decision in *Bailey v Ministry of Defence* where divisibility of damage was not clearly distinguished from the question of 'divisibility' of the exposures.[149] The claimant in *Bailey* was in a weakened

---

[142] Smith, 'Causation—the Search for Principle' (n 115).
[143] ibid 102.
[144] *Sienkiewicz* (n 89) [90] (Lord Phillips).
[145] Bailey (n 131) 173.
[146] ibid.
[147] *Wardlaw* (n 5) 621.
[148] ibid 626.
[149] *Bailey v Ministry of Defence* [2008] EWCA Civ 883, [2009] 1 WLR 1052.

state which, when she vomited, caused her to be unable to respond naturally to the vomit, instead aspirating it leading to cardiac arrest and brain damage. The defendant hospital had negligently failed to resuscitate her adequately following an operation, thus causing her to be weaker than she would otherwise have been. At the same time she developed pancreatitis which also caused her to become weaker but this was a natural complication and not attributable to the negligence of the hospital. The question was whether the negligent failure to resuscitate the patient after her first operation was a cause of her ultimate injury but there is confusion in the way the damage was, and has subsequently been, defined.

The immediate cause of the claimant's brain damage was clear in *Bailey*: the aspiration of the vomit led to cardiac arrest which resulted in brain damage, so Waller LJ focused on the question of what had caused her to aspirate her vomit,[150] later saying 'the question is what caused her weakened state'.[151] He effectively seems to regard the weakness as the damage forming the focus of the causal inquiry, asking 'Is it enough for the claimant to establish that, on the balance of probabilities, a lack of care made a material contribution—something greater than negligible— to the weakness of her condition …?'.[152] The Court of Appeal in *AB v Ministry of Defence* also stated that the damage in *Bailey* had been the claimant's weakness which is a divisible (ie dose-related) condition.[153] Given that we have also learnt since *Wardlaw* was decided that the severity of pneumoconiosis is dose-related,[154] the Court in *AB v MOD* held that the test of material contribution to harm 'applies only where the disease or condition is 'divisible' so that an increased dose of the harmful agent worsens the disease'.[155] Subsequently in *Jones v Secretary of State for Energy and Climate Change*, Swift LJ argued that although pneumoconiosis is now known to be divisible the Court in *Wardlaw* treated it as indivisible,[156] and that 'the "injury" in *Bailey* was in reality the claimant's brain damage, which was indivisible'.[157]

The confusion in *Bailey* is exacerbated by Waller LJ's later, unelaborated, reference to this as a case of 'cumulative causes':

> In my view one cannot draw a distinction between medical negligence cases and others. I would summarise the position in relation to cumulative cause cases as follows. If the evidence demonstrates on a balance of probabilities that the injury would have occurred as a result of the non–tortious cause or causes in any event, the claimant will have failed to establish that the tortious cause contributed. *Hotson* exemplifies such a situation. If the evidence demonstrates that 'but for' the contribution of the tortious cause the injury

---

[150] ibid [2].

[151] ibid [33].

[152] ibid [35]. See also Sarah Green, 'Contributing to the Risk of Confusion? Causation in the Court of Appeal' (2009) 125 *Law Quarterly Review* 44, 45.

[153] *AB v Ministry of Defence* [2010] EWCA Civ 1317, (2011) 117 BMLR 101, [150] (Smith LJ giving the judgment of the Court).

[154] *Cartledge v E Jopling & Sons Ltd* (n 85).

[155] *AB* (n 153) [150].

[156] *Jones v Secretary of State for Energy and Climate Change* (n 131) [6.49].

[157] ibid.

would probably not have occurred, the claimant will (obviously) have discharged the burden. In a case where medical science cannot establish the probability that 'but for' an act of negligence the injury would not have happened but can establish that the contribution of the negligent cause was more than negligible, the 'but for' test is modified, and the claimant will succeed.[158]

There is a similar lack of consensus in the use of the terms 'divisible' and 'cumulative' in academic commentary; for example, Gullifer has suggested that harm is divisible if there is a temporal or spatial separation between the causes as in *Performance Cars v Abraham*,[159] and indivisible if the candidate causes are cumulative causes of the same type that combine together as in *Wardlaw*.[160] Stauch says that where the disease is indivisible it should not matter whether the causal process is cumulative or alternative.[161] In order to resolve these cases it is essential to define the damage at the outset and to maintain a clear separation of damage from any 'divisibility' of the exposures.

III. Using NESS to Clarify the Material Contribution to Harm Test

A. Asking the Right Questions: The Limits of the But-For Test

Analysis of the *Wardlaw* test often begins with the question of whether it is an exception to, or an application of, the but-for test. Indeed, Bailey asks this question,[162] and his analysis of material contribution to harm begins from the premise that 'as a matter of principle, satisfying the normal but-for test of causation should almost invariably be an essential part of the case to be established by a claimant in tort'.[163] The conceptual deficiencies of the but-for test mean, however, that this is not a particularly helpful question to ask.

As Steel and Ibbetson have highlighted,[164] there are two elements to a test of causation: the conceptual element and the evidential element. In the orthodox approach to factual causation the but-for test fulfils the conceptual element; the claimant is required to prove that the defendant's negligence was necessary for the damage that occurred. The evidential element concerns the standard to which the claimant must prove but-for causation, ie the balance of probabilities. A key

---

[158] *Bailey* (n 149) [46].

[159] *Performance Cars v Abraham* [1962] 1 QB 33 (CA).

[160] Louise Gullifer, 'One Cause after Another' (2001) 117 *Law Quarterly Review* 403, 406.

[161] Marc Stauch, '"Material Contribution" as a Response to Causal Uncertainty: Time for a Rethink' (2009) 68 *Cambridge Law Journal* 27, 29.

[162] Bailey (n 131) 167.

[163] ibid 169.

[164] Sandy Steel and David Ibbetson, 'More Grief on Uncertain Causation in Tort' (2011) 70 *Cambridge Law Journal* 451, 452.

uncertainty with the *Wardlaw* test of material contribution to harm is that it seems to respond both to evidential issues and to conceptual inadequacies of the but-for test.

B. Evidential Element: A *Material* Contribution to Harm

In *Wardlaw* itself, one effect of using the test of material contribution to harm was to maintain a clear separation of the conceptual and evidential parts of causation. The defendant in *Wardlaw* had argued that since the innocent dust was by far the greater of the two sources, it was the 'most probable' cause of the claimant's illness. Yet if, as Lord Reid explained, the disease was caused by the whole of the dust,[165] then on the balance of probabilities both sources were necessary for the outcome. Viewed in this light, one function of the material contribution to harm test is to remind us that the civil standard of proof requires us to ask whether on the balance of probabilities the negligence was *a* cause; satisfying the 'balance of probabilities' is not the same as being 'the most probable' cause.

If the emphasis is placed on the requirement of a *material* contribution to harm, the test also addressed the evidential problem that the Court was unable to determine precisely the proportion of dust coming from the negligence source except that it was more than *de minimis*. This has led to a perceived injustice between the outcome in *Wardlaw* and that in *Hotson*. The claimant in *Hotson* fell from a tree injuring his hip and the defendant hospital negligently failed to diagnose this injury on his initial visit resulting in a delay in treatment.[166] The blood vessels in his hip were damaged, and bleeding continued during the period of delay, and the claimant eventually suffered avascular necrosis caused by insufficient blood vessels remaining intact in the joint. The House of Lords held that there was only a 25 per cent chance that sufficient blood vessels had remained intact at the time of the hospital's negligence, so on the balance of probabilities the delay had made no difference to the outcome. Smith has criticised this decision on the basis that 'if the medical experts had been *unable* to assess the contributions and had said only that the delay had made a more than minimal contribution, the claimant would have succeeded in full'.[167] However, this is to misinterpret the House of Lords' decision in *Hotson*. The claim failed not because the negligence contributed fewer than half of the damaged blood vessels, but because on the balance of probabilities the blood vessels damaged by the delay did not make a contribution to the harm at all since too many blood vessels had been damaged by the fall for the condition to be treatable.[168] This highlights the importance of separating the conceptual issue

---

[165] *Wardlaw* (n 5) 621.

[166] *Hotson v East Berkshire Health Authority* [1987] AC 750 (HL). The loss of chance argument advanced in *Hotson* is examined in detail in ch 4.

[167] Smith (n 115) 103.

[168] The correctness of this analysis of the causal process will be discussed in the final section.

of whether the negligence made a contribution to the damage, from the evidential issue of whether the balance of probabilities standard of proof requires that the contribution can be quantified in order for the court to form the requisite degree of belief that the negligence made a contribution.

C. Conceptual Element: A Material *Contribution to Harm*

Bailey seeks to show that the test of material contribution to harm is an application of the but-for test. It is important that he regards the but-for test as being synonymous with factual causation, so any departure would be exceptional. For him, the but-for test must be satisfied, and when we say that a claimant must prove that the negligence 'caused or materially contributed to' the loss, this is a more elaborate way of saying that the claimant must prove but-for causation that resolves 'the need to find words that cover both cases arising (effectively) from single causes and those arising from multiple causes'.[169] For example, he says that 'an omission (ie a failure to prevent harm occurring) cannot ever be the sole effective cause of an injury, and so the term 'material contribution' rather than 'cause' is entirely appropriate'.[170] We know, however, that no outcome has a single cause.[171] This means that when Bailey says that 'caused' relates to cases arising *effectively* from single causes he is making recourse to the Hart and Honoré type approach that uses common sense to distinguish 'causes' from 'mere conditions'. He is selecting between all of the necessary conditions, so his approach is evaluative rather than purely factual. This is why he finds it significant to remind us that in any given causal set, more than one factor may be identified as 'a cause' rather than as a 'mere condition'. While this evaluative inquiry is a part of the negligence inquiry, as discussed in the first part of this chapter, it goes beyond the question of factual causation. It is also unsatisfactory because it does not help us to distinguish between the myriad scenarios that might be deemed *effectively* to involve multiple causes: cases involving omissions, cases like *Wardlaw* where there were multiple sources of one harmful agent (silica dust) and cases where there were multiple different harmful agents. Instead, all instances of harm arise from 'multiple causes' in the sense of being caused by a sufficient set of conditions. So what negligence law needs is a test that is capable of functioning with that understanding of causation.

The NESS analysis of causation enables the causal question to be clearly articulated, making the resolution of cases more straightforward. The following sections consider a number of cases where there has been confusion in application of the *Wardlaw* test and in the question of 'apportionment' and seeks to show that approaching these cases via the NESS test clarifies the issues.

---

[169] Bailey (n 131) 178.
[170] ibid 177.
[171] See text to n 40.

D. Applying NESS to Divisible Damage

One case that could have been resolved more simply if the damage had been properly defined at the outset is *Ingram v Williams*.[172] The claimant in this case was born prematurely (his prematurity was not attributable to negligence) and suffered disabilities. The alleged negligence lay in the defendant doctor's failure to conclude that the membranes of the mother's womb might have ruptured, with the result that the baby was not born in hospital and was suffering hypothermia when he finally arrived at a hospital. Whilst in hospital he suffered several infections during the neonatal period but these were not attributable to negligence. The expert witnesses were agreed that all three factors contributed to the degree of the claimant's disability. The defendant thus argued that his liability should be limited to the extent that his negligence had worsened the claimant's disability rather than extending to the entirety of his disability.

Causation was addressed only briefly because the Court found that the defendant had not acted negligently. Proof of causation should have been straightforward because 'the experts' joint view was that all causal factors made an unquantifiable contribution to [the claimant's] disability' such that 'if he had been born in hospital there would have been a material reduction in his disability'.[173] This is therefore a case involving divisible damage, and the alleged negligence was a cause of a portion of the disability. Following *Holtby v Brigham & Cowan*, in cases of divisible damage liability is apportioned across each of the causes because each is a cause of only a portion of the damage, and where this cannot be done with precision then the court should take a 'broad brush' approach.[174]

Yet there was confusion in the argument and judgment applying *Bailey* to the facts. The claimant argued that 'as in *Bailey*, there are indivisible but different causes with the result that the claimant succeeds in full'.[175] The claimant thus focused on the fact that the sources of weakness in *Bailey* combined together, so that their effects could not be distinguished, as being the defining characteristic of 'cumulative cause cases'. In contrast, the defendant rightly understood that the damage itself was divisible and that where damage is divisible the but-for test can be satisfied. He therefore sought to distinguish this case from *Bailey* because 'the principle in *Bailey* … only came into play in a case where the 'but for' test was not met'.[176] The Court accepted the defendant's argument that *Bailey* is limited to

---

[172] *Ingram v Williams* [2010] EWHC 758 (HC), [2010] Med LR 255.
[173] ibid [85].
[174] *Holtby v Brigham & Cowan (Hull) Ltd* [2000] 3 All ER 421 (CA).
[175] *Ingram* (n 172) [82].
[176] ibid [84].

indivisible damage cases but did not accept that this case involved 'divisible causes of damage' explaining that

> it was not possible to quantify the extent to which his disabilities would have been avoided or mitigated if he had been born in hospital. All that could be said was that if he had been born in hospital there would have been a material reduction in his disability.[177]

Beyond the difficulties the judge would have faced in quantifying the portion of the damage attributable to the defendant's negligence, the case is made more difficult by the failure to distinguish clearly between the divisibility of the damage and the 'divisibility' of the causes of that damage. Since the damage was divisible, causation could be established relatively simply since the defendant's negligence was a cause of a portion of the disability and, as we have seen, the NESS test effectively collapses into the but-for test in respect of that portion.

E. Applying NESS to Indivisible Damage

The Court of Appeal did maintain a clear distinction between the damage and the triggers in *Environment Agency v Ellis* where the claimant had suffered a back injury due to the defendant employer's negligence.[178] Two years later, before commencing negligence proceedings in relation to the back injury, his back gave way resulting in a fall that damaged his right knee. Between these two events he had also had an accident when he lost his footing on a ladder, and additionally he was found to be suffering from previously undiagnosed spinal degeneration. The trial judge found that the spinal degeneration would have caused problems in the future anyway, so he reduced damages to take account of this as a vicissitude of life. The remaining sum made up 100 per cent of the award of damages, but the judge only awarded 90 per cent of this, reducing the award by 10 per cent to reflect the fact that the ladder accident was a contributory cause of the fall which damaged the claimant's knee. The claimant argued that this reduction was inappropriate because the ladder accident was simply part of the chain of causation, while the defendant argued that damages should be apportioned 70 per cent to the spinal degeneration, 20 per cent to the negligence, and 10 per cent to the ladder accident, as this reflected the extent to which each of these causes contributed to the fall. The Court of Appeal correctly held that this was 'essentially ... a single indivisible injury case'.[179] Although the trigger for the fall could conceivably be described as 'divisible' or 'cumulative' in the sense that the negligence and the ladder accident both led to the fall, there was a single injury to the claimant's knee, caused in a one-off event, and not dose-related, so the damage was indivisible. There was a single actually occurring set of conditions for that damage, and the Court had found that the defendant's negligence was a necessary element of that set.

---

[177] ibid [85].
[178] *Environment Agency v Ellis* [2008] EWCA Civ 1117, [2009] PIQR P5.
[179] ibid [31].

Similarly in the Canadian decision in *Athey v Leonati*, the claimant, who had a history of back problems, was injured in two car accidents resulting from the defendants' negligence. He later suffered a disc herniation which reduced his earning capacity. The trial judge had only awarded 25 per cent of the full damages to reflect his assessment of the contribution of the accidents to the disc herniation. The Supreme Court awarded full damages because the damage was indivisible so the only basis for a reduction in damages would have been evidence that the claimant was likely to suffer a disc herniation in the future even without the accidents.[180] These were therefore straightforward cases where the but-for test could be used as shorthand for the NESS test and each factor was a cause of the whole damage, so joint and several liability applied.

F. Over-determined Indivisible Damage: Causation in *Bailey*

The decision of the Court of Appeal in *Bailey* was notable for showing confusion over the meaning and applicability of the *Wardlaw* test of material contribution to harm. Waller LJ, with whom Sedley and Smith LJJ concurred, approached the issue by asking 'was this a case in which the judge was entitled to depart from the but-for test?'[181] As this chapter has argued, the legal issues cannot be fully articulated if the but-for test is taken as the frame of reference, because the but-for test is conceptually inadequate. Using the NESS test makes the resolution of the case simpler and reduces the potential for future confusion.

To briefly recap the facts, the claimant in *Bailey* was in a weakened state and therefore aspirated her vomit leading to cardiac arrest and brain damage. The defendant's negligence had led to weakness, and she was also weakened by a naturally occurring illness. The question was whether the negligent failure to resuscitate the patient after her first operation was a cause of her ultimate injury.

The first step is to determine whether the damage is divisible; the damage in *Bailey* was the brain injury which in this case was indivisible. The cause of the brain damage was the claimant's weakened state which prevented her from responding naturally to her vomit. Miller has expressed concern that 'lack of care and pancreatitis are very different entities',[182] so in order for them to form an indecipherable mass we are required to assume that they 'operate in essentially the same way when adding to the body's weakness; and their respective contributions must, at least in theory, be measurable on a common scale'.[183] He is concerned that 'to the layperson at least' it is unclear that the factors operate in the same way where the case, as in *Bailey* involves 'a pathological condition, which cannot be described more precisely than "weakness"'.[184] One response to his concern is that, as he says,

---

[180] *Athey v Leonati* [1996] 3 SCR 458 (SCC).

[181] *Bailey* (n 149) [36] (Waller LJ).

[182] Chris Miller, 'Causation in Personal Injury after (and before) *Sienkiewicz*' (2012) 32 *Legal Studies* 396, 405.

[183] ibid 405.

[184] ibid 406.

it arises from a layperson's perspective whereas the explanation was accepted by the relevant experts in the case. In other cases where the non-negligent factor involves a different causal mechanism, such as in *Hotson* where the fall caused bleeding into the joint, negligently caused weakness will not be relevant because a different mechanism is at work, but *Bailey* seems to be a straightforward case where failure to respond naturally to vomit can be ascribed to weakness.

The Court faced a practical difficulty in applying the but-for test in this case because the evidence did not establish that the weakness due to negligence was necessary for the harm; the pancreatitis alone may have left her in a sufficiently weak state that she may still have aspirated her vomit and suffered brain damage in any event. In part this is because 'weakness' is not a quantifiable, measurable factor; it is not possible to say that pancreatitis added x units of weakness, the negligence added y units, and that the threshold of weakness required for being unable to respond to vomit is z units. There was, therefore, a degree of uncertainty in the sense that the various sources of the trigger could not be quantified. In part, however, the but-for test is simply conceptually inadequate to deal with this kind of scenario where the various sources combine together in an indecipherable mass. The fact that there is a variety of sources means that there may be pre-emption or duplication, and since the but-for test is unable to cope with either kind of scenario, it can no longer help us ask the right questions in *Bailey*.

Applying the NESS test, the question is whether the weakness that was due to the defendant's negligence was a necessary element of a sufficient set that *actually occurred*? A sufficient set included a certain degree of weakness, plus the patient vomiting, plus nobody noticing and clearing her airway etc. Pre-empted factors are those that occur after a sufficient set has come together, so if the negligence contributed weakness after the patient vomited then it would be pre-empted from forming part of an *actually occurring* sufficient set. However, this is not the case. The weakness from the failure to resuscitate combined with the weakness due to pancreatitis in the period before the patient vomited. This means that it formed a part of an actually occurring sufficient set. As the NESS test has shown, this is the case whether there was just enough weakness to form a sufficient set (ie the threshold level of weakness was just reached) or if there was weakness in excess of the threshold (ie it was a case of asymmetrical duplication).

The judge at first instance seems to have understood that this was a relatively simple issue, explaining that although he could not say 'whether the contribution made by [the negligence] was more or less than that made by the pancreatitis ... the natural inference is that each contributed materially to the overall weakness and it was the overall weakness that caused the aspiration', so he found that the causal link had been established.[185] The NESS test may have enabled him to articulate the justification for this conclusion more robustly.

---

[185] *Bailey v Ministry of Defences, Portsmouth Hospitals NHS Trust* [2007] EWHC 2913 (QB), [61] (Foskett J).

The facts in *Bailey* can be contrasted with those in *Hotson*. The claimant in that case fell from a tree injuring his hip. The defendant hospital negligently failed to diagnose the injury to the hip when the claimant first visited, resulting in a delay in diagnosis and treatment. The claimant suffered avascular necrosis which occurs when there is an insufficient supply of blood to the epiphysis. A number of blood vessels were damaged by the fall. During the period of delay in diagnosis these blood vessels continued to bleed into the joint, blocking the blood vessels that had remained intact. Although the claimant advanced a claim for the loss of a chance of avoiding the injury, the House of Lords adhered to traditional principles, retaining the avascular necrosis itself as the gist of the action and applying the but-for test on the balance of probabilities to decide whether the delay in treatment was a cause of this injury.[186] They held that on the balance of probabilities at the time of the negligence there were already insufficient blood vessels remaining intact to keep the epiphysis alive. Effectively they considered that the claimant was already doomed to suffer avascular necrosis. Stapleton criticises this approach.[187] She effectively argues that because avascular necrosis occurs when the level of damaged blood vessels passes a particular threshold this case can be equated with a river pollution type scenario. She explains:

> Both the weakening of the blood supply due to the fall and the weakening resulting from the breach began to starve the hip joint of blood leading later to an avascular necrosis: that is, the necrosis only happened after Hotson's blood supply had been weakened by both the fall and the breach.[188]

However a key distinction between *Bailey* and *Hotson* is that the former involves (asymmetrical) duplication because both sources of weakness operated on the claimant simultaneously, whereas in the latter the damage to the blood vessels operated on the claimant consecutively. This means that while causation was over-determined in the sense of being duplicated in *Bailey*, in *Hotson* any over-determination takes the form of pre-emption. So while the NESS test is more inclusive than the but-for test, it is not so inclusive that it would find causation where, in fact, causation has been pre-empted. This point is made clearer if we consider another hypothetical example on which Stapleton relies:

> On a certain train line the trains weigh 10 units each; a bridge carrying the line was built to withstand a weight of 20 units. A train will pass across the bridge at noon. Before noon *X* deposits a weight of 6 units within the bridge structure, then *Y* deposits another 6-unit weight, then *Z* deposits another 6-unit weight. *X, Y,* and *Z* act independently and are unaware of the conduct of each other. At noon the train attempts to cross the bridge which collapses, killing a passenger on the train.[189]

---

[186] *Hotson* (n 166).
[187] Stapleton, 'Unnecessary Causes' (n 91) 48–50.
[188] ibid 49.
[189] ibid 48–49.

Asking whether *Z* was a cause of the passenger's death, she observes that the passenger seems to be doomed once the second weight is placed on the bridge but argues that

> this dooming question is irrelevant to the question of whether the third weight physically contributed to the collapse or not ... The law cannot ignore what it knows to be true: that the third weight was exerting its force on the bridge when the train arrived.[190]

She therefore concludes, correctly, that *Z*'s weight was a cause of the death. This is comparable to *Bailey* where 'a threshold point of physical weakness had become oversubscribed before an external stress, in this case the vomit, came on the scene to complete the mechanism'.[191] It is not, however, analogous to the facts in *Hotson*. In the train example, *Z*'s weight is a necessary element of an *actually* occurring sufficient set because the set only becomes sufficient once the train's weight is also added. Until that moment *Z* could choose to remove her weight and it would not form part of an actually occurring sufficient set. Her weight therefore forms part of an 'indecipherable mass' when the set becomes sufficient. In *Hotson*, the negligent damage to blood vessels occurs after the initial damage rather than simultaneously. The negligently damaged blood vessels are not part of an *actually occurring* sufficient set if the damage was already untreatable at that time because 'being treatable' is a necessary part of such a set. This was not a case where an 'external stress' was needed to complete the sufficient set, so once enough blood vessels were damaged there would be a sufficient set. The question was simply at what point enough blood vessels were damaged, and the House of Lords was satisfied on the balance of probabilities that this moment was reached before the negligence occurred.

This shows that it is not enough to focus on the fact that a threshold level of the harmful agent was needed for the harm to occur. We must also ask whether the exposures were consecutive or simultaneous. This is why Wright's observation that asymmetrical duplication is distinct from pre-emption should not have been confined to a footnote, and why Wright's 'at least enough' formulation is to be preferred to the more ambiguous formulation in his more recent account of NESS or Stapleton's 'extended but-for' test.[192] Only if the exposures are simultaneous will we be dealing with asymmetrical duplication and be able to say that the defendant's exposure was a necessary element of an actually occurring sufficient set. If they are consecutive then once the threshold is reached any later exposures will be pre-empted from being causes because they simply cannot form part of an *actually occurring* sufficient set since an essential ingredient of any sufficient set is 'the damage can still be avoided'. It is therefore clear that while the NESS test is more inclusive than the but-for test, it is not over-inclusive.

---

[190] ibid 49.
[191] ibid 50.
[192] See text to n 104.

IV. Conclusion

Chapter one showed that causation has a vital but limited role in interpersonal responsibility and this chapter has drawn this issue out in greater detail to isolate factual causation, the fact of being *a* cause, from evaluative conclusions that a condition was *the* responsible cause. It was shown that the NESS test is preferable to the but-for test as a test of factual causation because it is better matched to the philosophical account of what it means to be a cause and is therefore able to resolve more complex causal problems that the but-for test is unable to resolve. Adopting the NESS test would ensure that courts are equipped to address a wider range of causal scenarios without resorting to exceptional tests. This is important because it has shown that cases such as *Wardlaw* and *Bailey* may involve an exception to the but-for test but they do not involve an exception to the causation requirement. Having addressed the conceptual aspects of causation in this chapter the remaining chapters turn to evidential problems that have arisen and consider how they can be resolved consistently with principles of corrective justice. Since the NESS test is conceptually more robust than the but-for test, the remaining evidential problems can be more clearly identified. The final chapters will also draw on the analysis of the role that causation has within interpersonal responsibility and of the roles of the other negligence doctrines in addressing the remaining aspects of interpersonal responsibility.

3

Proof of Causation

The previous chapter explored the conceptual aspect of causation, considering the function of factual causation within the negligence inquiry, and how best to translate the idea of factual causation into a workable legal test. Later chapters will turn to address cases involving particular evidential difficulties and judicial responses to those difficulties, notably the idea of loss of a chance in medical negligence and the evidentiary gap arising in cases such as *Fairchild*.[1] Before addressing those specific problems of proof of causation, this chapter seeks to address proof of causation more generally. Just as it is essential to have a clear approach to the conceptual aspect of causation in order to properly identify the problems arising in loss of chance and evidentiary gap cases, it is essential to have a clear understanding of broader evidential issues in causation. As before, this also enables us to make full use of the evidence available before considering resorting to exceptional approaches. This chapter therefore considers how evidence can be used to satisfy an orthodox test for causation, and begins by examining what the balance of probabilities standard of proof actually entails.

Problems of proof arise in particular in cases involving injuries or diseases whose aetiology is not well understood since resort must then be made to scientific evidence that is explicitly probabilistic in nature. Study of such cases shows that the relationship between legal and scientific approaches to causation and standards of proof is rife with misunderstandings and contradictions. While there is a perception that science is more demanding than civil law, insisting upon a 95 per cent confidence limit in contrast to law's perceived acceptance of anything over 50 per cent, there is also widespread judicial and academic scepticism of some disciplines, most notably epidemiology. Epidemiological evidence is often equated with statistical evidence, with commentators questioning its value in proving causation in an individual case.[2] Yet there is also a growing tendency to regard the balance of probabilities standard of proof of causation as being nothing more than a statistical requirement, with a test of doubling of the risk at a nascent stage.

---

[1] *Fairchild v Glenhaven Funeral Services (t/a GH Dovener & Son)* [2002] UKHL 22, [2003] 1 AC 32.
[2] See eg Michael Dore, 'A Commentary on the Use of Epidemiological Evidence in Demonstrating Cause-in-Fact' (1983) 7 *Harvard Environmental Law Review* 429; Richard Wright, 'Causation, Responsibility, Risk, Probability, Naked Statistics, and Proof: Pruning the Bramble Bush by Clarifying the Concepts' (1988) 73 *Iowa Law Review* 1001; Richard Wright, 'Liability for Possible Wrongs: Causation, Statistical Probability and the Burden of Proof' (2008) 41 *Loyola of Los Angeles Law Review* 1295; Richard Wright, 'Proving Causation: Probability versus Belief' in Richard Goldberg (ed), *Perspectives on Causation* (Hart Publishing, 2011).

The 'doubles the risk' test has emerged in recent case law as a means of establishing causation in cases involving indivisible damage where there are competing sources of risk and the aetiology of the disease is not sufficiently well understood to pinpoint the causes without resort to probabilistic evidence.[3] For example in *Novartis v Cookson* the claimant developed bladder cancer following negligent occupational exposure to carcinogenic substances in addition to exposure to carcinogens through smoking cigarettes. The Court of Appeal considered that 'in terms of risk, if occupational exposure more than doubles the risk due to smoking, it must as a matter of logic be probable that the disease was caused by the former'.[4] The test is therefore based on the idea that if negligence more than doubled the risk of the claimant's damage then it was more probably than not the cause of that damage. The 'doubles the risk' test is inappropriate since it is based on a flawed understanding both of the balance of probabilities standard and of epidemiological evidence. It is, however, important that criticisms of the doubling of the risk test should not also be taken as criticisms of epidemiology which can provide valuable evidence of causation.

The first part of this chapter identifies some of the concerns arising from the interaction of science and law, focusing in particular on how to reconcile the standards of proof in the two disciplines. The second section then turns its attention to epidemiological evidence since this branch of science is particularly relevant in negligence scenarios yet there are sharp divisions over its use in proof of causation. Epidemiology is thus used as a lens through which to view some broad points about the interaction of law and science, as well as narrower points that are specific to negligence and epidemiology. While it is beyond the scope of this work to provide a detailed account of epidemiology, it is feasible to identify key features of epidemiological evidence and, importantly, to identify points that are most commonly misunderstood by lawyers. The final section considers the value of epidemiological evidence in proof of causation in negligence, considering first the ways it has been misused by courts before identifying the ways in which it can be beneficial. It seeks to adopt a reasoned middle ground between those who consider that epidemiological evidence 'is neither useful nor relevant in establishing what actually happened in a particular situation',[5] and those who would readily accept that epidemiological evidence of a doubling of risk is sufficient to prove causation in negligence.[6]

---

[3] *Novartis Grimsby Ltd v Cookson* [2007] EWCA Civ 1261; *Jones v Secretary of State for Energy and Climate Change* [2012] EWHC 2936 (QB).

[4] *Novartis* (n 3) [74] (Smith LJ).

[5] Wright, 'Proving Causation' (n 2) 207.

[6] See eg Alex Broadbent, *Philosophy of Epidemiology* (Palgrave Macmillan, 2013) ch 11.

I. Standards of Proof in Science and Law

Before we can engage with the substance of scientific evidence of causation in a negligence inquiry it is essential to understand the standard of proof, and here two key concerns emerge. The first is to understand the legal standard of proof in its own terms: what does the 'balance of probabilities' standard actually entail? Central to the current confusion is the perception that the 'balance of probabilities' standard of proof can be satisfied by proof of at least a 50 per cent probability that the defendant's breach of duty was a cause of the damage suffered.[7] This approach misconceives what the 'balance of probabilities' standard of proof entails by conflating the fact to be proved with the standard to which it must be proved. The balance of probabilities is not merely a quantitative probabilistic concept. Instead it is a qualitative concept relating to the fact-finder's degree of belief in a given proposition, and the value of this qualitative element will be explored.

The second key concern is to understand the relationship between the standards of proof in civil law and in science. The perception that scientific standards are higher than in civil law is a source of tension. By identifying differences in the nature of scientific and legal inquiries, and differences in the function of the standard of proof in both types of inquiry, we can begin to reconcile the two disciplines.

A. The Balance of Probabilities Standard of Proof

Just as the criminal standard of proof, 'beyond reasonable doubt', concerns the fact-finder's degree of belief in a particular fact, the civil standard, 'the balance of probabilities', also reflects the requisite degree of belief that should be satisfied.[8] Causation will be proved to the requisite degree if the fact-finder believes it is more probable than not that the breach of duty was a cause of the damage suffered.[9] The use of the word 'probabilities' and the availability of statistical or probabilistic evidence should not mislead us into viewing the balance of probabilities as requiring or accepting a statistical probability of causation of over 50 per cent. The probability of a fact and the degree of belief in the truth of that probability are distinct concepts as Gold has notably explained:

> The standard of persuasion, as that term is used here, defines the level of confidence that the jury must feel in order to find a fact 'true' in favor of the party with the burden of

---

[7] See eg *Gregg v Scott* [2005] UKHL 2, [2005] 2 AC 176 and the discussion of *McGhee v NCB* [1973] 1 WLR 1 in *Sienkiewicz v Greif* [2011] UKSC 10; [2011] 2 AC 229 at [28] (Lord Phillips) and [149]–[156] (Lord Rodger).

[8] *Sienkiewicz v Greif* [2011] UKSC 10, [2011] 2 AC 229 at [217]–[222] (Lord Dyson), citing Steve Gold, 'Causation in Toxic Torts: Burdens of Proof, Standards of Persuasion, and Statistical Evidence' (1986) 96 *Yale Law Journal* 376, 395.

[9] *Miller v Minister of Pensions* [1947] 2 All ER 372 (KBD): 'If the evidence is such that the tribunal can say: "We think it more probable than not", the burden is discharged, but, if the probabilities are equal, it is not' at 374 (Lord Denning).

proving that fact. A standard of persuasion represents a degree of certainty in the jury's collective mind, which can be characterized as a 'probability.' Thus, in a conventional case, only the issue of the sufficiency of the jury's *belief* in certain facts, measured against the standard of persuasion, involves probability. The facts themselves, defined as elements on which one party has the burden of proof, are deemed true or false, with no room for intermediate probabilities. Suppose, however, that the issue in a case involved an allegedly unfair coin that had been tossed to start a football game. Then, a question of fact would itself be about a 'probability'—whether the coin, when flipped, really gave a fifty-fifty chance of heads or tails. In toxic torts, the nature of statistical proof similarly introduces probability into the arena of fact.[10]

In negligence the fact that must be established is that the defendant's negligence was a cause of the claimant's damage, so the claimant must persuade the court to form a probable belief in this fact. The statistical probability of causation may be relevant to proof of that fact, but ultimately the court is seeking to form a sufficient degree of belief in the fact that the negligence was a cause of the damage.

Like Gold, Barnes labels these two concepts 'fact probability' and 'belief probability'.[11] He explains that belief probability refers to 'the credibility— the believability—of the evidence in support of a party's factual claims'.[12] Fact probability refers to the statistical likelihood of a causal relationship, one element of which is the 'relative risk'.[13] As Miller explains, fact probability and belief probability are independent:

> It is not illogical for me to have a high (>90%) degree of belief in the relative risk of 2.7, which emerges from a study undertaken by a renowned epidemiologist, and a lower belief (<50%) in the higher figures (3.2) cited in paper whose author is unknown to me … or if I know that her earlier study of … risk was found, by other statisticians, to have been methodologically flawed'.[14]

The conflation of fact probability and belief probability is evident in decisions such as *Gregg v Scott*.[15] In that case the expert witness, Professor Goldstone, gave a 'working example' of the fate of a cohort of 100 patients with the same disease as the claimant, and concluded that only 42 would survive.[16] The claim failed because the claimant's pre-tort chance of recovery was less than 50 per cent, so the Court held that on the balance of probabilities he was destined not to survive even with proper treatment. Lord Nicholls considered that '[t]he patient could recover damages if his initial prospects of recovery had been more than 50%'.[17]

---

[10] Gold, 'Causation in Toxic Torts (n 8) 381–82.

[11] David W Barnes, 'Too Many Probabilities: Statistical Evidence of Tort Causation' (2001) 64 *Law and Contemporary Problems* 191. See also Gold (n 8) 376.

[12] ibid 192.

[13] ibid 193. These probabilities are discussed more fully below in s II: Epidemiological Evidence'.

[14] Chris Miller, 'Causation in Personal Injury: Legal or Epidemiological Common Sense?' (2006) 26 *Legal Studies* 544, 551.

[15] *Gregg v Scott* (n 7).

[16] The reliability of this evidence will be scrutinised in a later section.

[17] *Gregg* (n 7) [2].

If the claimant had a 51 per cent chance of recovery then, on Lord Nicholls' reasoning, causation would be established to the requisite degree, yet the reality is that the fact in question is merely the fact that the claimant had a 51 per cent chance of recovery. The court should assess the reliability of the evidence of that 51 per cent chance in order to form a rational, probable belief in its accuracy. And this is still a step removed from being convinced on the balance of probabilities that the defendant's negligence actually caused harm to the claimant since there is a large and not insignificant chance (49 per cent) that the claimant was destined not to recover. A pre-tort chance of 51 per cent would, therefore, almost certainly not suffice to convince a court on the balance of probabilities that the claimant's cancer was, as a matter of fact, curable. As the House of Lords had made clear in the earlier decision in *Hotson*, the patient does not have a personal 'chance', he is either in the survivor group or the non-survivor group and this is the fact that the court needs to determine.[18] What is required is evidence particular to the claimant to support the belief that he was in fact a member of the 51 per cent who would have survived with proper treatment.

The significance of the balance of probabilities standard of proof is that it allows a court to find causation to be established even when it harbours significant doubt, so long as it is marginally more convinced than not that the fact is true.[19] In *McGhee*, Lord Kilbrandon said that proof of causation 'depends on drawing a distinction between the possibility and the probability of the efficacy of the precautions. I do not find it easy to say in the abstract where one shades into the other'.[20] The line between possibility and probability in the degree of belief is not a bright one because it necessarily involves a qualitative assessment of the evidence which introduces an element of subjectivity. But it is the role of the judge to decide on which side of the line a particular case falls. This would be clearer if the 'balance of probabilities' were not expressed as a numerical probability as McIvor argues:

> Since belief values are impossible to quantify in precise terms, in the sense that ordinary human beings cannot differentiate between, for example, a 51% degree of belief and a 58% degree of belief … we should dispense with the practice of expressing the balance of probabilities standard in numerical terms.[21]

This is uncontroversial in cases that do not involve probabilistic evidence as Miller explains:

> We have no conceptual difficulty in judging the credibility of causal accounts which have no explicit reliance on probability or statistics—the collision resulted from the defendant's driving round a blind corner on the wrong side of the road.[22]

---

[18] This reasoning is analysed in ch 4.

[19] Claire McIvor, 'Debunking some Judicial Myths about Epidemiology and its Relevance to UK Tort Law' (2013) 21 *Medical Law Review* 553, 558.

[20] *McGhee v National Coal Board* [1973] 1 WLR 1 (HL), 10 (Lord Kilbrandon).

[21] McIvor, 'Debunking some Judicial Myths about Epidemiology and its Relevance to UK Tort Law' (n 19) 581.

[22] Miller, Causation in Personal Injury' (n 14) 555.

Courts should not feel restricted by the availability of statistical or epidemiological evidence; the fact that part of the evidence can be quantified or assigned a numerical probability does not make it intrinsically more valuable than the qualitative aspect of proof.

Stauch has criticised the balance of probabilities as being a crude test in comparison to statistical evidence:

> [W]hereas statistics derived systematically from our previous experience of similar cases, provide us with a very accurate probability-weighting for each candidate [cause], the balance of probabilities test attempts to perform the same operation by appealing crudely to what we *feel* the likely cause to have been. The relevant feeling must, once again, derive from our previous experience of similar cases, but this time in its rawest form.[23]

There are a number of observations to make in relation to this statement. The first is that the balance of probabilities will necessarily seem less objectively measureable than statistical probabilities because it is a qualitative concept. As a belief probability it measures the judge's degree of belief in a proposition so necessarily involves her assessment of how credible the assertion is. Rather than being a weakness of the balance of probabilities standard of proof, Barnes' work has shown that the qualitative aspect is vital to assessing the credibility of the scientific evidence and its implications in an individual case. His work shows that, in addition to establishing the fact probability, the court must weigh up other factors affecting the reliability of the scientific study from which those probabilities were derived, and must extrapolate to the individual case.[24] While statistical probabilities may have an outward appearance of objectivity, they only tell part of the story and they certainly do not provide a definitive answer about causation in an individual case.

Additionally, Stauch presents us with a choice between statistical probabilities and the balance of probabilities test and implies that by insisting on the balance of probabilities test the courts are making a conscious and deliberate decision to rely on a feeling rather than on scientific and statistical evidence. It is essential to remember that these two types of probability are not mutually exclusive; indeed, as Barnes' article shows, a rational belief probability must be based on an assessment of the credibility of the scientific evidence which includes, but is far wider than, the relative risk or fact probability. As Haack argues:

> To deny that degrees of proof are mathematical probabilities is emphatically not to deny that statistical evidence—the random-match probabilities that by now are a routine part of DNA testimony, for example, or the epidemiological evidence common in toxic-tort cases, etc etc—plays a significant role in many cases.[25]

The belief probability required to satisfy the balance of probabilities is a more holistic approach that cannot be equated with fact probability, but incorporates it

---

[23] Marc Stauch, 'Loss of Chance in Medical Negligence' (1997) 17 *Oxford Journal of Legal Studies* 205, 219.

[24] These factors will be considered in greater detail in s II: 'Epidemiological Evidence'.

[25] Susan Haack, *Evidence Matters: Science, Proof, and Truth in the Law* (Cambridge University Press, 2014) 19.

as one element of an analysis that takes account of all the available evidence. Haack describes this kind of approach as 'foundherentist':

[I]t is intermediate between the traditionally-rival families of theories of epistemic justification, foundationalism and coherentism—which, however, don't exhaust the options. Unlike coherentism, but like (some forms of) foundationalism, foundherentism allows a role for experiential evidence as well as for reasons; unlike foundationalism but like coherentism, it allows pervasive relations of mutual support among beliefs.[26]

She likens this to the way we solve a crossword puzzle:

[E]xperiential evidence is the analogue of the clues, and reasons (a person's background beliefs, ramifying in all directions) the analogue of already-completed crossword entries.[27]

And Haack later explains that 'this kind of reliance on a whole mesh of evidence is ubiquitous—the rule, not the exception', it is 'commonplace in everyday life', for example 'after reading a startling story in a newspaper, I buy a different paper, or turn on the television news, to check whether other sources confirm it'.[28]

This holistic approach, looking at the overall picture presented by the evidence, is often apparent in judicial decision-making. In *Sienkiewicz*, Lady Hale suggests that 'most judges will put everything into the mix before deciding which account is more likely than not'.[29] The Court in *Reay and Hope v British Nuclear Fuels* took such an approach, engaging in a qualitative assessment of the evidence.[30] The claimant's case centred on one particular epidemiological study, and French J considered that for the study to provide evidence of causation on the balance of probabilities:

it must do so not necessarily alone but in the context of all the other evidence and the admitted facts in the case and including the evidence called by each side as to the possible biological route or routes, if any, by which the radiation could have caused the two diseases or either of them.[31]

This meant engaging not only with the figures produced by the study, but also with the reliability of the study itself as well as how far the results of the study fitted with the other available evidence. Although this exercise was undertaken in *Reay* it is by no means done consistently, particularly where the 'doubles the risk' test is applied as later analysis will highlight.[32] The Court in *Reay* did also observe that:

The fact that an epidemiologist or another scientist would not find an association and/or a cause to be established to his satisfaction is, of course, most helpful to a judge but only within the limits imposed by their respective disciplines.[33]

---

[26] ibid 13.
[27] ibid 13–14.
[28] ibid 218.
[29] *Sienkiewicz* (n 8) [172].
[30] *Reay and Hope v British Nuclear Fuels Plc* [1994] Env LR 320. It is perhaps notable, however, that this decision preceded the development of the 'doubles the risk' test discussed in more detail below.
[31] ibid 335.
[32] See s III.A below.
[33] *Reay* (n 30) 336.

It is important, therefore, to turn to the different concerns and standards applied in science and law.

B. Scientific Standards of Proof

Two conflicting concerns emerge from recent judicial treatment of scientific and epidemiological evidence. On one hand there is a concern that scientific standards of proof are far higher than the balance of probabilities standard applied by civil courts, meaning that a court could be satisfied that a causal link is established when a scientific expert might not be similarly satisfied. One significant error is the belief that the scientific standard of proof is 95 per cent,[34] but, far from being a standard of persuasion, the 95 per cent figure relates solely to the 'p-value' or 'sampling error probability' that is 'a statistical property of data underlying evidence offered to prove a relevant fact'.[35] The p-value will be explored in greater detail in section II, but it is important to observe from the outset that it is just one statistical property of data that does not reflect the quality of a study but simply tells us the likelihood that the study sample is unrepresentative of the broader population.

Yet the belief that scientific standards are higher than legal standards of proof is accompanied by judicial scepticism surrounding the value of epidemiological evidence with Lord Kerr going so far as to say 'there is a real danger that so-called "epidemiological evidence" will carry a false air of authority',[36] suggesting a belief that epidemiological standards are low and the discipline unscientific in nature. Beside concerns about epidemiological methods, which will be addressed at a later stage, this highlights the need for clarity about the different standards and about the nature of the legal and scientific inquiries more broadly.

i. The Standards of Proof in Law and Science

The standard of proof in science is perceived to be higher than in civil law as Lord Prosser explained in *Dingley v The Chief Constable of Strathclyde Police*:

> Whether one uses the word 'scientific' or not, no hypothesis or proposition would be seen as 'proved' or 'established' by anyone with any form of medical expertise merely upon the basis that he had come to regard it as probably sound … And even if, in relation to any possible proposition or hypothesis, such an expert even troubled to notice that he had come to the point of regarding it as not merely possible but on balance 'probable', then I think he would regard that point as one from which he must set off on further inquiry, and by no means as being (as it is in the courts) a point of arrival. Mere marginal probability will not much interest him. But it must satisfy a court.[37]

---

[34] See text to n 83 below.
[35] Barnes, 'Too Many Probabilities' (n 11) 193.
[36] *Sienkiewicz* (n 8) [206].
[37] *Dingley v The Chief Constable, Strathclyde Police* 1998 SC 548, 603.

Knowledge in science will usually be regarded as incomplete so it will be common for scientific experts to acknowledge their doubts; this pervasive doubt should not act as an obstacle to proof of causation in negligence in itself since it will almost always exist to some degree. As Bradford Hill argued:

> All scientific work is incomplete—whether it be observational or experimental. All scientific work is liable to be upset or modified by advancing knowledge. That does not confer upon us a freedom to ignore the knowledge we already have.[38]

It is worth reiterating at this stage that the balance of probabilities standard requires merely probability rather than certainty. As McIvor explains:

> In weighing up all the evidence about causation, the court has to be at least slightly more convinced by the claimant's case than the defendant's before the court can find in favour of the claimant. Or perhaps a more apposite explanation, bearing in mind the manner in which the standard of proof was actually applied in *Sienkiewicz*, is that the standard *requires* a court to find in favour of the claimant if they are at the very least marginally more convinced by the claimant's case than by the defendant's, and *notwithstanding* the fact that it may still harbour serious doubts in this respect.[39]

While it is arguable that the evidentiary gap in relation to mesothelioma meant that the Court in *Sienkiewicz* was right to hold that causation could not be established on the balance of probabilities, there has been startling reluctance to give due weight to epidemiological evidence in other cases that do not involve an evidentiary gap, particularly apparent in *McTear*.[40] In that case, the Court required such a high degree of proof that it was not willing to find on the balance of probabilities that there exists a general causal link between cigarette smoking and lung cancer. It is widely accepted that cigarette smoking is a cause of lung cancer, so where there is convincing scientific evidence of causation the courts should be more ready to accept it.[41] Indeed, even when there is still scientific doubt, if the court is marginally more convinced than not by the claimant's case they should be willing to accept that causation is established.[42] After all, as Haack reminds us:

> What the legal finder of fact is asked to do is *not*, strictly speaking, to determine whether the defendant is guilty, or is liable, but ... to determine whether the evidence establishes the defendant's guilt or liability to the required degree.[43]

This means making full use of the evidence that is available and giving it the full weight it deserves, which would be simpler if courts explicitly articulated the

---

[38] Sir Austin Bradford Hill, 'The Environment and Disease: Association or Causation?' (1965) *Proceedings of the Royal Society of Medicine* 295, 300.

[39] McIvor, 'Debunking' (n 19) 577–78.

[40] *McTear v Imperial Tobacco Ltd* [2005] 2 SC 1 (Court of Session (Outer House)).

[41] See Miller (n 14) 544; Alex Broadbent, 'Epidemiological Evidence in Proof of Specific Causation' (2011) 17 *Legal Theory* 237, 245. Both authors highlight that the Court in *McTear* refused to accept that a causal link exists between cigarette smoking and lung cancer at the same time that the Scottish Parliament was legislating to ban smoking in public places on the basis of the same evidence as to causation.

[42] McIvor, 'Debunking' (n 19).

[43] Haack, *Evidence Matters* (n 25) 56.

fact that the balance of probabilities standard enables them to be satisfied that causation is established in circumstances where science may not be adequately satisfied, because the scientific standard is higher than that of civil law. Instead, in *Sienkiewicz*, Lord Phillips expressed the view that where a scientific expert cannot 'postulate with confidence the chain of events that occurred, ie the biological cause ... he is unlikely to be of much assistance to the judge who seeks to ascertain what occurred on a balance of probability'.[44]

A key consideration is clarity in communication between lawyers and scientific or medical experts. The trial judge in *Hotson* noted that the claimant's expert witness 'speaks of likelihood as something involving a less than 50% chance in contradistinction to a probability as denoting more than that'.[45] In other words, the medical expert drew a significant distinction between something being 'likely' and it being 'probable'. Given the importance of the 'balance of probabilities' in determining the outcome of a case it is essential that all parties understand the concept and use the term 'probable' consistently. As previously explained, in civil law the balance of probabilities standard requires the fact-finder to be marginally more convinced than not by the claimant's account.[46] It will, of course, be difficult for a court to express a bright dividing line where the balance of probabilities lies, and to provide clear reasons for finding the balance of probabilities to be satisfied when there remains significant scientific doubt. But as Bradford Hill tells us, there will always be some degree of doubt surrounding scientific findings, and the fact that there is some uncertainty should not lead courts to reject the scientific evidence entirely.

This pragmatism is also required by the practical constraints of civil litigation. As Haack explains, while a court is searching for the truth:

> a trial is very different from an open-ended scientific or scholarly investigation sifting for as long as it takes through all the evidence that can be had; legal determinations of fact are subject both to limitations of time and to constraints on how evidence may lawfully be obtained and what evidence may lawfully be presented.[47]

This means that courts cannot wait until more or more reliable scientific evidence becomes available; as Miller states, 'civil courts cannot commission laboratory experiments or epidemiological studies, but nor can they suspend a case until someone else does'.[48] Courts must reach a decision based on the available evidence and it is a valuable feature of the balance of probabilities standard that it allows them to reach a decision in spite of residual uncertainties.

---

[44] *Sienkiewicz* (n 8) [9] (Lord Phillips).
[45] *Hotson v East Berkshire HA* [1985] 3 All ER 167 (QBD), 173.
[46] See text to n 39.
[47] Haack (n 25) 55–56.
[48] Chris Miller, 'Coal Dust, Causation and Common Sense' (2000) 63 *Modern Law Review* 763, 769.

ii. The Nature of the Legal and Scientific Inquiries

The legal inquiry is not only subject to the practical constraints outlined above, but its broad focus or nature is backwards-looking and therefore distinct from scientific inquiries which are usually forwards-looking in nature. Dawid explains:

> As a very loose generalisation, *Science* is more typically concerned with general EoC [effect of cause] type queries, and *Law* with individual, CoE [cause of effect] type queries. Because of this mismatch we must be particularly careful when we try to bring scientific evidence and reasoning to bear on questions of legal causality.[49]

This is sometimes also expressed as the difference between 'general' causation, eg 'does cigarette smoking cause lung cancer?' and 'specific' or 'individual' causation, eg 'was this individual's lung cancer caused by smoking cigarettes?'. The negligence inquiry focuses on individual causation, although courts will sometimes have to grapple with questions of general causation since this is a prerequisite of specific causation; for example, the Court in *McTear* had to address the question of whether cigarette smoking *can* cause lung cancer before it could determine whether the victim's cigarette smoking was a cause of his lung cancer.[50]

Where there is genuine scientific debate the task of a court examining issues of general causation is a delicate one that needs to acknowledge the potential for future scientific developments whilst reaching a decision on legal liability on the basis of what is currently known. In *XYZ v Schering*, Mackay J explained the role of the judge faced with a debate he described as 'unyielding' and 'devoid of willingness to countenance that there may be two sides to the question':

> He cannot transform himself into some form of super-scientist with access to a level of expertise superior to those who have given the evidence. Rather his role, and my role here, is to evaluate the witnesses and decide after 42 days of evidence and submissions, undoubtedly a more extensive debate on this topic than has ever been carried out to date, which parts of the evidence are sound and reliable and which are not.[51]

Although a court need only be persuaded on the balance of probabilities that the defendant's negligence was a cause of the particular claimant's harm, in order to form a rational belief it will generally need to be more strongly convinced that there exists a general causal relationship. For example, in *McTear* the claimant was the widow of a lung cancer victim who brought a claim against the manufacturer of the cigarettes her husband had smoked on the basis that they had caused his lung cancer. For her claim to be successful she needed first to establish the general causal link between cigarette smoking and lung cancer, before going on to establish the specific causal link between cigarette smoking and her husband's lung cancer. The Court was presented with detailed epidemiological evidence and found

---

[49] A Philip Dawid, 'The Role of Scientific and Statistical Evidence in Assessing Causality' in Goldberg (ed), *Perspectives on Causation* (n 2) 134. See also *Sienkiewicz* (n 8) [170] Lady Hale.
[50] *McTear* (n 40).
[51] *XYZ v Schering* [2002] EWHC 1420 (QB), [33]–[34].

that the claimant had failed to establish either limb. If, hypothetically, the Court had accepted that there is a general causal relationship between smoking and lung cancer but had been only marginally more convinced than not of this fact, then it is unlikely that the claimant would have been able to go on to convince them that it was this causal mechanism at play in her husband's disease. As it is, however, the Court's approach to both stages was too demanding and virtually amounted to requiring certainty.

In order to extrapolate from evidence of general causation to a question of specific causation, it will be essential to draw on testimony from experts in the relevant field and to ensure clarity and consistency in the discourse between lawyers and scientists, such as clinicians and epidemiologists. Furthermore, pressure from lawyers to express causal claims in statistical terms may conflict with the expert witness's reluctance to assign a precise numerical value. For example the medical experts' position in *Gregg* was that a figure could not be put on the claimant's individual chance of recovery from his cancer. With regard to the claimant's pre-tort chance of cure, Inglis J noted:

> Professor Goldstone was unable to put a percentage figure on that chance. It has to be taken as less than evens ... It might be said that since neither he nor Dr Bunch put a figure on it, the court should not. I do not agree ... The experts thought it possible that his individual prognosis had been reduced to less than 50% of what it would have been intrinsically at the outset.[52]

Since the balance of probabilities involves a qualitative assessment of the evidence it is important not only to avoid the temptation to map statistical probabilities directly onto it but also to avoid pressuring expert witnesses to quantify the risk if they are unable to. Yet courts should not go too far in the other direction as it has been suggested that the proliferation of expert evidence 'may also put pressure on judges to appear to address more general issues of scientific causation or appeal to common sense models of causation in order to differentiate their views from those of the experts'.[53] As noted earlier, while the balance of probabilities has a qualitative aspect, conclusions about causation should still be justified by reference to the available evidence, whether it is scientific or otherwise.

The remaining concern about standards of proof in science is the idea that scientists require a 95 per cent probability before they will accept that a causal link is established, so the scientific standard is much higher than the mere balance of probabilities required by civil law. Indeed, in *Sienkiewicz* Lord Phillips cited with approval the passage from *Dingley*,[54] and stated:

> When a scientific expert gives an opinion on causation, he is likely to do so in terms of certainty or uncertainty, rather than probability. Either medical science will enable him

---

[52] Para [51] (cited in *Gregg* (HL) (n 7) [164] (Lord Phillips)).

[53] Gary Edmond and David Mercer, 'Rebels without a Cause?: Judges, Medical and Scientific Evidence and the Uses of Causation' in Ian Freckleton and Danuta Mendelson, *Causation in Law and Medicine* (Ashgate, 2002) 88.

[54] (n 37).

to postulate with confidence the chain of events that occurred, ie the biological cause, or it will not. In the latter case he is unlikely to be of much assistance to the judge who seeks to ascertain what occurred on a balance of probability.[55]

The origins and meaning of this belief will be considered in the next section, which moves on from the broad differences of approach in law and science and explores a branch of science which has increasing significance in negligence cases, epidemiology.

II. Epidemiological Evidence

It has already been noted that while some courts have accepted epidemiological evidence of doubling of the risk of harm as satisfying the balance of probabilities standard of proof, others have expressed scepticism with Lord Kerr in *Sienkiewicz* questioning its validity as a discipline.[56] The final section of this chapter will consider how epidemiological evidence can be used in proof of causation in negligence. This section provides a preliminary account of what epidemiology is, including an overview of the different types of epidemiological study, the information that it can provide etc. This is important because, as McIvor explains, judicial scepticism 'stems largely from a lack of understanding of epidemiology as a discipline. In particular, Lord Phillips' leading speech [in *Sienkiewicz*] seriously misconceives what epidemiologists actually do and the type of evidence that they can bring to the legal table'.[57] This does not set out to be a definitive guide to epidemiology; indeed, a central argument is that epidemiology is a specialist discipline and that epidemiological evidence ought to be presented in court by epidemiologists rather than other scientific or medical experts. While it would therefore be ambitious for a legal academic to claim to understand all the finest details of epidemiology it is important to have an understanding of key principles such that it is possible to identify how it relates to the negligence inquiry. The aim is therefore to provide an overview to give a sense of what epidemiology is, and to highlight some areas where there is currently a lack of clarity in the judicial treatment of epidemiological evidence, and to explore how it can be used to satisfy the legal standard of proof.

Epidemiology is described by Broadbent as 'the study of the distribution and determinants of disease and other health states in human populations by means of group comparisons, for the purpose of improving population health'.[58] A key misconception identified by McIvor is the belief that epidemiologists are 'mere statisticians, concerned solely with the calculation of incidence rates and capable

---

[55] *Sienkiewicz* (n 8) [9] (Lord Phillips).
[56] See text to n 36.
[57] McIvor (n 19) 554.
[58] Alex Broadbent, *Philosophy of Epidemiology* (Palgrave Macmillan, 2013) 17.

only of producing "naked statistics".[59] This is evident in Lord Phillips' speech in *Sienkiewicz* where he describes epidemiology as:

> the study of the occurrence and distribution of events (such as disease) over human populations. It seeks to determine whether statistical associations between these events and supposed determinants can be demonstrated. Whether those associations if proved demonstrate an underlying biological causal relationship is a further and different question from the question of statistical association on which the epidemiology is initially engaged.[60]

But epidemiologists do seek evidence of an underlying biological causal relationship as McIvor explains:

> While statistics are certainly an important tool used by epidemiologists, they are no more than a tool and epidemiologists are more than just statisticians. In addition to designing and executing studies to collect relevant data, epidemiologists use various sophisticated techniques for interpreting the data precisely in order to determine whether any indicated statistical associations provide evidence of an underlying biological relationship of cause and effect. Epidemiologists are trained in statistics, research methodologies, and also in medicine. The highly specialised techniques that they use for drawing causal inferences from empirical data are informed by all three disciplines.[61]

Some courts have shown an appreciation of this; for example, French J explained in *Reay* that 'epidemiology is the study of disease and disease attributes in defined populations. It is concerned with aetiology and distribution of disease',[62] but courts are by no means consistent in recognising that epidemiologists go beyond producing mere statistics.

This basic view of epidemiology was strikingly apparent in *Sienkiewicz*, where Lord Phillips focused on the output of epidemiological studies being the calculation of relative risk, and showed little appreciation for what the relative risk tells us.[63] He also showed a lack of insight into the significance of the 95 per cent confidence limit, adhering to the view it indicates the reliance that can be placed on the relative risk.[64] It is crucial that lawyers and judges understand these epidemiological concepts, at least in sufficient depth to be able to ask the right questions of epidemiologist expert witnesses. The following sections outline how the design of a study can affect its reliability, the relevance of particular statistics such as the 'relative risk' and the 'p-value' and factors affecting the causal inferences that might be drawn on the basis of a study.

---

[59] McIvor (n 19) 554.
[60] *Sienkiewicz* (n 8) [80].
[61] McIvor (n 19) 570.
[62] *Reay* (n 30) 335.
[63] *Sienkiewicz* (n 8) [72]–[82].
[64] ibid [82].

A. Epidemiological Studies: Design

The design of a study affects its reliability so it has a significant impact on the potential for a court to form a rational belief in the conclusions derived from that study. Studies can broadly be divided into those that are experimental and those that are observational.[65] Barnes explains that the 'well-known gold standard for experimental design is the randomized, controlled, double-masked study'.[66] A clinical trial is perhaps the best known form of experimental epidemiology.[67] Yet there are ethical barriers to conducting such studies in many cases, certainly if a particular factor is suspected to have a harmful effect:

> There have been few experiments where people are randomly allocated to 'experimental' or 'control' groups and then deliberately exposed to possible harms in order to prove that a potential cause was indeed responsible for the disease. Most of the scientific evidence about causation therefore comes from observational studies, although randomised studies of interventions likely to be beneficial sometimes provide sound evidence of harm as well.[68]

This means that majority of epidemiological studies will be observational,[69] and while this is not the 'gold standard' such studies are highly valuable so long as they are well designed and we are alert to their limitations. Indeed in the hierarchy of evidence-based medicine they both outrival expert opinion or clinical examples that more typically feature in the evidence of clinicians.[70] The two main types of observational study are cohort studies and case control studies, both of which look at a group of subjects over a period of time. A cohort study takes a disease-free group of people with a particular exposure and follows them over a period of time to discover whether they suffer harm. A case control study is retrospective, and starts by identifying a group of people suffering a particular harm and works backwards through their history to identify possible causes. Both types of study involve use of a control group: in a cohort study this will be a group that does not have similar exposure, in a case control study it will be a group of people who do not have the disease but have a similar background to those subjects who do have the disease. The case control study is therefore quicker to conduct, and has the potential to identify multiple risk factors for one disease whereas the cohort study takes longer to complete since it follows the cohorts over a period of time

---

[65] For an accessible introduction to types of epidemiological study, see Kenneth J Rothman, *Epidemiology: An Introduction* (Oxford University Press, 2002) Ch 4; Kenneth J Rothman, Sander Greenland and Timothy L Lash, *Modern Epidemiology* (3rd edn, Wolters Kluwer, 2008) ch 6.

[66] Barnes (n 11) 200.

[67] Rothman, *Epidemiology* (n 65) 60; Rothman, Greenland and Lash, *Modern Epidemiology* (n 65) 88–93.

[68] Peter Greenberg, 'The Cause of Disease and Illness: Medical Views and Uncertainties' in Freckleton and Mendelson, *Causation in Law and Medicine* (n 53) 43.

[69] Rothman, Greenland and Lash (n 65) 93.

[70] Kevin C Chung, Jennifer A Swanson, Delaine Schmitz, et al, 'Introducing Evidence-based Medicine to Plastic and Reconstructive Surgery' (2009) 123 *Plastic and Reconstructive Surgery* 1385–89.

UNIVERSITY OF WINCHESTER
LIBRARY

and generally requires a higher number of subjects in order to produce reliable results, but has the potential to identify multiple diseases flowing from a single risk factor.[71] In any study it is important to guard against bias, or systematic error, for example in properly randomising the subjects, ensuring effective 'blinding' of subjects and in following up with subjects.[72] Another concern is identifying possible 'confounders', for example people who smoke may also be more prone to drink alcohol so it is important to design the study in a way that allows the effects of smoking and drinking alcohol to be separated so that the ill-effects of one are not incorrectly attributed to the other. Already it is clear that qualitative evaluation of any study is essential to forming a rational belief in the accuracy of the results it produces.

B. The Relative Risk

The relative risk (RR), or risk ratio, is just one of the calculations that can be performed on epidemiological evidence, but it is this figure that is central to the 'doubles the risk' test. It is obtained by comparing the exposed group and the control group: 'Risk ratios measure the percentage change in the incidence of a specified harm, such as a disease. A risk ratio compares a background rate, where the stimulus in question is not present, to the rate that obtains when the stimulus is present'.[73] Broadbent provides the example of smoking:

> Suppose (roughly correctly) that 15 percent of British male smokers get lung cancer, whereas 1.5 percent of British male non-smokers do. Then RR = 15%/1.5% = 10. This tells us that lung cancer is ten times as common among British male smokers than British male non-smokers.[74]

It is important to note that the relative risk is not absolute but is calculated for a specified population:

> In fact, RR … is a function of exposure, disease, and population. To see why, recall that I do not specify an age range for the (fictitious) RR associated with smoking among British males. Suppose we select an age range of fourteen to eighteen. If RR was close to 1 in that group, that would not show that smoking does not cause lung cancer. The likeliest explanation would be that few teenagers get lung cancer regardless of whether they smoke. It follows that there is no such thing as the RR of lung cancer for smoking, independent of the specification of an exposed population and an unexposed population that is suitable to act as a control.[75]

In *Sienkiewicz*, Lord Phillips suggested that the 'doubles the risk' test applies to epidemiological evidence as a function of the relative risk, explaining 'if statistical

[71] Rothman (n 65) 91; Rothman, Greenland and Lash (n 65) chs 6–8.
[72] Rothman, Greenland and Lash (n 65) 93–94; Rothman (n 65) ch 4.
[73] Barnes (n 11) 193.
[74] Broadbent 'Epidemiological Evidence' (n 41) 241.
[75] ibid 243.

evidence indicates that the intervention of a wrongdoer more than doubled the risk that the victim would suffer the injury, then it follows that it is more likely than not that the wrongdoer caused the injury'.[76] The 'doubles the risk' test is crude in that it misconceives not only the balance of probabilities standard of proof, but also the function of relative risk in epidemiology, and will be explored in greater detail below once further epidemiological concepts have been outlined.

C. The p-value and Confidence Intervals

The idea that scientific standards of proof are higher hangs to a large degree on the requirement of a 95 per cent confidence limit, or a p-value of less than 0.05, and it is important that we have a clear understanding of what this standard signifies. Crucially it does not represent the standard of proof applied, nor does it reflect the quality of the study, but relates to the specific concept of 'sampling error probability'. It is 'a statistical property of data underlying evidence offered to prove a relevant fact',[77] so it aids the assessment of the reliability of a particular fact probability, such as relative risk. Barnes explains that:

> Even when a sample is composed of randomly chosen subjects, those subjects may not represent accurately the population. That possibility means that any observed statistical relationship between acts like the defendant's and harms like the plaintiff's revealed by a study of a sample may be due to the happenstance of having drawn randomly an atypical sample.[78]

Barnes explains that in all studies based on a sample of the population there will be a sampling error and that this 'is not an error in the design of the sample. Indeed, it is not an error attributable to any person. It is an unavoidable property of inferential statistics, the process of estimating attributes of a population by examining a sample'.[79] The p-value is an indicator of statistical significance and tells us how likely it is that a relative risk of, for example, 3, would occur in a sample if there were in fact no association (so the true relative risk is 1.0). The sampling error probability is expressed as a 'p-value' ranging from 0 to 1.00, and a p-value closer to 0 indicates a smaller probability that error is due to the make-up of the sample. The greatest sampling error probability that is accepted in science is 5 per cent, meaning that on the basis of sampling error there must be at least a 95 per cent chance that the relationship is causal and not due to the chance that the sample is unrepresentative of the population. So a p-value of 0.05 tells us that

---

[76] *Sienkiewicz* (n 8) [72] (Lord Phillips). McIvor highlights the inconsistencies in the application of the 'doubles the risk' test, pointing to cases where it has been applied to probabilistic evidence other than epidemiology: 'The "Doubles the Risk" Test for Causation and Other Related Judicial Misconceptions about Epidemiology' in Stephen GA Pitel, Jason W Neyers and Erika Chamberlain (eds), *Tort Law: Challenging Orthodoxy* (Hart Publishing, 2013) 229–33. These issues will be discussed below.

[77] Barnes (n 11) 193.

[78] ibid 193.

[79] ibid 198.

there is only a 1 in 20 chance that a study has shown an association when in fact there is not one and the true relative risk is 1.0. A confidence interval of 95 per cent provides a range of RRs that are compatible with the data, giving upper and lower limits that could still be produced by chance in 1 in 20 studies. A narrower range reflects a higher degree of power in the study, for example the larger the size of the cohort studied the narrower the 95 per cent confidence interval is likely to be.

It is essential to observe that the p-value does not reflect the quality of the study:

> A sampling error probability may as easily be calculated from a poorly designed study as from a randomized, controlled, double-masked study. The credibility of that probability and any fact probability derived from that study, however, depends on the quality of the study design.[80]

In other words, '[t]he p-value does not measure the probability that the design was perfect; rather, it assumes the design was perfect'.[81] As such, a p-value below 0.05 does not provide 'unassailable support for a causal relationship ... [since] the p-value tells us nothing about possible systematic errors'.[82] Since a sampling error probability can be calculated for a poorly-designed study as easily as for a well-designed study it would be a doing a disservice to scientific experts to suggest that they are only concerned with the p-value.

Despite this, legal discourse commonly states that the standard of proof in science is 95 per cent; for example, even Goldberg states that 'for medical science ... rules of epidemiology require evidential proof on a balance of probabilities of at least 95 per cent to establish causation'.[83] Since the 95 per cent confidence limit concerns only one aspect of statistical and epidemiological evidence, it is not a belief probability and it cannot meaningfully be compared to the balance of probabilities standard of proof as Barnes explains:

> Judges and lawyers first encountering statistical evidence want to believe that scientific standards are tougher than legal standards. A court will reject an assumption that there is no causal connection between an act and an injury if the evidence makes causation 'more likely than not.' A scientist will reject an assumption that there is no relationship between two variables only if there is less than a five percent probability that the statistical evidence showing a relationship is due to chance. The law appears willing to accept no more than a forty-nine percent chance of error while science appears willing to accept no more than a five percent chance of error.[84]

He argues that '[t]his perception is incorrect, but hard to change'.[85] Just as the balance of probabilities standard is qualitative, any assessment of epidemiological

[80] ibid 200.

[81] ibid 204.

[82] Peter Feldschreiber, Leigh-Ann Mulcahy and Simon Day, 'Biostatistics and Causation in Medicinal Product Liability Suits' in Goldberg (n 2) 184.

[83] Richard Goldberg, 'Using Scientific Evidence to Resolve Causation Problems in Product Liability: UK, US and French Experiences' in Goldberg (n 2) 150.

[84] Barnes (n 11) 191.

[85] ibid.

evidence is also qualitative. Epidemiologists do not focus solely on the relative risk, nor on the p-value, but look at these figures whilst also evaluating the design of the study in order to be satisfied about their reliability. Moreover, these figures indicate the existence of an association between exposure and harm, and the Bradford Hill criteria must also be applied in order to draw a conclusion about whether that association arises because of a causal relationship.

D. Moving from Association to Causation: The Bradford Hill Criteria

Once the quality of a study has been established, if it shows evidence of an association between a potential cause and effect, epidemiologists then test the reliability of the causal inferences that can be drawn from the data. Miller has explained, '[i]n the UK, the nine criteria articulated by Professor Bradford Hill are perhaps the best known'[86] criteria to test causal inferences. These are: the strength of association, how high is the relative risk?; consistency, have the results been replicated elsewhere?; specificity of cause and of effect, does the 'cause' produce only one effect? Does the 'effect' have only one cause?; temporality, the effect must follow the cause; biological gradient, is a 'dose relationship' identifiable?; plausibility, is it consistent with prevailing biological knowledge?; coherence, does it conflict with any known biology of the disease?; experiment, does the frequency of the effect fall when the 'cause' is removed?; analogy, is the cause-effect relationship of any comparable disease accepted?[87]

These factors relate to the question of whether there is a general causal relationship between the 'cause' and 'effect', ie the harmful agent for which the defendant is responsible and the type of illness suffered by the claimant. Bradford Hill emphasised that this is not a checklist of factors that must all be satisfied before a causal inference can be drawn:

> None of my nine viewpoints can bring indisputable evidence for or against the cause-and-effect hypothesis and none can be required as a sine qua non.[88]

Haack notes that this is in tension with legal tendencies:

> The legal *penchant* for convenient checklists has led many to construe his list of (as he says) 'viewpoints' as criteria for the reliability of causation testimony, and though he himself seems to have grasped the quasi-holistic character of the determinants of evidential quality ... his partial sketch-map has led many astray.[89]

The decision in *McTear* is particularly unsatisfactory in this regard. In that case, the claimant's husband had died from lung cancer and she sought to establish that

---

[86] Miller (n 14) 544, 545.
[87] ibid 548 and Sir Austin Bradford Hill, 'The Environment and Disease (n 38).
[88] Bradford Hill (n 38).
[89] Haack (n 25) 243.

the defendant was negligent in selling cigarettes without appropriate warnings and that smoking the defendant's cigarettes was a cause of her husband's lung cancer. The claimant was required not only to prove specific causation, but first to prove general causation, ie that cigarette smoking can cause lung cancer. The epidemiological evidence showed a strong association between cigarette smoking and lung cancer but the Court was not satisfied that the relationship was causal:

> The finding of an association between exposure and a condition or disease, even if judged to be statistically significant, does not of itself connote that a causal connection between the two is established. This is a matter for a further exercise of judgment, taking account of such criteria as the consistency, the strength, the specificity, the temporal relationship and the coherence of the association.[90]

The Court was particularly troubled by the lack of specificity:

> People who have never smoked cigarettes die from diseases that smoking can cause, and to that same extent some cigarette smokers too can die of the disease but not as a result of their smoking.[91]

This reasoning effectively treats the Bradford Hill criteria as a checklist, denying a causal relationship because of the lack of specificity and this is precisely what Bradford Hill cautioned against. Indeed he provided cigarette smoking and lung cancer as an example to warn against such an approach:

> Coming to modern times the prospective investigations of smoking and cancer of the lung have been criticised for not showing specificity—in other words the death rate of smokers is higher than the death rate of non-smokers from many causes of death ... But here surely one must return to my first characteristic, the strength of association. If other causes of death are raised 10, 20 or even 50% in smokers whereas cancer of the lung is raised 900–1,000% we have specificity—a specificity in the magnitude of the association ... In short, if specificity exists we may be able to draw conclusions without hesitation; if it is not apparent, we are not thereby necessarily left sitting irresolutely on the fence.[92]

This demonstrates that it is essential that the Bradford Hill criteria are not treated as a checklist, but as factors that contribute to a more holistic assessment of the evidence.

This overview of epidemiological evidence has shown that it is far more rich and sophisticated than the picture painted by Lord Phillips in *Sienkiewicz* which focused almost exclusively on relative risk.[93] In addition that relative risk should be accompanied by a low p-value, preferably no greater than 0.05, it should be derived from a well-designed study, and the Bradford Hill criteria should then be applied to evaluate whether this evidence of an association actually reflects a

[90] *McTear* (n 40) [6.158].
[91] ibid [6.176] citing Christine Callum, *The UK Smoking Epidemic: Deaths in 1995* (Health Education Authority, 1998).
[92] Bradford Hill (n 38) 297.
[93] See text to n 63 above.

causal relationship. It would be reductive to think of epidemiological evidence as merely furnishing us with statistics just as it is also reductive to think of civil law's 'balance of probabilities' standard as merely a statistical requirement. Qualitative evaluation of the evidence is vital to drawing a reasoned and rational conclusion, and epidemiologists are trained to engage in such a qualitative exercise. Scepticism about epidemiological evidence should not attach to the discipline of epidemiology itself but the legal tendency to simplify the evidence to the degree that it loses value, by treating the Bradford Hill criteria as a checklist, by interpreting the p-value as being a standard of proof, by claiming that a relative risk of 2 is sufficient to establish causation on the balance of probabilities. The real issue, therefore, is how courts engage with epidemiological evidence and it is to this that we turn next.

E. Expert Evidence

Two key concerns emerge when we examine the way in which courts engage with epidemiological evidence. First, courts rely too frequently on clinicians rather than epidemiologists to interpret epidemiological evidence, and they lack sufficient expertise in this specialist discipline. Second, judges too frequently resort to their own guesswork, which risks them reaching inaccurate conclusions and also damages the wider perception of the value of epidemiological evidence.

i. Expert Witnesses

As noted earlier, epidemiologists are trained in research methodologies, statistical techniques, and in medicine, so where a case involves epidemiological evidence, the appropriate expert witness to speak to that evidence is an epidemiologist, yet clinicians are frequently relied upon. Greenberg observes that 'the capacity of the expert may be seen as very broad indeed ... it follows that a medical practitioner nearly always is permitted to give evidence on any branch of medicine'.[94] This is problematic because it results in clinicians being regarded as authoritative on evidence that is actually outside of their discipline. This leads him to describe the legal approach as being 'more like the medical paradigm that preceded EBM [evidence based medicine]. It is relatively hierarchical and based more on authority than scientific evidence'.[95] In other words it is outdated. This has contributed to judicial aversion to epidemiological evidence; indeed, Miller describes the Court's approach in *McTear* as showing 'dogmatic aversion' to epidemiological evidence, because the Court felt that it had not been sufficiently trained in epidemiological techniques.[96] The Court in *Smith v McNair*, although less averse, still found

---

[94] Greenberg, 'The Cause of Disease and Illness' (n 68) 53.
[95] ibid 52.
[96] Miller (n 14) 566.

the epidemiological evidence unhelpful in the absence of epidemiologist expert witnesses.[97] Lord McEwan suggested that it would have been helpful to hear from the authors of the epidemiological studies since the Court was 'at once disabled from being able properly to evaluate the worth of the study or to draw on the proper conclusions'.[98] It may not always be realistic for the authors of the studies relied upon to act as expert witnesses, but at the very least epidemiologists should interpret and speak to the reliability of epidemiological evidence. The evidence in *Gregg v Scott* was a worked example of the fate of 100 hypothetical patients, devised by the medical expert witness, so it cannot be equated with epidemiological evidence but instead reflected his personal clinical opinion. McIvor notes that in *Novartis v Cookson* the evidence of a clinician was preferred over the evidence of an epidemiologist in determining the cause of the claimant's bladder cancer. This case involved two potential causes: occupational exposure to carcinogenic substances and the claimant's own cigarette smoking. It was accepted that these two factors would have had an additive, if not synergistic, effect and the epidemiologist expert witness who had published extensively on the subject of bladder cancer concluded that the occupational risk from carcinogenic dyes was so low that the claimant's smoking had to be regarded as the main cause of his illness. The other expert witness was a consultant urologist who concluded that smoking contributed 25–30 per cent of the claimant's risk while the occupational exposure contributed the remaining 70–75 per cent of the total risk.[99] Although the defendant argued that the clinician's opinion was not supported by the published literature and was beyond his expertise, Smith LJ said:

> The proposition that a clinician is not capable of fully understanding the published epidemiological literature on the causation of a condition within his own speciality seems unsustainable and would, I think, surprise many clinicians and epidemiologists.[100]

McIvor argues that:

> This comment provides a good illustration of the general UK judicial belief that epidemiology is a very simple and unsophisticated branch of science and that clinicians are the only real medical experts … there is a lack of appreciation that medical science is a huge discipline encompassing numerous specialist sub-disciplines.[101]

She therefore advocates strongly in favour of 'the routine use of appropriately qualified and experienced epidemiologists as expert witnesses'.[102] This requirement derives from the function of the evidence and the type of decision that is being made. A clinician is surely capable of understanding the relevant literature so far as it impacts on her practice and treatment options, but this is prospective

---

[97] *Smith v McNair* [2008] CSOH 154, [81].
[98] ibid [80].
[99] These figures will be discussed in s III.A, 'Misusing Epidemiological Evidence'.
[100] *Novartis Grimsby Ltd v Cookson* (n 3) [57].
[101] McIvor, 'Debunking' (n 19) 586.
[102] ibid 586.

and treatment may be justified if it has merely a possibility of success. This is significantly different in nature from the backwards-looking exercise of attributing causation in a negligence action. For this particular purpose it is preferable to draw on epidemiologists who have a deeper understanding of the evidence so can speak to the finer details that might not concern a clinician when determining a patient's prognosis or course of treatment.

McIvor also suggests that there is a lack of appreciation that epidemiology is a sub-discipline of, and therefore a part of, medical science. This is evident in the way the terms 'epidemiologist' and 'statistician' are frequently used interchangeably,[103] and this error is pervasive. Indeed Kobyasheva has written that McIvor 'emphasises the importance of using qualified statisticians to analyse the data' despite McIvor explicitly emphasising the importance of using qualified *epidemiologists*.[104] As noted earlier in this section, epidemiologists are not simply statisticians; while they are trained in statistical techniques they also have training in research methodologies and medicine. This means that epidemiologists are the appropriate experts to interpret epidemiological evidence. Statisticians will lack the medical knowledge needed to appreciate the finer details of the evidence, just as clinicians will similarly lack the necessary statistical knowledge.

ii. Avoiding Judges' Guesswork

A balance must be struck between courts' reluctance to engage with epidemiological evidence in some cases, and judges who are overly eager to embark on their own personal guesswork in other cases. In *McTear*, Lord Nimmo Smith expressed concern that he had not been educated sufficiently in epidemiological techniques to be able to engage with the available evidence.[105] Goldberg suggests:

> The mere placing of an obligation on the pursuer to teach the epidemiology to the court suggests that the court can act passively in this process. This is surely an unhelpful approach in cases such as *McTear*, where there is a clear societal function of a judge to resolve these matters to the satisfaction of both parties.[106]

At the other end of the spectrum, judges have engaged in personal guesswork which is equally, if not more, unsatisfactory. In *Sienkiewicz*, the appellant raised serious concerns about the trial judge's calculations, arguing that they were speculative, lacked accurate readings, were based on estimates and involved errors of calculation.[107] Although the Court of Appeal was not satisfied that the trial judge had significantly erred in his calculations, Smith LJ expressed concern about the

---

[103] See eg Sarah Fulham-McQuillan, 'Judicial Belief in Statistics as Fact: Loss of Chance in Ireland and England' (2014) 30 *Professional Negligence* 9, at 15 and 18.
[104] Aleksandra Kobyasheva, 'Using Epidemiological Evidence in Tort Law: a Practical Guide' (2014) 30 *Professional Negligence* 125, 134.
[105] *McTear* (n 40) [6.155]–[6.156].
[106] Goldberg, 'Using Scientific Evidence' (n 83) 160.
[107] *Sienkiewicz v Greif (UK) Ltd* [2009] EWCA Civ 1159; [2010] QB 370, [11].

judge's calculations and was uncertain about the whole process of quantitative assessment.[108]

In addition, it is unhelpful for courts and academics to treat personal calculations of the probability of causation as though they are the equivalent of epidemiological evidence since this risks discrediting actual epidemiological evidence. The trial judge in *Hotson* estimated the claimant's chance of recovery had he received proper treatment as being 25 per cent. This figure seems to be an attempt to quantify the degree of belief he had in the fact that the harm could have been prevented, based on the scientific papers and clinical evidence.[109] It has since been taken as an estimate of the claimant's statistical chance of a cure, and it appears to derive from being a mid-point between one paper that suggested the claimant had no prospect of a cure and another which indicated that he had a roughly 50 per cent chance of a cure.[110] This 'technique' of picking an intermediate figure lacks a scientific basis. It is disappointing, therefore, that Miller recognises that the estimate in *Hotson* is 'crude' and 'lacking in statistical power' but since it is based upon empirical data he 'take[s] it as comparable with epidemiological data in estimating an objective chance'.[111] In light of the judicial tendency, evident in *Sienkiewicz*, to view epidemiology as being unscientific, treating such a crude estimate as being comparable to epidemiological data can only serve to deepen this perception and to weaken confidence in epidemiological evidence more widely.

In terms of training for judges, Haack acknowledges that it 'really isn't feasible to bring—let alone keep—judges up to speed with cutting-edge genetics, epidemiology, toxicology, or whatever' but suggests that

> it *should* be feasible, however, to educate judges in the elements of probability theory, to give them a sense of how samples may be mishandled or this or that kind of mistake made at the laboratory, to explain how such information about the probability that the lab made a mistake is such-and-such affects the significance of random match probability, and so forth.[112]

Since such statistical techniques will be relatively unchanging, it does indeed seem feasible for judges to be trained at least in basic techniques and to be aware of common errors of design or interpretation whereas this would be unrealistic in constantly changing disciplines. She does note, of course, that 'when the issues are subtle, the subtleties need to be conveyed',[113] and it is here that the role of the appropriate expert witness is vital.

---

[108] ibid [37].

[109] This is discussed in ch 4, text to n 5.

[110] *Hotson v Fitzgerald and others* [1985] 3 All ER 167, 173.

[111] Chris Miller, 'Causation in Personal Injury Law: The Case for a Probabilistic Approach' (2014) 33 *Topoi* 385, 389.

[112] Haack (n 25) 117.

[113] ibid 117.

III. Using (and Misusing) Epidemiological Evidence in Negligence

In law, the use of epidemiological evidence has become closely associated with the notion that causation can be proved on the balance of probabilities if the defendant's negligence more than doubled the risk of harm. The so-called logic of this emerging approach to causation is that if the negligence more than doubled the risk of harm then it is the most probable cause of the harm.[114] The source of the evidence of a more than doubling of risk is usually epidemiological evidence showing a relative risk >2. The flaws in this approach are numerous: the concept of causation has been shown in chapter two to involve a set of factors which together are sufficient to bring about the effect, so it makes no sense to speak of a single factor as being 'the most probable cause';[115] the balance of probabilities has been shown in this chapter to concern belief probability not fact probability so it does not require us to identify the most probable cause; epidemiologists do not regard a relative risk of >2 as having any intrinsic value, and relative risk alone does not indicate a causal relationship. The first part of this section expands upon these criticisms to show that the so-called 'doubling of the risk' test is flawed and ought not to be allowed to take hold as a legal test of causation. The second part has a more positive focus, looking at how epidemiological evidence might be used in proof of causation in negligence.

A. Misusing Epidemiological Evidence: The Flaws of the 'More than Doubles the Risk' Test

The 'more than doubles the risk' test has been applied in only a handful of cases so far but, in light of its flaws, it should not be allowed to take root as an accepted test of causation. Its origins lie in the decision in *XYZ v Schering*.[116] The claimants in that case had suffered venous-thromboembolisms (VTE) which they alleged were caused by third generation combined oral contraceptive pills (COC3s) which were said to be defective under the Consumer Protection Act 1987. Their claims followed a letter from the UK Committee on the Safety of Medicine to prescribers explaining that three unpublished studies showed there to be around a twofold increase in the risk of VTE compared with second generation COCs. At the outset, Mackay J identified the relevant issues as follows: do COC3s carry an excess risk of VTE that is more than twice that carried by COC2s; if so, are the products defective within the meaning of the relevant legislation; if so, and in the absence of the

---

[114] *Sienkiewicz v Greif* (CA) (n 107) [20] and [23] (Smith LJ).
[115] See ch 2, text to n 40.
[116] *XYZ v Schering* (n 51).

availability of defences specified within the legislation, would the claimants have been prescribed the pills but-for the defect; and if so, did the exposure to the pills cause or contribute to the harm suffered? The first question as to doubling of risk was considered capable of disposing of the claims: if there was a more than doubling of the risk then the product was defective and, Mackay J stated, if there was a more than doubling of the risk then causation would also be established:

> If factor X increases the risk of condition Y by more than 2 when compared with factor Z it can then be said, of a group of say 100 with both exposure to factor X and the condition, that as a matter of probability more than 50 would not have suffered Y without being exposed to X. If medical science cannot identify the members of the group who would and who would not have suffered Y, it can nevertheless be said of each member that she was more likely than not to have avoided Y had she not been exposed to X.[117]

In its bare form this would therefore allow all 100 people to establish causation even though up to half of the cases were not actually caused by factor X.[118] This approach was subsequently adopted in *Novartis v Cookson*,[119] where the claimant had developed bladder cancer which had two potential causes: occupational exposure to carcinogens, and the claimant's own former smoking habit. This case was therefore different in that there were two candidate causes operating on the claimant concurrently and the question was whether the occupational exposure was a cause. The judge at first instance accepted the evidence of the claimant's expert witness that the claimant's smoking contributed 25–30 per cent of the total risk and the occupational exposure contributed 70–75 per cent. The 'more than doubles the risk' approach was adopted by the Court of Appeal:

> The natural inference to draw from the finding of the fact that the occupational exposure was 70% of the total is that, if it had not been for the occupational exposure, the claimant would not have developed bladder cancer. In terms of risk, if occupational exposure more than doubles the risk due to smoking, it must as a matter of logic be probable that the disease was caused by the former.[120]

Indeed, the finding that the negligence had more than doubled the risk due to smoking meant that it was 'inevitable' that causation would be proved.[121]

In the Court of Appeal decision in *Sienkiewicz*, Smith LJ concluded that

> it must now be taken that, saving the expression of a different view by the Supreme Court, in a case of multiple potential causes, a claimant can demonstrate causation in a case by showing that the tortious exposure has at least doubled the risk arising from the non-tortious cause or causes.[122]

---

[117] ibid [21].
[118] The claims ultimately failed on the first issue because the RR was found to be around 1.7 so the product could not be found to be defective, although Mackay J suggested that he was inclined to conclude that there was a causal relationship at that level: 'Though it is very weak it is based on the 1995 studies which are broadly consistent and impressive pieces of epidemiology', ibid [344].
[119] *Novartis* (n 3).
[120] ibid [74] (Smith LJ).
[121] ibid [62] (Smith LJ).
[122] *Sienkiewicz* (CA) (n 107) [23].

In the Supreme Court, Lord Phillips then described the 'doubles the risk' test as 'one that applies epidemiological data to determining causation on balance of probabilities in circumstances where medical science does not permit determination with certainty of how and when an injury was caused'.[123] He suggested that there was no place for the 'doubles the risk' test when *Wardlaw* applies,[124] but saw no reason in principle why it should not apply in other cases (which will be discussed later), although he expressed concern that a mere doubling of risk is a 'tenuous basis' on which to find causation because of the potential flaws in epidemiological evidence.[125] More recently, in *Jones v Secretary of State for Energy and Climate Change*,[126] Swift J elevated the doubling of risk test to the status of an additional test for causation. She considered that it was necessary first to decide whether the *Wardlaw* test could be applied,[127] and in the case that it did not apply she should then decide whether it was appropriate to apply the 'doubles the risk' test.[128] So the 'doubles the risk' approach, which started life as a particular interpretation of the balance of probabilities standard of proof, has gradually come to be regarded as an alternative test of causation to be applied after the but-for test and *Wardlaw* test of material contribution to harm have been exhausted.

i. The Conflation of the Conceptual and Evidential Elements of Causation in the 'Doubles the Risk' Approach

As Steel and Ibbetson have highlighted, there are two elements to a test of causation: the conceptual element, ie what the claimant must prove, and the evidential element, ie the standard to which she must prove it.[129] In the orthodox approach, the claimant must satisfy the but-for test (the conceptual element) on the balance of probabilities (the evidential element). The 'doubles the risk' test seems to have been conceived in *XYZ v Schering* as a way of satisfying the balance of probabilities standard of proof of the but-for test, therefore as an evidential standard. As seen above, it has come to be regarded as an alternative test of causation that might apply once the but-for test and *Wardlaw* test have been exhausted. This is unsound because it conflates the conceptual and evidential aspects of causation since the

---

[123] *Sienkiewicz* (n 8) [72] (Lord Phillips).

[124] In his view the *Wardlaw* test applies to cases of both divisible and indivisible damage so long as the causal process involves 'cumulative and simultaneous' rather than 'alternative' causes: *Sienkiewicz* (n 8) [90].

[125] ibid [83].

[126] *Jones v Secretary of State for Energy and Climate Change* (n 3).

[127] Although noting that the Court of Appeal in the Atomic Veterans case (*Ministry of Defence v AB and others* [2010] EWCA Civ 1317) considered that the *Wardlaw* test applied only in cases of divisible damage, Swift J preferred the position adopted by Lord Phillips in *Sienkiewicz* that the *Wardlaw* test applies to cases of both divisible and indivisible damage so long as the negligence was one of a number of 'cumulative and simultaneous' causes: *Jones* (n 3) [6.51].

[128] ibid [6.50]–[6.53].

[129] Sandy Steel and David Ibbetson, 'More Grief on Uncertain Causation in Tort' (2011) 70 *Cambridge Law Journal* 451, 452.

doubling of risk has become not only a standard of proof but the very thing to be proved.

This is a worrying development because in this form the 'doubles the risk' test merely amounts to a more stringent version of the *Fairchild* test: rather than simply requiring an ill-defined 'material increase' in the risk of harm it requires a doubling of the risk. The only advantage it has over the *Fairchild* test is that it is clear that courts are making an inductive leap to regard proof of doubling of risk as being satisfactory as proof of causation rather than reformulating the gist of the negligence action as the risk of harm. A serious concern, however, is that it involves just as much of a departure from corrective justice-based principles of liability as the *Fairchild* test since a claimant is able to recover for the physical harm when she has only proven that the defendant caused an increase in risk. This test has not, however, attracted the same degree of scrutiny as the *Fairchild* test, nor has an attempt been made to define the circumstances in which it should apply, and its application should surely be tightly circumscribed given its unorthodox nature. The ultimate argument of this section, however, is that the 'doubles the risk' test is unacceptable regardless of whether it is an evidential standard or a distinct test of causation because it simply does not make appropriate use of epidemiological concepts.

ii. Doubling of Risk in Epidemiology

Lord Phillips held in *Sienkiewicz* that the 'doubles the risk' test applies when the only evidence in a case is epidemiological, so it corresponds to evidence of a relative risk greater than 2 (RR>2).[130] There are a number of reasons why this is an inappropriate use of the relative risk calculation.

First, as previously explained, epidemiology 'looks at the distribution and determinants of diseases in *human populations*' (emphasis added).[131] This means that when a relative risk is calculated, it relates to a particular, defined population within a defined time period:

> There is no such thing as the RR of lung cancer for smoking, independent of the specification of an exposed population and an unexposed population that is suitable to act as a control.[132]

There is no evidence that the Court in *Novartis* appreciated this. It was unclear in that case whether the risk of cancer from occupational exposure to carcinogens and from cigarette smoking was simply additive or whether it was multiplicative.[133] The risks are not expressed in relation to specified populations; indeed, the evidence accepted by the Court was that of a clinician who estimated that occupational exposure contributed 70–75 per cent of the total risk and smoking contributed

---

[130] See eg *Sienkiewicz* (n 8) [82] (Lord Phillips).
[131] McIvor, 'Debunking' (n 19) 554.
[132] Broadbent (n 41) 243.
[133] *Novartis* (n 3) [44].

25–30 per cent of the total risk, so that the figures added up to 100 per cent to reflect the fact that the claimant had developed cancer. As McIvor notes, this is not an assessment of relative risk, but a personalised calculation of the probability that it was each of the sources of carcinogens that caused the cancer.[134] Indeed, when looking at the causes of a given disease within a population, the percentages will again usually add up to over 100 per cent. Rothman provides an example of a disease in people who drink or smoke or do both. Among those who both smoke and drink, in his example 75 per cent of cases are caused by smoking, and 67 per cent are caused by drinking, adding up to well over 100 per cent. This is because a number of cases will have been caused by both smoking and drinking. The idea that the percentage should add up to one hundred, he says, 'is based on the naïve view that every case of disease has a single cause and that two causes cannot contribute to the same case ... The sum of disease attributable to various component causes in reality has no upper limit'.[135]

Assuming that a court were to be provided with evidence of the relative risk arising from a particular agent in a defined population, we have seen that the relative risk alone is not proof of causation but of an association. In addition, it is necessary to assess the reliability of the study from which the RR is calculated, to find a p-value of 0.05 or less, and to apply the Bradford Hill criteria before concluding that there is a causal relationship. Even if this can all be done, however, the RR still does not tell us how many cases were actually caused by the harmful agent; the number of cases actually caused by exposure is represented by the 'etiologic fraction'.[136] Since writers do not always use technical terms consistently,[137] it is worthwhile giving a brief definition of the relative risk and etiologic fraction at the outset and they will be provided in square brackets when citing writers who use different terms.

The relative risk represents the number of cases of a particular outcome in an exposed population divided by the number of cases in an unexposed population. So if there are 6 cases of a disease per 100 people in the exposed population and only 2 cases per 100 in the unexposed population, the relative risk associated with exposure is 6/2 = 3 (also expressed as RR = 3). The 'excess fraction' is closely related and tells us how many *excess* cases there are in the exposed population as a fraction of the total number of cases in that population. It is calculated as 1 − (1/RR), so if the RR is 3 then the excess fraction is 1 − 1/3 = 2/3. This therefore tells us that 2/3 of the cases in the exposed population would not have occurred in the absence of the harmful agent. The 'doubles the risk' test equates the excess fraction with the probability that the harmful agent caused the claimant's injury. If the RR is greater

---

[134] McIvor, 'The "Doubles the Risk" Test' (n 76) 232.

[135] Rothman (n 65) 13.

[136] Rothman, Greenland and Lash (n 65) 63.

[137] Sander Greenland, 'Relation of Probability of Causation to Relative Risk and Doubling Dose: a Methodologic Error that has Become a Social Problem' (1999) 89 *American Journal of Public Health* 1166. He explains 'writers often use terms such as attributable risk, attributable proportion, attributable fraction, etiologic fraction, and the probability of causation in an interchangeable fashion' at 1168.

than 2 then the excess fraction is greater than 1/2 so more than 1/2 of cases in the exposed population would not have occurred in the absence of the harmful agent so, the idea goes, on the balance of probabilities the harmful agent caused the outcome. The problem with equating the *excess* fraction with the probability of causation is that the excess fraction does not actually tell us how many cases were *caused* by the exposure. That figure would be the 'etiologic fraction' and this simply cannot be calculated accurately from epidemiological studies. The etiologic fraction will often be higher than the excess fraction so that if the relative risk is 3, making the excess fraction 2/3, exposure will actually have played a causal role in *at least* 2/3 of cases. The reason why the etiologic fraction is often higher is that exposure could have played a causal role in some cases of harm that would have occurred in the unexposed population anyway, eg smoking may be a cause of lung cancer in a person who would eventually have developed lung cancer even if they had not smoked.[138] Equating the excess fraction with the probability of causation assumes that the risk factor being studied does not interact with other background risks of the same harm, and this is often a false assumption. Greenland and Robins explain:

> We know of no cancer or other important chronic disease for which current biomedical knowledge allows one to exclude mechanisms that violate the assumptions needed to claim that PC = RF [probability of causation equals 'rate fraction' or 'excess fraction'].[139]

This is because cancer requires a sequence of distinct mutations, so exposure to the candidate risk factor could cause only one of the mutations and still be a cause of the overall disease: 'any factor that increases the rate of other necessary mutations will multiply the incidence of cases caused and not caused by exposure to the same degree'.[140] Greenland and Robins give an example of a study of women with occupational exposure to a risk factor for bone cancer, which shows three cases of bone cancer at age 45 compared to a cohort without the occupational exposure where there are two cases of bone cancer at age 45. The relative risk is 1.5, so the excess fraction is 1/3. Application of the 'doubles the risk' test would lead to the conclusion that occupational exposure did not cause any individual's bone cancer. Greenland and Robins explain how wrong this may be:

> Consider that the three cases that occurred at age 45 *may not overlap at all* with the two cases that would have occurred at this age absent exposure. For example, it is possible that exposure interacts with background factors to advance the incidence time of *all* bone cancer cases. This would happen if the cancer is the endpoint of a pathologic process whose rate is accelerated by radiation exposure. Thus, it could be that the two background cases (the two women who would have gotten bone cancer at age 45 even without exposure) instead got their cancer years earlier because of exposure; while the three cases that occurred at age 45 would not have occurred until years later absent exposure. In fact,

---

[138] Broadbent (n 41) 242–43.

[139] Sander Greenland and James M Robins, 'Epidemiology, Justice, and the Probability of Causation' (2000) 40 *Jurimetrics* 321, 325.

[140] ibid 325.

it could be that exposure causally contributed to *all* cancers at *all* ages by accelerating *all* the incidence times. If so, the probability of causation would be 100%. Yet, despite this ubiquity of harm, the causal rate ratio [relative risk] would remain 3/2 = 1.5 and the causal rate fraction [excess fraction] would thus remain 33%.[141]

This is a striking example because the 'doubles the risk' test would lead us to the conclusion that occupational exposure was not a cause in any case when in fact it was a cause in every case. What epidemiological evidence can do, therefore, is 'to place a nonzero lower bound on the probability of causation when RF>0'.[142] This means that epidemiological evidence does not tell us how probable causation is, 'but how improbable it is not'.[143] Consequently the 'doubles the risk' test is not valid where the various risk factors are not mutually exclusive,[144] yet this eluded the Court in *Novartis*,[145] and in *Shortell v BICAL Ltd*.[146]

In *Shortell*, Mackay J considered that where the claimant had succeed in showing a more than doubling of risk it was 'not relevant as between the claimant and the defendant to argue that another agent (tortious or otherwise) may also have contributed to the occurrence of the disease'.[147] In *Novartis*, the claimant suffered bladder cancer and the Court found that the risk from occupational exposure to amines and the risk from amines in cigarette smoke 'would have had at least an additive, if not multiplicative, effect'.[148] It was further noted that 'a certain level of exposure to carcinogen was required to overcome the body's natural defence mechanisms so as to trigger an abnormal cell development'.[149] These findings indicate that the two risk factors were not independent, so the etiologic fraction would have exceeded the excess fraction, so the occupational exposure could have had a causal role even if the 'doubles the risk' test was not satisfied.

As Greenland explains elsewhere:

> Epidemiologic data cannot distinguish accelerated occurrences from unaffected occurrences. The only way one can estimate the relative proportion of accelerated and unaffected occurrences—and hence estimate the probability of causation—is by positing a specific biological model for the disease process.[150]

This means that in any case, but particularly where the relative risk is less than 2, courts should be alert to the fact that the etiologic fraction will likely exceed the

---

[141] ibid 327.
[142] ibid 326. See also Dawid, 'The Role of Scientific and Statistical Evidence in Assessing Causality' (n 49) 143.
[143] Broadbent (n 41) 258.
[144] See also Jane Stapleton, 'Factual Causation, Mesothelioma and Statistical Validity' (2012) 128 *Law Quarterly Review* 221, 223–25.
[145] *Novartis* (n 3).
[146] *Shortell v BICAL Construction Ltd* Queen's Bench Division District Registry (Liverpool), 16 May 2008.
[147] ibid [51].
[148] *Novartis* (n 3) [44].
[149] ibid [45].
[150] Greenland, 'Relation of Probability of Causation to Relative Risk and Doubling Dose' (n 137) 1167.

relative risk and should also look to evidence as to the underlying biological process. It is therefore questionable whether the Court was right to reject the claim in *Loveday v Renton* in which the claimant alleged that her brain damage was caused by the whooping cough vaccine.[151] The evidence showed a relative risk of 2.5, but the 95 per cent confidence interval ranged from RR 0.67–10.94, so the Court rejected the causal link on the basis that the confidence interval included RR = 1. Given that the etiologic fraction will usually exceed the relative risk, and the confidence interval included much higher relative risks, this alone is a weak basis on which to reject the claim.

In light of this knowledge, the conditions cannot exist for Lord Phillips' suggested role for the 'doubles the risk' test identified in *Sienkiewicz*. As noted earlier, Lord Phillips' view was that where 'two agents have operated cumulatively and simultaneously in causing the onset of a disease' there is no scope for the 'doubles the risk' test, and instead the *Wardlaw* test applies (with joint and several liability for indivisible disease and apportionment for divisible diseases).[152] In a case where 'the initiation of the disease is dose related, and there have been consecutive exposures to an agent or agents that cause the disease, one innocent and one tortious, the position will depend upon which exposure came first in time'.[153] If the tortious exposure was first then it will necessarily be a cause, but where the innocent exposure occurred first, the tortious exposure may or may not have been necessary to trigger the initiation of the disease, and the 'doubles the risk' test may have a role in such cases. Likewise, he suggested,

> where there are competing alternative, rather than cumulative, potential causes of a disease or injury, such as in *Hotson*, I can see no reason in principle why epidemiological evidence should not be used to show that one of the causes was more than twice as likely as all the others put together to have caused the disease or injury.[154]

In this schema, Lord Phillips requires us to have some understanding of the underlying biological process in order to determine whether it is a case of two agents acting cumulatively and simultaneously, a case of the initiation being dose related, or a case of alternative potential causes. And yet his premise for the doubles the risk test was that:

> The 'doubles the risk' test is one that applies epidemiological data to determining causation on balance of probabilities in circumstances where medical science does not permit determination with certainty of how and when an injury was caused.[155]

It is illogical to suggest that the 'doubles the risk' test applies when medical science cannot determine how and when an injury was caused, but to then argue that it only applies to certain types of biological process. If we have enough information

[151] *Loveday v Renton (No1)* [1989] 1 Med LR 117.
[152] *Sienkiewicz* (n 8) [90].
[153] ibid [92].
[154] ibid [93].
[155] *Sienkiewicz* (n 8) [72] (Lord Phillips).

to identify the biological process then we have more than just epidemiological evidence so we would not need to resort to the 'doubles the risk' test. Moreover, the simple fact that medical science cannot explain with *certainty* how and when an injury is caused is not a barrier to establishing causation for the purposes of negligence liability since the balance of probabilities standard does not require certainty, it merely requires probable belief.

In summary, the 'doubles the risk' test is based upon a seriously flawed understanding of what epidemiological evidence is and the figures which can be derived from it, and as such it should not be allowed to gain traction as a test of causation in negligence. The test should not be regarded as synonymous with the use of epidemiological evidence which can provide courts with valuable evidence of causation for the purposes of negligence liability.

B. Using Epidemiological Evidence: The Place of Epidemiological Evidence in Standard Tests of Causation

Although the 'doubles the risk' test is seriously flawed this is not a reflection of epidemiological evidence itself which remains useful in proof of causation although there is some uncertainty surrounding its value in proof of specific causation. In *Gregg v Scott*, Lord Nicholls observed:

> Statistical evidence ... is not strictly a guide to what would have happened in one particular case. Statistics record retrospectively what happened to other patients in more or less comparable situations. They reveal trends of outcome. They are general in nature. The different way other patients responded in a similar position says nothing about how the claimant would have responded.[156]

The focus of this section is to address this concern and identify ways in which epidemiological evidence can meaningfully be used in proof of specific causation. It first addresses the question of reliability of epidemiological evidence and then considers how the evidence might be 'personalised' to the individual claimant.

i. Admissibility

Concerns have been raised regarding the quality of evidence, including epidemiological studies, with McIvor suggesting that 'the very fact that methodologically problematic evidence can end up before a trial court is indicative of the need for a pre-trial admissibility test for scientific evidence in UK civil law'.[157] Whilst it is important that courts are presented with reliable evidence, the controls should be well founded and reflect good scientific practice. Epidemiological evidence should not be rejected simply because the p-value is greater than 0.05 since this holds

---

[156] *Gregg* (n 7) [28].
[157] McIvor, 'Debunking' (n 19) 574.

no intrinsic value. Magnusson warns that it has become 'the obligatory standard for "statistical significance"' and that 'courts are told that data slightly more
deviant than the 95 per cent confidence level variety are unacceptable for human
consumption of any kind. Usually they are not told, the data being ejected before
ever reaching court'.[158] Yet he cautions that it was not selected for any sound
mathematical reason, so it should not necessarily be regarded as absolute, entailing the rejection of any study with a p-value of just over 0.05. Rothman similarly
advises that it is more useful to know the p-value than to know simply whether
the data is statistically 'significant' ($p<0.05$) or 'not significant' ($p>0.05$) which
is a 'less informative dichotomy'.[159] Since the balance of probabilities standard is
qualitative it allows for flexibility in giving a court the freedom to be more convinced than not by evidence that in all other respects is strong yet has a p-value
marginally over 0.05.

Similarly, the doubling of risk should not be treated as an admissibility test
as has occurred in many cases in the United States in the wake of *Daubert*.[160]
Edmond and Mercer note that in *Daubert* the Supreme Court 'actually stipulated
the types of methodological strictures scientists should adopt in producing their
knowledge for it to be classed as scientific and sufficiently reliable for admissibility in legal proceedings'.[161] Given the scope for small deviances from the 'ideal'
evidence, it seems preferable that courts assess the reliability of evidence on a case
by case basis.

Moreover, as Haack convincingly argues, the overall body of evidence may be
greater than the sum of its parts so that one less reliable study may still help form
a convincing overall picture when combined with other studies:

> If courts decide *with respect to each expert* whether his testimony should be admitted, in
> whole or in part, they may fail to recognise that the testimony of several experts might,
> in some instances, fit together in an explanatory story to give more credibility to a fact in
> issue than the testimony of any one would do.[162]

She continues:

> As the way a crossword entry interlocks with others may reasonably raise our confidence
> that it is correct, the way that, e.g., an epidemiological study suggesting a weak correla-
> tion of substance S with disorder D interlocks with toxicological results suggesting a pos-
> sible mechanism by which S might sometimes cause this or that physiological damage,
> may reasonably increase our confidence that the statistical results are not misleading.[163]

---

[158]   Eric Magnusson, 'Statistical Proof of Causation' in Freckleton and Mendelson (n 53) 406–07.
[159]   Rothman (n 65) 117.
[160]   *Daubert v Merrell Dow Pharm., Inc.*, 509 US 579 (1993). Detailed discussion of *Daubert* is beyond
the scope of this book but Susan Haack includes a detailed chapter addressing it in her book (n 25)
ch 5. See also Mark Geistfeld, 'Scientific Uncertainty and Causation in Tort Law' (2001) 54 *Vanderbilt
Law Review* 1011, 1012.
[161]   Edmond and Mercer, 'Rebels without a Cause?' (n 53) 91.
[162]   Haack (n 25) 43.
[163]   ibid.

As previously highlighted, the qualitative nature of the legal standard of proof is an invaluable feature which allows the courts to view the overall picture created by the evidence rather than adopting a rigid, formulaic approach to each individual piece of evidence. It would be unfortunate if a strict quantitative admissibility test were introduced that removed this characteristic.

ii. Personalising the Evidence: The Straw Man of 'Naked Statistics'

The dominant concern regarding epidemiological evidence is that it provides us with statistics that relate to a population rather than to individuals within that population so it cannot speak to the individual claimant's case. The example that commonly accompanies this concern about the use of so-called 'naked statistics',[164] is Justice Brachtenbach's blue cab scenario:

> Assume there are two cab companies in a town; one has three blue cabs and the other has one yellow cab. A pedestrian is hit by a cab, but doesn't know what color it was. In a suit for personal injury, plaintiff wants to admit the statistical fact that there is a 75 percent chance that she was hit by a blue cab. This fact has relevancy; it is admissible. But is it sufficient to prove the blue cab company more probably than not committed the act? No. If this were not the case, the blue cab company could be held liable for every unidentified cab accident that occurred.[165]

Three objections are raised in response. First, the statistical evidence in this example is being deployed not only to determine causation but also to determine breach of duty so the degree of uncertainty in this case is much more vast than in the causation cases that are being addressed. It would be inappropriate to use 'naked statistics' to plug the gaps in evidence of both breach of duty and factual causation, and courts have not considered using epidemiological evidence in such circumstances; for example, in *Novartis* it was known that the defendant was negligent and exposed the claimant to a risk factor for the harm that eventuated. The second objection relates not to 'naked statistics' themselves, but to the fact that the absence of any other kind of evidence in a road traffic accident is odd in itself, so we are disinclined to form a strong belief in the conclusions that might otherwise be drawn from the statistics:

> Common sense is not easily instructed to ignore the fact that when buses strike, there is usually more than just statistical evidence available. This is because buses are big, noisy, and full of people. However, diseases are not like buses. When trying to prove specific causation using epidemiological evidence, there is no possibility of eyewitness testimony. When only epidemiological evidence is used, that is generally because clinical science cannot produce anything better. If a claimant sought to rely on epidemiological evidence to prove causation for a harm that was comfortably within the scope of clinical science,

---

[164] The term 'naked statistics' is used by Richard Wright, 'Proving Causation' (n 2) 210; 'Causation, Responsibility, Risk, Probability, Naked Statistics, and Proof' (n 2).
[165] *Herskovits v Group Health Cooperative of Puget Sound* (1983) 664 P 2d 474 at [187].

they would be on shakier epistemic ground, because the total evidential picture, taking into account the evidence that might in principle have been available to the claimant, would be weaker.[166]

It will be rare that the only evidence available is epidemiological. It should be considered as part of the whole body of evidence and, to draw on Haack's analogy of a crossword, it should fit with the other clues. She also reminds us that it would be essential to assess the reliability of the statistics in the blue cab example:

> The statistical evidence may itself be more or less *independently secure*—more so if, e.g., it is based on a careful search of good records of what franchises were issued, less so if, e.g., it is based merely on the word of someone or other who answered a phone at the Town Hall.[167]

The third objection is that, as discussed above, epidemiology does not deal only in naked statistics. In his analysis of the blue cab example, Lord Phillips suggested that 'much more significant would have been the care taken by the rival taxi firms in employing competent drivers, and the past accident record of the firms in question'.[168] It has already been seen that epidemiologists do go beyond mere statistical analysis and engage with the plausibility of the underlying biological mechanism.

The decision in *Novartis* is problematic because the way the Court handled the available evidence was akin to its use in the blue cab scenario. The claimant had been exposed to carcinogenic amines both through occupational exposures to dyestuffs and through his own cigarette smoking, and subsequently developed bladder cancer. Although there was epidemiological evidence available in that case, and it was provided by an epidemiologist, the Court preferred the evidence of a consultant urologist. The Court found that the disease had been triggered by the cumulative effect of exposure to amines from both sources, and that the combined effect of the two exposures increased the overall risk either additively or possibly multiplicatively. Notably, Smith LJ also concluded that 'this was not a case in which the extent of the occupational exposure could be quantified'.[169] Despite these findings, the Court *did* quantify the exposure, accepting the urologist's evidence that the occupational exposure contributed 70–75 per cent of the total risk while the claimant's smoking habit contributed the remaining 25–30 per cent of the total risk. Based on this evidence Smith LJ concluded that '[i]n terms of risk, if occupational exposure more than doubles the risk due to smoking, it must, as a matter of logic, be probable that the disease was caused by the former'.[170] This approach is simplistic and effectively ignores the underlying aetiology of the disease to treat 'amines from dyestuffs' and 'amines from cigarette smoke' as the equivalent of blue and yellow cabs. The criticisms of 'naked statistics' should be directed not at

---

[166] Broadbent (n 41) 269.
[167] Haack (n 25) 20.
[168] *Sienkiewicz* (n 8) [96]. See also *Herskovits* (n 165) [188].
[169] *Novartis* (n 3) [57].
[170] ibid [74] (Smith LJ).

epidemiological evidence, but at the Court's willingness in this case to prefer questionable statistics over the more nuanced epidemiological evidence and to seek the 'most probable cause' when the evidence as to the aetiology shows that there are a multiple stages in the development of cancer and that carcinogens play a role at a number of points. Given that epidemiology can provide us with more than just 'naked statistics', the question becomes how to personalise the epidemiological evidence so that we can draw conclusions about an individual.

iii. Personalising the Evidence: Using Epidemiological Evidence in Proof of Individual Causation

One possibility is that where the epidemiological evidence is reliable and the relative risk is unusually high we may rationally believe that the negligence caused the individual claimant's harm. In *Sienkiewicz*, Lord Dyson suggested that:

> there is no *a priori* reason why, if the epidemiological evidence is cogent enough, it should not be sufficient to enable a claimant to prove his case without more. Our civil law does not deal in scientific or logical certainties. The statistical evidence may be so compelling that, to use the terminology of Steve Gold, the court may be able to infer belief probability from fact probability. To permit the drawing of such an inference is not to collapse the distinction between fact probability and belief probability. It merely recognises that, in a particular case, the fact probability may be so strong that the court is satisfied as to belief probability.[171]

This suggests that if epidemiological evidence is robust and establishes a particularly high relative risk, then we might be able to adduce causation in an individual case without more. Steel and Ibbetson offer some support for this view in their analysis of the decision in the *Creutzfeldt-Jakob Disease Litigation, Group A and C Plaintiffs* where claimants had developed CJD after having injections of human growth hormone and the disease was caused by a single injection.[172] Where claimants had received injections both before and after the date at which the administering of the injections became tortious, the Court accepted that a claimant could establish that her disease was caused by negligence if she had received more injections after the cut-off date than before. This seems to be an example of 'naked statistics' being used to establish causation, and indeed an example where evidence that a claimant had received marginally more injections after the cut-off date would not be sufficient to convince us on the balance of probabilities that it was actually one of the tortious injections that caused the disease. Steel and Ibbetson ask:

> What if 95 injections had occurred after the cut-off date and only 5 before? It seems compelling here to say that it was more probable than not that the disease was caused by a tortious injection (*i.e.* that fact was more probable than not). In other words, sometimes

---

[171] *Sienkiewicz* (n 8) [222].
[172] *Creutzfeldt-Jakob Disease Litigation, Group A and C Plaintiffs* (2000) 54 BMLR 100.

probabilities ought to alter our degree of belief in a proposition about a fact; and some probabilities ought to alter that degree enough as to satisfy the balance of probability standard.[173]

This is a compelling argument, yet Wright is particularly cautious about this approach, explaining that 'the demand for particularistic evidence is not based on the notion that such evidence is "uniquely highly probabilifying" but rather on the fact that it is uniquely instantiating'.[174] It would be rare that the risk attributable to the negligence was so high that a court could form a probable belief that the negligence was in fact a cause of the harm, but it would also be rare that a court was presented with purely statistical evidence, so there seems to be little practical place for Wright's objection.

Broadbent notes that Wright's objection to epidemiological evidence is not simply that it is class-based rather than individual.[175] Instead, he explains, in Wright's view the nature of such evidence is that it is an *ex ante* probability, ie the kind of probability that would guide us in 'placing a bet' whereas the nature of civil proof is such that the evidence must meet a standard or 'clear a bar' and requires an *ex post* probability, ie 'a case-specific probability, based solely on the particularistic evidence specific to a particular occasion'.[176] Even if epidemiological evidence is particularised to the claimant it is still the same *kind* of evidence. Broadbent accepts that *if* this is the nature of civil proof then epidemiological evidence is ineffective as proof of specific causation,[177] but he accepts epidemiological evidence since he disagrees with Wright over the nature of civil proof.

The position adopted here is situated between these two stances, maintaining that the nature of civil proof requires evidence to clear a bar, but instead arguing that epidemiology does not deal only in *ex ante* statistics. As we have seen, the Bradford Hill criteria are qualitative, and epidemiologists use these criteria to draw inferences about general causal relationships based on the probabilistic evidence as well as evidence pertaining to the underlying biological process. In the same way it is, therefore, appropriate to draw inferences about specific causation based on epidemiological evidence, where there is some further particularistic evidence that helps convince us that the claimant is more likely in the 'caused' or 'uncaused' category.

Green thus highlights that in Wright's view, 'particularistic evidence connects a possibly causal generalization to the particular occasion by instantiating the abstract elements in the causal generalization, thereby converting the abstract generalization into an instantiated generalization',[178] so, she says, 'on Wright's analysis, evidence of a claimant's exposure to a given agent *is* particularised

[173] Steel and Ibbetson, 'More Grief on Uncertain Causation in Tort' (n 129) 466.
[174] Wright, 'Proving Causation' (n 2) 208.
[175] Broadbent (n 6) 176–77.
[176] Wright, 'Causation, Responsibility, Risk' (n 2) 1050.
[177] Broadbent (n 6) 177.
[178] Wright, 'Pruning' (n 2) 1051.

evidence sufficient to link epidemiological information about a condition to that claimant'.[179] Effectively particularistic evidence is merely evidence of the specific claimant's circumstances that gives us reason to believe that, had she taken part in the epidemiological study, she would have been in the cohort whose harm was caused by the relevant agent. Greenberg suggests that we should work backwards to identify any reasons why the epidemiological evidence should not apply to the individual claimant:

> It is useful to begin by asking if there are compelling reasons why the results of the study should *not* apply to this particular patient. Possible reasons include differences in genetic predispositions, gender, age, inclusion and exclusion criteria, settings, use of medications, and other 'co-morbidities' (e.g. medical, social and psychological circumstances). Additional reasons are differences in the degree of exposure to the possible cause and how the disease outcome was measured and detected.[180]

This occurred to a degree in *Gregg v Scott* since the recovery rates for the cancer from which the claimant was suffering varied depending on a particular genetic trait.[181] This meant that the broad recovery rates did not apply to the individual claimant and instead had to be modified to take account of his genetic subgroup.

Another epidemiological technique that can assist is 'stratification', identifying particular characteristics of subjects of the study in order to observe whether exposure affects people differently depending on age, genetic makeup, lifestyle factors etc. Dawid explains that 'whether or not we have conducted such "pre-stratification" at the design stage, when the data are in it would be sensible to conduct a "post-stratified" analysis, looking at the results within each of these groups, rather than overall'.[182] Epidemiological experts are not restricted to presenting the results of a single study and instead may conduct a systematic review using a range of databases and studies to collect information.[183] Reconciling the accumulated studies and drawing reasoned conclusions requires specialist knowledge which again highlights the need for epidemiologists rather than clinicians to be used as expert witnesses and for courts to avoid doing their own guesswork to interpret the studies.

Goldberg has advocated the use of Bayes' theorem to obtain a probability of causation that is personal to the claimant.[184] This chapter will not engage with the detail of Bayes' theorem and the calculations that take place, in large part because its practical significance is limited by it being premised on the assumption that the risk factors are independent rather than synergistic,[185] while many cases do

---

[179] Sarah Green, 'Causation in Negligence' (Hart Publishing, 2015) 119.
[180] Greenberg (n 68) 47.
[181] The details of this evidence will be analysed in the next chapter on loss of chance.
[182] Dawid (n 49) 136.
[183] McIvor, 'Debunking' (n 19).
[184] Goldberg (n 83); Richard Goldberg, *Causation and Risk in the Law of Torts: Scientific Evidence and Medicinal Product Liability* (Hart Publishing, 1999) 38–43.
[185] Goldberg, *Causation and Risk* (n 184) 42.

involve synergistic interaction.[186] Furthermore, the end-product of this technique is still a statistic (albeit one that has been narrowed down to reflect the individual claimant's characteristics by accounting for known risk factors such as age, gender etc) so it espouses and lends itself to a quantitative interpretation of the balance of probabilities standard. As Haack explains, in a method that relies on Bayes' theorem, its role 'is to transform the mathematical sense of "probable" into the epistemic. Of course, no theorem of the probability calculus could possibly perform such a miracle of "translation".[187] Indeed, as she argues:

> It does not follow ... that the calculus of probabilities can illuminate the epistemic role such evidence plays in the context of the larger body of evidence in a case...On the contrary, in fact: by tempting us to confuse statistical probabilities with degrees of proof, legal probabilism can seduce us into forgetting that the statistical evidence in a case should be treated as *one piece of evidence among many.*[188]

Using Bayes' theorem encourages us to express every piece of information as a statistic to feed into the equation, but ultimately leaves us with a statistic. For example, Miller returns to the blue cab example and suggests that an eyewitness statement would be particularistic, but then if we had information about the fallibility of the witness then this could be expressed as a statistic and fed into Bayes' theorem.[189] He cites Lawrence Tribe who concedes that '*all* factual evidence is ultimately "statistical", and all legal proof ultimately "probabilistic", in the epistemological sense that no conclusion can ever be drawn from empirical data without some step of inductive inference'.[190] This may be true, but in reality the constraints of a court setting mean that not everything will be expressed in such statistical terms. A court will not undertake Miller's suggested 'carefully controlled experiment, with conditions comparable to those which obtained at the time of the accident'[191] to determine how frequently the witness correctly identifies the colour of the cab. Likewise, a court cannot assess the fallibility of an expert witness in statistical terms, but will instead have to be satisfied with the consistency of the expert's testimony, their credentials and experience etc. This is not a peculiarly legal approach: in evidence-based medicine 'the value of experience is not completely ignored as the practice of EBM involves an integration of the practitioner's clinical expertise and judgement with the best available evidence'.[192] Indeed it is for this reason that Greenberg advocates using epidemiologists rather than clinicians to deal with epidemiological evidence—the focus should be on the relevance of the witness's expertise rather than on their status in a hierarchy where clinicians are held in the highest esteem. As discussed above, it is a positive attribute of the

---

[186] See text to n 139 above.
[187] Haack (n 25) 73.
[188] ibid 71–72.
[189] Miller (n 14) 554.
[190] ibid 554 citing Laurence H Tribe, 'Trial by Mathematics: Precision and Ritual in the Legal Process' (1971) 84 *Harvard Law Review* 1329, 1330.
[191] Miller (n 14) 554.
[192] Greenberg (n 68) 46.

balance of probabilities standard of proof that it involves a qualitative assessment of the evidence and is based on the whole picture.[193]

When assessing the impact of particularistic evidence on the claimant's case, it is again important to be informed by epidemiologist expert testimony rather than to rely on the judge's own intuitions. After the epidemiological expert in *Novartis* had produced a report assessing the risks attributable to occupational exposure to amines and to cigarette smoking, further detail emerged about the extent of the occupational exposure. The epidemiologist accepted that 'when he had formed his opinion, he had been handicapped by the inaccuracies of his understanding of the exposures' yet he did not change his opinion.[194] At first instance, the Recorder 'was not impressed by the Professor's unwillingness to reconsider his opinion on causation in the light of the new information brought to his attention'.[195] Yet the epidemiologist's opinion was that although the occupational exposure was greater than he originally thought, it was still too low to impact on the risk of bladder cancer. Although his assessment may be contrary to our instincts it should have been trusted if he was able to explain it.[196]

IV. Conclusion

The approach advocated here is, in summary, a middle ground between, on the one hand, the scepticism of Wright and others who do not accept that epidemiological evidence has a role to play in proof of specific causation and those, on the other hand, who willingly accept that proof of a doubling of risk can satisfy the balance of probabilities standard of proof even if, like Broadbent, they do not go so far as to insist on a doubling of risk. The balance of probabilities requires courts to form a sufficiently strong belief in the fact of causation, and for this they must engage not only with the statistics such as the relative risk, but evaluate the reliability of the studies and the statistical significance of the results, and engage with the Bradford Hill criteria where appropriate. In order to move from epidemiological evidence to draw conclusions about an individual, a court should be guided by epidemiologist expert witnesses who have the relevant expertise to engage fully with the data, and should seek to personalise it to the individual claimant, but it important to understand basic epidemiological concepts in order to ask the right questions. Particularistic evidence has achieved an almost mythical status in approaches dismissive of epidemiological evidence, and it is important that courts are not overly demanding; after all, the standard of proof is one of mere probability which, as we have seen, should not be implemented in a manner that requires near certainty.

---

[193] See text to nn 24–28.
[194] *Novartis* (n 3) [54] (Smith LJ).
[195] ibid [55] (Smith LJ).
[196] ibid [54]–[56].

4

Loss of a Chance

The loss of a chance argument has been raised by claimants who have been unable to prove on the balance of probabilities that the defendant's negligence was a cause of their physical damage. The claims in *Hotson v East Berkshire Health Authority*[1] and *Gregg v Scott*[2] arose in the medical negligence context and in both cases the negligence consisted of the doctor's failure to diagnose and treat an existing illness. In both cases, the Court found that on the balance of probabilities the patient's existing illness could not have been cured with careful treatment, so the delay was not a cause of any eventual physical damage. The claimants argued instead that although it was less than probable that their condition could have been cured, the 'chance' of a cure had been reduced by the negligence and this 'chance' was something of value. They therefore sought to reformulate the actionable damage as the 'chance' of avoiding physical injury rather than the physical harm itself. If it succeeded, this action for loss of a chance would lead to proportionate recovery of damages for the physical harm, for example in *Hotson* the loss of a 25 per cent chance of avoiding avascular necrosis was valued at 25 per cent of the total loss caused by the avascular necrosis. Although this argument therefore centres on the question of whether a 'chance' of a better outcome can constitute actionable damage in negligence, it is an attempt to sidestep the difficulties of proof of causation of the physical harm on the balance of probabilities standard of proof.

This chapter is in two parts. The first addresses the claims for proportionate recovery for the loss of a chance of a better medical outcome and argues that the House of Lords was correct to reject the claims in *Hotson* and *Gregg*. In corrective justice-based interpersonal responsibility, liability is for 'wrongful loss' and the loss can only be characterised as wrongful if it was, in fact, caused by the defendant's negligence. Causation is a factual relationship, so the negligence either was or was not a cause of the damage. The claimant need only persuade the court of this fact on the balance of probabilities and if the court is, on balance, persuaded that the negligence was a cause of the damage then it accepts the fact of causation to be proved and the claimant recovers in full. Although the loss of chance argument ostensibly reformulates the damage as the chance of avoiding physical harm, it will

---

[1] *Hotson v Fitzgerald and others* [1985] 1 WLR 1036 (QBD); *Hotson v East Berkshire Health Authority* [1987] 2 WLR 287 (CA); *Hotson v East Berkshire Health Authority* [1987] AC 750 (HL).
[2] *Gregg v Scott* [2002] EWCA Civ 1471, [2003] Lloyd's Rep Med 105 (CA); [2005] UKHL 2, [2005] 2 AC 176 (HL).

be argued that what it in fact achieves is to 'discount' liability to reflect the degree of doubt over the fact of causation.

The second part of the chapter argues for recognition of a different conception of loss of a chance in the form of the opportunity to access treatment before the patient's prospects of recovery declined. The essence of this argument is that within the doctor-patient relationship, when the patient visits the doctor with an existing illness, the opportunity to access treatment is something of value to the patient because it is logically prior to the claimant's right to give informed consent to any such treatment. This opportunity therefore reflects an aspect of the patient's autonomy interest and is lost when there is a worsening in the patient's statistical chance of cure by the time she is properly diagnosed and given the opportunity for treatment. In part it is the specific nature and focus of the doctor's duty of care that justifies protection of this particular aspect of the patient's autonomy. Crucially, the prospective uncertainty at the time of treatment as to whether the patient can be cured is shared by both parties and it is this shared epistemological uncertainty that gives the opportunity value even though, with the benefit of hindsight, we may eventually discover that the patient's condition was untreatable. Since the damage is to the patient's autonomy interest rather than her physical welfare, this damage would be actionable whether or not the patient also suffers the eventual physical harm she sought to avoid. This also entails that it should be valued independently rather than as a proportion of the physical outcome. While the practical effect is that loss of chance would 'assist' claimants by providing compensation even where the doctor's negligence is not proved to have caused physical harm, this compensation would be very modest and is certainly not a way to bypass the causation requirement regarding the physical harm.

Part I: Loss of a Chance: Proportionate Recovery for Physical Harm

When analysing the loss of a chance argument advanced in *Hotson* and *Gregg* it is easy to lose sight of how these cases would be resolved on orthodox negligence principles. This section therefore takes the preliminary step of analysing each case within the framework of the existing negligence doctrines in order to set aside any possible misconceptions about how orthodox negligence principles operate. This involves building on chapter one to separate clearly the concepts of damage, causation and quantification. This will allow an analysis of the loss of chance argument to be based on a clear understanding of the concepts involved and of precisely where the problem lies. Two main strands of *Hotson* emerge here: the definition of damage and its relation to the so-called 'hook' argument, and the relationship between damage and quantification, in particular the vicissitudes principle. *Gregg* further highlights the tension between the medical definition of cure in that case as 10 years' disease-free survival and the formulation of the damage in respect of lost years in a negligence action. Beyond the negligence doctrines, both cases also involved misapplication of the balance of probabilities standard of proof, and these issues will be examined in arguing that proportionate recovery for the loss of a 'chance' of avoiding physical harm merely discounts damages to reflect the degree of doubt over the causal link.

I. Orthodox Negligence Principles in *Hotson* and *Gregg*

A. The Facts of *Hotson*

The claimant in *Hotson* was a boy who had fallen from a tree and sustained an injury to his hip, specifically a fracture to the left femoral epiphysis. He was taken to hospital (for which the defendant health authority was responsible) where he was examined, his knee was x-rayed and bandaged. The medical staff negligently failed to x-ray his hip so they did not diagnose the injury to his hip and instead sent him home untreated. He continued to suffer severe pain for the next five days after which he returned to hospital where his hip was x-rayed, the correct diagnosis was made, and emergency treatment begun. The boy suffered avascular necrosis in the epiphysis which involved deformity of the hip, with loss of movement and a limp, and would worsen in future due to osteoarthritis developing in the joint because of the injury. The femoral epiphysis is a layer of cartilage between the head and neck of the femur and avascular necrosis of the epiphysis develops because of a failure of the blood supply to the epiphysis. The award of damages for the five-day period of suffering was unproblematic. The difficulty arose in relation to the avascular necrosis. The injury clearly constituted actionable damage, the defendant owed the claimant a duty of care and had breached that duty. The difficulty was in establishing on the balance of probabilities that the negligence was a cause of the injury. At first instance, Simon Brown J found that there was only a 25 per cent chance that the claimant would have avoided avascular necrosis if his injury had been treated appropriately, so a traditional claim would have failed. However, he awarded the claimant damages to compensate the loss of a 25 per cent chance of avoiding avascular necrosis. These damages were 25 per cent of the value of the overall injury. He effectively treated the case as involving an issue of quantification of the loss caused by the delay in diagnosis, leading to proportional recovery, rather than as involving a difficulty of establishing a causal link between the delayed diagnosis and the final injury. The Court of Appeal upheld the claim, but it was rejected by the House of Lords. The House of Lords did not reject the concept of the loss of a chance, but held that in this instance the finding of fact was that, on the balance of probabilities, at the time of the negligence insufficient blood vessels remained intact for the injury to be treatable. Thus he was destined to suffer avascular necrosis and there was no 'chance' that had been lost.

With regard to the causal process involved in this case, the judge at first instance had found that avascular necrosis occurs when there are insufficient blood vessels to keep the epiphysis alive. When the claimant first went to hospital some blood vessels remained intact although distorted, but the delay in commencing treatment meant that already ruptured blood vessels continued to bleed into the joint thus increasing pressure in the joint and blocking the intact blood vessels. The delay in diagnosing and treating the injury therefore caused damage to those blood vessels that had remained and sealed the claimant's fate by turning his injury into an inevitability.[3]

The judge thought it 'possible but improbable' that sufficient vessels remained intact after the fall because the injury to the joint was at the upper end of the spectrum of severity. He found that there was a 25 per cent chance that following the fall sufficient blood vessels had remained intact to keep the epiphysis alive and avoid avascular necrosis. Lord Mackay, in the House of Lords, suggested that Simon Brown J had arrived at this figure because it was midway between the figures given by the two expert witnesses.[4] Simon Brown J said himself that he was 'unattracted to, and finally unable to accept, either of the competing extreme views',[5] so his conclusion seems to attempt a compromise between the views of the two expert witnesses.

B. Distinguishing Damage, Causation and Quantification

As argued in chapter one, it is essential to maintain a clear distinction between the negligence doctrines, notably damage, causation and quantification. At first instance, Simon Brown J said that

> [i]n the end the problem comes down to one of classification. Is this on true analysis a case where the plaintiff is concerned to establish causative negligence or is it rather a case where the real question is the proper quantum of damage? Clearly the case hovers near the border.[6]

The orthodox approach to negligence is that a claimant must show that she has suffered actionable damage and that the negligence was a cause of this damage. Physical injury is a recognised form of damage, but the loss of a chance of avoiding physical injury was previously not recognised as being capable of forming the gist of a negligence action. Once all the elements of a negligence claim have

---

[3] *Hotson v Fitzgerald and others* [1985] 1 WLR 1036 (QBD), 1040 (Simon Brown J).

[4] *Hotson v East Berkshire HA* [1987] AC 750 (HL).

[5] *Hotson v Fitzgerald and others* [1985] 3 All ER 167, 173 (Simon Brown J's evaluation of the evidence is available in this report but omitted from that of the Weekly Law Reports).

[6] *Hotson* (QBD) (n 3) 1043.

been established and the court is concerned with valuing the claimant's loss, the principle of *restitutio in integrum* means that the claimant should be compensated for all the losses that flow from the personal injury. Certain lost chances are recoverable at this stage. Simon Brown J explained:

> Time and time again courts evaluate past and future medical risks and award damages based on an assessment of the likelihood (a) of some adverse medical condition, like epilepsy or osteo-arthritis, developing consequent on the injury, or (b) that some pre-existing, perhaps degenerative, condition would in any event have manifested itself so as to cause the same or at any rate some lesser degree of disability as has been occasioned by the injury.[7]

This is simply an aspect of returning the claimant to his pre-tort position. But the judge then went on to overstate the significance of this, suggesting that:

> There is really no significant difference between that exercise and what the court is being invited by the plaintiff to do in the instant case.[8]

In fact, there is a significant difference between these principles and the loss of a chance argument in that they address issues of quantification whereas the loss of chance argument involves a prior issue of damage and causation. The following sections will therefore distinguish the aspects of damage, causation and quantification in those traditional principles in order to show that the loss of a chance of avoiding avascular necrosis is not analogous with existing negligence principles.

C. The 'Hook' Argument

Simon Brown J considered that the claimant's five days' pain and suffering constituted actionable damage, and that the lost chance of recovery could simply be regarded as a question of quantification.[9] This is referred to by Stapleton as the 'hook' argument, the idea being that once it has been proved that the negligence caused some physical damage, albeit minimal, any lost chance of avoiding further harm can be 'hooked' on to this claim as an issue of quantification.[10] But he went on to say 'this very point underlines how unsatisfactory it would be to suppose that the case should turn entirely on whether there is any directly provable injury, however slight. That will itself often be a matter of chance'.[11] However Simon Brown J has overstated the 'hook' concept here. In his earlier explanation of conventional principles he had noted that courts regularly assess the likelihood that the claimant will develop a medical condition *consequent* on the injury.[12] It is

---

[7] ibid 1045.
[8] ibid.
[9] ibid 1045.
[10] Jane Stapleton, 'Cause in Fact and the Scope of Liability for Consequences' (2003) 119 *Law Quarterly Review* 388; 'Loss of the Chance of Cure from Cancer' (2005) 68 *Modern Law Review* 996.
[11] *Hotson* (QBD) (n 3) 1045–46.
[12] See text to n 7.

necessary to show that there is a causal link between the injury that the defendant has actually caused and the anticipated future illness. A defendant is not required to pay for all future illnesses that the claimant might suffer, she is required to compensate for those illnesses that the claimant might suffer *because* of the harm the defendant has negligently caused her. In *Hotson*, the claimant was unable to prove that the delay in treatment had caused the avascular necrosis, so he would have been equally unable to prove that his five days' pain and suffering was causally related to the avascular necrosis. Lord Bridge explained this in the House of Lords:

> The damages referable to the plaintiff's pain during the five days by which treatment was delayed in consequence of failure to diagnose the injury correctly, although sufficient to establish the authority's liability for the tort of negligence, have no relevance to their liability in respect of the avascular necrosis. There was no causal connection between the plaintiff's physical pain and the development of the necrosis. If the injury had been painless, the plaintiff would have to establish the necessary causal link between the necrosis and the authority's breach of duty in order to succeed. It makes no difference that the five days' pain gave him a cause of action in respect of an unrelated element of damage.[13]

By understanding that the hook argument can only succeed where there is a causal relationship between the actionable injury and the risk of future illness it is clear that it is not arbitrary as Simon Brown J suggested.[14] The hook idea should continue to be used where actionable injury causes the claimant an increased risk of future illness, but cannot apply in *Hotson* where there is no causal relationship between the five days' pain and suffering and the increased risk of avascular necrosis.

D. The Vicissitudes Principle

As noted above, Simon Brown J also observed that courts regularly take into account the likelihood that some pre-existing condition would have resulted in the same degree of disability when valuing the loss caused by the defendant.[15] This is known as the vicissitudes principle. When calculating loss of earnings the multiplier used by the court is reduced to take account of the 'vicissitudes of life', ie the risk that the claimant's earnings would have been reduced by other unrelated accidents or illnesses.[16] Simon Brown J said that this amounts to holding that

> if the risk, or chance [of avoiding injury], is less than 50 per cent then the plaintiff gets nothing. If, however, it is over 50 per cent then the court should proceed to determine the matter as one of quantum, which involves having regard to the chances and contingencies and making discount accordingly.[17]

---

[13] *Hotson* (HL) (n 4) 780 (Lord Bridge).
[14] See also *Wright v Cambridge Medical Group* [2011] EWCA Civ 669, [2012] 3 WLR 1124, [49]–[51] (Lord Neuberger).
[15] See text to n 7.
[16] *Lim Poh Choo v Camden & Islington AHA* [1980] AC 174 (HL).
[17] *Hotson* (QBD) (n 3) 1049.

This, he said, 'smacks somewhat of heads I win, tails you lose'.[18]

He is right to say that such a position would discriminate in favour of defendants, yet once again he has overstated the issue. The discount made for the vicissitudes of life is made to reflect as accurately as possible the true value of the loss suffered by the claimant. Damages should return the claimant to the position she would have been in without the negligence so the court must do its best to account for the events that would have befallen her anyway including the likelihood that unrelated illness or accident would have impacted on the claimant's earning capacity in the future. It is an issue of quantification. The fact that the defendant's negligence was a cause of the injury actually suffered is not in doubt. In *Hotson*, the claimant did not establish that the defendant's negligence caused him to suffer avascular necrosis so the subsidiary task, of taking the pre-existing chance of injury into account when valuing the loss caused by the negligence, never arises.

The difference is apparent if *Hotson* is compared with *Smith v Leech Brain*.[19] In that case, the defendant's negligence caused the claimant to suffer a burn on his lip which triggered a pre-cancerous condition and led to his eventual death. The pre-cancerous condition meant that independently of the negligence there was an increased likelihood that he would have developed cancer in the future, so his damages were reduced by 5 per cent to account for this possibility. Stapleton suggests that this is indistinguishable in effect from the loss of chance-based claim for proportionate recovery:

> The 'discount' is made not to reflect that chance that the triggering had been due to a cause other than the defendant's fault (because it was clear that this had not been the case) but to reflect the true value of the loss which the defendant had caused the plaintiff to suffer. In many cases, if not all, this approach will give a result indistinguishable from that produced had the claim been framed in terms of loss of a chance.[20]

Even though the *result* might look indistinguishable from a claim for proportionate recovery framed as a claim for the loss of a chance, it does not mean, as Stapleton suggests, that valuing a lost chance as a proportion of the physical harm to which the chance relates is conceptually sound. There was no doubt in *Smith* that the defendant's negligence had caused the claimant to suffer the harm at that particular time. Yet when making a discount for the vicissitudes of life at the valuation stage, account was taken of the pre-cancerous condition to personalise the likelihood that the claimant would have died prematurely anyway. In *Hotson*, the doubt surrounded the question of whether the defendant's negligence had caused him to suffer avascular necrosis at this time. If proportional recovery were allowed in *Hotson* it would not reflect the chance that the claimant would have suffered the same loss due to an unrelated illness at some stage in the future; it would reflect

---

[18] ibid 1049.

[19] *Smith v Leech Brain & Co* [1962] 2 QB 405 (QBD).

[20] Jane Stapleton, 'The Gist of Negligence: Part 2 the Relationship between "Damage" and Causation' (1988) 104 *Law Quarterly Review* 389, 398.

the degree of doubt over whether the defendant had caused him any loss at all. In the House of Lords, Lord Ackner correctly stated that:

> Once liability is established, on the balance of probabilities, the loss which the plaintiff has sustained is payable in full. It is not discounted by reducing his claim by the extent to which he has failed to prove his case with 100 per cent certainty.[21]

Understanding that the vicissitudes principle relates to valuation of loss once a causal link has been established makes it clear that it is distinct from the loss of chance argument which seeks to solve a difficulty relating to proof of causation. Simon Brown J suggested that the rejection of the loss of chance argument would be inconsistent with the conventional approach in this respect, yet it has been shown that this is not the case.

Stapleton has criticised the decision of the House of Lords for failing to resolve the essence of the claimant's argument, 'namely whether reformulation of the gist in terms of loss of a chance should now be acceptable'.[22] It is clear that this is what the claimant was trying to do, and that he was trying to do this because of his inability to prove a causal link between the negligence and the physical outcome. The above discussion should also have added some clarity to what happens at each stage of a conventional claim in terms of damage, causation and valuation, so that arguments for and against reformulating the gist in terms of loss of a chance are considered against an accurate picture of traditional recovery.

E. The Facts of *Gregg v Scott*

The loss of chance argument for proportionate recovery was subsequently raised again in the medical negligence context in the case of *Gregg v Scott*.[23] The claim once again failed. The claimant in *Gregg* went to the defendant doctor complaining of a lump under his arm which the defendant negligently diagnosed as a benign fatty lump rather than referring the patient for further tests which would have shown that it was cancerous. This resulted in a nine-month delay in the diagnosis and commencement of treatment of the claimant's disease. The claimant argued that the nine-month delay due to the defendant's negligence had caused him to lose a chance of being cured because his chance of cure had been reduced from a statistical 42 per cent at the time of negligence to 25 per cent at the time of trial.[24] The medical definition of cure is 10 years' disease-free survival, so the claim was that the negligence had caused him to lose a chance of 10 years' disease-free

---

[21] *Hotson* (HL) (n 4) 793 (Lord Ackner).

[22] Stapleton, 'The Gist of Negligence' (n 20) 393.

[23] *Gregg v Scott* [2002] EWCA Civ 1471, [2003] Lloyd's Rep Med 105; [2005] UKHL 2, [2005] 2 AC 176.

[24] The reliability of these statistics will be considered below in addition to asking whether the loss of such a chance can constitute damage.

survival.[25] Since the details of the facts are relatively dense they will be presented in more depth in relation to each issue rather than being repeated here.

The claimant presented a claim that was destined to fail; there are barriers to accepting the loss of a chance argument in itself, but even more so in a case such as this where the 'chance' has not been definitively lost. This is not because the claimant's 'chance' was reduced to 20–30 per cent,[26] but because the claimant was still alive, and until he either died or survived disease-free for 10 years it could not be said that this 'chance' had run its course. The problem seems to arise because the claimant used the loss of a chance argument to try to avoid the difficulty of proving a causal link between the negligence and the physical harm. But given that the claimant had not yet suffered the 'outcome' to which the chance related, ie dying before 10 years had elapsed, even if the evidence had favoured finding a causal link between the doctor's negligence and the claimant's probable death, he would still have been unable to claim for this because he had not yet suffered the damage. Effectively, faced with a case where it was going to be difficult to prove that the defendant's negligence had caused damage to the claimant, he decided to advance a case based on loss of a chance, yet his loss of a chance argument was less readily acceptable than it might otherwise have been because he was claiming for the loss of the chance of avoiding a harm that he had not yet, and may never, suffer. However, it seems that the claimant could have advanced a more modest claim based on traditional principles and that such a claim ought to have succeeded. Similarly to the discussion of *Hotson* in the previous section, the following analysis seeks to clear away any misconceptions surrounding how orthodox negligence principles would apply to this case in order to be left with a clearer understanding of what problems remain that might be solved by taking a loss of chance approach to recovery.

F. Pain and Suffering

During the nine months that elapsed between the defendant's negligence and the eventual diagnosis of the claimant's illness the cancer had 'gradually enlarged'.[27] Following the referral for a biopsy he was admitted to hospital with 'acute and intense chest pain which was a result of the lymphoma having spread, in particular to the left pectoral region'.[28] The spread of the cancer is a personal injury, and

---

[25] The start date for measuring the 10-year period is unclear. The medical evidence referred to 10 years' disease-free survival which suggests it is measured from the date that the tumour has been eliminated. Lord Phillips thought that it probably started at the date of commencement of treatment (*Gregg v Scott* [2005] UKHL 2, [2005] 2 AC 176, [132]). At trial and in the Court of Appeal reference was made to the chance of 5 years' disease-free survival but this seems to be because of the number of years that had elapsed between the negligence and the trial, so the medical definition of cure was still premised on 10 years' disease-free survival.

[26] The difficulty of giving an accurate figure will be addressed later.

[27] *Gregg v Scott* [2002] EWCA Civ 1471, [2003] Lloyd's Rep Med 105, [1] (Latham LJ).

[28] ibid [2].

the claimant ought to have been able to recover for this physical injury and the consequential pain and suffering.[29]

The next issue is the extent of the treatment that the claimant had to undergo. The claimant underwent chemotherapy, supplemented by radiotherapy. The tumour responded but not completely, so the claimant underwent a more aggressive treatment of high dose chemotherapy, with harvesting of stem cells. He suffered side effects from the treatment, and these were severe in the case of the high dose chemotherapy. He had to give up work, felt ill and had felt weak ever since. At first instance, Inglis J found that 'it is possible to say on the basis of Professor Goldstone's model that he would more probably than not have achieved complete remission with initial CHOP therapy and without high dose chemotherapy with stem cell harvesting'.[30] Baroness Hale, despite rejecting the claim for loss of a chance, still acknowledged that this amounted to a finding that 'the claimant would have achieved initial remission had he been treated earlier'.[31] She ultimately considered that it was probable that the claimant would still have suffered the same setbacks and that the relapses would have happened anyway, but she did say:

> Even on conventional principles, this does not necessarily mean that the claimant is not entitled to anything at all. The defendant is liable for any extra pain, suffering, loss of amenity, financial loss and loss of expectation of life which may have resulted from the delay. If, without the delay, the claimant would have achieved a longer gap before more radical treatment became necessary, then he should be entitled to damages to reflect the acceleration in his suffering. If the pain and suffering he would have suffered anyway was made worse by the anguish of knowing that his disease could have been detected earlier, then he should be compensated for that.[32]

It is therefore clear that, even if she thought that the delay had no effect on the overall prognosis for cure such that the spread of the cancer did not affect the final outcome of death/survival, she did think that the spread of the cancer was physical damage and that this had affected the treatment necessary which caused him greater pain and suffering. Again, he could have recovered for this if he had formulated his claim in terms of the spread of the cancer and the consequences of the spread.

G. Loss of Life Expectancy

The claimant argued that the defendant's negligence caused him to lose a chance of a cure by reducing this chance from 42 per cent to 25 per cent. Given that the

---

[29] *Gregg* (HL) (n 25) Lord Hope, who ultimately would have allowed the claim for loss of a chance, recognised that he was in the minority and that the claim would therefore fail, but expressed his hope 'that it was not too late for the pain and suffering which the appellant suffered due to the tumour's enlargement ... to be brought into account by way of an award of general damages' [123]. See also Baroness Hale [206] and Lord Phillips [169].

[30] ibid [202].

[31] ibid [203].

[32] ibid [206].

medical definition of cure is 10 years' disease-free survival, the claim for lost years was that the negligence had caused him the loss of a chance of 10 years' disease-free survival. By incorporating the medical definition of cure into the claim for lost years the claimant seems to have made it easier for the Court to reject his claim. This is because introducing a cut-off date of 10 years adds a binary quality to the inquiry—he either will or will not live for 10 years, and the delay in diagnosis either has or has not prevented him for living for 10 years. If he had advanced a more modest yet conventional claim for loss of life expectancy, which is open-ended in nature, then it seems likely that he would have been able to establish that the delay in diagnosis did reduce his life expectancy. Admittedly his life expectancy was already quite short at the time of the negligence, but the spread of the cancer due to the delay reduced it even further. Lord Phillips highlighted this problem which was created by the way the claim for lost years was formulated:

> The conventional way of determining the effect of the injury on expectation of life is as follows. The court determines what the claimant's expectation of life would have been but for the injury. The court then determines what the claimant's expectation of life is having regard to the effect of the injury. The difference between the two constitutes the 'lost years'.[33]

It is important to note that a conventional claim for loss of life expectancy is not the same as the 'hook' argument. The hook argument consists of arguing that once a claimant can point to some actionable damage that was caused by the defendant's negligence, all other chances are recoverable as a matter of quantification. As discussed above in relation to *Hotson*, a claimant will actually only be compensated where the reduction in the chance of avoiding future illness or of making future gain is *as a consequence* of the actionable damage, ie causally related to the actionable damage.[34] This is an area where the importance of distinguishing clearly between issues of damage, causation and quantification, is very apparent yet often overlooked. Mr Gregg was unable to show that there was a causal link between the spread of the cancer and the final outcome of being cured (or failing to survive for 10 years) because on the balance of probabilities he would not have survived 10 years even with timely diagnosis. But if he had advanced a conventional claim for the physical harm constituted by the spread of the cancer, the additional pain and suffering caused by the spread, and the more aggressive treatment, then it would seem likely that having more extensive cancer would have reduced his life expectancy somewhat, even if his life expectancy was already short because he was suffering from cancer at the time of the negligence. If a claimant with an identical disease was shot and killed by a defendant, in valuing the lost years the court would assess his life expectancy with cancer at the time he was shot and compensate the lost years. It ought therefore also to be feasible for the Court in *Gregg* to have assessed the claimant's life expectancy at the time of the negligence and his life expectancy nine months later when the cancer had spread.

---

[33] ibid [131].
[34] See text to n 13.

Indeed this approach was subsequently adopted in the High Court decision in *JD v Mather*,[35] a case which similarly involved a doctor's negligent failure to diagnose the claimant's cancer, resulting in a delay in diagnosis and treatment during which time the cancer had upstaged. The Court accepted evidence that the claimant's life expectancy had been reduced from seven and a half years to four years as a consequence of the upstaging of the cancer.[36] Damages were therefore awarded for the physical damage constituted by the upstaging of the cancer and for the reduction in life expectancy which was caused by the upstaging.[37]

Lord Phillips summarised the various 'adverse events' that Mr Gregg had suffered 'beyond the initial development of his cancer' as: (i) the spread of the cancer to the pectoral region accompanied by acute pain; (ii) high dose chemotherapy with harvesting of stem cells; (iii) relapse when a tumour developed in the right axilla accompanied by chemotherapy; (iv) psychiatric distress on being told that the relapse meant that he would die; (v) further suspected relapse with additional chemotherapy.[38] He correctly explained that 'the chance that the delay in commencing his treatment has caused each of these adverse events is not the same'.[39] This highlights the need for claimants to be careful and specific in how they detail the loss for which they are claiming, and also the need for a claimant to be realistic about what she can prove. Given that corrective justice requires that a defendant only pay for that loss that she caused through her negligence, a claimant will only recover if she can prove the causal link between the negligence and the damage. It is surely preferable for a claimant to receive modest compensation for that portion of the loss the defendant can be proved to have caused, rather than to attempt to combine the losses into one claim for the loss of a chance of a better outcome. Lord Phillips concluded that

> On balance of probability I suspect that one is now in a position to conclude that the delay in commencing Mr Gregg's treatment has not affected his prospect of being a survivor but has caused him all the other adverse events which I have set out above.[40]

If Mr Gregg had advanced a traditional claim for these limited heads of damage it is therefore likely that he would have been successful.

II. Loss of a Chance and the Balance of Probabilities Standard of Proof

This chapter has illustrated that it is essential to have a clear understanding of the concepts of damage, causation and quantification and their interrelationship

---

[35] *JD v Mather* [2012] EWHC 3063 (QB), [2013] Med LR 291.
[36] ibid [46]–[48].
[37] See also *Oliver v Williams* [2013] EWHC 600 (QB), [2013] Med LR 344 [42].
[38] *Gregg* (HL) (n 25) [167].
[39] ibid [168].
[40] ibid [169].

before it is possible to analyse the loss of chance argument for proportional recovery. In light of this it is clear that if courts recognised that the loss of a chance of a better medical outcome could constitute the gist of a negligence action, this would represent a significant departure from traditional principles.

The loss of chance argument has been raised by claimants because of difficulties they faced proving the causal link between the defendant's negligence and their loss. In both *Hotson* and *Gregg*, the claimant was already unwell and the defendant's negligence consisted of a failure to diagnose and treat that existing illness. Proof of causation is naturally complicated in this scenario because there is routinely a candidate cause other than the defendant's negligence—the court must determine whether the illness alone would have caused the harm even with careful diagnosis and treatment. Since the civil standard of proof is the balance of probabilities, and recovery in negligence law is 'all-or-nothing', it is often said that where the patient's pre-tort chance of a cure exceeded 50 per cent the courts regard her as having been destined to be cured, but if her chance of cure was below 50 per cent the courts regard her as being doomed to suffer the harmful outcome even with careful treatment so the doctor's negligence is deemed not to be a cause and the claimant receives nothing.[41] As discussed in chapter three, the balance of probabilities relates to the degree of belief the judge must form in the fact of causation,[42] and statistical evidence is just one element in informing a rational belief. The statistical evidence should be personalised to the individual as far as possible, and in order to form a rational belief based on such evidence the judge must also be persuaded of the reliability of the evidence. The judge's degree of belief is not easily quantified as a percentage because it involves a qualitative assessment of the available evidence, and it would be wrong to think that statistics are somehow more useful or objective because they express probabilities. Understanding that the balance of probabilities relates to the judge's degree of belief highlights the error of proportionate recovery, which would actually equate to discounting damages to reflect the judge's doubt as to causation.

A. Resolving *Hotson* and *Gregg* on the Balance of Probabilities

In the previous chapter we saw that the balance of probabilities is often misconceived as a purely statistical requirement and expressed in numerical terms such that causation is proven if the claimant adduces evidence of at least a 51 per cent statistical likelihood that the defendant's negligence was a cause. This error was evident in *Gregg*, where Lord Nicholls began his speech by stating that '[t]he

---

[41] See Allan Beever, '*Gregg v Scott* and Loss of a Chance' (2005) *University of Queensland Law Journal* 201, 201. See also Stapleton 'Loss of the Chance of Cure' (n 10) 997; Sarah Green, 'Coherence of Medical Negligence Cases: a Game of Doctors and Purses' (2006) 14 *Medical Law Review* 1, 3.

[42] See Richard Wright, 'Proving Causation: Probability versus Belief' in Richard Goldberg (ed), *Perspectives on Causation* (Hart Publishing, 2011) 205–12.

patient could recover damages if his initial prospects of recovery had been more than 50%. But because they were less than 50% he can recover nothing'.[43] This is also common in academic commentary, for example Beever has suggested that '[t]he problem facing the plaintiff was that, before the defendant's negligence, his chance of being cured was only 42%. This meant that, on the balance of probabilities, the defendant did not deprive the plaintiff of a cure'.[44]

Mr Gregg had not suffered the harmful outcome to which this 'chance' related since he was still alive, so in reality there was not a causation question to answer. This means that even if the his pre-tort 'chance' of recovery had exceeded 50 per cent he would not have had a successful claim on traditional principles unless he could prove that he had suffered actionable damage, ie the harmful physical outcome. Lord Nicholls was therefore wrong to suggest that '[t]he patient could recover damages if his initial prospects of recovery had been more than 50%'.[45] The causation question is not the open-ended question of 'what position would the claimant be in if the defendant had acted carefully?', but the focused questions of 'has the claimant suffered actionable damage?' and 'was the defendant's negligence a cause of that damage?'. Had he died, however, the causation question would have been whether the negligent delay in diagnosis was a cause of his death, so it should be established on the balance of probabilities that his disease could have been cured.

This tendency to map the patient's statistical chance directly onto the balance of probabilities is perhaps more common in cases of medical negligence because a doctor explaining a patient's prognosis will routinely refer to the statistical likelihood of recovery. But once the patient has suffered the harmful outcome then it is a question of fact whether the condition was treatable, and the balance of probabilities is a matter of belief in this fact and is designed to deal with the uncertainty— the court does not need to be convinced that the injury was certainly treatable, it needs only be convinced that it is more likely than not that it was treatable.[46] In *Gregg*, Lord Nicholls expressed concern that:

> Statistical evidence ... is not strictly a guide to what would have happened in one particular case. Statistics record retrospectively what happened to other patients in more or less comparable situations. They reveal trends of outcome. They are general in nature. The different way other patients responded in a similar position says nothing about how the claimant would have responded.[47]

---

[43] *Gregg* (HL) (n 25) [2].
[44] Beever, '*Gregg v Scott*' (n 41) 201. See also Stapleton, 'Loss of the Chance of Cure' (n 10) 997; Green, 'Coherence of Medical Negligence Cases' (n 41) 3.
[45] *Gregg* (HL) (n 25) [2].
[46] See ch 3, text to n 10.
[47] *Gregg* (HL) (n 25) [28].

He continued to ask

> Who can know whether Mr Gregg was in the 58% non-survivor category or the
> 42% survivor category? There was no evidence, peculiar to him or his circumstances,
> enabling anyone to say whether on balance of probability he was in the former group of
> the latter group.[48]

In both *Hotson* and *Gregg* there was, however, evidence to indicate which group
the claimant was in, so there was no inherent obstacle to deciding the cases on the
balance of probabilities.

B. Proof in *Hotson*

The details of the decision at first instance in *Hotson* show clearly that the judge
did undertake a detailed qualitative assessment of the conflicting evidence. Confusion arose subsequently because he went on to quantify his doubt in order to
award proportionate recovery and that figure has since been interpreted as being a
statistical probability of cure.[49]

The evidence did not consist simply of conflicting statistical probabilities of
avascular necrosis following a fall. The 25 per cent 'chance' was not a quantitative assessment of the likelihood of harm, but was a numerical expression of the
judge's degree of belief in the fact that the injury could be avoided; it reflected
his qualitative assessment of the evidence. He looked at how severe the displace-
ment of the bone was, how easily the fracture was reduced, the different interpretations of the x-rays, disagreement over whether the blood vessels would have
continued to bleed and build up pressure on those remaining intact or would
have sealed themselves, a paper from a medical journal that considered different
treatment options, and a paper that analysed nine cases of fracture separation of
the epiphysis in children. He found that there were internal inconsistencies in the
evidence of the claimant's expert witness as well as between the two conflicting
experts. On one issue he said 'I am not *persuaded* by the published material before
me ... Rather I am *on balance persuaded* to the contrary view' (emphasis added).[50]
Eventually he concluded:

> I regret that I found certain parts of the evidence of both experts, highly qualified and
> experienced although they both undoubtedly are, difficult to accept, either as a result of
> internal inconsistency within their evidence or because of what seemed to be an intrinsic
> want of logic in some particular expressed view ... In the result I find myself unattracted
> to, and finally unable to accept, either of the competing extreme views.[51]

---

[48] ibid [29].
[49] *Hotson v East Berkshire HA* [1985] 3 All ER 167 (QBD). This is set out in the All England Law
Reports but unfortunately is omitted from the Weekly Law Reports.
[50] ibid 173.
[51] ibid.

This was the basis for his finding that it was 'possible but improbable' that the fall had 'left intact sufficient vessels to keep the epiphysis alive'.[52] Whilst he expressed the 'chance' as a percentage, it is clear from the language used throughout the judgment that this 25 per cent 'chance' was not a statement of how likely it was, given the number of blood vessels remaining intact, that the claimant could be cured, but a statement of how likely it was that enough vessels remained intact for him to be cured. It therefore reflected his degree of belief in the proposition that enough blood vessels remained intact for the epiphysis to be kept alive. It was expressed numerically to allow the calculation of damages at the valuation stage. Normally, if approaching this as an orthodox claim for the physical harm, the judge would not need to put a figure on the extent of his doubt. The balance of probabilities merely requires him to find, as he did, that on balance he was persuaded that insufficient vessels remained intact. But because he was willing to approach it as a loss of a chance case, he quantified the extent of the remaining doubt in his mind as being 25 per cent so that he could then calculate a proportionate award of damages. This is in no way the same as saying that the doctor created a 25 per cent risk, or caused the claimant to lose a 25 per cent chance, or contributed 25 per cent of the chance of harm.

C. Proof in *Gregg*

In *Gregg*, the expert evidence at first instance consisted of a joint report by a consultant haematologist Professor Goldstone (instructed by Mr Gregg) and Dr Bunch (instructed by Dr Scott) concerning the claimant's disease and the effect of the delay in diagnosis, and oral evidence by Professor Goldstone alone. In the period between the claimant's pleading of the particulars of the claim in April 2000 based on Professor Goldstone's evidence, and the writing of the joint report in 2001, Professor Goldstone became aware of a paper that had been published in 1999 by the American Society of Hematology, written by Falini et al (the 'Falini paper') which suggested that the particular type of lymphoma could be further divided into two sub-categories, ALK positive and ALK negative. Those who fell into the ALK negative subset had a significantly worse prognosis than those in the ALK positive category. The claimant's lymphoma was ALK negative. The joint report by Professor Goldstone and Dr Bunch took account of the Falini paper. Only Professor Goldstone gave oral evidence and there he developed a 'working example' of the fate of a cohort of 100 ALK negative patients based on the evidence in the joint report. Latham LJ noted that '[t]he assumption was that the cohort consisted of patients with the same stage of disease as that from which the appellant suffered at the time when treatment should have been commenced'.[53]

---

[52] ibid 171.
[53] *Gregg* (CA) (n 27) [14].

The working example showed:

> Of those with initial treatment by CHOP chemotherapy with or without field radio-therapy 55 will achieve complete remission. 45 will not achieve complete remission, and of those 41 will then die. Four who did not achieve complete remission immediately will be brought to achieve it by further treatment of various kinds. Thus of the initial 100 59 manage to achieve complete remission. Of those 35 do not relapse. They are described by Professor Goldstone as the core group of survivors. 24, however, do relapse (usually, if they are going to, within two years or so of achieving remission). Of those 24 half, a further 12, will not be responsive to further treatment and will die. The remaining 12 will be responsive to further treatment, typically high dose chemotherapy with stem cell harvesting such as the claimant himself went through. Of those 12 half, a further six, will not relapse again and will become survivors. Of the remaining six who do relapse again, only one will survive. The number of survivors from the 100 who started out will therefore be 42.[54]

During the period of delay following the negligence the cancer upstaged from stage 1 (presence in the lymph nodes) to stage 1E (spread to other tissues out-side the lymph nodes). There appears not to be a similar working example for a cohort of 100 ALK negative patients at stage 1E,[55] but the expert evidence in the joint report was that 'it was "quite possible" that his individual prognosis had been reduced to less than 50% of what it would have been intrinsically at the outset'.[56] At the time when the disease was actually diagnosed and treated the likelihood of cure was 'no more than 10–15%',[57] but at the time of trial '[h]is actual prognosis they considered to be dependent now more on the fact that he had survived for three years' which meant that his chances of 10 years' survival 'had increased from a statistical 10% to 20–30%'.[58] Thus

> the Statement of Facts and Issues agreed by the parties included a statement that the judge found that the effects of the delay in commencing Mr Gregg's treatment meant that his 'chances of long-term survival fell as a result of the negligence from 42% (on initial presentation to [Dr Scott]) to 25% (as at the date of trial)'.[59]

There are two areas of concern in this case: first, the reliability of the evidence; second, the Court's failure to personalise the statistical evidence to the claimant.

D. Reliability of the Evidence in *Gregg*

Lord Phillips' examination of Professor Goldstone's evidence led him to conclude that it was 'a very inadequate tool for assessing the effect of the delay in treatment on

---

[54] Findings at first instance, cited in *Gregg* (HL) (n 25) [146] (Lord Phillips).

[55] As will be discussed later, this is because the working model was actually based on patients at all stages of the disease (see text to n 67).

[56] *Gregg* (CA) (n 27) [13] (Latham LJ).

[57] ibid.

[58] ibid [15].

[59] *Gregg* (HL) (n 25) [147] (Lord Phillips).

Mr Gregg's progress and prognosis'.[60] McIvor has identified a number of concerns regarding Professor Goldstone's evidence which affect the degree of belief that can be placed in the statistics he presented to the Court.[61] She notes that as a consultant haematologist his expertise was medical rather than statistical or epidemiological so, whilst skilled in diagnosis and treatment of certain illnesses, he was less skilled in the interpretation of data.[62] She further highlights that he had initially suggested that the statistical probability of survival was 84 per cent because he had not taken into account the paper by Falini et al which showed that ALK negative patients had a much lower chance of survival than ALK positive patients. This paper had been available at the time of writing of his first report so its omission casts doubt on the overall quality of his evidence.[63] The Falini paper itself was based on a very small sample consisting of only 78 patients, 53 of whom were ALK positive and only 25 of whom were ALK negative.[64] Given the small sample size the accuracy of this data is probably limited. Furthermore, the 'working example' that Professor Goldstone devised to predict the likely fate of 100 ALK negative patients seems to be based on his own experience.[65] Presumably given that he had only recently become aware of the Falini paper, and therefore was only recently alerted to the reduced survival rate of ALK negative patients, it can only have been a rough model. This does not suggest that the statistics he produced are especially reliable, it suggests that they are the best that he could do based on his clinical experience and that a different expert could have given quite different figures.

E. Personalising the Evidence in *Gregg*

Even if this evidence was reliable, in order to form a rational belief as to whether the claimant's disease could have been successfully treated it is essential, as seen in chapter three, to personalise it to the individual as far as possible. Professor Goldstone had made some attempt to personalise the statistics to Mr Gregg's post-tort chances in light of the progress of his treatment, suggesting that the likelihood of survival had increased from 10–15 per cent at the time of diagnosis to 20–30 per cent at the time of trial. But there was no corresponding attempt to personalise the statistics in relation to his pre-tort chance of survival despite there being information on which this attempt could have been based. Stapleton explains the significance of this omission:

> The unpersonalized estimate of [Mr Gregg's pre-tort chance of being cured] was 42%. But by the time of trial we had an important piece of information about the actual

---

[60] ibid [157].
[61] Claire McIvor, 'The Use of Epidemiological Evidence in UK Tort Law' in Sana Loue (ed), *Forensic Epidemiology in the Global Context* (Springer-Verlag, 2013) 75–76.
[62] See ch 3, text to n 101.
[63] McIvor, 'The Use of Epidemiological Evidence in UK Tort Law' (n 61) 76.
[64] *Gregg* (CA) (n 27) [11].
[65] ibid [14].

experience of this particular claimant after the commencement of treatment, which could have been used to 'personalize' that estimate. By the trial we knew that, even after breach, Mr Gregg was able to achieve complete remission in 1996. Does this not show that, *a fortiori*, had there been no breach, Mr Gregg would have been one of the 59 out of 100 who initially achieved complete remission? A member of *that* group had a pre-tort chance of cure of 42/59 = 71%, not 42%.[66]

It was noted above that it was assumed that Professor Goldstone's working example applied to a cohort of 100 patients whose disease was at the same stage as the claimant's pre-tort disease, and that he did not provide a similar working example for 100 patients whose disease was at the more advanced stage that Mr Gregg's cancer had reached when treatment commenced. It is thus unclear where the assessment of the claimant's post-tort likelihood of cure at 10–15 per cent was derived from. Furthermore, Lord Phillips questioned this assumption, explaining '[w]hen describing Professor Goldstone's model, the judge stated: "The 100 patients in the worked example include all ages, and also people with other unrevealed personal characteristics, *one of which is the stage of the disease at diagnosis*".[67] This means that the Court could have made some attempt to personalise the statistics by considering the claimant's age, and the stage of his disease. Surely, given the early stage of his disease he was more likely to belong to the survivor category than somebody whose disease was more advanced?

As seen in chapter three, the court must seek to personalise the evidence to the individual claimant in order to form a rational belief in the likely causes of the damage, and should also evaluate the reliability of the evidence. Mr Gregg's claim was fatally flawed because he had not suffered actionable damage in the form of the final outcome, yet even if he had suffered this harmful outcome the evidence pertaining to causation had not been personalised and in any case was not reliable. It seems unlikely that he would have been able to prove causation on the balance of probabilities even if he had suffered actionable damage, but there is nothing to suggest that this is a particularly unusual problem requiring an exceptional solution.

F. Rejecting 'Chance' Conceived as a Proportion of the Physical Outcome

The House of Lords in *Hotson* avoided the question of whether 'loss of a chance' was actionable because it was held that the patient did not have a chance of recovery when he first went to hospital. Instead, it was held, he either had sufficient blood vessels remaining undamaged and treatment would have succeeded, or insufficient blood vessels remained intact and he was doomed to develop avascular necrosis. Likewise, in *Gregg* it was held that the 42 per cent chance of recovery

---

[66] Stapleton, 'Loss of the Chance of Cure' (n 10) 1000.
[67] *Gregg* (HL) (n 25) [148].

meant that in a cohort of 100 patients, 42 would recover and 58 would not.[68] The claimant either was one of the 42 or one of the 58, but he did not personally have a 'chance'. Such arguments are broadly based on the idea that the physical process of disease is 'deterministic' in nature. It is this issue of determinism of causal processes that will be examined in further detail. These cases were correctly decided. The fact that the claimants were unable to prove causation but put forward the loss of chance argument seeking to recover a proportion of the value of the relevant physical harm shows that they were effectively asking to be compensated for the mere possibility that the defendant had caused them physical harm. As the previous section showed, the 'chance' in *Hotson* was actually a quantification of the judge's doubt over the causal link. This is inconsistent with corrective justice where a wrongdoer is required to repair a loss because she caused it through her wrongdoing.

Following the decision in *Hotson*, the concept of chance was elaborated in an article by Helen Reece,[69] in which she sought to reconcile *Hotson* with the earlier decision in *Chaplin v Hicks*.[70] In *Chaplin*, the claimant was a woman who had entered a beauty contest organised by the defendant. Entrants were narrowed down to a final group of 50 women who were then invited to an appointment with the defendant who would select 12 winners from this group. The claimant was unable to keep her appointment and sued the defendant for breach of contract for failing to give her a reasonable opportunity to present herself for an appointment. The defendant argued that damages could not be quantified, but the Court of Appeal held that since the claimant had roughly a one in four chance of winning (ie 12 out of 50 chance) she should be awarded 25 per cent of the value of the prize that she would have received had she won the competition.

Reece argues that the distinction lies in the causal process itself which was 'deterministic' in *Hotson* but '(quasi) indeterministic' in *Chaplin*. By 'deterministic' she means the 'hypothetical chain of events is *fully determined by the events which have occurred*'.[71] This means that in a deterministic world, given sufficient knowledge, the cause of anything could be discovered and the future could be predicted with certainty. In contrast, if a process is indeterministic it occurs randomly and cannot be predicted even with unlimited knowledge. Reece explains that in an indeterministic process, probability is an objective concept. The likelihood of a future event occurring has an objective probability that is a property of the natural

---

[68] Assuming these figures were based on reliable evidence.

[69] Helen Reece, 'Losses of Chances in the Law' (1996) 59 *Modern Law Review* 188.

[70] *Chaplin v Hicks* [1911] 2 KB 786 (CA).

[71] Reece, 'Losses of Chances in the Law' (n 69) 192. She provides the following explanation from Laplace: 'We ought then to regard the present state of the universe as the effect of its anterior state and as the cause of the one which is to follow. Given for one instant an intelligence which could comprehend all the forces by which nature is animated and the respective situation of the beings who compose it—an intelligence sufficiently vast to submit these data to analysis—it would embrace in the same formula the movements of the greatest bodies of the universe and those of the lightest atom; for it, nothing would be uncertain and the future, as the past, would be present to its eyes' (Laplace, *Philosophical Essay on Probabilities* (1819, Springer-Verlag English translation 1995) 4).

world. In contrast, in a deterministic process there is no objective probability of something occurring—either it will or it will not and theoretically this can be predicted with certainty. So when probability is used to describe the chance of such an event, the probability is not objective but epistemological; it is an expression of the likelihood of an event given the limited knowledge that is available. Reece explains, for example, that in an accident where a motorist drives into a pedestrian who then suffers broken bones, the bones break because the force of the car is applied to them 'and bones do not break in the same way on a random basis'.[72] Similarly, given sufficient knowledge it would be possible to predict with certainty whether or not a pedestrian's bones would be broken in any particular case. So when road safety advertisements say that if a car hits a child at 40mph there is an 80 per cent chance that the child will die, but at 30mph there is an 80 per cent chance that the child will live, this is an epistemological assessment of the 'chance' that the child will die, but in any particular case the outcome (life or death) would be determined by the precise conditions. Given sufficient knowledge, in the instant that a child is hit by the car it would be possible to say with certainty that this child will live or die. Often we lack sufficient knowledge and the residual uncertainty is managed, in negligence law, through the balance of probabilities standard of proof. In contrast, the decay of a Uranium atom is random, as is the outcome of a lottery which cannot be predicted so the holder of a lottery ticket has an objective chance of winning.[73] In these indeterministic cases, Reece concludes, the balance of probabilities standard of proof simply cannot cope so the courts turn to a loss of chance approach which reflects the underlying existence of an objective probability.[74] So she rejects the notion of 'loss of a chance' as damage unless there was an objective chance.

Reece argues that the causal process involved in *Hotson* was deterministic:

> [T]here was a time in the past when the cause of the necrosis could have been determined. If the blood vessels had been examined after the fall, then it would have been humanly possible to decide whether or not the plaintiff would develop necrosis even if he were treated. At the time of the trial the cause was uncertain, but the uncertainty was epistemological not objective.[75]

Since the claimant did not have an objective chance of recovery, Reece concludes that the 'loss of a chance' cannot form the gist of the negligence action. This echoes the analysis in chapter two where the NESS test was applied to the facts of *Hotson* and it was seen that the 'sufficient set' for avascular necrosis is 'insufficient blood vessels intact to keep the epiphysis alive'. The relevant question is whether the blood vessels damaged due to the delay were necessary for the sufficiency of this set. In other words, when the claimant first went to hospital were there sufficient blood vessels remaining intact for the epiphysis to stay alive? It is clear that

---

[72] Reece (n 69) 195.
[73] ibid.
[74] ibid 204–05.
[75] ibid 196.

once a claimant has suffered physical harm the causes of this are fixed because the physical process was deterministic, so there is not a 'chance' that the defendant was a cause there is merely uncertainty as to whether she was a cause. Indeed, Lord Bridge was quite clear that the difficulty in *Hotson* was a problem of individual proof and did not involve any deeper problem that would necessitate resort to statistics. He said

> [i]n some cases, perhaps particularly medical negligence cases, causation may be so shrouded in mystery that the court can only measure statistical chances. But that was not so here. On the evidence there was a clear conflict as to what had caused the avascular necrosis.[76]

In other words, if the problem was more akin to the evidentiary gap cases where there was a lack of understanding of the causal process and the medical evidence could only furnish statistical assessments of risk then there may be a reason for considering the loss of chance approach. But in this case the causal process was understood, the problem was simply one of proof in the individual case and the claimant had not managed to persuade the judge on the balance of probabilities. This means that the loss of chance argument, as it was presented in *Hotson*, cannot be accepted.

In his dissent in *Gregg*, Lord Nicholls accepted the deterministic view of *Hotson* but appeared to assert that the causal process in *Gregg* was indeterministic:

> There was no significant uncertainty about what would have happened to Stephen Hotson's leg if treated promptly, once his condition at the time of the negligence has been determined on the usual probability basis ... Identifying Mr Gregg's condition when he first visited Dr Scott did not provide an answer to the crucial question of what would have happened if there had been no negligence. There was considerable medical uncertainty about what the outcome would have been had Mr Gregg received appropriate treatment nine months earlier.[77]

Yet the majority considered the process to be deterministic, with Lord Hoffmann explaining:

> There is no inherent uncertainty about what caused something to happen in the past or about whether something which happened in the past will cause something to happen in the future. Everything is determined by causality. What we lack is knowledge and the law deals with lack of knowledge by the concept of the burden of proof.[78]

Although there was greater uncertainty in *Gregg* in that there were more variables than simply the number of blood vessels left intact, and in that less is known about how those variables affect a patient's progress, this does not entail that the process is indeterministic. Although medical understanding of the aetiology of cancer is incomplete, a range of risk factors are known so the statistical information may

---

[76] *Hotson* (HL) (n 4) 782.
[77] *Gregg* (HL) (n 25) [38].
[78] ibid [79] (Lord Hoffmann).

be personalised taking into account characteristics of the claimant such as age, general health, spread of the cancer etc, raising the belief probability to a sufficient level for a court to accept that causation is established on the balance of probabilities. It is clear that the majority felt that there was sufficient information regarding the aetiology of this cancer to form a belief on the balance of probabilities as to whether the delay in diagnosis was a necessary element of a sufficient set. The line that Lord Nicholls sought to draw between the degree and nature of the uncertainty in *Hotson* and in *Gregg* is not a clear one. Moreover, in cases of physical injury it would be impracticable and undesirable to seek to differentiate between the degrees of uncertainty and to engage courts in proof that a process is indeterministic in order to limit the scope of an exceptional approach to causation.

Lord Nicholls' willingness in *Gregg* to accept the loss of chance argument seems to reflect a clear desire to help a claimant overcome evidentiary difficulties in the medical negligence context. He explained that 'in cases of medical negligence assessment of a patient's loss may be hampered, to greater or lesser extent, by one crucial fact being unknown and unknowable: how the particular patient would have responded to proper treatment at the right time'.[79] That, however, is the nature of a counterfactual inquiry, and it is addressed by using the balance of probabilities standard of proof. It is true that the existing disease makes it harder for a court to determine what would have happened to the claimant. In other contexts a claimant could expect to carry on unharmed unless something unusual occurs, such as a defendant's negligence; in cases such as these where the claimant is already unwell then he would have expected to suffer harm unless the doctor could cure his illness. The loss of chance argument is therefore a solution to help claimants overcome the evidentiary difficulty, as Lord Nicholls makes plain:

> In suitable cases courts are prepared to adapt their process so as to leap an evidentiary gap when overall fairness plainly so requires. *Fairchild v Glenhaven Funeral Services Ltd* is a recent illustration of this in a different context. In the present context use of statistics for the purposes of evaluating a lost chance makes good sense.[80]

Indeed, the *Fairchild/Barker* exception contributes to pressure to allow proportionate recovery for loss of chance claims because 'loss of a chance of avoiding harm' and 'increase in risk of suffering harm' are often seen as two ways of expressing the same thing. Jones has noted the apparent similarities between chance and risk:

> Although their Lordships would no doubt protest that the facts of *Barker* are at some remove from *Gregg v Scott*, the acceptance that an increase in the risk of harm can constitute actionable damage (where the harm has actually materialised) indicates that there is no conceptual objection to a claim based on the loss of a chance of a better medical outcome. The explanation for the different outcomes comes down to a choice as to which claimants, faced with causal uncertainty, deserve to be given a helping hand in the litigation lottery.[81]

---

[79] ibid [27] (Lord Nicholls).
[80] ibid [31].
[81] Michael Jones, 'Proving Causation—Beyond the 'But For' Test' (2006) 22 *Professional Negligence* 251, 268.

If loss of a chance did lead to proportionate recovery then it would be conceptually close to risk. The claimant in *Barker* suffered mesothelioma caused by asbestos inhalation but the 'evidentiary gap' in relation to the aetiology of that disease means that where the asbestos has come from a number of former employers it is impossible to say on the balance of probability that any individual source was a cause of the harm.[82] Exceptionally, the *Fairchild* test of 'material contribution to the *risk* of harm' applies. In *Barker*, the House of Lords held that the *Fairchild* test should lead to several liability so that each defendant is liable only for the extent of her contribution to the overall risk. Given that the overall risk was a risk of the physical harm that the claimant suffered, this amounted to liability for a portion of the physical harm. This was a defendant-focused solution, the claimant was still notionally entitled to compensation for the full value of the physical harm (subject to contributory negligence) but each defendant was only liable for a portion of the total loss according to the extent of her contribution to the total risk of harm. The loss of chance approach proposed by the claimants in *Hotson* and in *Gregg* awards partial recovery for the claimant although the effect would be comparable for the defendant doctor who would compensate a proportion of the physical harm corresponding to her contribution to the overall risk.

Yet the risk-based approach was applied in *Barker* in part because of an evidentiary gap relating to the overall causal process whereas in *Hotson* and in *Gregg* the problem was that despite the understanding of the causal process the claimant was unable to prove his individual case. In terms of the NESS test, the claimants in *Hotson* and in *Gregg* were unable to prove that the negligence was a *necessary* element of the sufficient set. With better evidence they would have been able to prove that the negligence was a cause of their losses. But in *Fairchild* and *Barker* the general lack of understanding of the aetiology of the disease, combined with exposure to asbestos from a number of sources, meant that one could never prove a causal link. The uncertainty there was what constitutes a *sufficient set* in the first place let alone requiring the claimant to prove that the negligence was *necessary* on this occasion.

The problems of proof are therefore very different in *Fairchild/Barker* and in the loss of chance cases, but if proportionate recovery was allowed in loss of chance cases it would effectively achieve the same outcome by holding the defendant liable for her contribution to the total risk. Proof of causation was impossible in *Fairchild/Barker*. By contrast, in *Hotson* and in *Gregg* it was merely difficult.

Part II: The 'Lost Opportunity' as Damage

In this section it will be argued that in the context of medical negligence, specifically the misdiagnosis of an existing illness, the loss of an epistemological chance

---

[82] See ch 5, text to n 75.

ought to be taken into account in recognising a distinct form of damage. Instead of approaching the question of loss of a chance as a way of assisting a claimant who faces difficulties of proof of causation of physical harm, the lost chance is examined in its own right as an interference with the patient's autonomy interest. In order to maintain a distinction between this and the loss of a chance argument advanced in *Hotson* and *Gregg* it will be labelled 'loss of opportunity'.

The essence of this argument is that within the doctor-patient relationship, when the patient visits the doctor with an existing illness, the opportunity to access treatment is something of value to the patient because it is logically prior to the claimant's right to give informed consent to any such treatment. This opportunity is an aspect of the patient's autonomy interest and is damaged when there is a worsening in the patient's statistical chance of cure by the time she is properly diagnosed and given the opportunity for treatment. In part, it is the specific nature and focus of the doctor's duty of care that justifies protection of this particular aspect of autonomy. Crucially, the prospective uncertainty at the time of treatment as to whether the patient can be cured is shared by both parties and it is this shared epistemological uncertainty that gives the opportunity value even though, with the benefit of hindsight, we may eventually discover that the patient's condition was untreatable.

Since the damage is to the patient's autonomy rather than her physical welfare it would be actionable whether or not the patient also suffers the eventual physical harm she sought to avoid. This also entails that the damage should be valued independently rather than as a proportion of the physical outcome so that it ought to have a place in the tariff set out in the Judicial College's *Guidelines for the Assessment of General Damages in Personal Injury Cases*.[83] Since this form of damage is independent of the physical outcome and would not lead to proportionate damages, it is conceptually distinct from an increase in risk, so its recognition would not have the expansionary effect that is often feared in relation to proportionate recovery for loss of a chance.[84]

I. The Patient's Autonomy Interest

An individual's autonomy, understood as the idea that 'a person controls aspects of their life, and determines their shape',[85] and the 'vision of people controlling, to some degree, their own destiny, fashioning it through successive decisions throughout their lives',[86] is a very broad interest which has not traditionally been protected in the tort of negligence. Instead, aspects of autonomy are protected

---

[83] Judicial College, *Guidelines for the Assessment of General Damages in Personal Injury Cases* (13th edn, Oxford University Press, 2015).
[84] See eg Jones, 'Proving Causation' (n 80).
[85] Joseph Raz, *The Morality of Freedom* (Clarendon Press, 1986) 144.
[86] ibid 369–70.

through other torts, notably the trespass torts. Nolan argues that the tort of negligence would expand beyond reasonable limits if it were to protect the autonomy interest comprehensively, and instead 'protection can only be accorded, as at present, to certain derivative autonomy interests—freedom of movement, reproductive autonomy and so forth—rather than to autonomy in the round'.[87] The proposal in this chapter involves only a modest expansion of the protection of autonomy, thus maintaining 'reasonable limits' on the tort of negligence.

The question of whether the setback to the patient's autonomy interest can be considered damage within the negligence inquiry depends on our definition of damage. Nolan has observed that 'it is impossible to define damage for the purposes of a negligence action without falling into circularity (for example "an interference with an interest protected by the law of negligence" or "a form of harm actionable in negligence")'.[88] Lord Hoffmann's definition of damage in *Rothwell*, as 'an abstract concept of being worse off, physically or economically',[89] is criticised because 'not all forms of being worse off count as damage' and 'in some cases the claimant may be better off, not worse off, as a result of the defendant's negligence, but this will make no difference'.[90] This is a form of being worse off that, it is argued, should be recognised as damage in negligence, and if the claimant is eventually better off in the sense of being cured it does not impact on the recognition of the loss of opportunity as damage since there are two different interests at stake, autonomy and physical welfare.

The House of Lords decision in *Rees v Darlington Memorial Hospital NHS Trust* protected a patient's reproductive autonomy through an award of damages in negligence.[91] In that case, the claimant became pregnant following a negligently performed sterilisation by the defendant doctor. It was held that the parents should be awarded a conventional sum of £15,000 for the injury to their 'right to limit the size of their family'.[92] This was also articulated as the parents' (particularly the mother's) 'opportunity to live her life in the way that she wished and planned',[93] and characterised as an injury to the parents' autonomy.[94] Nolan acknowledges that conceiving of this award of damages as compensatory rather than vindicatory

> represents a significant departure from established principles of actionable damage, since loss of autonomy would no longer be merely a compensatable aspect of a more orthodox form of damage (as with loss of amenity and personal injury): it would instead amount to an actionable injury in its own right.[95]

---

[87] Donal Nolan, 'New Forms of Damage in Negligence' (2007) 70 *Modern Law Review* 59, 87. He notes that Raz makes a similar argument: Raz (n 85) 247.

[88] Donal Nolan, 'Damage in the English Law of Negligence' (2013) 4 *Journal of European Tort Law* 259, 265.

[89] *Rothwell v Chemical and Insulating Co Ltd* [2007] UKHL 39, [2007] 3 WLR 876.

[90] Nolan, 'Damage' (n 88) 265.

[91] *Rees v Darlington Memorial Hospital NHS Trust* [2003] UKHL 52, [2004] 1 AC 309.

[92] ibid [122] (Lord Millett).

[93] Ibid [8] (Lord Bingham).

[94] ibid [125] (Lord Millett).

[95] Nolan 'New Forms' (n 87) 79.

Yet he argues that it is best understood as constituting a new form of actionable damage since the damage requirement is central to negligence.[96] Stevens objects, however, that 'if loss of autonomy is a form of harm for which damages are recoverable, should it not always be recoverable? Puncturing the tyres of my bicycle reduces my autonomy as well'.[97] Recognising harm to the claimant's autonomy as a form of actionable damage is clearly not uncontroversial but it will be argued that this particular aspect of a patient's autonomy ought to be protected and that the justifications for its protection arise because of the considerations of interpersonal justice that are specific to the doctor-patient relationship. These justifications therefore also act to tightly circumscribe its application so that negligence is not extended to cover autonomy interests more widely.

In arguing that a particular loss should constitute damage within the negligence inquiry, Priaulx identifies two questions that must be addressed: 'how and in what way had [the claimant] been made "appreciably worse off"?', and in recognising this as damage, what are 'the normative reasons as to why that step *should* be taken'?[98] It is to these questions that we now turn.

A. The Loss Suffered by the Claimant

The first limb of this argument is that the patient is worse off in a case where negligent misdiagnosis reduces her epistemological chance of a cure, even if she is ultimately cured, because she suffers an interference with her autonomy interest since the diagnosis is a necessary prerequisite of making informed decisions about treatment.

Autonomy is not the sole principle at stake in the doctor-patient relationship but sits alongside the others of the four ethical principles identified by Beauchamp and Childress: non-maleficence, beneficence and (distributive) justice.[99] While patient autonomy currently dominates medical ethics,[100] in the negligence context the focus is generally on the patient's physical well-being, so non-maleficence and beneficence are usually prioritised, but Clark and Nolan suggest that while the 'healthcare professional's more general duty of care … would usually be thought of as protecting the patient's *welfare*, as opposed to her *autonomy*',[101] it 'would

---

[96] See also Nicolette Priaulx 'Joy to the World! A (Healthy) Child is Born! Reconceptualising "Harm" in Wrongful Conception' (2004) 13 *Social & Legal Studies* 5, 15–17.

[97] Robert Stevens, 'Rights and Other Things' in Donal Nolan and Andrew Robertson (eds), *Rights and Private Law* (Hart Publishing, 2012) 135.

[98] Nicky Priaulx, 'Injuries That Matter: Manufacturing Damage in Negligence' ExpressO Available at: http://works.bepress.com/nicolette_priaulx/2.

[99] Tom L Beauchamp and James F Childress, *Principles of Biomedical Ethics* (7th edn, Oxford University Press, 2012)

[100] Charles Foster, *Choosing Life, Choosing Death: The Tyranny of Autonomy in Medical Ethics and Law* (Hart Publishing, 2009) 3.

[101] Tamsyn Clark and Donal Nolan, 'A Critique of *Chester v Afshar*' (2014) 34 *Oxford Journal of Legal Studies* 659, 675.

be foolish to deny its central significance for the doctor-patient relationship'.[102] One aspect of autonomy that they describe is as 'a function of the range of choice realistically available to the individual'.[103] They argue that there is an autonomy violation in cases of medical non-disclosure of risk such as *Chester v Afshar*,[104] despite the fact that the patient still chooses whether or not to undergo the procedure, because:

> The better our understanding of the choice, the more autonomous the choice is, and the more information we have about the choice, the better our understanding is likely to be.[105]

This is evident in the shift that has taken place in determining the doctor's breach of duty towards a patient in relation to advice about treatment and its risks, which has moved away from the medical paternalism of *Sidaway*,[106] to recognise the importance of respect for patient autonomy in the recent decision in *Montgomery v Lanarkshire*.[107] The violation of the patient's autonomy interest is arguably even clearer in cases of negligent failure to diagnose than in cases of negligent failure to warn of risk: in the latter the patient is at least presented with the *choice* of undergoing treatment, in the former the misdiagnosis means that the patient is not aware of her condition so is not given the option or opportunity for treatment. It should not matter whether the patient lacks proper information regarding treatment or information regarding the existence of the illness itself; in both instances the patient is effectively unable to make an informed decision regarding treatment.[108]

It could be argued that the patient in a failure to warn case is required to make an informed decision about a positive intervention that itself carries risk, whereas a patient in a failure to diagnose case is denied knowledge about an existing illness and the risks of not receiving treatment. In other words, the failure to warn concerns the risks of intervention, failure to diagnose concerns the risks of non-intervention. If the concern was merely to protect informed consent, then this would perhaps be persuasive since it serves to legitimate the doctor's intervention, for instance, Maclean states that 'the role of consent is to give the actor permission

---

[102] ibid 677.
[103] ibid 680.
[104] *Chester v Afshar* [2004] UKHL 41; [2005] 1 AC 134.
[105] Clark and Nolan (n 101) 678. See also Kumaralingam Amirthalingam, 'Causation and the Medical Duty to Refer' (2012) 128 *Law Quarterly Review* 208, 210; Jose Miola, 'Autonomy Rued, Ok?' (2006) 14 *Medical Law Review* 108, 113. The decision in *Chester* and the autonomy-based analysis of it will be discussed below.
[106] *Sidaway v. Governors of the Bethlam Royal Hospital* [1985] AC 871.
[107] *Montgomery v Lanarkshire Health Board* [2015] UKSC 11, [2015] 2 WLR 768. See Tracey Elliott, 'A Break with the Past? Or More of the Same? *Montgomery v Lanarkshire Health Board*' (2015) 31 *Professional Negligence* 190.
[108] Note that the patient's autonomy interest is not limitless; eg, there is no right to insist on treatment that is not clinically indicated: *R (on the application of Burke) v General Medical Council* [2005] EWCA Civ 1003, [2005] 3 WLR 1132 (CA).

to do something that would otherwise be illegitimate'.[109] The focus here, however, is on the patient's autonomy interest more broadly conceived. Although there is not a single accepted definition of autonomy,[110] it is generally defined more broadly than simply involving the right to make our own decisions and also incorporates 'the ability to determine the shape of our own lives'.[111] Dworkin says 'What makes an individual the particular person he is his life-plan, his projects. In pursuing autonomy, one shapes one's life, one constructs its meaning'.[112] This allows us to see the risks of intervention and of non-intervention as two sides of the same coin: a patient deciding whether to undergo treatment will not necessarily be weighing competing treatment options but may well be weighing treatment against non-treatment. The patient may have good reasons, or indeed bad reasons, for declining treatment; the law on informed consent seeks to protect her autonomy so it does not only protect 'good' decisions, it protects the making of informed decisions.

Where there has been the loss of an epistemological chance, the patient has lost the right to make decisions about her treatment with their original likelihood of success. She has also lost the right to make such decisions at the particular time, and her own priorities and personal life may have altered during this delay. This is important because protection of the patient's autonomy requires respect for the patient's medical and non-medical priorities as McLean argues:

> While doctors are committed to being guided by the best interests of their patients, the competent patient is, and needs to be, the ultimate arbiter of what these interests actually are, and this will often be informed by a variety of non-medical matters.[113]

This subjective nature of decision-making was recognised in the Supreme Court decision in *Montgomery v Lanarkshire* which prioritised autonomy over medical paternalism in setting the standard of care in respect of warning of risks involved in treatment:

> The relative importance attached by patients to quality as against length of life, or to physical appearance or bodily integrity as against the relief of pain, will vary from one patient to another. Countless other examples could be given of the ways in which the views or circumstances of an individual patient may affect their attitude towards a proposed form of treatment and the reasonable alternatives.[114]

It may seem contradictory to accept that Stephen Hotson would have suffered physical harm even with proper diagnosis and treatment and still claim that he would have done better to have had that diagnosis and treatment. But denying that the reduction in the epistemological chance is a setback to his physical integrity

---

[109] Alasdair Maclean, *Autonomy, Informed Consent and Medical Law* (Cambridge University Press, 2009) 196.

[110] See Foster, *Choosing Life, Choosing Death* (n 100) 7–9 for four senses in which it is used.

[111] Sheila McLean, *Autonomy, Consent and the Law* (Routledge Cavendish, 2010) 1.

[112] Gerald Dworkin, *The Theory and Practice of Autonomy* (Cambridge University Press, 1988) 31.

[113] McLean (n 111) 43.

[114] *Montgomery* (n 107) [46] (Lord Kerr and Lord Reed).

does not entail denying that it is a setback to an aspect of his autonomy. Crucially, at the time of the misdiagnosis both the doctor and the patient regard the outcome of treatment as being uncertain, and this shared prospective uncertainty lends a focus to the doctor's duty meaning both regard the opportunity for treatment as something of value. After all, at the time of diagnosis and treatment, the outcome is uncertain for both the patient and the doctor. Perry explains:

> The plaintiff in *Hotson*, for example, would clearly have done better if he had gone, either initially or immediately following his first examination by the defendants, to doctors who would have given him proper treatment. This is not to say that he would ultimately have been better off if he had received such treatment, but only that he would have made a better choice if he had gone to persons who were able to provide it; at least where the outcome of treatment cannot be known with certainty in advance, which was the case in *Hotson*, it is clearly preferable to be treated competently rather than incompetently.[115]

Where the patient's autonomy rather than welfare underlies the gist damage, the idea of being better or worse off turns not on the physical outcome but on the patient's ability to make choices leading to that outcome.

The question of course arises whether this form of damage loses its significance where the patient is a child, as was the case in *Hotson*, and lacks competence to consent to treatment.[116] It is the child's parents who consent to medical treatment, but 'where the patient lacks competence to make his or her own treatment decisions … beneficence stakes a claim for priority',[117] so decisions must be made in the child's best interests and her physical well-being is prioritised. It is helpful to consider what the outcome would have been in *Chester* if the victim there had been a child, so supposing there was a negligent failure to inform her parents of the risks involved in the treatment to which they consented, and to which they may or may not have consented at a later date having sought a second opinion. It would be strange for a court to refuse a remedy simply because the claimant is a child, but this alone is not a strong justification. Although it is the parents who give consent, it would not be argued that their autonomy interest has been violated by the failure to give adequate warning of the risks of treatment since their consent in this situation is not so much an exercise of their autonomy as their parental responsibility. Despite that, there surely remains a duty on the part of the doctor to warn the parents of the risks involved in treatment so that their consent is informed consent, so what would be the damage where there is a failure to warn the parents of the risks to their child? Although a child does not have a right to consent, it could be argued that they still have an interest in autonomy and that this is exercised, to a degree, through the parents. McLean suggests that 'children *do* have rights, but decisions are taken for them in order that they may ultimately be able

[115] Stephen Perry, 'Protected Interests and Undertakings in the Law of Negligence' (1992) 42 *University of Toronto Law Journal* 247, 309.
[116] Note that a *Gillick* competent child can consent to treatment: *Gillick v West Norfolk and Wisbech Area Health Authority* [1986] 1 AC 112.
[117] Elizabeth Wicks, *Human Rights and Healthcare* (Hart Publishing, 2007) 91.

to do so for themselves'.[118] Ost suggests that children do have autonomy rights, but they are overridden by concerns for the child's physical welfare.[119] For example where a child is involved in research and reveals that she is potentially at risk of harm, Ost highlights that the National Children's Bureau guidelines state that if the researcher decides to inform others they should discuss this with the child and 'hopefully' obtain their consent. She explains that 'whilst the guidelines start from a position of perceiving children as subjects with autonomy rights, the "children as objects" approach is then adopted and prioritised if a child is considered to be at risk of harm'.[120] This indicates that children do have an autonomy interest, but that it can be overridden in order to protect the child's physical well-being. Hollingsworth distinguishes de facto autonomy, the 'competence and opportunities necessary to exercise that right', from de jure autonomy, the 'legal right to self-government'.[121] In her opinion the difference between children and adults relates to their 'procedural enjoyment of their rights', so that 'where the child does not have de jure autonomy, the decision to exercise "remedial rights" is made on her behalf by a third party ... often ... on the basis of her perceived best interests'.[122] Whilst very young children will lack de facto autonomy in the sense of lacking competence, a doctor's negligent misdiagnosis deprives them of the 'opportunities necessary to exercise that right', so we can still see damage to the child's limited autonomy interest. Given that '*Gillick* competence' in medical law depends not on the child's age but on her development, it would be untenable to suggest that the 'opportunities' aspect of her autonomy interest only comes into existence at the same time as competence. The ability for anyone to make a decision in the child's best interests, whether it is the parents or the doctor, remains dependent on there being a diagnosis in the first place, so the loss of an epistemological chance retains significance for a child even if the child has less control over subsequent treatment.

The focus so far has been on the question of how the patient can be said to be appreciably worse off where negligent misdiagnosis causes the loss of an epistemological chance of cure, and this has been premised on the idea that it involves damage to the patient's autonomy interest. The analysis now turns to the remaining question whether there are convincing normative reasons why this should be recognised as damage in negligence.

---

[118] Sheila McLean, *A Patient's Right to Know: Information Disclosure, the Doctor and the Law* (Dartmouth Publishing, 1995) 43.

[119] Suzanne Ost, 'Balancing Autonomy Rights and Protection: Children's Involvement in a Child Safety Online Project' (2013) 27 *Children and Society* 208, 210.

[120] ibid 210; NCB, *Guidelines for Research* (NCB, 2003).

[121] Kathryn Hollingsworth, 'Theorising Children's Rights in Youth Justice: The Significance of Autonomy and Foundational Rights' (2013) 76 *Modern Law Review* 1046, 1058.

[122] ibid 1058.

B. The Place of Autonomy within the Doctor-Patient Relationship

Chapter one highlighted the importance of coherence and the need for the negligence doctrines to 'articulate a single normative sequence'.[123] Since negligence is a corrective justice-based system of interpersonal responsibility, the reasons for recognising the loss of opportunity as damage are therefore sought in the relationship between the doctor and patient. The doctor's duty of care is particularly focused on diagnosis and, because the doctor shares the patient's prospective uncertainty about the outcome of treatment, the epistemological chance has value in the eyes of both the patient and the doctor. In respect of the physical outcome the deterministic model is appropriate, but a patient weighing up the risks of treatment in order to give consent is necessarily dealing with epistemological risks because of the prospective nature of her decision, and the doctor is similarly only able to provide her with epistemological risks. When we are considering damage to the patient's autonomy interest it is therefore appropriate to focus on her epistemological chance and the opportunity for treatment associated with it.

i. The Focus of the Doctor's Duty of Care

A particular feature of the doctor-patient relationship is its practical focus on this aspect of the patient's autonomy. Amirthalingam considers it important that in cases where recovery is allowed for loss of a chance, such as *Chaplin v Hicks*[124] and *Kitchen v RAF*,[125] 'the purpose of the duty in question was either to protect the claimant from being deprived of economic opportunity or to provide the claimant with an opportunity to recover losses'.[126] McGregor similarly identifies a distinguishing characteristic of those cases as involving relationships where 'the provision of the chance is the object of the duty that has been breached'.[127] Given that a doctor cannot generally guarantee a cure, a distinct objective of her duty is to give the patient the opportunity for treatment. In *Wright v Cambridge Medical Group*,[128] the defendant doctor's negligence lay in the failure to refer the claimant to hospital for appropriate treatment, resulting in a three-day delay in admission to hospital. In that case, Dame Janet Smith observed that 'it was not within

---

[123] Ernest Weinrib, 'The Jurisprudence of Legal Formalism' (1993) 16 *Harvard Journal of Law and Public Policy* 583, 593.

[124] *Chaplin* (n 70)

[125] *Kitchen v Royal Air Force Association* [1958] 1 WLR 563.

[126] Kumaralingam Amirthalingam, 'The Changing Face of the Gist of Negligence' in Jason W Neyers, Erika Chamberlain and Stephen GA Pitel (eds), *Emerging Issues in Tort Law* (Hart Publishing, 2007) 481.

[127] Harvey McGregor, 'Loss of a Chance: Where Has it Come From and Where is it Going?' (2008) 24 *Professional Negligence* 2, 6.

[128] *Wright (A Child) v Cambridge Medical Group* [2011] EWCA Civ 669, [2013] QB 312.

the scope of [the defendant's] duty to treat [the claimant], only to refer her as expeditiously as was practicable so as to reduce her period of suffering and to give her the best possible opportunity for recovery'.[129] Indeed, Amirthalingam argues:

> The general practitioner of today is more often than not a gate keeper, whose principal role is to make a diagnosis and refer the patient to the relevant specialist for treatment. In cases of potentially serious illness or disease, a patient goes to the general practitioner in order to be referred to the appropriate specialist who is trained to treat the particular problem. The sole purpose of the general practitioner's duty in such cases is to provide the patient with the opportunity of a timely referral to the appropriate specialist.[130]

This reasoning is not limited to general practitioners since experience shows that referral to a specialist nowadays does not necessarily involve treatment by that specialist, who will instead refer the patient to a range of other doctors for diagnostic tests and eventual treatment. So much depends not only on the chance of the treatment being successful, but on its performance by other healthcare practitioners, that each doctor involved in diagnosis can meaningfully be said to provide a patient with the opportunity for treatment.

Given that this is a key component of the doctor's duty towards her patient there is not a concern that it would be unforeseeable to the doctor that the opportunity is valued by the patient. Where autonomy is currently protected in negligence in cases of wrongful conception, Nolan argues that it is significant that the pregnancy was unwanted by the individual in question rather than whether pregnancy is more generally considered desirable, because it is the *individual's* autonomy that is at stake. The relationship between the parties is important there as he explains:

> Where the existence of damage depends not only on what takes place, but also on the claimant's attitude towards it, there is a possibility that a defendant could be held liable for causing an outcome which the claimant considers harmful, but which the defendant could not reasonably have foreseen would be perceived in such terms. Clearly, though, this line of argument is not open to a doctor who has negligently carried out a sterilisation or a vasectomy.[131]

This is an important consideration since it was recognised in chapter one that coherence requires that '[t]he negligence concepts form an ensemble that brackets and articulates a single normative sequence'.[132] Cases of misdiagnosis do not suffer from the objection that the patient is unusual in desiring the opportunity for proper treatment,[133] and it is more than simply foreseeable to the doctor that the patient will value this opportunity—the patient has presumably gone to see her doctor because she suspects she is unwell and is seeking a diagnosis and possible treatment, and a key element of the doctor's duty is to provide this opportunity.

---

[129] ibid [129] (Dame Janet Smith).

[130] Amirthalingam, 'The Changing Face of the Gist of Negligence' (n 126) 482.

[131] Nolan, 'New Forms' (n 87) 75.

[132] Weinrib, 'The Jurisprudence of Legal Formalism' (n 123) 593.

[133] Of course not all patients will desire treatment, particularly where such treatment will be aggressive and the prognosis is weak, but the interest at stake here is the opportunity to make that decision.

Beyond foreseeability, a further defining characteristic of the doctor-patient relationship, identified by Perry, is that it involves an undertaking on the part of the doctor that further justifies protection of the patient's opportunity to access treatment:

> A doctor who treats a patient is implicitly representing that he or she has a certain level of medical skill and competence and that the patient, in submitting to treatment, can rely on the doctor to exercise that skill and competence. The doctor can, in other words, be reasonably taken as intending to induce a belief in the patient that he or she may rely on the doctor to provide treatment that will be in accordance with appropriate standards. In so relying the patient shifts his or her position to the extent that other choices, such as going to a different doctor or seeking a second opinion, are foregone and eventually foreclosed.[134]

Since this form of loss is not only foreseeable within the doctor-patient relationship, but also forms a distinct focus of the doctor's duty of care, considerations of interpersonal responsibility weigh in favour of its recognition as damage.

ii. The Nature and Extent of the Uncertainty

There is a logical force to recognising loss of an epistemological chance as damage because the epistemological uncertainty is shared by the doctor and patient and underpins the need for informed consent. Although the physical process may be described as deterministic on Reece's definition, at the time of diagnosis the outcome remains unknowable for both parties. The epistemological uncertainty shapes the exercise of the patient's right to give informed consent—she must be informed of the risks so that she can measure them against her own concerns and priorities. Essentially, the law ought to recognise reduction in the epistemological chance as damage because it is this epistemological chance that the patient ultimately is weighing up when she exercises her autonomy through the right to give or withhold consent to treatment.

Reece's definition of determinism may be an acceptable theoretical and philosophical definition relating to the physical outcome,[135] but it does not reflect the experience of the doctor and the patient at the time of diagnosis and treatment, and it is this perspective that is relevant to the patient's autonomy interest since the exercise of autonomy necessarily involves weighing prospective risks. Even with her medical knowledge and understanding, the doctor is unable to predict the outcome with certainty, instead describing the patient as having a chance of recovery and then treating the illness. Providing appropriate treatment is the way the doctor finds out whether the patient could or could not be cured.

---

[134] Perry, 'Protected Interests and Undertakings in the Law of Negligence' (n 115) 308.
[135] See text to n 71.

UNIVERSITY OF WINCHESTER
LIBRARY

As Lord Nicholls argued, the doctor regards the patient as having a chance of being cured, explaining:

> the law should be exceedingly slow to disregard medical reality in the context of a legal duty whose very aim is to protect medical reality. In these cases the doctor's duty to act in the best interests of his patient involves maximising the patient's recovery prospects, and doing so whether the patient's prospects are good or not so good.[136]

In a case such as *Hotson* the process is deterministic, and medical science has advanced enough to understand that it is the state of the blood vessels that determines whether the damage will occur. But, in any individual case, when the doctor commences treatment both she and the patient regard the outcome as involving a chance because they simply do not know whether sufficient blood vessels remain intact. Even with careful treatment the doctor cannot guarantee that the treatment will succeed or fail because there are factors beyond her control and because she does not know whether there are enough blood vessels remaining intact.

Similarly, in a case such as *Gregg* the doctor effectively treats the patient as though he has a chance of recovering. When Mr Gregg was eventually referred to a specialist who diagnosed the lump as cancer his chance of survival if treated was assessed at 10–15 per cent.[137] Although the doctor may explain that this chance is not personal to the patient and that it means 10–15 per cent of patients in his position will survive, the doctor still provides treatment. Even armed with knowledge of the extent and location of the cancer, and with understanding of factors that affect survival rates, the doctor was unable to say whether Mr Gregg was one of the 10–15 out of 100 who would survive or one of the 85–90 out of 100 who would die even with treatment. Since the delay has reduced the epistemological chance, and the epistemological chance is all that is currently available to the parties for the weighing of risks and decisions regarding treatment in the exercise of her autonomy, reduction in this chance ought to be recognised as damage.

C. The Limited Scope of Loss of Opportunity as Damage

Since this approach focuses on the restriction of the patient's choice through the denial of the opportunity for treatment, it does not suffer from conceptual proximity to the notion of risk in the way that proportionate recovery for the loss of a chance of cure suffers. This means that it does not put pressure on decisions such as *Wilsher* in the way that proportionate recovery has the potential to do. In *Wilsher*,[138] the claimant was a baby who had been born prematurely and later

---

[136] *Gregg* (HL) (n 25) [42]. I am grateful to Tracey Elliott for pointing out the caveat that the duty can only be to maximise the patient's recovery prospects within the framework of the available NHS resources since there may be treatments that the NHS will not fund.

[137] *Gregg* (CA) (n 27) [13] (Latham LJ). This was his 'chance' at the time of diagnosis—by time of trial his chance was assessed at 20–30%.

[138] *Wilsher v Essex Area Health Authority* [1988] AC 1074 (HL).

suffered blindness caused by a condition called retrolentalfibroplasia ('RLF'). While in hospital he received negligent medical treatment when a catheter was inserted into a vein rather than an artery leading to incorrect measurement of the oxygen levels in his blood and the hospital therefore administering excess oxygen. Excessive oxygen in the blood is known to cause RLF, but due to his being born prematurely the baby also suffered four other conditions that each also carried a risk of RLF. He was unable to prove on the balance of probabilities that it was the excess oxygen rather than one of the naturally occurring conditions that caused his blindness and the House of Lords refused to apply the *McGhee* test of material contribution to the risk of harm in this case.[139] Since it was not possible to identify on the balance of probabilities which harmful agent (eg oxygen) had caused the illness, it was not possible to say that the defendant had contributed to the relevant risk factor. Stapleton has argued:

> [T]he pure loss-of-a-chance claim in *Gregg* might indirectly have put pressure on the decision on *Wilsher* which has been recently and unanimously approved by the Lords in *Fairchild*. At the moment after breach might baby Wilsher have had a loss of a chance claim of the sort contemplated by Lord Nicholls because his premature condition gave rise to a 'significant medical uncertainty'? Even the adoption of the control mechanism, or 'artificial hook', of requiring that the breach had caused a physical change might not prevent such a pre-blindness claim being made by baby Wilsher, who could argue that the excessively oxygenated blood resulting from breach was such an 'injury'.[140]

There are two issues to address here. The first relates to the 'hook' argument. This has already been discussed in detail to show that there would have to be a causal relationship between the physical 'hook' and the related chances. It is important to note that a physical change does not constitute damage until it makes the claimant worse off, so excessively oxygenated blood would not constitute a 'hook'.[141]

The second issue is that in *Wilsher* the doctor exposed the baby to a discrete risk, independent of the naturally occurring risks, so any interference was with the patient's physical welfare rather than his autonomy interest. When there is a negligent failure to warn of risk there are two issues at stake: whether the negligence has interfered with the patient's autonomy interest embodied by the right to give informed consent, and whether the negligence has also interfered with the patient's bodily integrity by causing physical damage. The physical exposure to the risk of RLF in *Wilsher* concerns the patient's physical welfare, and is separate from any informational deficit that impacts on autonomy via consent.

The above analysis has shown that the doctor-patient relationship is special because of its focus not only on the patient's welfare but also her autonomy. The opportunity for treatment, and the opportunity to weigh up the risks of treatment with the initial prospects of success, are aspects of the patient's autonomy interest

---

[139] The *McGhee* test was applied in *Fairchild* and is more commonly known as the *Fairchild* test today, but *Wilsher* was decided in the interval between those two decisions.

[140] Stapleton, 'Loss of the Chance of Cure' (n 10) 1003.

[141] *Rothwell* (n 89).

and ought to be protected. The provision of this opportunity is an important function of the doctor's duty of care, and within the doctor-patient relationship it is not only foreseeable that the patient values this opportunity, but also that the patient relies on the doctor's advice. Although epistemological chance cannot be protected in a claim relating to the patient's physical welfare, epistemological chances form the basis of the patient's weighing of her treatment options and ought properly to be protected in respect of her autonomy interest.

II. Orthodox Application of the Remaining Negligence Doctrines

Since this approach concerns only the damage that forms the gist of the negligence action, the remaining negligence principles would continue to apply in the traditional way. The claimant must establish that the defendant doctor did breach her duty of care, so she must show that the reasonably competent doctor would have diagnosed the condition, or would have referred her for the relevant tests or treatment.

For there to be damage to the patient's autonomy interest the opportunity for treatment with the original chance of success must have been lost. When loss of chance is presented as a solution to the difficulty of proving causation, one objection is that it is not possible to say that the chance has been 'lost' unless it has been reduced to zero. In other words, it is only once the claimant has suffered physical harm that her chance has been definitively lost. In *Gregg*, Lord Phillips therefore left open the question of whether proportionate recovery for loss of a chance would be appropriate where physical harm had actually occurred, but on the facts of *Gregg* he considered it impossible to say whether a chance had been lost because the physical harm had not yet occurred.[142] This problem simply does not arise in the approach proposed in this chapter where the question is whether the claimant has been prevented from exercising her choice to undergo treatment with the original prospects of cure. This means that it is the fact of a reduction in the statistical chance that entails a 'loss' of the opportunity, rather than the reduction of that chance to zero. The requirement does remain, however, that there must be a reduction in the statistical chance of a cure, otherwise the patient's opportunity for treatment remains intact. The claimant must therefore prove on the balance of probabilities that the negligence caused the reduction in her statistical chance of cure. In *Hotson*, the judge found that the delay had allowed the bleeding to continue to build pressure in the joint and block those blood vessels that had remained intact, turning his injury into an inevitability. This meant that his physical state had worsened so his chance of cure was reduced by the delay caused

---

[142] *Gregg* (n 2) [190].

by the negligence. In *Gregg*, the claimant's cancer spread during the nine months' delay so it was clear that his physical state had worsened and this was responsible for the reduction in the statistical likelihood of cure. If the cancer had remained unchanged during that time then it would be hard to see that the delay caused any reduction in the chance of cure. In practice then, proof of a loss of the opportunity for proper treatment will usually require proof of a worsening of the patient's physical state in order to ground the belief that the statistical chance of cure has been reduced, so this will not have a substantial expansionary effect on liability.

It is important to note that this lost opportunity would not constitute a 'hook' on which the claimant could subsequently seek to recover damages for his lost chance of avoiding the physical outcome as a simple matter of quantification. As already discussed, there must be a causal relationship between the hook and the related chances. Since neither Stephen Hotson nor Mr Gregg were able to 'hook' their claims for loss of a chance to the physical worsening of their condition during the period of delay, they would also be unable to hook such claims to the lost opportunity for treatment.

For the purposes of limitation, in practical terms the claimant will usually acquire knowledge that the injury is significant when they receive the delayed, correct diagnosis. Although section 14(3) Limitation Act 1980 provides for constructive knowledge, including knowledge that the claimant might reasonably be expected to acquire from facts ascertainable by the claimant or with the help of medical advice, courts should be slow to find that this date occurred prior to the correct diagnosis because the doctor's negligence will have played a role in giving the patient false reassurance about her condition. Only where the claimant was manifestly unreasonable in not returning to the doctor sooner should the limitation period start prior to diagnosis, for example if there was a significant worsening of symptoms and the claimant did not seek medical advice.

A. Quantifying the Loss

The final question is how to value this damage to the patient's autonomy. In this approach the lost opportunity exists independently of the physical outcome and this has important consequences for its valuation because it means that the valuation must also be independent of the final outcome. It also means that where a chance has been lost, it is actionable regardless of whether or not the illness was cured. If a claimant suffers the physical harm and has a successful claim in respect of that outcome she should still be able to recover for the loss of a chance because that was valuable to her during her treatment—it is a distinct head of damage.[143]

---

[143] Clark and Nolan make a similar argument in relation to cases of negligent failure to warn of medical risk since the patient's autonomy is violated in those cases regardless of whether the patient would have undergone the same operation had she been properly informed of the risks (n 101) 684.

Since the damage is to an aspect of the claimant's autonomy rather than her physical well-being, the damages awarded should not be for the physical outcome. This seems obvious, yet the decision of the House of Lords in *Chester v Afshar* was based on the need to vindicate the patient's right to give informed consent, in other words it protected an aspect of her autonomy, but she was compensated for the physical damage.[144] The defendant doctor in *Chester* negligently failed to warn the claimant of a small risk involved in undergoing an operation, and that risk materialised resulting in physical harm. The claimant sought to recover damages for the physical harm, but encountered difficulty in proving the causal link between the negligent failure to warn of the risk and the harmful outcome because, even if she had been properly warned, she may still have chosen to undergo the operation at a later date having sought a second opinion. Despite finding that factual causation had not been established, in a majority decision the House of Lords awarded damages for the physical harm suffered in order to give force to the doctor's duty to warn,[145] and in order that 'her right of autonomy and dignity ... be vindicated'.[146] The claimant should instead have received a modest sum to compensate the violation of her autonomy as Clark and Nolan argue:

> The claimant in *Chester* did suffer an injury for which the defendant was responsible, but the harm was not the physical injury to her body but the violation of her autonomy. Compensating her for that injury would have obviated the need perceived by the majority to *over*-compensate her by allowing her to recover for the physical harm, while also opening the way to remedying the *under*-compensation that occurs in the no-difference and no-injury cases, where the autonomy violation still goes without redress.[147]

It is admitted that the proposed approach to misdiagnosis cases may increase pressure to recognise as damage the interference with a patient's autonomy in cases of negligent failure to warn of risk such that patients would be compensated for their autonomy damage alongside any compensation in respect of proven physical damage. What it does not do is provide a basis on which claimants in either type of case could be compensated for the physical harm that they suffer where the only damage is to their autonomy interest. It would be wrong for the law to allow a claim for one kind of damage but compensate another so this would be a positive development in opening the way for the award of a conventional sum in a case such as *Chester*.

Similarly, since the damage is to the patient's autonomy, it would be inappropriate to award damages as a proportion of the value of the claimant's physical injury since this would be indistinguishable from the loss of chance claims advanced in *Hotson* and *Gregg*. In *Hotson* the trial judge found that the claimant had lost a 25 per cent chance of avoiding avascular necrosis and awarded 25 per cent of the

---

[144] *Chester* (n 104).
[145] ibid [86]–[87] (Lord Hope) and [101] (Lord Walker).
[146] ibid [24] (Lord Steyn).
[147] Clark and Nolan (n 101) 684. See also Kenyon Mason and Douglas Brodie, 'Bolam, Bolam— Wherefore Are Thou Bolam?' (2005) *Edinburgh Law Review* 298, 305.

value of this physical damage. In *Gregg*, the claimant argued that his chance of survival had been reduced from 42 per cent to 25 per cent and the claim was for a proportion of the value of the loss that he would suffer if he failed to survive, ie a proportion of the value of the physical injury itself and of the loss of lifetime's earnings. The damage to the claimant's autonomy is much more modest, and does not entail compensation for loss of amenity, loss of earnings etc. Damages should not be awarded as a proportion of the physical harm as Voyiakis explains:

> Knowing how much risk I have imposed on you and how much compensation I would have to pay you if I had caused you actual physical harm does not by itself suggest how much I should pay for having exposed your physical health to danger. To take a crude example, when I make it 40 per cent more likely that you will suffer lung cancer, I am not causing you 40 per cent of the harm that lung cancer brings about. The quantity of risk and the quantity of physical harm do not seem to be related in any such straightforward way. We therefore have reason to object to the latter being taken as a measure of the former.[148]

This much is apparent if we recall the more straightforward causal models addressed in chapter two. There it was said that if the harm is indivisible then each of the necessary elements of the sufficient set is a cause and each is a cause of the whole loss. Apportionment of *liability* might be appropriate as a matter of moral responsibility, but each cause has causal responsibility for the whole of the harm. In contrast, where the harm is divisible, ie dose-related, then each causal factor contributes/causes a portion of the overall harm. So it seems illogical to say that a doctor who has contributed a 40 per cent risk to an indivisible harm should pay 40 per cent of the value of the physical harm. Valuing the chance as a percentage of the physical harm reinforces the sense that the loss of a chance argument as it was advanced in *Hotson* and in *Gregg* is simply an attempt to assist a claimant to bypass the causation requirement.

The argument made here, instead, is that the loss of the opportunity for treatment involves damage to the patient's autonomy rather than her physical integrity so it ought to be assessed independently of the physical outcome. It should, therefore, be treated as any other loss and assigned a value within the Judicial College's *Guidelines for the Assessment of General Damages in Personal Injury Cases*.[149] Jansen has addressed the 'pragmatic objection [which] emphasizes the difficulties of assessing the value of chances':

> [T]here are difficulties in assigning a financial value to lost chances, especially if they are related to physical harm ... It is difficult to evaluate physical injuries financially. The widely differing amounts which courts award to physically injured parties illustrate that. But this indicates only that there is no 'objective' measure as such, and that the measure, therefore is to be determined by policy considerations. Courts do manage to deal with this consistently.[150]

---

[148] Emmanuel Voyiakis, 'The Great Illusion: Tort Law and Exposure to Danger of Physical Harm' (2009) 72 *Modern Law Review* 909, 917.

[149] Judicial College, *Guidelines for the Assessment of General Damages in Personal Injury Cases* (n 83).

[150] Nils Jansen, 'The Idea of a Lost Chance' (1999) 19 *Oxford Journal of Legal Studies* 271, 293.

In other words, the value assigned to any physical injury is necessarily artificial. This has been addressed by using the tariff system so that the level of damages is commensurable with the seriousness of the injury, and the loss of opportunity could similarly be included in the tariff.

The final question is whether the loss of opportunity for treatment should be a fixed, conventional sum, or whether there should be a scale reflecting the seriousness of the physical harm to which the opportunity related. Since the claim in *Rees* concerned autonomy, namely reproductive autonomy, Wheat suggests that the award there of £15,000 might be regarded as 'a useful starting point' in valuing autonomy infringements.[151] This suggests that reproductive autonomy has a fixed value—one person's choice to limit the size of their family is not worth any more or less than another person's same choice, regardless of their background circumstances or the financial/physical consequences that flow from it. This does not mean that all cases of misdiagnosis should attract a single, conventional sum. While the £15,000 in wrongful conception cases does not vary to take account of the individual's circumstances, it does reflect the 'seriousness' of the outcome that they sought to avoid. In relation to risk, Voyiakis argues that while the value of the risk is not necessarily an equivalent percentage of the physical harm, we have an intuitive notion that some risks are more serious than others. He explains:

> This intuition seems to follow naturally from the idea that protecting oneself against risk of some harm is a means to protecting oneself against the actual harm. It also seems to tally with our intuitive comparisons across risks of different seriousness: the effect of being exposed to a 40 per cent risk of lung cancer is more serious than the effect of being exposed to a 40 per cent risk of a broken toe exactly because getting lung cancer is much more serious than getting a broken toe.[152]

This means that it would be possible to set a tariff for a lost chance. Any physical injury is represented by a range of values in the tariff, with the judge being able to use the range of the scale to reflect the impact the injury had on the individual. 'Loss of an opportunity' could have a similar scale. It would be possible to set a value for the loss of a chance of avoiding a life-threatening illness with a scale of damages to reflect a small reduction in chance or a large reduction in chance, another value for the loss of the chance of avoiding a less serious illness (or disability or temporary illness) with a similar scale to reflect the extent of the reduction in the chance. In misdiagnosis cases, sums could similarly be fixed in as much as they would not vary to take account of the individual patient's circumstances such as their epistemological chance, but could still vary along a scale to reflect the seriousness of the outcome that they sought to avoid, e.g. death, permanent disability, temporary disability etc.

---

[151] Kay Wheat, 'Progress of the Prudent Patient: Consent after *Chester v Afshar*' (2005) 60 *Anaesthesia* 217, 219.
[152] Voyiakis, 'The Great Illusion' (n 148) 917.

In recent years, medical paternalism has given way to patient autonomy as a key ethical principle in healthcare. This is apparent in the decision in *Montgomery v Lanarkshire* which cements a subjective, patient-centred approach to the standard of care in respect of a doctor's advice as to treatment options and associated risks. Whilst misdiagnosis most obviously impacts on the patient's physical well-being if it causes physical harm by denying a cure, the misdiagnosis also impacts on the patient's autonomy interest if it lowers her epistemological chance of a cure because it denies her the right to make treatment decisions and weigh up the risks against her own plans, priorities and desires. If the law is committed to prioritising patient autonomy within the doctor-patient relationship then it must be prepared to recognise interference with the patient's autonomy interest as a form of damage in negligence.

5

The Evidentiary Gap

In the remainder of this work, attention is turned towards the problem of the 'evidentiary gap' that arose in *McGhee*[1] and in *Fairchild*.[2] In this chapter it is necessary first to analyse the relevant case law in order to understand what exactly the so-called 'evidentiary gap' is. The first section will draw on the NESS analysis of causation presented in chapter two to locate the problem that arose in these cases. Whereas claimants more commonly face the problem of proving that the negligence was a *necessary* element of a sufficient set of conditions that actually occurred, it will be shown that where there is an 'evidentiary gap' the claimant faces the prior problem that the state of scientific uncertainty prevents the definition of a sufficient set of conditions for the harm that she has incurred. The subsequent sections will turn to the legal solutions that have been adopted to address the evidentiary gap. Beginning with *McGhee*, and continuing through *Fairchild* and *Barker*,[3] the courts have considered it sufficient for the claimant to prove that the defendant's negligence materially increased the risk of the relevant injury, or materially contributed to the risk of the relevant harm, in cases involving an evidentiary gap.

One interpretation of this test is that it simply alters the legal standard of proof that the claimant is required to meet, or that it allows the drawing of an inference of causation, so section II will consider whether this is an appropriate solution. Drawing on the discussion of the standard of proof in chapter three, ultimately it will be argued that given the nature of the gap in scientific understanding surrounding the aetiology (the 'evidentiary gap') it is inappropriate for the law to attempt to bridge this gap—such resort to intuition in the face of explicit scientific uncertainty would base liability on a fiction. The result is that the defendant may be held liable even though her negligence was probably not a cause of the harm.

Section III will therefore turn to the alternative interpretation of the *Fairchild* test, as proposed in *Barker*, that in cases where the test applies the damage which forms the gist of the negligence action is the increase in risk.[4] Liability

---

[1] *McGhee v National Coal Board* [1973] 1 WLR 1 (HL (Sc)).

[2] *Fairchild v Glenhaven Funeral Services (t/a GH Dovener & Son)* [2002] UKHL 22, [2003] 1 AC 32.

[3] *Barker v Corus* [2006] UKHL 20, [2006] 2 AC 572.

[4] Although the majority in *BAI v Durham* [2012] UKSC 14, [2012] 1 WLR 867 considered that the gist of the action was still the physical harm and that the decision in *Barker* had simply equated 'materially increasing the risk' with 'contributing to the cause', Lord Phillips (dissenting) insisted that the rule in *Barker* was that where the *Fairchild* test of 'material increase in the risk of harm' is applied the gist of the action is the risk of harm.

under *Barker* was several (rather than joint and several) and the extent of an individual defendant's liability was to be measured by the extent of her contribution to the total risk to which the claimant was exposed. At first glance this solution appears to conform to corrective justice because a defendant is held liable only for that loss which she has been proved to have caused, ie since she has only been proved to have increased the risk of the claimant's injury, she is only held liable for this increase in risk. However, closer analysis shows a number of flaws in this approach. By insisting that the claimant have suffered the relevant physical harm before allowing her to bring a negligence action for exposure to the risk of this harm the effect is that the physical harm remains the gist of the action and the apportionment of liability that takes place reflects the possibility that the defendant caused the harm. This echoes the criticism of proportionate recovery for 'loss of a chance'—the reality is that it is liability for possible causation of harm. Furthermore, liability for risk is a more deeply problematic concept. Risk is a forward-looking concept so is mismatched with the backward-looking causation enquiry. More importantly, risk lacks moral significance as damage in the context of the negligence enquiry because it does not add anything to the breach of duty requirement. Conduct is wrongful if the defendant failed to take reasonable care, ie she exposed the claimant to an unreasonable risk of harm. If 'exposure to risk' also constitutes actionable damage then the damage requirement would effectively be subsumed into the breach inquiry. This is inconsistent with corrective justice which is concerned with 'wrongful loss' not with wrongdoing in isolation.

The final section will refocus on corrective justice and argue that these claims ought to fail for want of proof of causation since the approaches explored in previous sections fail to achieve consistency with corrective justice. Since the defendant is liable in circumstances where she may not have been a cause of the loss, corrective justice is abandoned in these cases in favour of the pursuit of consequentialist goals. The effect of this has been to throw negligence into the state of incoherence that is inherent in the pursuit of consequentialist goals within the bipolar framework of the tort action. *Barker* seems to achieve a fair balance between the competing interests of claimants and defendants, but this is simply the author's personal preference since there is no logical demand on the limits of liability. Ultimately it is preferable that the scope of application of the *Fairchild* test be as tightly circumscribed as possible so that the incoherence that has affected liability in these cases is not repeated in other contexts.

I. Defining the Evidentiary Gap

The so-called 'evidentiary gap' problem was first addressed in *McGhee v National Coal Board*[5] in relation to the cause of dermatitis, and subsequently in relation

---

[5] *McGhee v National Coal Board* 1972 SLT (notes) 61 (Court of Session, Scotland); [1973] 1 WLR 1 (HL (Sc)).

to the cause of mesothelioma in *Fairchild v Glenhaven Funeral Services* (and later cases).[6] The defendant in *McGhee* was held liable for the claimant's dermatitis where the claimant was only able to prove that his negligence had materially increased the risk of dermatitis. Following this decision it was unclear whether 'material increase in the risk of harm' constituted an exceptional new test for causation or whether the Court had simply taken a 'robust' view of the evidence before it. The House of Lords held that this approach could not assist the claimant in *Wilsher v Essex AHA*,[7] but it was resurrected and construed as an exceptional test in *Fairchild*. The purpose of this section is to examine the causal problem that arose in each of these cases, and the scientific evidence that was available, in order to understand precisely what the 'evidentiary gap' consists of. Approaching this from the basis of the NESS test will be shown to have a dual advantage over the but-for test. It first enables the causal problem to be conceptualised more accurately. This then means that the possible legal responses to the problem of the evidentiary gap can be analysed with greater clarity.

A. The Evidentiary Gap Relating to Dermatitis: *McGhee v National Coal Board*

The claimant in *McGhee* developed dermatitis as a result of damage to his skin from brick dust. He became covered in dust while emptying brick kilns for the defendant employer. This exposure to brick dust at work was unavoidable, so it was not negligent. The defendant's negligence consisted of failure to provide shower facilities to enable the claimant to wash the brick dust off his skin before cycling home. The medical evidence was that the claimant's dermatitis was caused by brick dust on his skin, so both the innocent and guilty periods of exposure to brick dust were potential causes of the dermatitis in this case. The problem facing the claimant was to prove that the negligent exposure in particular was an actual cause of his dermatitis. On the basis of the available legal tests he was required to prove that but-for the negligent exposure he would not have developed dermatitis, or, applying the *Wardlaw* test,[8] that the negligent exposure had materially contributed to his dermatitis.

The difficulty the claimant faced in this particular case was that although medical science was able to state that brick dust *does* cause dermatitis, it was unable to explain *how* it causes dermatitis.[9] This meant that proof that the negligent exposure had actually contributed to the claimant's disease was problematic. Lord Wilberforce noted that the experts 'had to admit that they knew little of the

---

[6] *Fairchild v Glenhaven Funeral Services (t/a GH Dovener & Son)* [2001] EWCA Civ 1881, [2002] 1 WLR 1052; [2002] UKHL 22, [2003] 1 AC 32.

[7] *Wilsher v Essex AHA* [1988] AC 1074 (HL).

[8] *Bonnington Castings v Wardlaw* [1956] AC 613 (HL).

[9] *McGhee v National Coal Board* [1973] 1 WLR 1 (HL) 3 (Lord Reid).

quantity of dust or the time of exposure necessary to cause a critical change'.[10] Lord Reid explained this gap in the medical experts' understanding more clearly:

> In the present case the evidence does not show—perhaps no one knows—just how dermatitis of this type begins. It suggests to me that there are two possible ways. It may be that an accumulation of minor abrasions of the horny layer of the skin is a necessary precondition for the onset of the disease. Or it may be that the disease starts at one particular abrasion and then spreads, so that multiplication of abrasions merely increases the number of places where the disease can start and in that way increases the risk of its occurrence.[11]

The 'evidentiary gap' in this case therefore concerns the aetiology of the disease, in particular the question of whether it is caused by an accumulation of abrasions or by a single abrasion. If it were caused by a single abrasion then the but-for test would apply, and if it were caused by an accumulation of abrasions the test of 'material contribution to harm' would apply. Since the causal process is unknown, neither test can be satisfied unless the defendant's negligence is the only source of the relevant harmful agent.[12]

B. The Evidentiary Gap Relating to Mesothelioma: *Fairchild v Glenhaven Funeral Services*

The victim in *Fairchild* had died from mesothelioma, a malignant tumour in the pleura (the membrane surrounding the lungs) and the negligence action was brought by his widow.[13] During his working life he had been exposed to asbestos by a number of his former employers, one of whom was the defendant employer. The problem facing the claimant was to establish that the defendant's negligence was a cause of the victim's disease. Similarly to *McGhee* it was known that inhalation of asbestos fibres *does* cause mesothelioma, but medical science was unable to explain *how* it causes mesothelioma. Once again, therefore, the problem of proof arose because of the scientific uncertainty combined with the fact that there was more than one period of exposure to the harmful substance.

---

[10] ibid 5 (Lord Wilberforce).

[11] ibid 4 (Lord Reid).

[12] Although the possibility that the disease is of idiopathic origin may still hamper proof. The claimant in *Australian Knitting Mills Ltd v Grant* (1933) 50 CLR 387 developed dermatitis after wearing garments manufactured by the defendant. The High Court of Australia was not satisfied that the disease was not of idiopathic origin so that the dermatitis could have been caused by the claimant having sensitive skin with the exposure to the external agent being merely coincidental, although the decision was eventually reversed by the Privy Council in *Grant v Australian Knitting Mills Ltd* [1936] AC 85. See generally Mark Lunney, 'Causation, Science and Sir Owen Dixon' (2004) 9 *Australian Journal of Legal History* 205; Chief Justice Robert French, 'Science and Judicial Proceedings: Seventy-Six Years On' (2010) 84 *Australian Law Journal* 244.

[13] *Fairchild v Glenhaven Funeral Services Ltd and others* [2002] UKHL 22, [2003] 1 AC 32, [7].

Lord Bingham explained the uncertainty:

> The mechanism by which a normal mesothelial cell is transformed into a mesothelioma cell is not known. It is believed by the best medical opinion to involve a multi-stage process, in which six or seven genetic changes occur in a normal cell to render it malignant. Asbestos acts in at least one of those stages and may (but this is uncertain) act in more than one ... It is accepted that the risk of developing a mesothelioma increases in proportion to the quantity of asbestos dust and fibres inhaled: the greater the quantity of dust and fibre inhaled, the greater the risk. But the condition may be caused by a single fibre, or a few fibres, or many fibres: medical opinion holds none of these possibilities to be more probable than any other, and the condition once caused is not aggravated by further exposure.[14]

The scientific uncertainty concerning the quantity of asbestos fibres required to cause mesothelioma, and the stage(s) at which the fibres are involved in the causal process, combined with the fact that the claimant had been exposed to asbestos by a number of former employers, meant that he was unable to establish causation, either on the but-for test or on the 'material contribution to harm' test because it was impossible to say what he needed to prove. Stapleton has explained:

> This means that there is as yet no means of telling whether the mesothelioma of a person subjected to a sequence of asbestos exposures was due to all exposures, only some or one, let alone which one. Importantly, there is no direct basis for saying that longer, more intense exposures are more likely to have been the cause ... than much shorter exposures, nor is there any basis for saying that earlier exposures are more likely to have been the cause than later exposures.[15]

Lord Bingham called this a 'rock of uncertainty', and it is generally known as the 'evidentiary gap'.[16] The evidentiary gap is therefore a very specific evidential problem. It is not simply a problem of a lack of evidence relating to the individual claimant. It goes to the general state of knowledge and understanding of the disease in medical science. The 'evidentiary gap' must also be described more accurately than 'scientific uncertainty about the aetiology of the disease'. The *disease* is known to be indivisible (ie its severity is not dose-related), and the harmful agent is known (eg brick dust, asbestos), but the *process* by which it is caused may have been a single fibre,[17] or an accumulation or interaction of a few or many fibres.[18]

---

[14] ibid (Lord Bingham).

[15] Jane Stapleton, 'Lords a'leaping Evidentiary Gaps' (2002) 10 *Torts Law Journal* 276, 281.

[16] See eg ibid.

[17] Although the single fibre theory has since been discredited it was an important factor in the *Fairchild* decision.

[18] It is therefore distinct from the problem that arose in *Wilsher*. The claimant there was a baby born prematurely who developed retrolentalfibroplasia ('RLF'). The defendant had negligently exposed the claimant to excess oxygen which is known to cause RLF, but the claimant also suffered a number of other conditions that were equally capable of causing RLF and which were due to his premature birth rather than to negligence. The case will be examined in greater detail at a later stage, but it is important to note that the problem in that case was not that medical science was unable to explain how RLF is caused, but that the claimant was unable to show that excess oxygen was a cause in his individual case.

Little has changed in the understanding of the aetiology of mesothelioma in the years since *Fairchild*, as Lord Phillips explained in the recent case of *Sienkiewicz v Greif*.[19] It is still believed that a small number of cases may possibly be idiopathic, meaning they have an unknown cause other than asbestos, but mesothelioma is 'always, or almost always, caused by the inhalation of asbestos fibres'.[20] One development since the decision in *Fairchild* concerns the minimum length of the latency period which is now believed to be five years rather than ten. This period is important because any exposure to asbestos during this period has no causative effect because the disease has already been caused. Furthermore, it is no longer believed that mesothelioma is triggered by a single asbestos fibre.[21] While it is therefore believed that mesothelioma is caused by multiple asbestos fibres, there remains significant scientific uncertainty as to how it is caused and at what stages the fibres are effective. Lord Phillips explained:

> It is believed that a cell has to go through 6 or 7 genetic mutations before it becomes malignant, and asbestos fibres may have causative effect on each of these.

> It is also possible that asbestos fibres have a causative effect by inhibiting the activity of natural killer cells that would otherwise destroy a mutating cell before it reaches the stage of becoming malignant.[22]

He also noted another possible causal mechanism, explaining that 'The Peto Report also raised the possibility (but no more) of synergistic interaction between early and later exposures. Causation may involve a cumulative effect with later exposure contributing to causation initiated by an earlier exposure'.[23]

C. Analysis of the Evidentiary Gap

The focus of the chapter has so far been confined to determining the factual basis of the evidentiary gap. The solution that was adopted in *McGhee* and applied in *Fairchild* was to hold the defendant liable on the basis that his negligence had materially increased the risk of the harm suffered. Before it is possible to engage in an analysis of this solution, and of the subsequent developments to it in later cases, it is essential to understand more precisely the causal problem that arises in these cases.

---

[19] *Sienkiewicz v Greif (UK) Ltd* [2011] UKSC 10, [2011] 2 AC 229. Lord Phillips based this understanding on a case control study by Peto and Rake, published in 2009 by the Health and Safety Executive, on 'Occupational, Domestic and Environmental Mesothelioma risks in Britain' ('the Peto Report'), which he explained 'is said to be the first representative study to quantify the relationship between mesothelioma risk and lifetime occupational and residential history in this country' (at [18]), and on 'the collation of data about mesothelioma set out by Rix LJ in his judgment in the series of appeals collectively described as *Employers' Liability Insurance "Trigger" Litigation* [2010] EWCA Civ 1096' (at [19]).

[20] *Sienkiewicz* (n 19) [19] (Lord Phillips).

[21] ibid [102] (Lord Phillips). See also *Amaca Pty Ltd v Booth* [2011] HCA 53, [19].

[22] ibid [19] (Lord Phillips).

[23] ibid [102] (Lord Phillips).

Steel and Ibbetson have explained that,

> [t]he normal rule of causation ... has two aspects: the evidential and the conceptual. In order to establish liability, P has to show on balance of probabilities (evidential) that but for D's wrongful conduct the injury would not have occurred (conceptual).[24]

Problems of causation divide into these two categories, the conceptual and the evidential. Stapleton has explained that the problem in evidentiary gap cases is an evidential one: '[the claimant's] difficulty was the antecedent one that there was simply inadequate factual information to feed into the but-for test'.[25] She therefore considers it irrelevant to address the conceptual inadequacies of the but-for test because 'this was not the problem facing the claimants in *Fairchild*'.[26] Since the NESS test addresses conceptual inadequacies of the but-for test, it has limited use in addressing this evidential problem. In this section it will be argued, however, that there remain a number of advantages to adopting the NESS test. First, since the NESS test is better matched to the underlying concept of causation than the but-for test it enables us to pinpoint precisely which aspect of causation the evidential problem relates to. Second, the NESS analysis highlights the fact that the *Wardlaw* test of material contribution to harm is distinct in nature from the *McGhee/Fairchild* test of material contribution to the risk of harm. The former addresses a conceptual weakness in the but-for test, so does not depart from the causation requirement, the latter addresses an evidential obstacle to proof of causation regardless of how causation is conceptualised so represents a significant exception to the causation requirement. Adopting the NESS test would not solve the evidential problem raised by the evidentiary gap, but it would make it easier to understand exactly what is at stake in these cases.

i. NESS and Identifying the Problem: Locating the Evidentiary Gap

In Wright's NESS account of causation, 'a particular condition was a cause of (condition contributing to) a specific consequence if and only if it was a necessary element of a set of antecedent actual conditions that was sufficient for the occurrence of the consequence'.[27]

The problem that a claimant usually faces in negligence is to establish the *necessity* of the defendant's negligence in order to complete the sufficient set of conditions. An example is the so-called 'single hit hunters' scenario that arose in

---

[24] Sandy Steel and David Ibbetson, 'More Grief on Uncertain Causation in Tort' (2011) 70 *Cambridge Law Journal* 451, 452.

[25] Stapleton, 'Lords a'leaping' (n 15) 280.

[26] ibid.

[27] Richard Wright, 'Causation in Tort Law' (1985) 73 *California Law Review* 1735, 1790.

the Canadian case of *Cook v Lewis*.[28] If two hunters have each negligently fired their guns in the victim's direction and the victim has been hit by only one bullet then the problem she faces is proving which hunter fired the bullet that hit her, ie which bullet was *necessary* for the sufficient set of conditions? Additionally the cases of *Hotson v East Berkshire HA*[29] and *Gregg v Scott*,[30] that were examined in the previous chapter involved an evidential problem concerning the necessity of the negligence, and the claimants attempted to avoid this problem of proof by proposing 'loss of a chance' as an alternative form of damage. It was clear in these cases what they were required to prove, the difficulty was in proving it to the balance of probabilities standard of proof. For example, in *Hotson*, the sufficient set of conditions for avascular necrosis is 'insufficient intact blood vessels to keep the epiphysis alive'. The problem for the claimant was to prove whether those blood vessels that were damaged during the delay caused by the defendant's negligence were *necessary* for this set, or whether they had been pre-empted from having any effect by the quantity of blood vessels damaged during the fall.[31]

In contrast, the claimants in the evidentiary gap cases of *McGhee* and *Fairchild* faced the prior problem of identifying what constitutes a *sufficient set* of conditions to cause the relevant disease since it was unknown whether the disease was caused by a single fibre, a few, or many fibres. This was essential to their claims because there were multiple exposures to the harmful agent so there were multiple potential causes meaning, for example, that it was not possible to identify those exposures that had been pre-empted from forming a sufficient set. If medical science is unable to explain what constitutes a sufficient set of conditions, then a claimant faces an insurmountable challenge—how can she prove that the defendant's negligence was necessary for the sufficiency of the set of conditions to cause her dermatitis or mesothelioma if uncertainty surrounding the aetiology of her disease means that medical science is unable to tell her what a sufficient set consists of? In other words, in most negligence cases we know what the claimant needs to prove and the problem for her is proving it to the requisite legal standard of proof. In cases involving this kind of evidentiary gap it is not possible to say what the claimant needs to prove let alone asking her to prove it to a particular standard.

The NESS test therefore facilitates the distinction to be made clearly between evidence of causation in the personal sense of proving that the negligence was *necessary* for the sufficiency of the set of conditions, and evidence of causation in the deeper, general sense of proving what a sufficient set of conditions is for a given disease. The next section builds on this NESS-informed understanding of the evidentiary gap in order to explore possible legal solutions with greater clarity.

---

[28] *Cook v Lewis* [1951] SCR 830.
[29] *Hotson v East Berkshire Health Authority* [1987] AC 750 (HL).
[30] *Gregg v Scott* [2005] UKHL 2, [2005] 2 AC 176 (HL).
[31] See ch 4, Part I, s II.F.

ii. NESS: Separating the Conceptual from the Evidential Aspects of the Legal Solution

The solution adopted by the majority of the House of Lords in *McGhee* built on the *Wardlaw* test of material contribution to harm and suggested that there is 'no substantial difference between saying that what the defender did materially increased the risk of injury to the pursuer and saying that what the defender did made a material contribution to the injury'.[32] It will be argued that there is, however, a significant difference between these two propositions since they are different in nature. The *Wardlaw* test addresses a conceptual inadequacy of the but-for test whereas *McGhee* addresses the evidentiary gap so it assists a claimant who faces an evidential barrier to proof on any test. Therefore, *McGhee* is not simply an extension of the *Wardlaw* test; it is an exception to it.

The problem with the decision in *McGhee* is that it seems to be built upon the misconceived idea that the *Wardlaw* test of 'material contribution to harm' is an exceptional approach which facilitates proof of causation and that making a further allowance where the claimant can only prove a material increase in the risk of harm is not a significant leap. This is partly due to the fact that, as chapter two illustrated, the speeches in *Wardlaw* did not adequately define the causal or evidential problems in that case so the scope and effects of the test of material contribution to harm are unclear. But it is also partly because the analysis in *McGhee* failed to define accurately the conceptual and evidential problems raised by either case.

In *McGhee*, Lord Salmon and Lord Reid both observed that a distinction could be drawn between the causal processes in *Wardlaw* and *McGhee* yet they chose to dismiss it as irrelevant. Lord Reid explained that dermatitis may be caused by an accumulation of abrasions, or by one particular abrasion, but continued to say:

> I am inclined to think that the evidence points to the former view. But in a field where so little appears to be known with certainty I could not say that that is proved. If it were, then this case would be indistinguishable from *Wardlaw's* case.[33]

He explained:

> Nor can I accept the distinction ... between materially increasing the risk that the disease will occur and making a material contribution to its occurrence.

> There may be some logical ground for such a distinction where our knowledge of all the material factors is complete. But it has often been said that the legal concept of causation is not based on logic or philosophy. It is based on the practical way in which the ordinary man's mind works in the everyday affairs of life. From a broad and practical viewpoint I can see no substantial difference between saying that what the defender did materially increased the risk of injury to the pursuer and saying that what the defender did made a material contribution to his injury.[34]

---

[32] *McGhee* (n 9) 5 (Lord Reid).
[33] ibid 4 (Lord Reid).
[34] ibid 5 (Lord Reid). See also 12–13 (Lord Salmon).

This highlights that the ordinary person's analogy between increasing the risk of harm and contributing to the harm is flawed because Lord Reid had previously explicitly stated that causation of dermatitis is *not* analogous with the pneumoconiosis in *Wardlaw*. The danger of regarding *Wardlaw* as taking an exceptional approach is that courts will not analyse the conceptual and evidential problems that necessitated the 'material contribution to harm' approach, and will instead focus on contextual similarities and policy considerations. Although Lord Wilberforce adopted a different solution in *McGhee*, reversing the onus of proof, he still drew on contextual similarities to *Wardlaw* in order to justify taking an exceptional approach. He focused on the fact that both cases involved industrial disease and explained '[i]n cases concerned with pneumoconiosis, the courts faced with a similar, though not identical, evidential gap, have bridged it by having regard to the risk situation of the pursuer'.[35] Likewise, in the later decision in *Fairchild*, Lord Nicholls held that '[o]n occasions the threshold "but for" test of causal connection may be over-exclusionary. Where justice so requires, the threshold itself may be lowered'.[36]

It is essential to understand why the but-for test is over-exclusionary in order to assess whether justice requires an exceptional approach. In the case of *Wardlaw*, the exception to the but-for test was necessary because the but-for test was conceptually inadequate as a test of causation. In *McGhee* and *Fairchild*, the problem is not the conceptual aspect of the test for causation, but the deeper evidential problem that it is not possible to define a sufficient set. As already stated, adopting the NESS test would not overcome the problems facing the claimant because the problem is an evidential one. The benefit of the NESS test is that it shows us that it is only possible to recognise liability in these cases if an exceptional approach is adopted.

Now that the problem of the evidentiary gap has been explained, the focus of the chapter can turn to the question of how to address this problem in a way that is consistent with corrective justice. Sections II and III will consider a range of legal and academic responses in terms of the concepts involved, before section IV returns the focus squarely to the demands of corrective justice. Solutions fall into two broad categories: those that focus on the legal standard of proof and those that seek to avoid the problem by reformulating the damage that forms the gist of the negligence action. Section II is therefore focused on proposals that relate to the evidential standard, and section III considers attempts to reformulate the damage in these cases.

II. Evidential Solutions: The Inferential Approach

The majority in *McGhee* found that the defendant had materially increased the risk of dermatitis, and considered this a sufficient basis for liability. Lord Kilbrandon

---

[35] ibid 6 (Lord Wilberforce).
[36] *Fairchild* (n 13) [40] (Lord Nicholls).

did not resort to reasoning based on a material increase in risk, simply finding that causation had been established on the balance of probabilities. Lord Wilberforce, however, pointed to the contradiction that lay at the heart of the majority approach. He had made a similar assessment of the facts of the case, explaining that pneumoconiosis involves a 'similar, though not identical, evidential gap'.[37] Yet he preferred to resolve the problem by reversing the onus of proof because 'to bridge the evidential gap by inference seems to me something of a fiction, since it was precisely this inference which the medical expert declined to make'.[38]

There were two competing interpretations of the significance of the finding of a 'material increase in risk' following *McGhee*. It was initially held in *Wilsher* that the majority had simply taken a 'robust and pragmatic' view of the available evidence in order to draw an inference of causation.[39] It was eventually held in *Fairchild* that this was an exceptional test for causation that was applicable in a tightly circumscribed set of cases to enable claimants to overcome the evidentiary gap.[40] However, in his corrective justice-based account of the tort of negligence, *Rediscovering the Law of Negligence*, Beever argues that the majority in *McGhee* did draw a factual inference of causation and that they were entitled to find that the claimant had succeeded in proving the causal link on the balance of probabilities.[41] Since the main arguments about causation in this work are premised on a corrective justice account of negligence it is essential to examine the validity of Beever's assertions.

It will be argued that the nature of the evidentiary gap means that it is simply not possible to establish on the balance of probabilities that the defendant's negligence was a cause of the claimant's disease. As discussed in chapter three, it is important to recognise that the balance of probabilities standard merely requires causation to be more probable than not, and should not be applied in a more restrictive manner that approaches requiring certainty.[42] There will, therefore, be cases where the expert evidence does not prove causation definitively yet a court can still justifiably conclude that causation has been established on the balance of probabilities. But where the expert evidence demonstrates an evidentiary gap there is simply insufficient information to feed in to any test or in to the balance of probabilities standard of proof—no explanation is more likely than any other. For a court to find that causation has been established on the balance of probabilities when the scientific evidence is that causation *cannot* be established because of an evidentiary gap, is to make a deliberately misinformed judgment based on intuition both as to causation and as to overall responsibility for the loss. It is one thing for the court to be satisfied on the balance of probabilities where there is some degree of doubt or uncertainty in the expert evidence because the law requires

---

[37] *McGhee* (n 9) 6 (Lord Wilberforce).

[38] ibid 7 (Lord Wilberforce).

[39] *Wilsher* (n 7) 1090 (Lord Bridge).

[40] *Fairchild* (n 13) [22] (Lord Bingham), [44] (Lord Nicholls), [65] (Lord Hoffmann), [142] (Lord Rodger).

[41] Allan Beever, *Rediscovering the Law of Negligence* (Hart Publishing, 2007) 465–72.

[42] See ch 3, text to n 39.

only probability not certainty, but it is entirely different for a court to resort to intuition about what probably happened where the expert evidence clearly states that causation cannot be established.

A. The Inferential Approach to *McGhee*

As Lord Reid explained, the medical evidence in *McGhee* showed that brick dust can cause dermatitis, and that the longer it is on the skin the greater the risk of developing dermatitis, but could not explain why this is so. He conjectured that:

> Plainly that must be because what happens while the man remains unwashed can have a causative effect, although just how the cause operates is uncertain. I cannot accept the view … that once the man left the brick kiln he left behind the causes which made him liable to develop dermatitis. That seems to me quite inconsistent with a proper interpretation of the medical evidence.[43]

According to Beever 'the most natural reading' of this passage is that 'Lord Reid said that, on the balance of probabilities, the defendant's negligence caused the claimant's injury'.[44] He says that this view was also supported by Lords Simon, Kilbrandon and Salmon so that they all 'rightly or wrongly, insisted that the claimant in *McGhee* could establish causation on the balance of probabilities'.[45] It is clear that there are two issues at stake here, first whether Lord Reid *did* find causation to be established on the balance of probabilities rather than applying a new principle of law and, second, whether the evidence in the case was actually capable of supporting such a finding.

The first of these questions was resolved by the House of Lords in *Fairchild* where the majority held that since Lord Reid had explicitly noted the distinction between the facts of *McGhee* and *Wardlaw*, he cannot have intended to make a logically flawed finding of fact. This means that the more interesting and more important question is the second question—was the evidence in *McGhee* capable of supporting a finding of causation on the balance of probabilities?

As we have seen, Beever argues that causation could be established on the balance of probabilities in *McGhee*. However, the first step to accepting the inferential approach is asking the right questions, and Beever does not distinguish adequately between general and specific causation. He argues that '[c]rucially, the experts did not say that there was no proof of a causal link between dust and dermatitis'.[46] This is true, but it was not suggested that the claimant was unable to prove the general link between brick dust and dermatitis. The problem was proving the link between the *negligent* exposure to brick dust and the dermatitis. Indeed, the fact that his

---

[43] *McGhee* (n 9) 4–5 (Lord Reid), cited by Beever, *Rediscovering the Law of Negligence* (n 41) 466.

[44] Beever (n 41) 466.

[45] ibid.

[46] Beever (n 41) 468.

dermatitis was caused by brick dust was what enabled the Court to say that the negligent exposure to brick dust had increased the risk of suffering dermatitis. It is, however, a significant leap from saying that brick dust can cause dermatitis to saying that the negligent dust was a cause of the particular claimant's dermatitis.

Beever's primary concern, however, is with the different standards of proof in law and in medical science. He explains that the medical experts in *McGhee*

> said that it was not possible to prove … that the defendant's negligence caused the claimant's injury, but, as the medical experts were not applying the balance of probabilities, that does not imply that it was proved that the defendant did not cause the plaintiff's injury.[47]

However the burden of proof rests on the claimant so we should not be troubled by Beever's concern that it was not proved in *McGhee* that the defendant did not cause the claimant's injury.

As previously discussed in chapter three, while there are tensions between the legal and scientific standards of proof, courts must engage fully with the available evidence rather than side-lining it as being too demanding. Lord Phillips emphasised the difference between legal and scientific standards in the later case of *Sienkiewicz v Greif (UK) Ltd*:

> When a scientific expert gives an opinion on causation, he is likely to do so in terms of certainty or uncertainty, rather than probability. Either medical science will enable him to postulate with confidence the chain of events that occurred, i.e. the biological cause, or it will not. In the latter case he is unlikely to be of much assistance to the judge who seeks to ascertain what occurred on a balance of probability.[48]

To an extent this is right, and in the context of a negligence claim there is a clear place for pragmatism in the law. The courts cannot postpone decisions until scientific certainty is achieved.[49] As Lord Rodger said in *Fairchild*, 'the House must deal with these appeals on the basis of the evidence as to medical knowledge today and leave the problems of the future to be resolved in the future'.[50]

But scientific or medical expert evidence cannot be written off as too demanding. Instead it is essential that the courts engage with the evidence so that they understand what it does and does not tell them in order to assess how persuasive the evidence is. Expert testimony does not cease to be useful to a court just because the expert is unable to identify a cause with near certainty. As Laleng has suggested:

> an understanding of the similarities and differences between the two methods [legal and scientific] is more likely to yield acceptable results than policy-based decisions that seem to be based on little more than sympathy for victims and a possible generalised chemo-phobia.[51]

---

[47] ibid 467.
[48] *Sienkiewicz* (n 19) [9] (Lord Phillips).
[49] See ch 3, text to n 48.
[50] *Fairchild* (n 13) [124] (Lord Rodger).
[51] Per Laleng, '*Sienkiewicz v Greif (UK) Ltd* and *Willmore v Knowsley Metropolitan Borough Council*: A Material Contribution to Uncertainty?' (2011) 74 *Modern Law Review* 777, 793.

Chapter three explained at length that the balance of probabilities standard of proof is a 'belief probability'.[52] The judge must be more convinced than not that the claimant's account is true. Forming a belief probability requires a qualitative assessment of the evidence, so a court cannot choose to overlook scientific evidence. It is important for judges to understand that the balance of probabilities standard requires them to form a belief based on the available evidence, rather than ignoring the scientific evidence in favour of a 'common sense' judgment of causation. This is particularly important when an 'inferential approach' is proposed.

B. The Issues Concealed by an Inferential Approach

Where courts resort to an inferential approach, taking a 'robust and pragmatic' approach to the evidence, there is a lack of clarity not only in articulating the reasons underlying the solution to proof of causation but also in identifying the problems of proof that such an approach is being used to address. Beever says that where there is scientific uncertainty '[c]rucially, the Court cannot simply side with the defendant when the expert witnesses cannot or will not express their views on probabilities'.[53] There is some truth to this assertion but it needs to be heavily qualified. The burden of proof in civil law rests on the claimant, so if the claimant is unable to persuade the court of her claim on the balance of probabilities then it must fail. If the causal process is understood, ie it is known what constitutes a sufficient set, and the question is whether the defendant's negligence was necessary for the sufficiency of that set, then some pragmatism is needed in law and care needs to be taken to see what the scientific evidence tells us and what are the limits of what it does and does not say. But in cases involving an evidentiary gap the scientific evidence is that it is impossible to say what constitutes a sufficient set of conditions. This means that the experts' refusal to say how likely it is that the negligence was necessary for the sufficiency of the set is not a symptom of their adherence to a higher standard of proof than the legal standard, but instead is based on the scientific impossibility of assigning a probability. In other words, where it is theoretically possible to determine whether the negligence was a cause but the expert witnesses are reluctant to express an opinion because they are observing a higher standard of proof then it is still appropriate for the judge to assess her own degree of belief, but where the evidentiary gap makes it impossible for the expert witnesses to express an opinion there is no logical basis for the judge to have any degree of belief.

Beever's argument echoes the approach of Canadian courts following *Snell v Farrell* which approved taking a 'robust and pragmatic' to the facts in proof of causation.[54] The claimant in *Snell* underwent surgery to remove a cataract and

---

[52] See ch 3, section I.A.
[53] Beever (n 41) 471.
[54] *Snell v Farrell* [1990] 2 SCR 311.

during the operation the defendant doctor noticed a retrobulbar haemorrhage, bleeding behind her eyeball, which was an inherent risk of the procedure and not attributable to negligence. The negligence lay in his decision to continue the operation rather than treat the haemorrhage. The claimant suffered damage to her optic nerve which resulted in blindness, but she faced difficulty in proving causation because this could have been caused by the haemorrhage but could also have been caused by any of three other conditions she suffered: diabetes, high blood pressure or glaucoma. It was not possible to say when the damage to the optic nerve occurred since the doctor was unable to examine it until eight months after the operation because the blood from the haemorrhage obscured his view. In the Supreme Court of Canada, Sopinka J cited Lord Bridge's speech in *Wilsher*:

> The conclusion I draw ... is that [*McGhee*] laid down no new principle of law whatever. On the contrary, it affirmed the principle that the onus of proving causation lies on the pursuer or plaintiff. Adopting a robust and pragmatic approach to the undisputed primary facts of the case, the majority concluded that it was a legitimate inference of fact that the defendant's negligence had materially contributed to the pursuer's injury.[55]

He explained:

> The legal or ultimate burden remains with the plaintiff, but in the absence of evidence to the contrary adduced by the defendant, an inference of causation may be drawn although positive or scientific proof of causation has not been adduced. If some evidence to the contrary is adduced by the defendant, the trial judge is entitled to take account of Lord Mansfield's famous precept [that 'all evidence is to be weighed according to the proof which it was in the power of one side to have produced, and in the power of the other to have contradicted' (*Blatch v Archer* (1774), 1 Cowp. 63, 98 ER 969, at p970)]. This is, I believe, what Lord Bridge had in mind in *Wilsher* when he referred to a 'robust and pragmatic approach to the ... facts'.[56]

In his analysis of the decision, Brown sums this up by explaining that:

> In Canadian law, then, a limited scientific understanding of the aetiology of a plaintiff's condition does not, in and of itself pose an insurmountable hurdle to proving cause-in-facts. The gap created by what we do *not* know can be bridged by an inference of cause-in-fact, drawn from what we *do* know, where such an inference is supported by 'common sense' and by a 'robust' and 'pragmatic' treatment of evidence.[57]

This resort to common sense, and a robust and pragmatic treatment of evidence, is essentially a fudge that allows courts to avoid articulating the reasons for a finding of causation. This is evident in the divergence in the outcomes in *Snell* and in *Wilsher* despite their strikingly similar facts.

Knutsen has defended the robust and pragmatic approach, arguing that

---

[55] ibid 324.
[56] ibid 330.
[57] Russell Brown, 'Inferring Cause in Fact and the Search for Legal "Truth"' in Richard Goldberg (ed), *Perspectives on Causation* (Hart Publishing, 2011) 94.

all it does is augment some evidence about causation to the level of a balance of probabilities, as long as there is not other competing evidence that is of a greater level of proof sufficiency, and as long as such augmentation accords with common sense.[58]

On this interpretation, this approach meddles with the balance of probabilities standard of proof by finding that causation is proved when the probabilities are even rather than requiring the claimant to tip the balance. He continues:

> The spirit of *Snell v Farrell* was to be a plaintiff-friendly assist in proving difficult causation cases in the face of inconclusive evidence. That is why the nods to common sense and the distancing from scientific precision are there. A causal inference is no more than an educated guess taking all the circumstances of the case together.[59]

It is difficult to see how this can be an acceptable approach to proof of causation in cases involving an evidentiary gap. In a case such as *Snell* or *Wilsher*, there was not an 'absence of evidence to the contrary adduced by the defendant'. The defendants advanced evidence that the claimant was suffering from a range of other conditions that were all capable of causing the damage ultimately suffered. The defendant is not required to prove that one of those conditions did cause the damage, but faced with evidence of those conditions the burden remains on the claimant to persuade the court on the balance of probabilities that the negligence was a cause of the damage.

This tension is not new and was evident in the diverging approaches of the High Court of Australia in *Grant v Australian Knitting Mills Ltd* in 1933.[60] The claimant in that case developed dermatitis shortly after starting to wear garments manufactured by the defendant, and in his dissenting opinion Evatt J was prepared to accept the common sense conclusion that the garment caused the dermatitis given the short lapse of time between starting to wear the clothing and developing the condition. Dixon J was not willing to accept this common sense view in light of the availability of scientific evidence which identified the possibility of other non-negligent causes. Extra-judicially he explained:

> Questions of fact, raised by the standards of legal liability, which formerly might have appeared simple, are now shown to contain ingredients calling for close and complicated examination. Where rough and ready answers of the practical man might have once sufficed, an exact and reasoned solution is now called for.[61]

As Mullany clearly explains, for a belief in the fact of causation to be rational it must be based on scientific evidence since, '[t]he educative effect of the expert evidence makes appeals to common sense notions of causation largely meaningless or produces findings which would not be made by an ordinary person

---

[58] Eric S Knutsen, 'Clarifying Causation in Tort' (2010) 33 *Dalhousie Law Journal* 153, 174.

[59] ibid 175.

[60] *Australian Knitting Mills Ltd v Grant* (1933) 50 CLR 387. This decision was eventually reversed by the Privy Council in *Grant v Australian Knitting Mills* [1936] AC 85.

[61] Sir Owen Dixon, 'Science and Judicial Proceedings' in Judge Wionarski (ed), *Jesting Pilate and Other Papers and Addresses by the Right Honourable Sir Owen Dixon* (WS Hein, 1965) 14. See generally Lunney, 'Causation, Science and Sir Owen Dixon' (n 12).

who had not been so instructed'.[62] Negligence law need not require the 'exact' solution advocated by Dixon J since the standard of proof is merely the balance of probabilities, but it is reasonable to maintain his requirement that the solution be 'reasoned'.

Although the majority in *Fairchild* rejected the inferential approach, Lord Hutton adopted it, explaining that 'I consider that this approach, whereby the layman applying broad common sense draws an inference which the doctors as scientific witnesses are not prepared to draw, is one which is permissible'.[63] This is unjustifiable given that the problem was not that the scientific evidence was inconclusive, but that it showed a clear evidentiary gap in being unable to define a 'sufficient set'. This made it impossible to have a rational belief that the defendant's negligence was necessary for an actually occurring sufficient set. Weekes has argued that:

> This reliance on 'broad common sense' is perplexing. Expert evidence is tendered for the purpose of proving or disproving matters which are beyond the ordinary knowledge, sense and experience of the tribunal of fact. Thus when causation is beyond the powers of even the experts, the inferential approach amounts to deliberately uninformed guesswork.[64]

So it is one thing to say that 'the law's task is to determine the nature and form of evidence the plaintiff should be permitted to adduce to prove the required historical link',[65] but it is not the law's task to find a link where the evidence is clear that the link cannot be established. As Lord Hoffmann said in *Fairchild*, 'however robust or pragmatic the tribunal may be, it cannot draw inferences of fact in the teeth of the undisputed medical evidence'.[66]

C. Closing the Evidentiary Gap

The evidentiary gap may be overcome in the future as scientific knowledge develops so it is important to note that it will not be a permanent problem. Once the evidentiary gap no longer exists courts should revert to orthodox principles of damage and causation. McIvor criticises the decision in *Sienkiewicz*, observing that many of the speeches suggest that 'a claimant in a mesothelioma case would always need to be able produce evidence which identifies the precise point in time at which the genetic process triggering the malignant mutation was initiated'.[67]

---

[62] Nicholas J Mullany, 'Common Sense Causation—an Australian View' (1992) 12 *Oxford Journal of Legal Studies* 431, 437.

[63] *Fairchild* (n 13) [100] (Lord Hutton).

[64] Robert Weekes, 'Not Seeing the Wood for the Trees—Risk Analysis as an Alternative to Factual Causation in *Fairchild*' (2003) 12 *Nottingham Law Journal* 18, 25.

[65] Jane Stapleton, 'Publication Review—Causation and Risk in the Law of Torts: Scientific Evidence and Medicinal Product Liability' (2000) 116 *Law Quarterly Review* 506, 506.

[66] *Fairchild* (n 13) [70] (Lord Hoffmann).

[67] Claire McIvor, 'Debunking some Judicial Myths about Epidemiology and its Relevance to Personal Injury Litigation' (2013) 21 *Medical Law Review* 553, 565.

This, she says, reflects a standard of proof much closer to the criminal law requirement of proof 'beyond all reasonable doubt' than the civil law balance of probabilities standard.[68] It is not necessary to prove the precise point in time when the mesothelioma was triggered, but it is necessary to prove that the particular causal process was more likely than not the process that occurred.

Since *Fairchild* was decided the single fibre theory has been discredited and this is a significant step in closing the evidentiary gap because it means that the causal mechanism cannot be equated directly with the 'single hit hunters' scenario. Although the process could be described as 'cumulative' in the sense that the disease develops in a number of stages at each of which fibres may play a role, there is still significant uncertainty as Lord Phillips explained in *Sienkiewicz*:

> The amount of exposure does not necessarily tell the whole story as to the likely cause of the disease. There may well be a temporal element. The Peto Report also raised the possibility (but no more) of synergistic interaction between early and later exposures. Causation may involve a cumulative effect with later exposure contributing to causation initiated by an earlier exposure.[69]

Once more is known as to the interaction of exposures and the effect of timing of exposure, then it may be possible to prove causation *on the balance of probabilities*.

This second section has shown that where there is an evidentiary gap surrounding the aetiology of a disease which prevents the determination of a 'sufficient set' of conditions, and there are multiple sources of the harmful agent, it is not possible for a claimant to prove on the balance of probabilities that a particular source of the relevant harmful agent was a cause. Since the content of a sufficient set is unknown, even in theory, it is not possible to show that the defendant's negligence was necessary for the sufficiency of any set of conditions that actually occurred. This means that the fact-finder's belief would be irrational if she chose to disregard clear scientific evidence as to causation and replace it with a 'common sense' view drawing on uninformed intuition. The leap made by the majority in *McGhee* from finding that the defendant's negligence had 'materially increased the risk of harm' to concluding that his negligence had made a material contribution to the harm itself cannot, therefore, be accepted as drawing an inference about factual causation. As Nolan has argued, '[t]his conflation of material increase in risk and material contribution was a fairly blatant judicial sleight of hand'.[70] Indeed, this interpretation was disapproved in *Fairchild* where it was held that the evidentiary gap prevented proof of causation, but that to assist claimants facing this insuperable problem of proof the defendant would be held liable on the basis that he had caused a material increase in the risk of harm. Under *Fairchild*, as developed in *Barker*, proof of a material increase in the risk of harm does not prove that the

---

[68] See ch 3, text to n 39.
[69] *Sienkiewicz* (n 19) [102] (Lord Phillips).
[70] Donal Nolan, 'Causation and the Goals of Tort Law' in Andrew Robertson and Tang Hang Wu (eds), *The Goals of Private Law* (Hart Publishing, 2009) 168.

negligence was a cause of the harm. Instead the basis of liability has changed from liability for causing the claimant's damage, to liability for increasing the risk of the claimant's damage. Liability is no longer based on the fiction of a causal link, but is explicitly based on the fact that the defendant increased the risk and this is enough to engage liability. The following section will therefore turn to this solution to the evidentiary gap and its place within a corrective justice-based account of negligence.

III. Risk of Harm as the Gist of the Negligence Action: *Barker v Corus (UK) plc*[71]

In order for negligence liability to be consistent with corrective justice, there must be a causal link between the defendant's negligence and the claimant's damage. The previous section has shown that the evidentiary gap prevents proof of a causal link between the negligence and the physical harm suffered by the claimant. The majority in the Supreme Court decision in *BAI v Durham* held that the *Fairchild* rule is a special rule that deems the defendant to have caused the claimant's mesothelioma if it is proved that her negligence materially increased the claimant's risk of mesothelioma.[72] However, an alternative approach is to reconceptualise the actionable damage in these cases as exposure to the risk of harm rather than the physical harm itself since the claimant is able to prove that the defendant's negligence caused this 'damage'. This was the approach Lord Hoffmann purported to follow in *Barker v Corus*,[73] and in his dissent in *BAI v Durham* Lord Phillips maintained that this was the correct interpretation of *Barker*.[74] It will be argued here, however, that this approach is still not consistent with corrective justice. There are two strands to this argument. First, Lord Hoffmann insisted that the risk must have materialised into physical harm before the claimant would be able to recover for the exposure to the risk of harm, and this requirement means that it is still the physical harm that forms the gist of the action. Secondly, even if the physical harm requirement were to be removed, risk exposure lacks the independent moral significance to form damage in the negligence inquiry.

A. The Decision in *Barker v Corus*

The claim in *Barker v Corus* raised the question of whether the *Fairchild* principle was applicable when the claimant had been exposed to asbestos not only

---

[71] *Barker v Corus (UK) plc* [2006] UKHL 20, [2006] 2 AC 572.
[72] *BAI v Durham* ('Trigger Litigation') (n 4) (Lords Mance, Kerr, Clarke and Dyson).
[73] *Barker* (n 71) [35].
[74] *BAI v Durham* (n 4) [124]–[132].

due to the negligence of his former employers including the defendant, but also by himself during a period of self-employment. In *Fairchild*, the House of Lords had said that any background exposure to asbestos was so small that it could be effectively discounted so all of the claimant's exposure was attributable to former employers.[75] This meant that, although the evidentiary gap prevented the claimant from proving that a particular defendant was a cause of his mesothelioma, it was accepted that his damage was certainly attributable to *somebody's* negligence. The claimant in *Barker* was not an 'innocent claimant' in this sense because the period of self-exposure meant that he could not say that his damage had definitely been caused by somebody else's negligence. Given the possibility that the claimant had caused his own damage the fairness of shifting the burden of the loss onto a negligent employer was less apparent. As an alternative argument, the defendant claimed that if the *Fairchild* principle was applicable in this case then liability ought to be several rather than joint and several.

The House of Lords held that the *Fairchild* principle did apply even though the claimant himself was responsible for some of the asbestos exposure. The Court did, however, accept the defendant's second line of argument and held that where the *Fairchild* principle is applied liability ought to be several rather than joint and several. Lord Hoffmann, with whom Lord Scott, Lord Walker and Baroness Hale agreed on the applicability of the *Fairchild* principle, based his finding on causal principles:

> For this purpose it should be irrelevant whether the other exposure was tortious or non-tortious, by natural causes or human agency or by the claimant himself. These distinctions may be relevant to whether and to whom responsibility can also be attributed, but from the point of view of satisfying the requirement of a sufficient causal link between the defendant's conduct and the claimant's injury, they should not matter.[76]

This echoes the argument made in chapter two that causation is a factual question of involvement so it is irrelevant to the causation inquiry whether a candidate cause is innocent or negligent. Instead this characterisation is relevant to the attribution of responsibility, of which causal involvement is just one element. In particular, the duty of care and principles of legal causation define the limits of legal responsibility.

Lord Rodger's dissent in *Barker* focused instead on balancing the interests of the claimant and defendant to achieve a just solution. He considered that the *Fairchild* principle had been motivated by the demands of fairness and the need to avoid injustice to the claimant. Assuming that liability remained joint and several, he was concerned that applying the *Fairchild* principle where the claimant was responsible for a period of asbestos exposure would tip the balance too far in his direction, resulting in injustice to the defendant.[77] However, given that the majority favoured

---

[75] The question of whether it was correct to ignore the background risk, and the related 'innocent claimant' argument, will be addressed in section IV.A.

[76] *Barker* (n 71) [17] (Lord Hoffmann).

[77] ibid [98]–[101] (Lord Rodger).

several liability he accepted that 'the balance of potential injustices favour applying the *Fairchild* exception'.[78]

Section IV will look at broader policy arguments and considerations of fairness. The aspect of the decision that is considered here is the reasoning behind the decision that liability ought to be several. The House of Lords was in agreement that the extent of the defendant's contribution to the total risk was an appropriate measure for the apportionment of liability that would take place. It remained a requirement that the claimant must have suffered physical harm in the form of mesothelioma, meaning that the risk must have materialised. The value of the total risk was therefore said to be the same as the value of the physical harm. The defendant would compensate the claimant for a portion of the value of the physical harm, with the extent of that portion measured by his contribution to the total risk. Lord Scott explained that this apportionment would be based on the duration of the exposure for which each defendant was responsible compared with the total duration of exposure to asbestos. It might also take into account the intensity of the exposure and, since different types of asbestos increase the risk more than others, the type of asbestos dust.[79]

The majority were divided in the reasons they gave for this decision. One approach was to retain the physical harm, mesothelioma, as the actionable damage or 'gist' of the negligence action, but to apportion liability according to contribution to risk on the basis that this achieved a fair balance between the competing interests of the claimant and defendant. The second approach was to hold that where the *Fairchild* principle is applied the gist of the action is no longer the physical harm but the exposure to risk itself. Baroness Hale favoured the first justification, that apportionment was a 'fair' solution:

> The law of tort is not (generally) there to punish people for their behaviour. It is there to make them pay for the damage they have done. These *Fairchild* defendants may not have caused any harm at all. They are being made liable because it is thought fair that they should make at least some contribution to redressing the harm that may have flowed from their wrongdoing. It seems to me most fair that the contribution they should make is in proportion to the contribution they have made to the risk of that harm occurring.[80]

The relevance of risk, in her approach, was no more than that it provided a 'sensible basis' on which liability could be apportioned.[81]

In contrast, risk took on much greater significance in Lord Hoffmann's justification for applying several liability. Under the *Fairchild* principle a defendant is held liable on the basis that her negligence caused a material increase in the risk of

---

[78] ibid [101] (Lord Rodger).
[79] ibid [62] (Lord Scott).
[80] ibid [127] (Baroness Hale).
[81] ibid [126] (Baroness Hale).

harm. This meant, in his opinion, that the increase in risk, rather than the physical harm, ought to form the gist of the negligence action:

> Consistency of approach would suggest that if the basis of liability is the wrongful creation of a risk or chance of causing the disease, the damage which the defendant should be regarded as having caused is the creation of such a risk or chance.[82]

He continued to explain:

> If that is the right way to characterize the damage, then it does not matter that the disease as such would be indivisible damage. Chances are infinitely divisible and different people can be separately responsible to a greater or lesser degree for the chances of an event happening.[83]

This solution has an appearance of consistency with corrective justice since the defendant is ostensibly being held liable only for the damage that he has been proved to have caused, ie exposure to the risk of mesothelioma. If the actionable damage is the risk of mesothelioma then the centrality of the causation requirement is maintained since the claimant must still prove on the balance of probabilities that the defendant's breach of duty caused this damage. On closer inspection, however, this approach is not consistent with corrective justice. There are two reasons for this. First, the continued insistence that the claimant must have developed mesothelioma undermines the claim that the gist has been changed to the risk of mesothelioma. In other words, the damage for which the claimant was compensated was still the mesothelioma itself, but liability was apportioned to reflect the degree of uncertainty surrounding proof of the causal link. Secondly, even if the courts were to abandon the requirement that the claimant must suffer the physical harm, exposure to risk cannot be considered to be damage within corrective justice because it adds nothing to the breach inquiry. Conduct is characterised as wrongful if it exposes the claimant to an unreasonable risk of harm. Corrective justice does not punish this wrongful behaviour, but requires the wrongdoer to repair the loss when her wrongdoing causes harm to another. If a defendant commits a wrong by exposing a claimant to an unreasonable risk of harm but this risk does not materialise then she is not liable because there is no loss for her to correct. If the law was to hold that exposure to risk does constitute harm then the requirement of damage would effectively be lost and the basis for liability would not be corrective justice but a retributive form of justice.

---

[82] ibid [35] (Lord Hoffmann).

[83] ibid [35] (Lord Hoffmann). Lord Hoffmann has acknowledged extra-judicially that he sought to create a new cause of action in respect of risk, explaining 'My own proposal to treat *Fairchild* as creating a special new cause of action, that is, creating a risk of injury which has subsequently eventuated, could not be found in any opinion in *Fairchild*, except possibly my own, and certainly not in *McGhee*. I was rewriting history' (Lord Hoffmann, 'Fairchild and after' in Andrew Burrows, David Johnston and Reinhard Zimmerman (eds), *Judge and Jurist: Essays in Memory of Lord Rodger of Earlsferry* (Oxford University Press, 2013) 67).

B. Analysis of the 'Risk as Gist' Approach

As noted above, Lord Hoffmann explained that

> [c]onsistency of approach would suggest that if the basis of liability is the wrongful crea-
> tion of a risk or chance of causing the disease, the damage which the defendant should be
> regarded as having caused is the creation of such a risk or chance.[84]

Even Lord Rodger, who ultimately did not support the risk-based analysis, thought
that the 'dominant aim' pursued by changing the gist of the action to the risk
of harm was 'to secure internal consistency between the basis of liability and the
nature of the damage'.[85] However, writing after the House of Lords' decision in
Fairchild, Stapleton has said:

> The majority of the House … firmly rejected the use of legal fictions. Refreshingly, they
> did not adopt any of a range of possible pretences. One would have been that the *McGhee/*
> *Fairchild* rule related to a special duty, such as a duty to avoid exposing the victim to an
> increased risk of mesothelioma which would have constituted a special type of wrong
> twinned with a special sort of 'damage'.[86]

It will be argued that, as Stapleton suggests, the 'risk as damage' approach rests on a
fiction and conceals the fact that the gist is actually still the physical harm and that
the apportionment exercise reflects the remaining doubt over causation.

It will also be argued that Lord Hoffmann's approach introduces confusion to
the interaction between the damage, causation and quantification elements of the
negligence inquiry. Stapleton has said that it 'cannot be over-emphasised that the
formulation of the "damage" forming the gist of the action *defines* the causation
question. Logically one can only deal with causation after one knows what the
damage forming the gist of the action is'.[87] This is problematic in Lord Hoffmann's
approach because he suggests that the gist of the action is 'risk' which is a divisible
damage, but the claim is only actionable when the claimant has suffered the physical outcome harm, mesothelioma, which is indivisible.

i. The Inconsistency of the Physical Harm Requirement

Although Lord Hoffmann said that the gist of the action was the risk of
mesothelioma, it was still a condition of liability that the claimant must have
developed mesothelioma. This requirement of physical harm may be a practical

---

[84] ibid [35] (Lord Hoffmann).

[85] ibid [84] (Lord Rodger). His aim was to maintain 'a consistency of approach with the main body
of law on personal injuries' (ibid [84]).

[86] Stapleton, 'Lords a'leaping' (n 15) 290.

[87] Jane Stapleton, 'The Gist of Negligence: Part 2 The Relationship Between "Damage" and Causation' (1988) 104 *Law Quarterly Review* 389, 393.

way of limiting the number of cases where the *Barker* principles applies, but it is conceptually problematic because it means that the gist was not actually redefined as the risk of harm. Lord Hoffmann stated:

> Although the *Fairchild* exception treats the risk of contracting mesothelioma as the damage, it applies only when the disease has actually been contracted. [Counsel for the defendant] was reluctant to characterise the claim as being for causing a risk of the disease because he did not want to suggest that someone could sue for being exposed to a risk which had not materialised. But in cases which fall within the *Fairchild* exception, that possibility is precluded by the terms of the exception. It applies only when the claimant has contracted the disease against which he should have been protected.[88]

This reasoning is inadequate to support his assertion that the gist could be redefined as the risk of harm whilst still requiring the claimant to have developed mesothelioma. If the gist of the action is exposure to risk but the risk must have materialised before the action can be brought then there is an internal inconsistency between the content of the rule and the scope of application of the rule. Far from justifying the risk as damage approach, this inconsistency undermines the rule. Indeed, Beever says that

> the refusal to compensate the defendant's former employees unless they suffer mesothelioma reveals that the actionable damage is the mesothelioma and the consequences thereof, and not the risk of mesothelioma … The idea that these cases involve liability for risk creation is an illusion.[89]

This was an important factor in the Supreme Court decision in *Durham v BAI*.[90] This decision addressed a number of conjoined appeals concerning employers' liability insurance in the context of mesothelioma claims. There were two issues to be resolved. The 'construction issue' required the Court to determine whether the words 'sustained' and 'contracted' used in the insurance contracts referred to the date at which the mesothelioma was caused or the date at which the disease actually developed. This in turn required the Court to address the 'causation issue' concerning the effect of the *Fairchild/Barker* principle. If the *Fairchild/Barker* principle is a special rule that adopts a relaxed approach to causation, and deems the employers who have exposed their employees to asbestos to be a cause of the employees' mesothelioma, then causation of the disease can be established for the purpose of triggering the employers' liability insurance. If, however, the *Fairchild/Barker* principle is correctly understood as creating liability for exposing the employee to the *risk* of mesothelioma, this is insufficient to trigger the employers' liability insurance to compensate for the disease itself. The majority

---

[88] *Barker* (n 71) [48] (Lord Hoffmann). Affirmed in *Rothwell v Chemical and Insulating Co Ltd* [2007] UKHL 39, [2008] 1 AC 281.

[89] Beever (n 41) 487. See also Nolan, 'Causation and the Goals of Tort Law' (n 70) 178; Lara Khoury, 'Causation and Risk in the Highest Courts of Canada, England and France' (2008) 124 *Law Quarterly Review* 103, 126.

[90] *Durham v BAI* (n 4).

in the Supreme Court adopted the first of these approaches, with Lord Mance explaining:

> In reality, it is impossible, or at least inaccurate, to speak of the cause of action recognised in *Fairchild* and *Barker* as being simply 'for the risk created by exposing' someone to asbestos. If it were simply for that risk, then the risk would be the injury; damages would be recoverable for every exposure, without proof by the claimant of any (other) injury at all. That is emphatically not the law.[91]

Lord Clarke similarly suggests that

> Lord Hoffmann cannot have intended to hold, without more, that the basis of liability was the wrongful creation of the risk or chance of causing the disease because there would be no liability at all but for the subsequent existence of the mesothelioma.[92]

Whilst it seems inevitable that the decision of the majority was motivated by the desire to trigger the employers' liability insurance in an area where liability rules have been shaped from the outset in *Fairchild* by a policy concern to compensate victims of mesothelioma,[93] their decision was evidently also justified by the continued physical harm requirement.

In his dissent in *Durham*, Lord Phillips sought to distinguish the *effect* of the *Fairchild/Barker* principle,[94] which is to impose liability to compensate the victim's mesothelioma, from the *juridical basis* of *Fairchild/Barker*, which in his view creates a cause of action in respect of the increase in risk, rather than the disease itself. He explained:

> It would, I think, have been possible for the House in *Barker* to have defined the *special approach* in *Fairchild* as one that treated contribution to risk as contribution to the causation of damage. The important fact is, however, that the majority did not do so. They were at pains to emphasise that the *special approach* was not based on the fiction that the defendants *had* contributed to causing the mesothelioma. Liability for a proportion of the mesothelioma resulted from contribution to the risk that mesothelioma would be caused and reflected the *possibility* that a defendant might have caused or contributed to the cause of the disease.[95]

Yet if it is possible to draw such a sharp distinction between the effect of a rule and the juridical basis of that rule, surely this highlights the conceptual weakness of that rule. The requirement that the claimant must have developed mesothelioma undermines the 'risk as damage' approach so severely that it cannot simply be explained away by Lord Hoffmann as a requirement for the application of the *Fairchild* principle. If he was willing to adopt the 'risk as damage' approach because he prioritised 'consistency of approach' then the physical harm requirement should have been abandoned in order to actually achieve consistency of

---

[91] ibid [65].
[92] ibid [82].
[93] See eg ibid [73] (Lord Mance), [88] (Lord Clarke).
[94] ibid [116].
[95] ibid [130]

approach. As noted by Scherpe, '[n]othing is gained by replacing one fiction with another but much can be lost'.[96]

ii. Physical Harm and Risk: A Shift in Perspectives

There is a danger that this argument seems to focus solely on the *appearance* of inconsistency that arises when the court says that the gist is the risk of mesothelioma whilst still insisting that the claimant must have developed mesothelioma. Examining the nature of 'risk', however, will show that this problem is not just apparent, but goes to the essence of the concept of risk. The following section will look more closely at what 'risk' is, to show that risk is a forward-looking concept and that, properly understood, the extent of the risk created by a particular defendant is measured at the time it is created. There is an inherent mismatch between risk as a forward-looking concept and the backward-looking role in which risk is being cast in Lord Hoffmann's approach. Here the extent of the defendant's contribution to risk is only measurable once the risk has materialised and all the other sources of the same kind of risk have been identified. This means that the extent of the risk that the defendant created will vary in size depending on how many other sources of asbestos the claimant was exposed to, whereas risk is actually a forward-looking concept and measureable independently of other sources of risk. This mistaken use of risk seems attributable to the subtle shift in the phraseology of the *Fairchild* exception which originated as 'material increase in risk' in *McGhee* and has morphed into 'material contribution to risk' in *Barker*.

iii. What is 'Risk'?

Perry has said that '[i]n ordinary language conduct is typically said to be risky when it gives rise to a chance of a bad outcome of some kind. The concept thus involves two main elements: first, a notion of chance or probability, and second, a notion of harm'.[97] It involves a state of uncertainty as to the future. The measure of a particular risk is a product of the extent of the possible harm that may be produced, and the probability of this harm materialising. Notably, probability is a factor in calculating risk but it is not synonymous with risk. In *Risks and Legal Theory*, Steele set out a range of different meanings assigned to the word 'risk'. She explained that for some theorists we can only truly speak of 'risk' when the probability of the relevant outcome can be calculated. If the probability cannot be calculated then the situation ought to be described as involving uncertainty, indeterminacy or ignorance. Others use the word 'risk' to describe any situation

---

[96] Jens Scherpe, 'A New Gist?' (2006) 65 *Cambridge Law Journal* 487, 488.

[97] Stephen R Perry, 'Risk, Harm, and Responsibility' in David G Owen (ed), *Philosophical Foundations of Tort Law* (Oxford University Press, 1995) 322.

involving a hazard regardless of whether the probability of harm can be calculated. She says that the latter approach 'reflects an increasing colloquial and theoretical understanding of risks as *threats*, rather than as statistical probabilities'.[98] Notably the notion of risk relates to the future in all of these forms. 'Risk' is also sometimes used as shorthand for a particular decision-making method. In this sense 'risk' does not refer to a danger that necessitates a decision-making method in order to be managed, but refers to a way of approaching a problem or danger.[99] Steele also notes that 'risk' and 'probability', 'though related, are distinct terms'.[100] Risk will sometimes depend on a formal assessment of probability, and always depends on the likelihood of an outcome. Probability can be used for analysis of past events, eg what is the probability that X caused Y?, so probability does not always entail a risk assessment. In contrast, risk generally concerns the future although it can be used to debate the past,[101] for example to assess what would in the past have been a rational way to behave.[102] Once again we see that probability is one element of risk, but it is not synonymous with risk. This means that it is crucial that the two terms, 'risk' and 'probability', are not used interchangeably.

So while probability may be used to analyse past events, risk is a forward-looking concept. It describes a situation of uncertainty as to whether a particular outcome, or range of outcomes, will occur. When a risk materialises it causes an outcome so it is no longer a 'risk' but a cause. Of course there may be uncertainty as to what caused a particular event, ie uncertainty as to which risk(s) materialised, and as Steele noted above, probability can aid the analysis of causation. It would be incorrect to say that if a risk has materialised it has contributed to the risk of the outcome—this is just circular. In other words a 'risk' is only a 'risk' while the outcome is still prospective. Once the outcome occurs then the relevant question is whether the risk materialised and made a causal contribution. Weekes explains:

> By definition the concept of risk is a limitless one. The meaning of a factual cause is binary: a given activity either causes or does not cause the damage in question. The limit of a factual cause is where a given activity does not result, in whole or in part, in the certain damage. Risk, however, is defined by degree. A risk which is proven to have resulted in damage is of course a risk that has been realized, or more properly, 'a cause'.[103]

Beever explains the same idea through the analogy of a raffle that is held with 100 tickets each costing £2 and a single prize of £1,000 (where the ticket has no value other than the fact it provides a chance to win the £1,000 prize). Before the raffle is drawn, he explains, 'your ticket is worth £10, that being onehundredth of £1,000. But imagine now that the raffle is held and you do not win. How much is your ticket worth now? It is worthless'.[104]

[98] Jenny Steele, *Risks and Legal Theory* (Hart Publishing, 2004) 7.
[99] ibid 7.
[100] ibid 19.
[101] ibid 20.
[102] ibid 9.
[103] Weekes, 'Not Seeing the Wood for the Trees' (n 64) 27.
[104] Beever (n 41) 486

iv. Can Risk Constitute Damage?

Lord Hoffmann held in *Barker* that mesothelioma is no longer the actionable damage for which the claimant recovers. Instead the actionable damage for which the claimant recovers is the risk of mesothelioma to which the defendant exposed him. However, the claimant cannot claim in respect of this exposure to the risk of mesothelioma until he actually develops mesothelioma, and on Lord Hoffmann's reckoning it is then possible to establish how much the defendant contributed to the total risk to which the claimant was exposed. It will be argued that what this approach actually achieves is to make the defendant liable for the mesothelioma itself, but to discount the extent of his liability to reflect the uncertainty over whether the risk he created was the risk that actually materialised. The method used to calculate the appropriate discount is the *probability* that it was the defendant's risk rather than another source of risk that materialised. It cannot be the case that exposure to risk is the damage that is being compensated here because risk is forward-looking and only exists before the outcome occurs. After the outcome has occurred, the risk that the defendant created either is or is not a cause of that outcome. Since risk is forward-looking the extent of the risk is measurable at the time of exposure to the risk and its value is fixed at that time. In contrast, in Lord Hoffmann's approach, the measure of the defendant's liability will vary with each subsequent exposure of the claimant to the same type of risk. This variability shows that it simply cannot be 'risk' that is actually being compensated in Lord Hoffmann's approach. Instead he is awarding partial compensation for the mesothelioma to reflect the *probability* that the defendant caused it. But we must remember that 'probability' is *not* synonymous with 'risk'—probability is one element of risk calculation, but whereas probability can look both forwards and backwards, risk only looks forwards. This means that so-called 'risk' employed as an arithmetical tool to calculate apportionment of damages is not truly risk, but probability. This is the argument that will be elaborated in more detail here.

v. Calculating Risk and Probability

As explained, risk is a forward-looking concept and is a product of the extent of possible harm and the probability of that harm occurring. When an employer negligently exposes an employee to asbestos dust she exposes the employee to the risk of a number of asbestos-related diseases such as lung cancer, asbestosis and mesothelioma. The risk can be measured at that time based on the extent of the loss the employee would suffer if the risk were to materialise and the probability of it materialising. If the employee chose to take out a health insurance policy it would take into account the increased risk of the employee suffering these illnesses in the future—it is the increase in the probability of the disease that we tend to focus on because the extent of the loss does not vary. This focus on the probability aspect of risk may explain why Lord Hoffmann uses the term 'risk' when he is actually referring to 'probability'.

The relevant risk in these cases is the risk of mesothelioma. To provide a concrete example, in *Sienkiewicz* the risk of mesothelioma created by the environmental exposure to asbestos was 24 cases per million. The risk of mesothelioma created by the occupational exposure to asbestos was 4.39 cases per million.[105] The occupational exposure was therefore said to have increased the risk of the claimant developing mesothelioma by 18 per cent.[106] 'Risk' here is a predictive tool that informs us how likely it is that the employee will develop mesothelioma. It does not cease to be a predictive tool just because, in the context of a negligence action, the actual assessment of the risk takes place after the exposure and harm since it is still based on the prospective number of cases across a population with the same level of exposure. Based on the duration and extent of the exposure to asbestos dust, and the type of dust, it tells us how much more likely it is that the employee will develop mesothelioma than if she had not been exposed to each source of asbestos dust. If, hypothetically, the claimant had then been exposed to the same kind of risk by a later employer this would not alter the fact that the defendant had increased the risk of mesothelioma by 18 per cent. The risk that was created by the defendant does not increase or diminish when the employee is exposed to the same kind of risk by subsequent employers.

This can be explained through an equivalent variation on Beever's raffle analogy. In that example, 100 tickets were sold for a raffle with a single prize of £1,000. If *A* has one ticket, her ticket is worth £10 since that is one hundredth of £1,000. In terms of 'risk', the value of the 'risk' is £10 because it is a product of the value of the possible outcome, £1,000, and the probability of that outcome, 1/100. If *B* gives her ticket to *A*, she has added another 1/100 to the probability that *A* will win £1,000. If *C* has two tickets and gives these to *A*, she has added another 2/100 to the probability that *A* will win £1,000. *A*'s initial ticket is still worth £10 because it has a 1/100 chance of winning, the ticket she got from *B* is still worth £10 because it has a 1/100 chance of winning.

Lord Hoffmann said that 'the basis of liability is the wrongful creation of a risk or chance of causing the disease'.[107] If this was the case then the value of the risk created by a particular defendant would be fixed at the time of the exposure to that risk and would not vary. But this is not how Lord Hoffmann's approach works, so liability cannot actually be being imposed in respect of risk. This means that his approach is not consistent with corrective justice which requires the negligence doctrines to articulate a single normative sequence; if liability is imposed on the basis of increasing the risk of a disease, there is a normative disjunction in awarding damages for something other than that risk. Starting with the raffle analogy,

---

[105] For the purposes of this example it is assumed that these figures are accurate although McIvor notes that the judge calculated them himself from limited evidence and without the help of epidemiologist expert witnesses (n 67).

[106] (4.39/24) * 100 = 18.29

[107] *Barker* (n 71) [35] (Lord Hoffmann).

the equivalent to developing mesothelioma would be *A* winning the raffle prize of £1,000. The 99 losing tickets are worthless; the one winning ticket is worth £1,000. In the first scenario where *A* only has one ticket, this is the ticket that has been drawn and Lord Hoffmann would say that *A* contributed the whole of the 'risk' of winning. In the second scenario where *A* had another ticket given to her by *B*, Lord Hoffmann would say that *A* contributed 50 per cent of the 'risk' of winning, and *B* contributed the remaining 50 per cent. And in the final scenario where *A* was given a further two tickets by *C*, Lord Hoffmann would say that *A* contributed 25 per cent of the 'risk' of winning, *B* contributed 25 per cent of the 'risk' of winning, and *C* contributed 50 per cent of the 'risk' of winning. So the extent of the 'risk' created by *A* varies, as does the extent of the 'risk' created by *B*. But we know that risk is a forward-looking concept and that its measure does not depend on other subsequent exposures to the same kind of risk, so Lord Hoffmann cannot actually have made 'risk' the actionable damage. Once again the problem appears to be that he treats 'risk' as synonymous with 'probability' perhaps because of the role that probability plays in allowing us to calculate risk. As noted above, we also have a tendency to focus only on the probability element of risk when comparing risks of the same outcome because the possible outcome is a constant and the risk-creator increases the probability of this outcome occurring. Since the outcome has occurred, *A* has won £1,000, one of her tickets is worth £1,000 and the remaining three are worth nothing. There is a 1/4 *probability* that it is her own ticket, a 1/4 probability that it is the ticket she received from *B* and a 2/4 probability that it is a ticket she received from *C*. If we made her divide up the prize according to these probabilities, keeping £250 for herself, giving £250 to *B* and £500 to *C* we would be allocating the prize according to the purely statistical *probability* that each person was responsible for the winning ticket. It may be that in cases of evidentiary gap this is the best the court can achieve, to apportion liability according to the statistical probability that the defendant caused the disease. But since causation of the physical outcome cannot be proven on the balance of probabilities, the decision to impose proportionate liability for possible causation cannot be based on corrective justice. If we want to recognise exposure to the risk of mesothelioma as actionable damage in itself, then we need to understand that this damage occurs at the time of the exposure and has value that is independent of other exposures to the same kind of risk.

vi. 'Increase in Risk' or 'Contribution to Risk'?

This conflation of risk and probability is hidden in the subtle, yet significant, shift in the wording of the *Fairchild* principle. The *Fairchild* principle is expressed both as a test of 'material increase in the risk' of harm, and of 'material contribution to the risk' of harm. These phrases seem similar but insight into the notion of risk gained in the previous section allows us to see that they actually imply different exercises, and so should not be used interchangeably. This issue was highlighted by the decision of the Court of Appeal in *Williams v University of Birmingham* which asked whether:

> the law requires a judge to do a comparison between the two (or more) sources to see if the wrongful exposure at the hands of the defendant is, by comparison with the other exposures, too insignificant to be taken into account. Or, is it enough for a judge to find as a fact that the wrongful exposure at the hands of the defendant materially increased the risk that the victim would contract mesothelioma?[108]

Asking whether the defendant's negligence materially increased the risk of harm reflects the forward-looking concept of risk. An increase in the risk is measurable at the time of the exposure and if it is a 'material' increase then this will not change because the measure of the risk is unaffected by later exposures. In contrast, asking whether the defendant's negligence made a 'material contribution to the risk' does require a comparison with the other sources of risk. The contribution that the defendant made to the total 'risk' will be greater or smaller depending on how many other employers exposed the claimant to asbestos, over what period and with what intensity. As discussed above, this variability in the measure of the so-called 'risk' shows that actually we have shifted to measuring probability of causation. This change in the terminology seems to have occurred in academic discussion following *Fairchild*.[109] It was firmly entrenched by the time of *Sienkiewicz* where Lord Phillips said

> the only circumstances in which a Court will be able to conclude that wrongful exposure of a mesothelioma victim to asbestos did not materially increase the victim's risk of contracting the disease will be where that exposure was insignificant compared to the exposure from other sources.[110]

Whether conscious or unconscious, it is possible that it reflects a desire to draw a parallel with the *Wardlaw* test of 'material contribution to harm' that is a standard test for causation. The discussion above shows that courts must be careful when making subtle changes to the wording of a legal test because this can open the way for the test to take on a very different meaning.

C. Can Risk Constitute Damage in Corrective Justice?

This section focuses on risk solely in the forward-looking sense that the term properly implies. The question is whether exposing somebody to the risk of mesothelioma or of other harm is capable of constituting damage within a corrective justice-based system of negligence law. In this forward-looking sense it is still

---

[108] *Williams v University of Birmingham* [2011] EWCA Civ 1242, [2012] PIQR P4 [69] (Aikens LJ).
[109] See eg Stapleton, 'Lords a'leaping' (n 15).
[110] *Sienkiewicz* (n 19) [11] (Lord Phillips). Although the Court of Appeal in *Williams* concluded that it does *not* require a comparative exercise (n 108) [72] (Aikens LJ).

important to draw a distinction similar to that in the previous chapter on loss of a chance. In that chapter it was seen that causal processes can be deterministic or indeterministic.[111] It is only in indeterministic processes that we can appropriately say that there is a 'chance' of an outcome occurring and that the probability of this outcome is 'objective'. In deterministic processes, as most physical processes are believed to be, there is not a 'chance' as such since the occurrence of a particular outcome can theoretically be predicted with certainty given limitless knowledge. Instead the probability used to describe the likelihood of the outcome occurring is an epistemological probability; it reflects our belief based on the limited knowledge that is available. Thus a patient who is unwell when she visits her doctor is either destined to recover, or destined to succumb; she does not have an objective chance of recovery. Generally speaking then we deal with epistemological and not objective probabilities.

Recalling that probability is one element of risk, along with the possible outcome, risk can be objective or subjective even though it is based on epistemological probability. The term 'risk' denotes uncertainty as to the likelihood of a future outcome, so it incorporates epistemological probability. The harmful agent/risk agent has the potential to cause an outcome, ie it has the potential to form part of a deterministic causal process, but the limits of our knowledge prevent us from saying whether it will or will not cause harm to a particular individual. But there is a limit to this because the relevant outcome has an objective nature. With an indivisible harm such as mesothelioma, one only creates an objective risk of mesothelioma if the potential victim has not already contracted the disease. Of course, an employer will not usually know whether the employee has already contracted mesothelioma, so from her perspective exposing the employee to asbestos exposes the employee to a risk of mesothelioma, so in this subjective/epistemic sense the conduct creates a risk of harm. So even though risk relies on epistemological *probability*, the objective nature of harm means that we can talk about objective *risk* and subjective/epistemic *risk*. The following sections will consider whether risk, in either sense, can constitute damage in the negligence inquiry.

i. Objective Risk: The Evidentiary Gap Prevents Proof that the Defendant Created an Objective Risk

A criticism of the 'risk as damage' approach that has emerged in academic writing is that the evidentiary gap also prevents the claimant from proving that the defendant's negligence increased the risk that he would develop mesothelioma.[112] Scherpe has explained:

> The aetiology of the disease is such that once contracted further exposure does not matter and certainly cannot increase the risk of contracting it. If the disease was contracted

---

[111] See ch 4, Part I s II.F.
[112] See Nolan (n 70) 178; Beever (n 41) 486; Scherpe (n 96) 488.

during the first employment, all following exposure did and could not increase the risk and hence there could not be a contribution to the risk. But whether that was the case, we do not know—which is exactly the point: we do not know whether all exposure actually increased the risk. Assuming that it did is therefore also resorting to a fiction.[113]

In other words, it is only before mesothelioma has been contracted that exposure to asbestos actually creates an objective risk that the individual will develop the disease. Since the evidentiary gap prevents us from saying when the disease was contracted it is also impossible to say that any exposures other than the first exposure actually created a risk of the disease for this individual.

Nolan has addressed a potential criticism of this argument:

> It could be argued that this is to adopt the wrong perspective. From the point of view of the defendant at the time of the breach of duty, a risk *was* imposed on the claimant ... and indeed this must always be the case where the defendant has been negligent *towards the claimant*, as he has to be in order to be liable. But even if we assume that this was the perspective the House of Lords had in mind when they said that in cases falling within the *Fairchild* principle, the defendant was deemed to have caused the injury when he could be shown to have materially increased the risk of its happening, this switch from objective risk to subjective risk cannot rescue the risk as damage idea. This is because even if we accept the premise that an unrealised risk is a form of harm, this claim can surely be sustainable only if the defendant's action did *in fact* create a risk for the claimant.[114]

Since the evidentiary gap prevents us from being able to say whether the defendant exposed the claimant to an objective risk of mesothelioma, risk in the objective sense cannot help overcome the problem of the evidentiary gap.

ii. Subjective/Epistemic Risk: Lacks the Moral Significance to be Damage

The only remaining sense in which risk may therefore constitute damage, if it is to assist the courts in overcoming the evidentiary gap, is in the subjective sense. As explained above, a lack of knowledge will often prevent an employer from knowing whether her employee has already developed mesothelioma, so exposing the employee to asbestos exposes her to a risk of mesothelioma in a subjective, or epistemic sense. This is what enables the conduct to be characterised as wrongful, or negligent.[115] Since the standard of care in negligence is an objective standard, for the avoidance of confusion the label 'epistemic' will be used instead of 'subjective'.

As noted above, Nolan argued that while the *Fairchild* principle may be based on the fact that from the defendant's perspective he exposed the claimant to the risk of mesothelioma this does not rescue risk as a form of damage. It will be argued that Nolan's assertion is correct and that epistemic risk cannot constitute

---

[113] Scherpe (n 96) 488.

[114] Nolan (n 70) 179.

[115] Clearly asbestos exposure is also wrongful because it creates a risk of other asbestos-related illnesses too.

damage in negligence. One barrier is the difficulty of explaining why this sort of risk matters and should be deserving of compensation. The other, far greater, barrier is that it adds nothing to the negligence inquiry. Corrective justice requires a wrongdoer to repair the loss that she caused the victim to suffer through her wrongdoing. If the concept of 'loss' is the same as the concept of wrongdoing, ie the creation of an unreasonable risk, then loss is effectively subsumed into the concept of wrongdoing and liability is imposed for the sole fact of wrongdoing towards the claimant. An entire aspect of the equation has been removed, and the focus is solely on the defendant's wrongdoing so the justification for liability can no longer be corrective justice but must be a defendant-focused form of justice such as retributive or distributive justice.

iii. The Difficulty of Explaining Why Epistemic Risk Deserves Compensation

In terms of the negligence doctrines, Stapleton has argued that the question of what constitutes 'gist damage' or actionable damage is 'rarely addressed squarely by courts', and that the word 'damage' is 'bandied about in a number of different contexts, usually without clear definition yet equally without apparent awareness of the importance of precision in its use'.[116] This highlights one of the key difficulties with accepting risk as damage in cases involving the evidentiary gap—should exposure to the risk of harm be considered damage for the purposes of corrective justice-based liability? This question was not addressed head-on by the House of Lords in *Barker*. Amirthalingam has therefore argued that '*Barker* is an unsatisfactory decision in that it does not explain why "increased risk" should qualify as the gist of negligence'.[117] Furthermore, it does not account for why the risk of mesothelioma, and possibly of other diseases whose aetiology involves the same kind of evidentiary gap, is considered to be damage but the risk of other physical harm is not regarded as damage. It will be argued that any limit on what kinds of risk qualify as damage will necessarily be arbitrary because of the more fundamental problem that the risk of harm simply cannot constitute damage. Each of these objections must be addressed in greater detail.

A significant barrier to accepting that the risk of harm constitutes damage is that it is difficult to say why risk has value and what that value is. Voyiakis explains that 'we cannot decide whether persons exposed to risk of physical harm should be entitled to claim compensation unless we have some rough idea of what they would demand to be compensated *for*'.[118] As discussed in the previous chapter, the

---

[116] Jane Stapleton, 'The Gist of Negligence: Part 1 Minimal Actionable Damage' (1988) 104 *Law Quarterly Review* 213, 213.

[117] Kumaralingam Amirthalingam, 'The Changing Face of the Gist of Negligence' in Jason W Neyers, Erika Chamberlain and Stephen GA Pitel (eds), *Emerging Issues in Tort Law* (Hart Publishing, 2007) 474.

[118] Emmanuel Voyiakis, 'The Great Illusion: Tort Law and Exposure to Danger of Physical Harm' (2009) 72 *Modern Law Review* 909, 915.

risk itself does not have a value as a proportion of the value of the physical harm to which it relates:

> [W]hen I make it 40 per cent more likely that you will suffer lung cancer, I am not causing you 40 per cent of the harm that lung cancer brings about. The quantity of risk and the quantity of physical harm do not seem to be related in any such straightforward way. We therefore have reason to object to the latter being taken as a measure of the former.[119]

Instead, Voyiakis focuses on the concrete effects that exposure to the risk of harm can create, notably preventative medical care and the increase in the cost of health insurance or life insurance. Finkelstein similarly argues that the costs of medical monitoring mean that risk exposure constitutes damage because it affects the individual's objective level of welfare.[120] Yet her account is problematic because she also supports what she labels the 'Absorption Thesis' that risk as damage is 'absorbed' into the physical damage if that outcome eventuates. So she argues, 'the person who is harmed in a car accident surely does not think of himself as worse off than the person who sustains the same injuries through an intentional battery'.[121] This means that the risk of harm only constitutes damage if the risk fails to materialise, but once the risk materialises and results in physical damage then the period of risk exposure no longer constitutes an independent form of damage. Yet as Perry argues, 'the status of agent-imposed risk as harm in itself should not depend on whether the threatened physical harm has materialized'.[122] If risk exposure itself is characterised as damage when the outcome remains prospective, then once physical harm occurs it is inconsistent to say retrospectively that the period of risk exposure is no longer considered damage. In respect of the concrete effects of risk, Steele has distinguished the 'utility value' of risk from its 'mathematical value' and explained that the utility value of any particular risk depends on the individual involved. She says that 'if the possible losses are *not* purely financial, it is much harder to attach the risk "value" in any calculable form at all'.[123] So even the question of whether a risk has a financial impact will depend on the individual and whether they are inclined to have health/life insurance anyway.

Similarly, risk cannot be valued according to the anxiety it causes the claimant. The House of Lords held in *Rothwell* that the risk of future asbestos-related illness is not actionable damage, nor is anxiety related to this risk, nor is the combination of the two.[124] Green supports this conclusion, noting that human beings necessarily operate within a notion of risk meaning that:

> the degree to which any individual might or might not actually be at risk of an adverse outcome need bear no resemblance whatsoever to his *perception* of that risk. Therefore, any anxiety founded upon such a necessarily epistemic conception of that risk is a step

[119] ibid 917.
[120] Clare Finkelstein, 'Is Risk a Harm?' (2003) 151 *U Pa L Rev* 963, 971.
[121] ibid 993.
[122] Perry (n 97) 331.
[123] Steele, *Risks and Legal Theory* (n 98) 25.
[124] *Rothwell* (n 88).

further removed from the defendant's breach of duty than is anxiety consequent upon actual harm resulting from the tort.[125]

This conclusion reflects the considerations of corrective justice that underpin negligence liability. Corrective justice operates to correct wrongful losses, and the characterisation of a loss as 'wrongful' depends not only on it being caused by wrongdoing, but also allows the law to limit the definition of wrongful loss to those losses that go beyond what everybody is expected to tolerate as part of everyday life.

It is also difficult to reconcile risk as damage with the decision in *Cartledge v E Jopling & Sons Ltd*.[126] The claimant there had suffered damage to his lungs caused by inhalation of silica dust and it was held that the fibres caused actionable damage before producing symptoms that were noticeable in everyday life. If physical damage is actionable before it is discoverable by the claimant then risk exposure ought to also be actionable regardless of whether the claimant is aware of the risk. Yet risk exposure only seems to acquire significance if the claimant is aware of it. If the claimant is unaware of the risk then she is unaffected unless it materialises in physical harm.

The argument that epistemic risk should be regarded as damage could be seen to be analogous with the argument that was made in the previous chapter that the loss of an epistemic chance entails damage to the claimant's autonomy interest in the limited context of medical negligence involving the misdiagnosis of existing illness. That argument, however, was based on the unique characteristic of the doctor's duty of care which is focused on diagnosing existing illness and providing the opportunity for treatment. Respect for patient autonomy is a driving force in the doctor-patient relationship so, it was argued, the law ought to recognise damage to the patient's autonomy as well as damage to her physical welfare. Since a patient deciding whether to undergo treatment is necessarily weighing up epistemic risks there is a strong case for relying upon epistemic risk in recognising damage. There is no such focus in this context. Amirthalingam has noted, therefore, that limiting recovery for risk to mesothelioma, or to risks arising in the course of employment, would be arbitrary—there is nothing marking these contexts out as ones in which the claimant and defendant regard the risk of harm as damage in advance of their interaction. Amirthalingam suggests that 'unacceptable risk' might be considered damage. He explains that this 'provides a normative framework for courts to determine what sort of risks should be classed as unacceptable, and incrementally develop the law'.[127] This solution is too vague to be applied in practice, and it still does not explain *why* a particular risk is 'unacceptable'.

---

[125] Sarah Green, 'Risk Exposure and Negligence' (2006) 122 *Law Quarterly Review* 386, 388.
[126] *Cartledge v E Jopling & Sons Ltd* [1963] AC 758 (HL).
[127] Amirthalingam, 'The Changing Face of the Gist of Negligence' (n 117) 475.

D. Epistemic Risk: The Conflation of Breach and Damage

The more fundamental obstacle to the recognition of epistemic risk as damage in negligence is that the damage requirement would be subsumed into the breach inquiry so liability would be based entirely on wrongdoing rather than on the interaction of the two parties, so it would no longer be a system of corrective justice.

In *Fairchild*, Lord Rodger suggested that '[a]t best, it was only good luck if any particular defendant's negligence did not trigger the victim's mesothelioma'.[128] This is true, but should not impact on corrective justice-based liability since this addresses wrongful *loss*. As discussed in chapter one,[129] the causation requirement has been criticised as introducing an element of 'moral luck' into negligence liability,[130] and if the focus of liability was the wrongdoing of the defendant alone then there may be some force to this argument. However, since the focus of corrective justice is not on either of the parties alone, but is on the inequality that occurs when the wrongdoing of one person causes a loss to another person, it is only concerned with equality in *transactions*. When two people interact there is only a transaction when something passes between them, ie one causes a loss to the other. As Steele has explained, 'if the defendant is lucky and does not cause damage, then potential victims are lucky too and do not suffer any'.[131] The claimants in these cases have not been 'lucky' overall because we know that they have developed mesothelioma but this does not mean that it was caused by the particular defendant. If the defendant was lucky and did not trigger the claimant's mesothelioma but simply created a risk of mesothelioma by exposing her to asbestos dust then there has been no corrective justice transaction between the defendant and the claimant.

The relationship between the *Fairchild* test and breach of duty was considered by the Court of Appeal in *Williams v University of Birmingham*.[132] The main issue to be decided in that case was whether the defendant had breached his duty of care towards the claimant. The judge at first instance said that the legal standard of care was 'to take all reasonable measures to ensure that [the claimant] was not exposed to a material increase in the risk of mesothelioma'.[133]

In the Court of Appeal, however, it was held that this was inaccurate:

> A reference to exposure '*to a material increase in the risk of mesothelioma*' brings the test for causation in mesothelioma cases into the prior questions of the nature of the duty and what constitutes a breach of it. There is nothing in *Fairchild* or [*Sienkiewicz v Greif*] to suggest that the House of Lords or the Supreme Court has altered the 'breach of duty'

---

[128] *Fairchild* (n 13) [155] (Lord Rodger).

[129] See ch 1, text to n 67.

[130] David Howarth, 'Many Duties of Care—or a Duty of Care? Notes from the Underground' (2006) 26 *Oxford Journal of Legal Studies* 449, 461.

[131] Steele (n 98) 116.

[132] *Williams* (n 108).

[133] (Belcher J) at first instance (unreported) cited in *Williams* (CA) (n 108) [39]

test in mesothelioma cases so that a claimant only has to demonstrate that the defendant failed to take reasonable steps to ensure that the claimant or victim was not exposed to a '*material increase in the risk of mesothelioma*'.[134]

Instead, the duty of care is 'to take reasonable care ... to ensure that [the claimant] was not exposed to a foreseeable risk of asbestos related injury'.[135] If the defendant did not materially increase the risk of harm then it was clear that he had not breached his duty of care. But if his conduct did materially increase the risk of harm then the court must still ask whether a reasonable person in the defendant's place would have taken further steps to reduce the risk of harm. The test of breach of duty is therefore more demanding than the test of material increase in the risk of harm that is applied at the causation stage, so it is clear that epistemic risk is already subsumed into the breach inquiry. Subsuming the damage requirement into the breach inquiry would mean that the only remaining elements of the negligence inquiry would be the duty of care and the breach of duty.

As previously noted, wrongdoing and loss are distinct aspects of an interaction that triggers a corrective justice response, so they must also be distinct in the negligence inquiry. So just as we know that negligence cannot coherently be explained as a system of compensation, neither can it be explained in terms that focus solely on the wrongdoer. Damage is therefore said to form the gist of the negligence action; it is an essential ingredient of negligence liability. If damage were to be subsumed into the breach inquiry, the negligence action would focus almost exclusively on the defendant, and would no longer be a system of corrective justice.

IV. Theoretical Approaches to the 'Evidentiary Gap'

In this chapter it has been argued that the 'evidentiary gap' presents an insurmountable obstacle to proof of causation. This obstacle cannot coherently be overcome by taking a more relaxed evidential approach and drawing a common sense inference of causation. Nor can it be avoided by moving the problem to a different aspect of negligence by reconceptualising the gist of the action. The final section therefore turns to the question of how to justify imposing liability, whether it is several or joint and several, when causation cannot be proven. The dominant theme in judicial reasoning in *Fairchild* and in *Barker* is that the solutions were justified by policy concerns and the demands of fairness and justice. It will be argued here that 'fairness' and 'justice' are not arguments of corrective justice. The first part seeks to clear away a number of possible misconceptions about this. In the second part it will be demonstrated that they reflect an instrumentalist approach to liability, although the exact content of these instrumentalist goals is not clearly articulated in the decisions. As a result of adopting an instrumentalist approach,

---

[134] *Williams* (CA) (n 108) [40] (Aikens LJ).
[135] ibid [40].

UNIVERSITY OF WINCHESTER
LIBRARY

the *Fairchild* principle lacks a coherent theoretical foundation since, as discussed in chapter one, instrumentalist theories cannot be properly implemented through the institution of negligence law. As Nolan has explained,

> [t]he trouble is that the logic of the instrumentalist approach has no obvious stopping point ... And because there are no logical stopping points—or rather because the logical stopping points are incompatible with the basic idea of tort law—the courts have had to resort to illogical ones instead.[136]

A. Dispelling Possible Misconceptions

First it is important to address a number of possible misconceptions that 'fairness' may have some claim on corrective justice.

i. McGhee: *The Defendant Definitely Caused the Damage*

In *Fairchild*, Lord Bingham noted that the Court of Appeal had sought to distinguish that case, where multiple former employers may have caused the disease, from *McGhee* where there was only one employer involved. He said that in *McGhee*, 'there was a risk that the defendant might be held liable for acts for which he should not be held legally liable but no risk that he would be held liable for damage which (whether legally liable or not) he had not caused'.[137] This, however, is not a corrective justice-based reason for imposing liability. In corrective justice, a person is only required to repair loss that is caused *by their wrongdoing*. If loss was caused by non-wrongful, ie non-negligent, conduct then it is not a wrongful loss. It is therefore irrelevant that the defendant employer in *McGhee* was responsible for all of the claimant's exposure to brick dust. Some of this exposure was negligent but some was innocent and unless it can be shown that the negligent exposure specifically was a cause of the claimant's dermatitis then the loss is not wrongful.

In a paper that approaches causal uncertainty from the perspective of corrective justice Weinrib suggests, however, that liability was appropriate in *McGhee*.[138] The essence of his argument is that in separating the 'innocent' and 'guilty' periods of exposure to brick dust, the defendant wrongly 'treats the employer's conduct as composed of two separate episodes each with its own legal character, rather than as a single arc of risk-creating action'.[139] Instead, Weinrib argues:

> The innocent segment is not truly innocent unless the defendant follows through by taking the precautions that make it so. In the absence of more specific evidence about

---

[136] Nolan (n 70) 189.
[137] *Fairchild* (n 13) [33] (Lord Bingham). See also Joe Thomson, '*Barker v Corus: Fairchild* Chickens Come Home to Roost' (2006) 10 *Edinburgh Law Review* 421, 424.
[138] Ernest Weinrib, 'Causal Uncertainty' *Oxford Journal of Legal Studies* (forthcoming).
[139] ibid.

the causal efficacy of the various segments of the defendant's conduct, causation of the injury can be attributed to the defendant's negligent risk-creating conduct as a whole.[140]

In other words, the negligent failure to provide showers to enable the claimant to wash the brick dust off his skin before cycling home means that the earlier exposure to brick dust takes on a negligent character: 'failure to undertake such measures means that the defendant is tortious in his conduct of the activity as a whole even if segments of it are innocent when done'.[141] This argument is persuasive, but ultimately it is not convincing. Chapter one highlighted the relationship between the causation inquiry and other elements of negligence, and here the specification of the defendant's breach of duty is instructive.[142] As Stapleton has highlighted, the definition of the defendant's breach of duty frames the causation question,[143] and she illustrates this through the example of *McWilliams v Arrol*.[144] The claimant in that case fell to his death from scaffolding and the defendant employer was negligent in failing to provide a safety harness. It is uncontroversial that in order to prove that failure to provide a harness was a cause of the death, it was necessary to show (on the balance of probabilities) that the victim would have worn a harness if it had been provided. The negligence action failed because the claimant was unable to prove this. If Weinrib's approach is applied to *McWilliams* then the failure to provide a harness makes the whole of the defendant's activity wrongful and removes the need to show that the precautions would have been effective, whereas Stapleton explains that for the claimant to succeed he would need to establish that reasonable care required not only the provision of safety harnesses but also instating a surveillance system to ensure that safety equipment was used.[145] Instead Weinrib's approach effectively assumes that the precautions would have been effective whereas, for example, the claim in *McGhee* would surely have faced a problem of causation if there was evidence that the claimant would not have used the showers even if they had been provided.

ii. Fairchild: *The 'Innocent Claimant' Argument*

In *Fairchild*, the House of Lords considered that any background risk of mesothelioma was so small it could effectively be discounted, so that it was possible to say that the claimant's harm had definitely been caused by the negligence of *a* former employer it was just impossible to say *which* former employer(s) in particular.[146] Lord Bingham said:

> [T]here is a strong policy argument in favour of compensating those who have suffered grave harm, at the expense of their employers who owed them a duty to protect them

---

[140] ibid.
[141] ibid.
[142] See ch 1, text to n 109.
[143] Jane Stapleton, 'Cause in Fact and the Scope of Liability for Consequences' (2003) 119 *Law Quarterly Review* 388.
[144] *McWilliams v Sir William Arrol Co Ltd* [1962] 1 WLR 295 (HL).
[145] Stapleton, 'Cause in Fact and the Scope of Liability for Consequences' (n 143) 391–92.
[146] *Fairchild* (n 13) [2] (Lord Bingham).

against that very harm and failed to do so, when the harm can only have been caused by breach of that duty.[147]

Similarly where the material contribution to risk approach is adopted in Canada, it is limited to cases where all sources of exposure to the harmful agent were negligent.[148] Green favours this requirement which is reflected in the first stage of her 'necessary breach analysis' that asks 'is it more likely than not that *a* defendant's breach of duty changed the normal course of events so that damage (including constituent parts of larger damage) occurred which would not otherwise have done so when it did?'.[149] She would therefore impose liability in *Fairchild* and *Barker* (since two out of his three periods of exposure were by the defendant employers) but not in *Sienkiewicz*.[150] Assuming that any non-negligent exposure could properly be disregarded, this would mean that the claimant could prove that he had suffered a 'wrongful loss' because he could prove that his loss had been caused by a defendant's negligence, so the claimant's side of the corrective justice equation would be fulfilled.

Two objections are raised here, one factual and one theoretical. The factual objection concerns the disregarding of the background risk of mesothelioma. In *Sienkiewicz*, Lord Phillips noted the possibility (although he was not willing to concede that it was any more than a possibility) of a small number of cases of mesothelioma being idiopathic, ie having an unknown origin.[151] In addition 'a significant proportion of those who contract mesothelioma have no record of occupational exposure to asbestos. The likelihood is that in their case the disease results from inhalation of asbestos dust that is in the environment'.[152] Mesothelioma can be caused by very fleeting exposures to asbestos.[153] Furthermore, even in *Fairchild*, not all of each claimant's former employers responsible for asbestos exposure were before the Court.[154] Even ignoring environmental risk, this meant that while the claimant was 'innocent' in *Fairchild* in the sense that he had been exposed to asbestos by his former employers, it was still possible that the disease had been caused entirely by other employers not before the Court. The defendants were 'guilty' in the sense that they had each negligently exposed the claimant to asbestos, but it was still not possible to say that even collectively they were 'guilty' in the sense that one or more of them had caused the disease.

In *Barker*, the claimant was responsible for a period of his own asbestos exposure, and in *Sienkiewicz*, the majority of the claimant's exposure to asbestos was not due to negligence but was present in the atmosphere of the area where she lived.

---

[147] ibid [33] (Lord Bingham). See also [41] (Lord Nicholls), [153] (Lord Rodger).
[148] *Clements v Clements* [2012] 2 SCR 181.
[149] Sarah Green, *Causation in Negligence* (Hart Publishing, 2015) 4.
[150] ibid 131.
[151] *Sienkiewicz* (n 19) [19].
[152] ibid [19] (Lord Phillips).
[153] Stapleton, 'Lords a'leaping' (n 15) 276–79.
[154] *Fairchild* (n 13) [33] (Lord Bingham).

This means that the 'innocent claimant' argument cannot justify the extension of the *Fairchild* exception to those cases. Nolan suggests that imposing liability on a defendant in these circumstances reflects an underlying assumption 'that somehow fault matters more than causation'.[155] But, as he explains:

> [W]ithin a corrective justice framework this assumption is simply false, for, as Allan Beever points out, 'from the perspective of corrective justice, the defendant is *entirely innocent* (with respect to the claimant) unless the claimant establishes *all* [the elements of the cause of action] against the defendant'.[156]

Imposing liability, whether joint and several or merely several, on a defendant whose negligence has not been proven to be a cause of the claimant's loss is simply not consistent with corrective justice-based interpersonal responsibility.

Turning to the theoretical basis of the innocent claimant argument, even if the *Fairchild* exception had been limited to cases satisfying the underlying factual assumptions, the innocent claimant argument fails to justify negligence liability in a way that is consistent with the demands of corrective justice because it requires the defendants to be collectivised rather than focusing on the individual interactions. In the Canadian decision in *Clements v Clements*, McLachlin CJ argued that such liability is consistent with corrective justice:

> The deficit in the relationship between the plaintiff and the defendants viewed as a group that would exist if the plaintiff were denied recovery is corrected. The plaintiff has shown that she is in a relationship of doer and sufferer of the same harm with a group of defendants as a whole, if not necessarily with each individual defendant.[157]

But corrective justice does not allow for the defendants to be aggregated in this way. As Beever explains:

> We cannot say that the claimant is deserving of recovery and leave it at that. It is irrelevant to corrective justice that the claimant deserves recovery from *someone* ... In corrective justice, it is necessary to say that the claimant is deserving of recovery *from some particular person*.[158]

This is because corrective justice is not concerned with the claimant and defendant separately, but with both of them in their interaction, so it is not enough to say that the claimant has suffered a wrongful loss. She must be able to say that her wrongful loss was caused by the particular defendant's wrongdoing before that particular defendant can have any corrective justice-based *interpersonal responsibility* to repair the loss. It is important that the responsibility is individual rather than collective as highlighted by Nolan. He argues that corrective justice cannot accommodate the focus on the claimant's wrongful loss because this 'refers not to

---

[155] Nolan (n 70) 175.
[156] ibid 175, citing Beever (n 41) 446.
[157] *Clements* (n 148) 202.
[158] Beever (n 41) 457.

each defendant as an individual but to the defendants as a collective entity'.[159] He explains:

> [W]hile it seems reasonable to say that, as between the claimant and the *defendants*, the equities favour the claimant, unless there is some good reason why we should 'collectivise' the defendants in this way, we still do not have a justification for the imposition of liability as between the claimant and each individual defendant.[160]

Moreover, 'from the individual defendant's point of view, it seems irrelevant that the other possible cause of the claimant's injury is the negligence of another person, as opposed to non-negligent conduct or a natural event'.[161] Even if the claimant has suffered a wrongful loss, in the sense that her loss was definitely caused by somebody else's negligence, corrective justice still only requires that loss to be repaired by the individual whose negligence caused it. There may be a strong reason to feel that the claimant is deserving of compensation, but if a particular defendant cannot be proved to have caused the loss then there is no corresponding reason to engage her individual responsibility.

iii. *Reformulating Damage in the Innocent Claimant Argument*

Indeed, although the attempt to reformulate the gist of the action as the risk of harm in *Barker* was ultimately flawed, it did highlight the House of Lords' awareness that the causation requirement is an indispensable element of the negligence inquiry. Commenting on similar approaches to redefining damage in American tort law, Ripstein and Zipursky explain:

> Some recent cases sidestep causation issues by redefining the category of injury that will permit recovery … All of these efforts tend to underscore, rather than to rebut, the centrality of causation in extant American tort law, as they indicate the need to shift to other categories, rather than abandoning causation itself.[162]

Beever's rationalisation of liability in the Canadian case of *Cook v Lewis*,[163] focuses on damage rather than on the causal link. In this case, two defendants each negligently fired their guns in the direction of the claimant whilst hunting and the claimant was hit by only one of the defendants but was unable to prove which one. The 'innocent claimant' argument arises on these facts because the physical damage was caused by negligence and the difficulty was in pinpointing whose negligence actually caused the damage. Similarly to the solution in *Fairchild*, the Court in *Cook v Lewis* held both defendants liable. Beever seeks to reconcile this decision with the demands of corrective justice by focusing on the defendants' interference with the claimant's right to bodily integrity. He explains that through

---

[159] Nolan (n 70) 174.

[160] ibid 174.

[161] ibid 175.

[162] Arthur Ripstein and Benjamin C Zipursky, 'Corrective Justice in an Age of Mass Torts' in Gerald J Postema (ed), *Philosophy and the Law of Torts* (Cambridge University Press, 2001) 219.

[163] *Cook v Lewis* [1951] SCR 830.

the tort of assault we can see that there can be a violation of the right to bodily integrity without contact with the claimant's body so it does not matter that the claimant is unable to prove that the defendant caused physical damage. Where a claimant suffers physical injury, the interference with her right to bodily integrity is repaired through damages, but in a situation like *Cook* the claimant would be unable to recover damages for the physical injury from any of the defendants on traditional principles of proof of causation. Beever argues that this inability to recover damages is, by extension, an interference with the right to bodily integrity.

Weinrib adopts a similar theory of 'remedial continuity' which conceives of the remedial right 'not as discrete from the substantive right but, so far as the relationship between the particular plaintiff and defendant is concerned, as its continuation'.[164] He explains:

> Of each defendant it can be said that their negligent act either injured the plaintiff or prevented the plaintiff from determining who injured them. But whichever of these either defendant actually did, both of them created a wrongful risk to the bodily security that was the plaintiff's right. The damage that then occurred was the materialisation of that risk. The shot that actually wounded the plaintiff damaged the plaintiff's right in its substantive aspect. The other shot interfered with that right in its remedial aspect, because, in the absence of a special doctrine to deal with this situation, it prevented the operation of the legal mechanism by which the plaintiff would receive damages equivalent to the restoration of their uninjured state.[165]

For both Beever and Weinrib this is distinct from a claim based on the loss of a right to sue or on evidentiary damage, and is more easily accepted because it is well established that the right to bodily integrity is protected through tort law. Porat and Stein, for example, have proposed an 'evidential damage' doctrine under which 'the defendant would be responsible for evidential damage if his wrongful actions have impaired the plaintiff's ability or reduced his chances to establish the facts necessary for prevailing in a direct-damage lawsuit'.[166] Rather than operating as an 'evidential remedy' by altering the burden of proof, they envision it as a 'compensatory remedy' that can be brought against a defendant whose negligence has prevented proof of causation. The basis for this solution is that 'the law should recognize that the plaintiff has a legitimate interest in ascertaining the cause of her or his direct damage whenever it is possible that this damage resulted from a wrongdoing'.[167] As Weinrib explains, solutions that are premised on the claimant having a remedial right to establish liability are problematic because 'the positing of an independent remedial right would have a broader implication: any person whose negligence rendered the plaintiff's case against someone else impossible to prove would be liable in tort even if innocent of the substantive negligence that

---

[164] Weinrib, 'Causal Uncertainty' (n 138).
[165] ibid.
[166] Ariel Porat and Alex Stein, *Tort Liability under Uncertainty* (Oxford University Press, 2001) 160–61.
[167] ibid 167.

lay at the root of the plaintiff's cause of action'.[168] For example he suggests, and indeed Porat and Stein intend, that 'a nurse whose negligence in keeping proper notes makes it impossible to determine whether a patient's death was due to medical malpractice would be held liable for interfering with the plaintiff's remedial right'.[169]

Beever avoids this difficulty by maintaining that the claimant's inability to recover damages is an interference with her right to bodily integrity and is only actionable against a defendant who has violated that right by negligently creating the risk of physical injury towards the claimant. This solution is problematic, however, because while the right to bodily integrity is protected through the tort of assault that is a trespass tort and actionable per se whereas negligence requires proof of damage. Beever does not engage with the question of whether the inability to restore bodily integrity through recovery of damages ought to be recognised as damage within the tort of negligence. Beever's solution also suffers from the circularity that Stevens highlights in relation to the evidentiary damage idea:

> In *Cook v Lewis*, if this argument works at all, it is impossible to distinguish its operation as against either hunter. This creates a circularity problem. If it is successful, then the claimant has a good claim against both hunters. The premise upon which the claim for loss is based is that the ability to bring a claim against the real culprit has been lost. If the argument succeeds against both hunters, this premise is incorrect. If it works against both, it works against neither.[170]

The question of whether interference with the remedial aspect of the claimant's right ought to be recognised as damage in negligence is not squarely addressed, and given the centrality of the damage requirement in negligence this claim needs to be addressed directly. Furthermore, it is arguable that this solution continues to aggregate the defendants in a way that is inconsistent with corrective justice which, as previously identified, is concerned with the defendants as individuals. The defendant only damages the remedial aspect of the claimant's right because of the presence of another defendant who also negligently interfered with the claimant's right, and the claimant is neither required nor able to distinguish between them, so the defendants are still being collectivised.

While it may be argued that there is a clear need to compensate the claimants in these cases, and that it is important to deter defendants from acting negligently, it is not the role of negligence liability to pursue these goals. The coherence of negligence law is dependent on its pursuit of corrective justice-based personal responsibility, so it cannot be adapted to plug the gaps in order to achieve these consequentialist goals. As seen in chapter one, if the law is 'stretched' to achieve compensation and/or deterrence then it will suffer in terms of coherence and tend to be measured in terms of how well it achieves these consequentialist aims

---

[168] Weinrib (n 138).
[169] ibid.
[170] Robert Stevens, *Torts and Rights* (Oxford University Press, 2007) 150.

leading critics, such as Atiyah, to suggest that negligence law should be abandoned in favour of a fairer compensation system.[171] It is important to recall that while negligence law gives effect to corrective justice this does not preclude distributive goals such as compensation and deterrence from being pursued through other, more appropriate, institutions. As Ripstein and Zipursky argue:

> [A]ll of the considerations put forward as reasons for attenuating the causation require-ment in tort law are more plausibly viewed as reasons for supplementing the legal system with public compensatory and deterrent systems, for tort law without causation will be both ineffective and arbitrary to the core.[172]

Indeed, distributive mechanisms may ultimately be more effective in respect of mesothelioma since, as Green highlights:

> Whilst ... *Sienkiewicz*, and s 3 Compensation Act 2006 have the appearance of being claimant friendly, this is only true if a discrete snapshot of claimants with a particular time frame is being considered. Over the long term, non-apportioned liability ... merely front-loads assistance to claimants ... The House of Lords' approach in *Barker* would have ensured that more claimants received at least some compensation. Parliament's intervention means that some claimants will now receive full compensation, but many more will receive nothing at all.[173]

In the absence of state schemes it may seem unjust to leave the claimant without compensation in negligence, and to allow the negligent defendant to escape liabil-ity, but this is unjust from a distributive perspective and from the perspective of corrective justice liability must be denied. As explained in chapter one, it is one thing to acknowledge that negligence liability has compensatory and deterrent effects, but it is another thing to say that it has compensatory and deterrent goals and to measure its success against those goals. As a system of compensation or deterrence it has been shown that negligence will necessarily be a failure because the goals are mutually truncating and incompatible with the correlative structure of the negligence action.[174] If we deny liability where causation is not proven then negligence law might be criticised for failing to achieve optimal compensation and deterrence but it is not appropriate to measure its success or failure on those terms. It would be like measuring a car in terms of how good it is as an aeroplane and criticising it because it is no good at flying—we are criticising it for failing to be something that it is not. Instead we are interested in how well negligence law succeeds at achieving corrective justice and, measured in those terms, negligence law is a success if it denies liability where causation cannot be proven.

---

[171] See ch 1 text to n 40; Patrick S Atiyah, *The Damages Lottery* (Hart Publishing, 1997) 32–95.
[172] Ripstein and Zipursky (n 162) 245.
[173] Green, *Causation in Negligence* (n 149) 146.
[174] See ch 1, text to n 37 and n 38.

B. Where Next?

This final section turns to the question of how the courts should resolve future cases that involve an evidentiary gap. Since the passing of the Compensation Act 2006, these cases must be divided into two categories: those cases involving mesothelioma, and those involving other diseases.

i. Mesothelioma

The House of Lords decision to impose several liability in *Barker* was reversed, and joint and several liability was reinstated in cases involving mesothelioma by section 3 of the Compensation Act 2006. The provisions of section 3 of the Compensation Act 2006 apply where the defendant is liable in tort in connection with damage caused to the victim by the disease 'whether by reason of having materially increased a risk or for any other reason'.[175] As Lord Phillips noted in *Sienkiewicz*, as and when more is understood about mesothelioma and the uncertainty surrounding the aetiology is removed the *Fairchild* test may no longer apply since there would be no need for an exceptional approach to causation if the evidentiary gap no longer existed.[176] The single fibre theory has already been discredited and courts must continue to assess future developments in the scientific evidence relating to the aetiology of mesothelioma. There is clear tension between judgments in this regard. In *Jones v Secretary of State for Energy and Climate Change*, one of the experts who had assisted the Court in *Fairchild* indicated that mesothelioma may now be addressed on the basis of a material contribution to harm:

> Dr Rudd was asked why, if his thesis was correct, there had been any need for the *Fairchild* exception. His response was that, in *Fairchild*, he and other experts had been instructed to consider from what source the asbestos fibre(s) that had caused the final step in the production of the malignant cell had come. They were unable to do so; hence the impossibility of establishing causation and the necessity for the creation of the *Fairchild* exception. He said that the expert evidence in *Fairchild* was given in the light of the knowledge of carcinogenesis at that time. Judgment at first instance was given in *Fairchild* in February 2001 and, since then understanding of the molecular basis of carcinogenesis has improved considerably. Dr Rudd said that, if he were asked the same questions now as he had been asked in *Fairchild*, he would say that it was probable that the asbestos fibres from each source had contributed to the carcinogenic process.[177]

---

[175] Compensation Act 2006, s 3(1).
[176] *Sienkiewicz* (n 19) [70] (Lord Phillips).
[177] *Jones v Secretary of State for Energy and Climate Change* [2012] EWHC 2936 (QB), [2012] All ER 271, [8.21]

More recently in *Heneghan v Manchester Dry Docks*, the Court noted that Dr Rudd 'has maintained a consistent position'.[178] Yet in *Sienkiewicz*, Lord Rodger indicated that the evidentiary gap still exists:

> If the day ever dawns when medical science can identify which fibre or fibres led to the malignant mutation and the course from which that fibre or those fibres came, then the problem which gave rise to the exception will have ceased to exist ... But, unless and until that time comes, the rock of uncertainty which prompted the creation of the *Fairchild* exception will remain.[179]

Crucially, however, there is no need to wait until science can provide a definitive answer since the legal standard is merely the balance of probabilities. McIvor observes that 'the Supreme Court in *Sienkiewicz* appeared to apply a much higher standard of proof, one more akin to the criminal law standard of "beyond all reasonable doubt"'.[180] It is essential that as courts examine claims in light of the developing state of scientific knowledge they apply the civil standard of proof correctly and are not unreasonably demanding.

ii. Other Diseases Involving an Evidentiary Gap

The Compensation Act 2006 only applies to mesothelioma which means that if the *Fairchild* test is applied to other diseases involving an evidentiary gap the *Barker* principle of several liability is applicable.[181] Although Lord Brown in *Sienkiewicz* suggested that the *Fairchild* exception should be limited to mesothelioma actions,[182] it has not been convincingly restricted in this way so it may potentially be applied more widely,[183] and the High Court in *Heneghan* recently held that the *Fairchild* exception was applicable to the claimant's lung cancer.[184] This final section considers whether the *Fairchild* exception can and should apply to claims involving any other diseases where there is an evidentiary gap. It will be argued that although the 'single harmful agent' rule adopted in *Wilsher* and approved in *Fairchild* seeks to provide a rational limit on when the *Fairchild* exception can apply, ultimately it cannot be justified. Turning to the question of whether the *Fairchild* exception should be applied outside the context of mesothelioma, it will be argued that since it lacks a coherent theoretical justification it ought not to be applied to other diseases. Although the application of several liability following

---

[178] *Heneghan v Manchester Dry Docks Ltd* [2014] EWHC 4190 (QB), [21].

[179] *Sienkiewicz* (n 19) [142].

[180] Claire McIvor, 'Debunking Some Judicial Myths About Epidemiology and Its Relevance to UK Tort Law' (n 67) 565.

[181] The *Barker* principle also applies to mesothelioma in Guernsey since the Compensation Act 2006 does not apply there: *International Energy Group Ltd v Zurich Insurance Plc UK* [2015] UKSC 33, [2015] 2 WLR 1471.

[182] *Sienkiewicz* (n 19) [187].

[183] Chris Miller, 'Causation in Personal Injury after (and before) *Sienkiewicz*' (2012) 32 *Legal Studies* 396, 410.

[184] *Heneghan* (n 178).

Barker is a 'fairer' solution than joint and several liability, this does not rescue the *Fairchild* exception from its lack of a theoretical basis.

iii. *The Single Harmful Agent Rule:* Wilsher v Essex Area Health Authority

As discussed in chapter four, the claimant in *Wilsher* was a baby born prematurely who later suffered blindness caused by retrolentalfibroplasia ('RLF'),[185] and his case was brought in the interval between *McGhee* and *Fairchild*. To recap the facts of this case, the defendant's negligence consisted of administering excess oxygen which carries a risk of RLF and the baby also suffered four other conditions due to being born prematurely, each of which also carried a risk of RLF. He was unable to prove on the balance of probabilities that the excess oxygen was a cause of his RLF using the but-for test. He therefore argued instead that the *McGhee* principle should be applied, and the defendant should be held liable on the basis that his negligence materially increased the risk of RLF. The majority of the Court of Appeal found that the *McGhee* principle was applicable because the aetiology of the claimant's RLF was unknown, and applying the *McGhee* test they found that the defendant's negligence had materially increased the risk of RLF. Browne-Wilkinson V-C dissented, and his dissenting opinion was approved in the House of Lords. He distinguished the facts in *Wilsher* because there was only one harmful agent in *McGhee*, ie brick dust, whereas in *Wilsher* there were five possible harmful agents, ie the excess oxygen created by the defendant and the four other naturally occurring conditions.

> The defendants failed to take reasonable precautions to prevent one of the possible causative agents (e.g. excess oxygen) from causing RLF. But no one can tell in this case whether excess oxygen did or did not cause or contribute to the RLF suffered by the plaintiff. The plaintiff's RLF may have been caused by some completely different agent or agents … To the extent that certain members of the House of Lords [in *McGhee*] decided the question on inferences from evidence or presumptions, I do not consider that the present case falls within their reasoning. A failure to take preventative measures against one out of five possible causes is no evidence as to which of those five caused the injury.[186]

Since it could not be proved that excess oxygen was a cause of the claimant's RLF it was not possible to say that the defendant's negligence had led to a material increase in an operative risk:

> [U]nless and until you can say that the plaintiff's RLF was caused by oxygen, it is impossible to say that the injury falls 'squarely within the risk'.[187]

---

[185] *Wilsher* (n 7).
[186] *Wilsher v Essex AHA* [1987] 1 QB 730 (CA), 779 (Browne-Wilkinson VC).
[187] ibid 780 (Browne-Wilkinson VC).

The House of Lords reversed the decision of the Court of Appeal in *Wilsher*, preferring Browne-Wilkinson's 'single harmful agent' rule.[188] Although Lord Hoffmann dissented on this point in *Fairchild*, arguing that the rule does not draw a 'principled distinction',[189] he later accepted a more nuanced form of the single harmful agent rule in *Barker* explaining:

> In my opinion it is an essential condition for the operation of the exception that the impossibility of proving that the defendant caused the damage arises out of the existence of another potential causative agent which operated in the same way. It may have been different in some causally irrelevant respect ... but the mechanism by which it caused the damage ... must have been the same. So, for example, I do not think that the exception applies when the claimant suffers lung cancer which may have been caused by exposure to asbestos or some other carcinogenic matter but may also have been caused by smoking and it cannot be proved which is more likely to have been the causative agent.[190]

The single harmful agent rule has been widely criticised. Nolan, for example, says that 'it is difficult to see any logic in this limitation',[191] and Beever says that it 'seems to be nothing more than an arbitrary restriction on the application of *Fairchild*'.[192] It will be argued that although this rule seeks to limit the level of scientific uncertainty under which a defendant may still be held liable, ultimately it falls victim to these criticisms for a number of reasons.

The *Fairchild* exception addresses a problem of proof of factual causation so it is essential to begin by identifying the exact nature of the causal problem before considering the appropriate solution. In terms of the NESS test for causation, it has been explained above that where there is an evidentiary gap it is impossible to describe a 'sufficient set' in general terms. But it is important here to specify precisely why this was impossible and also to restate the terms of the NESS test:

> [A] particular condition was a cause of (condition contributing to) a specific consequence if and only if it was a necessary element of a set of antecedent *actual* conditions that was sufficient for the occurrence of the consequence.[193]

In both *McGhee* and *Fairchild* it was known that the sufficient set that *actually* occurred contained the type of substance to which the defendant had exposed the claimant. The sufficient set that actually occurred in *McGhee* contained abrasions from brick dust, and in *Fairchild* it contained inhalation of asbestos fibres. What was unknown was *how* the particular substance forms a sufficient set—does a

---

[188] It will be recalled Lord Bridge held that *McGhee* had not laid down a new legal principle but that the Court had taken a 'robust and pragmatic approach' to the facts in order to draw a legitimate inference of causation. The House of Lords in *Fairchild* subsequently overruled this aspect of Lord Bridge's reasoning, holding that *McGhee* had in fact laid down a new legal principle and that the inferential approach was inappropriate, but it affirmed the outcome in *Wilsher*, so the 'single harmful agent' rule still applies.

[189] *Fairchild* (n 13) [72].

[190] *Barker* (n 71) [24] (Lord Hoffmann).

[191] Nolan (n 70) 173.

[192] Beever (n 41) 475.

[193] Wright, 'Causation in Tort Law' (n 27) 1790 (emphasis added).

sufficient set contain just one or many abrasions/asbestos fibres? In *Wilsher*, there
was an extra degree of uncertainty because it was impossible to say that the sufficient set that *actually* occurred even contained excess oxygen. A sufficient set
can contain excess oxygen. A sufficient set might also contain excess oxygen in
combination with one or more of the other conditions.[194] On these facts the single
harmful agent rule looks straightforward, and in the Court of Appeal decision in
Wilsher Lord Browne-Wilkinson saw the 'common sense' underlying it. The weaknesses of the rule become apparent, however, when attempts are made to refine
and justify it.

iv. What is a Single Harmful Agent?

In *Barker*, Lord Hoffmann suggested that the relevant question was not simply
whether there was a single harmful agent involved, but whether there was 'another
potential causative agent which operated in the same way'.[195] This will be called
the 'single causal mechanism' rule to distinguish it from the simple single agent
rule. The reality is that it is unclear when agents can be said to operate in the same
way. In *Novartis Grimsby v Cookson*, the claimant had contracted bladder cancer
after being exposed to amines through his own cigarette smoking as well as being
negligently exposed to amines in dyestuffs by the defendant employer. Although
the case was ostensibly resolved on a conventional basis through the application
of the 'doubles the risk' test,[196] Smith LJ said that it would be 'highly arguable that
the two sources of amines acted in a similar causative way'.[197] In contrast, Lord
Hoffmann had explicitly stated in *Barker*, albeit *obiter*, that carcinogens in asbestos
and cigarette smoke cannot be said to operate in the same way, but did not articulate why this is so. Wellington highlights a practical obstacle to applying the single
harmful agent rule:

> In many cases to which the *Fairchild* exception applies, the evidentiary gap that neces-
> sitates invoking the exception will be a lack of knowledge as to the mechanism by which
> the causative agents affect the body. In such cases, how can the claimant show that two
> potential causes operate via the same mechanism?[198]

It is difficult to see that the single agent rule can apply in the way described by
Lord Hoffmann in *Barker* so in reality it would apply only where there is truly a
single agent involved and would draw an arbitrary line that is not grounded in an
understanding of the causal mechanism.

The 'similarity' of the causal mechanism will depend on whose perspective this
is judged from as Miller argues. The claim in *XYZ v Schering* centred on the risks of

---

[194] *Wilsher* (CA) (n 186) 764-5 (Mustill LJ).
[195] *Barker* (n71) [24] (Lord Hoffmann).
[196] ch 3 argues that the 'doubles the risk' test is, in fact, misconceived.
[197] *Novartis Grimsby v Cookson* [2007] EWCA Civ 1261 [62].
[198] Kate Wellington, 'Beyond Single Causative Agents: The Scope of the *Fairchild* Exception post-
Sienkiewicz' (2013) 20 *Torts Law Journal* 208, 231.

harm associated with third generation (COC3), as opposed to second generation (COC2), oral contraceptive pills. Miller highlights the difficulty of determining whether the two different pills would constitute a 'single harmful agent':

> The difference between the generations lay in the relative proportions of two synthetic hormones—progestogen and oestrogen. To the teams of pharmacologists and biochemists who spent many years developing these COC3s, they will doubtless be seen as a great advance and very different from the inferior product they replaced. But to most women, after being advised by their GPs to make the change, they will be seen as 'substantially similar': they are simply 'the pill'; they are taken in the same way and for the same reason.[199]

This highlights the artificial nature of the rule. Indeed, Lord Hoffmann has more recently commented, focusing on the evidence in *Novartis* that the amines from dyestuff and cigarette smoke act upon the body in the same way, 'that liability should depend upon this interesting biochemical fact shows how absurd the test is'.[200] In *Sienkiewicz*, Lord Phillips sought to justify the single causal mechanism rule by reference to the type of causal process it implies:

> The possibility that mesothelioma may be caused as the result of the cumulative effect of exposure to asbestos dust provides a justification, even if it was not the reason, for restricting the *Fairchild* rule to cases where the same agent, or an agent acting in the same causative way, has caused the disease, for this possibility will not exist in respect of rival causes that do not act in the same causative way.[201]

Yet as Wellington identifies, the central assumption that agents acting through different causal mechanisms cannot operate cumulatively 'is not borne out by the case law'.[202] She points to the decision in *Shortell v BICAL Construction Ltd*,[203] where the victim was a smoker who was negligently exposed to asbestos and contracted lung cancer. Lord Hoffmann had explicitly stated in *Barker* that cigarette smoke and asbestos fall outside the scope of the single causal mechanism rule, yet the evidence in *Shortell* showed that cigarette smoke and asbestos could have acted cumulatively to cause lung cancer since there was a multiplicative interaction between the two factors.[204] The single harmful agent rule does not stand up to scrutiny in either of its forms so it would, indeed, place an arbitrary limit on the scope of the *Fairchild* exception.

---

[199] Chris Miller, 'Causation in Personal Injury: Legal or Epidemiological Common Sense?' (2006) 26 *Legal Studies* 544, 562.

[200] Lord Hoffmann, 'Fairchild and after' (n 83) 66.

[201] *Sienkiewicz* (n 19) [104] (Lord Phillips).

[202] Wellington, 'Beyond Single Causative Agents' (n 198) 214.

[203] *Shortell v BICAL Construction Ltd* Queen's Bench Division District Registry (Liverpool), 16 May 2008.

[204] ibid [37].

v. Limiting the Fairchild Exception to Mesothelioma

The recent decision in *Heneghan* has raised the question of whether the *Fairchild* exception can be applied to lung cancer.[205] The victim in that case had smoked cigarettes and had been exposed to asbestos by a number of negligent employers throughout his working life, not all of whom were before the Court. Indeed, the employer responsible for the longest period of employment, assessed at 56 per cent of the victim's asbestos exposure,[206] was not before the Court. The six defendant employers together were responsible for just 35.2 per cent of the exposure. Although the victim had smoked, it was agreed by both parties' experts that the extent of the total asbestos exposure meant that, on the balance of probabilities, he would not have developed lung cancer but for the asbestos exposure. In the High Court, Jay J found that since the contribution to the total asbestos exposure from each defendant was proportionately small it could not be said that 'but for' any particular exposure the victim would not have developed lung cancer.[207] Furthermore, the evidence did not allow him to conclude that all exposures had contributed to the disease, so the material contribution to harm test could not be satisfied. The claim was allowed to succeed on the basis of the *Fairchild* exception and, since the disease was not mesothelioma, the Compensation Act 2006 did not apply so liability was apportioned applying the *Barker* principle. It is not clear that the 'evidentiary gap' in *Heneghan* shares the same characteristics as the evidentiary gap that was present in *Fairchild*.

Jay J suggested that if a claim had been brought against the employer responsible for 56 per cent of the victim's asbestos exposure then, on the balance of probabilities, that exposure caused the claimant's lung cancer.[208] Steel comments:

> If that is so, then, assuming that this earlier exposure was in breach of duty, the claimant could establish a good claim against that earlier employer. The fundamental reason for applying the *Fairchild* rule then falls away. It is no longer impossible to attribute liability to a particular person and so it is no longer the case that the victim of a tort loses their right to compensation simply due to the multiplicity of wrongdoers.[209]

This highlights just how unsatisfactory the 'doubles the risk' test is. If medical understanding of the aetiology of the disease is so shrouded in mystery that it is not possible to establish that any of the shorter periods of employment contributed to the causal process, then there is little foundation for forming a rational belief that longer period of employment contributed, particularly where it represents barely more than 50 per cent of the exposure. The ability of any claimant to receive compensation would turn on the chance that slightly more than 50 per cent of her asbestos exposure had been with one employer. Meanwhile, a claimant

---

[205] *Heneghan* (n 178).
[206] ibid [61].
[207] ibid [20].
[208] ibid [61].
[209] Sandy Steel, 'On When *Fairchild* Applies' (2015) 131 *Law Quarterly Review* 363, 367.

whose exposure to asbestos was entirely attributable to the negligence of former employers, but with no single period of employment responsible for over 50 per cent of her exposure, would be unable to claim even if she brought all the employers before the Court. The applicability of the *Fairchild* exception cannot depend solely on the particular claimant being unable to prove causation on the balance of probabilities, but should be restricted to cases involving the same type of 'evidentiary gap' concerning the aetiology of the disease that makes it impossible for any claimant with multiple exposures to prove causation.

The evidence in *Heneghan* was that the causal mechanism of lung cancer is 'cumulative' in the sense that it is a multi-stage process and asbestos fibres play a role at each stage but there was disagreement between the experts as to whether this meant that each source of fibres had contributed to the process or had merely contributed to the risk. It is clear that expert evidence occupies a central role in determining causation in such cases, but courts must also ask the right questions. Labelling the process as 'cumulative' is unhelpful because it fails to illuminate the underlying causal mechanism. One of the experts in *Heneghan*, Dr Rudd, said that the process was cumulative and 'it was highly more likely that some of the fibres involved in these processes came from each source of exposure'.[210] But he also conceded that

> had the deceased not been employed by the Fourth Defendant (which contributed 2.5% of the total exposure), then he would still probably have developed lung cancer. Indeed, it was possible to go further: the same conclusion flows if any of the six Defendants were notionally removed from the frame

and Jay J reached the same conclusion on the question of what the position would be if all six defendants were notionally removed.[211] This is reminiscent of the issue encountered in chapter two in respect of the double hit hunters scenario—if we remove Hunter *A* then the victim would still have suffered the harm as he would have been shot by Hunter *B*. We saw that 'whereas the but-for test told us that Hunter *A* *made no difference to the outcome* because the walker would have died anyway so Hunter *A* is not a cause, the NESS test tells us that in order for the walker's death to have been prevented Hunter *A*'s shot *would have to be absent* so Hunter *A* is a cause, and that Hunter *B*'s shot would also have to be absent so Hunter *B* is also a cause'.[212] However, the asbestos does not form an 'indecipherable mass' in the sense envisioned in chapter two because while the sources of asbestos do combine together over time, they are sequential and the causal mechanism is sequential. In this case, and other cancers involving multi-stage causal processes, the problem of over-determination is therefore complicated by the extended time period covered, so proof of causation will not be simple but nothing is to be gained by proceeding to develop a solution that fails to give due weight to the underlying causal mechanism.

---

[210] *Heneghan* (n 178) [20].
[211] ibid [20].
[212] See ch 2, text to n 74.

The decision in *Fairchild* was quite openly motivated by considerations of 'fairness' and 'justice' and other 'policy' considerations. Similarly in *Barker*, the legal rules were adapted to achieve what was perceived as a fair solution, with Lord Walker going so far as to say 'I prefer to start with the more fundamental issue of apportionment, since it must have a bearing on how far and how fast the boundaries of the new principle are to be extended'.[213] This openness has received some praise, with Morgan commenting that the 'open acknowledgment [in *Fairchild*] that policy had to be considered was welcome',[214] and Khoury suggesting that in *Barker*:

> The House of Lords has arguably been more transparent and honest than the French Cour de cassation by recognising that proportional liability is, in such cases, imposed *without proof of causation* between the negligence and the *actual loss*, due, essentially, not to logical conceptual reasons, but to the existence of overriding policy objectives.[215]

But it is not sufficient merely to acknowledge openly that a decision departs from traditional principles because of policy concerns. In order to be justifiable, those policy concerns must be articulated and defended. Morgan thus criticised the *Fairchild* decision because '[t]he court must explain precisely which policies are at stake, and such analysis is missing in *Fairchild*'.[216] Broad reference to 'fairness' and 'justice' is also insufficient as Morgan explains:

> While these are noble sentiments, they should not be dignified with the label of policy. Such a 'policy' says nothing more than that 'injured claimants should recover', and therefore it is much too wide to be of any use in setting the boundaries of what, after all, is said to be an exceptional approach ... A convincing justification must explain why recovery is allowed in certain cases, *and in those cases only*.[217]

The argument that it is unjust to leave claimants uncompensated is also criticised by Nolan who says 'this position was not really fully articulated, no justification being given for the assertion that irredeemable evidential uncertainty should operate to the detriment of the negligent defendants rather than the blameless employee'.[218] It is also difficult to reconcile with the fact that under *Barker* there is a significant chance that the claimant will not be fully compensated if defendants can no longer be traced or have become insolvent. Kramer argues that 'while it is clearly unfortunate that the victims are not fully compensated, arguably this is a result of tortfeasors becoming insolvent and not of the apportionment rule itself'.[219] But if the *Fairchild* exception was devised to achieve a fair outcome for

---

[213] *Barker* (n 71) [107] (Lord Walker). See also [40]–[43] (Lord Hoffmann), [101] (Lord Rodger), [109] Lord Walker, [127] (Baroness Hale).

[214] Jonathan Morgan, 'Lost Causes in the House of Lords: *Fairchild v Glenhaven Funeral Services*' (2003) *Modern Law Review* 277, 279.

[215] Khoury, 'Causation and Risk in the Highest Courts of Canada, England and France (n 89) 130.

[216] Morgan, 'Lost Causes' (n 215) 279.

[217] ibid.

[218] Nolan (n 70) 172.

[219] Adam Kramer, 'Smoothing the Rough Justice of the Fairchild Principle' (2006) 122 *Law Quarterly Review* 547, 550.

claimants in the face of a practical problem of proof, surely this entire area of law is shaped by the desire to achieve a particular outcome in practice, so it does not make sense to ignore the practical impact of insolvency of defendants when designing the legal rule. As the decision in *BAI v Durham* attests, the decision in *Barker* has potential to impact on the interpretation of the terms of insurance contracts relating to the date that the injury was 'sustained' or 'contracted' because this may depend on whether the relevant damage is the risk or the physical harm.[220] The impact of the *Fairchild* exception on other areas further troubled the Court in *IEG v Zurich* which addressed the liability of insurers in Guernsey where the *Barker* apportionment principle continues to apply. As Lord Sumption bemoaned in his dissenting judgment:

> The argument continues, it is incumbent upon us now to develop what is called the '*Fairchild* enclave' by devising ancillary rules which appear to do justice to cases within the enclave, even if they are also out of line with the ordinary principles of law. The difficulty about this approach is that a measure of legal coherence seems desirable even within the *Fairchild* enclave.[221]

It should be remembered that section 3 of the Compensation Act 2006 only applies to mesothelioma, so the *Barker* principle of apportionment would apply to other evidentiary gap disease cases.[222] The decision to apply several liability in *Barker* seems fairer than joint and several liability, but what is fairness being measured against? Green has argued that

> although there may well exist strong arguments in favour of maintaining the rule against apportionment where causation can be established on an orthodox basis, it is perfectly reasonable to argue for a modification of that rule where the causal criteria have themselves been altered.[223]

This shows the significance of the *Barker* decision—the abandonment of the causation requirement in *Fairchild* meant that liability was no longer based on corrective justice which meant that other negligence doctrines could also be altered to achieve a particular vision of liability. As such, Steel explains '[t]he real function of 'risk' in *Barker* is as a practical tool for devising apportionment of liability in the interests of fairness'.[224] Steel goes on to explain that '[s]uch a consideration of fairness is only intelligible against the background that there is a (moral) difficulty with the proposition that a defendant who has not caused the mesothelioma may be liable for it'.[225]

---

[220] *BAI v Durham* (n 4).
[221] *Zurich* (n 181) [114] (Lord Sumption).
[222] The *Barker* principle also applies in Guernsey: *Zurich* (n 181).
[223] Sarah Green 'Winner Takes All' (2004) 120 *Law Quarterly Review* 566, 568.
[224] Sandy Steel, 'Uncertainty Over Causal Uncertainty: *Karen Sienkiewicz (Administratrix of the Estate of Enid Costello Deceased) v Greif (UK) Ltd*' (2010) 73 *Modern Law Review* 646, 653. See also *Barker* (n 71) [120]–[128] (Baroness Hale).
[225] Steel, 'Uncertainty Over Causal Uncertainty' (n 224) 653.

One proposal for providing a rational limit to *Fairchild* is that it could be limited to cases of 'industrial risk', but it will be argued that this does not provide a sound theoretical basis for the rule. As noted above, Lord Hoffmann considered that it was appropriate to apply the *Fairchild* principle in a claim brought by an employee against a former employer but not one brought by a patient against their doctor. Similarly, Amirthalingam has argued that to avoid throwing causation 'into the abyss of intuition and policy ... it would have been better if the case had been analysed squarely as one about liability for industrial (or unacceptable) risk'.[226] The difficulty with characterising the *Fairchild* exception as involving industrial risk is that this focuses on defendants to the detriment of the claimants. As discussed in chapter one, deterrence is a distributive goal centred on defendants and it cannot be properly achieved through the institution of negligence law which involves claimants too. If deterrence is to be implemented through the negligence system, which requires a claimant to bring an action, then there ought to be a focus on the needs of the claimant too. However, if the *Fairchild* exception applied only to industrial risk then a claimant exposed to asbestos in school (or university) would be unable to bring a successful claim against the school or the workmen employed by the school.[227] Although Amirthalingam's focus on the industrial context emphasises the deterrent effect of liability, he also seems concerned by the vulnerability of the claimant in the industrial context because he favours joint and several liability (subject to reduction for contributory negligence) since this 'leaves the risk of insolvency of other potential defendants on the defendants'.[228] As chapter one demonstrated, the structure of negligence law prevents distributive goals from being achieved in a comprehensive way, and within a negligence claim the competing distributive arguments relate to the claimant and the defendant separately and are mutually truncating.

Given that negligence law cannot fully achieve goals relating to either the claimant or the defendant, the decision about where the balance between the competing interests ought to lie is subjective. Morgan has highlighted this by contrasting the decisions of the Court of Appeal and the House of Lords in *Fairchild*:

> The perceived unfairness of [leaving the claimant without compensation] had ... not swayed the Court of Appeal ... who set against the unpalatability of denying recovery to sympathetic claimants the injustice of requiring a defendant who may well have had no causal connexion with the relevant injury to compensate the claimant's entire loss ... The House of Lords were content to assert that this injustice was 'plainly' outweighed by the injustice of the claimants recovering nothing, which reasoning is (equally plainly) contestable and certainly not much of an explanation.[229]

With this in mind, the decision in *Barker* to apply several liability seems to be the fairest solution because it seeks to find a balance between the competing interests

---

[226] Amirthalingam (n 117) 470–71.

[227] Such as occurred in *Knowsley Metropolitan Borough Council v Willmore* [2011] UKSC 10, [2011] 2 WLR 523, and *Williams v University of Birmingham* (n 108).

[228] Amirthalingam (n 117) 474.

[229] Morgan (n 215) 281.

of the claimant and the defendant. But it must be made clear that this is a personal preference as to which distributive arguments ought to be prioritised over others in a context where such a choice simply has to be made and articulated clearly because of the underlying incompatibility of achieving distributive goals through a system of corrective justice. Given that proportionate liability cannot be justified by principles of corrective justice-based interpersonal responsibility it is preferable for the *Fairchild* exception to be restricted to claims in respect of mesothelioma.

Lord Hoffmann recently conceded that it would have been preferable for the Court to have denied liability in *Fairchild*:

> In retrospect, I think the most satisfactory outcome would have been for their Lordships in their judicial capacity to have adhered to established principle, wrung their hands about the unfairness of the outcome in the particular case, and recommended to the Government that it pass appropriate legislation. Then judiciary and legislature would each have been functioning within its proper sphere: the judges not creating confusion in the common law by trying to legislate for special cases and Parliament amending the common law where fairness and the public interest appeared to demand it.[230]

This has been echoed in the decision in *IEG v Zurich* where Lord Neuberger and Lord Reed said:

> When the issue is potentially wide-ranging with significant and unforeseeable (especially known unknown) implications, judges may be well advised to conclude that the legislature should be better able than the courts to deal with the matter in a comprehensive and coherent way. It can fairly be said that the problem for the courts in taking such a course is that the judges cannot be sure whether Parliament will act to remedy what the courts may regard as an injustice.
>
> The answer to that may be for the courts to make it clear that they are giving Parliament the opportunity to legislate, and, if it does not do so, the courts may then reconsider their reluctance to develop the common law. For the courts to develop the law on a case-by-case basis, pragmatically but without any clear basis in principle, as each decision leads to a new set of problems requiring resolution at the highest level, as has happened in relation to mesothelioma claims, is not satisfactory either in terms of legal certainty or in terms of public time and money.
>
> In the case of mesothelioma claims, there can be no real doubt but if *Fairchild* had been decided the other way, in accordance with normal common law principles, Parliament would have intervened very promptly. That may very well have been a better solution, but it can fairly be said that that observation is made with the wisdom of hindsight.[231]

Although courts facing future problems of causation cannot know how Parliament will respond, the repercussions of the *Fairchild* decision for the coherence of negligence law that can be seen with the benefit of hindsight should not be forgotten easily.

---

[230] Lord Hoffmann (n 83) 68.
[231] *IEG v Zurich* (n 181) [210]–[211] (Lord Neuberger and Lord Reed).

V. Conclusion

This chapter has shown that it is important to understand the different approaches in *Barker* in detail. On first impression, Lord Hoffmann's reconceptualisation of the gist of the action as the risk of harm appears to reconcile the *Fairchild* test with the principles of corrective justice; since the claimant can only prove that the defendant's negligence exposed him to the risk of harm he is only compensated for the risk exposure rather than the physical harm. The subtle change in the formulation of the *Fairchild* test also appears to bring it in line with the *Wardlaw* test of material contribution to harm, the only difference being that the 'harm' where *Fairchild/Barker* applies is 'the risk of harm'. In comparison, the reasoning adopted by Baroness Hale seems flimsy and unprincipled since it is based on vague notions of what she feels is a 'fair' balance between the competing interests of the claimant and defendant. This chapter has shown, however, that Lord Hoffmann's approach is conceptually problematic and is not consistent with corrective justice. This means that just like the *Fairchild* exception, the *Barker* apportionment rule is motivated by considerations of distributive justice and instrumentalism. Given that such considerations cannot provide a coherent foundation for negligence liability, Baroness Hale's open acknowledgement that the solution was based on vague considerations of fairness more accurately reflects the inherent uncertainty created by instrumentalist accounts of negligence.

The developments of the *Fairchild* test therefore serve to illustrate the incoherence that is inevitable when courts adapt the rules of causation to pursue instrumentalist goals rather than corrective justice. Since causation is an essential ingredient of corrective justice-based personal responsibility, there should be no liability when the causal link cannot be proved. While this may leave a pressing social need to compensate victims of a particular disease, as well as a need to deter defendants from engaging in risky conduct, it is not the primary function of negligence law to pursue these objectives. Compensation, deterrence and other instrumentalist goals do not provide a coherent theoretical justification for negligence, so the success of negligence law should not be measured against how well it achieves these goals. As noted in chapter one, Weinrib has observed that 'the legal regime of personal injuries can be organised either correctively or distributively ... nothing about personal injury as such consigns it to the domain of a particular form of justice'.[232] In light of the evidentiary gap relating to mesothelioma which prevents attribution of interpersonal responsibility in most cases this is a particular type of personal injury that ought to be addressed through a distributive mechanism.

---

[232] Ernest Weinrib, 'Corrective Justice' (1992) 77 *Iowa Law Review* 403, 415.

Conclusion

This work set out to identify a coherent legal solution to a range of problems of evidential uncertainty in causation in negligence but, as explained in the introduction, it was first necessary to situate the issue within the broader context of causation in negligence more generally. This involved addressing both the nature and function of the tort of negligence as well as the role played by causation within that tort.

In chapter one, it was argued that the tort of negligence is most coherently conceived as a system of corrective justice. It was seen that Aristotelian corrective justice and Kantian Right together form an account of interpersonal responsibility that prioritises coherence and morality. Causation was shown to be an essential element of interpersonal responsibility, but it was also seen that it has a limited role; causation provides the factual nexus between the claimant and the defendant but it must be supplemented by notions of wrongdoing and damage which sculpt the boundaries of interpersonal responsibility. This must be reflected in the negligence doctrines, so while the various doctrines must join together to 'articulate a single normative sequence', the doctrine of causation must have a clearly defined role within that sequence. Chapter one therefore explained the interrelationship between the causation requirement, and the elements of actionable damage, duty of care, breach of duty and quantification of loss.

Having shown in chapter one that causation has a vital but limited role in interpersonal responsibility, chapter two considered the demands that negligence law makes of the causation doctrine and argued that it is essential to isolate factual causation, ie the fact of being *a* cause, from evaluative conclusions that a condition was *the* responsible cause. As a test of factual causation, the NESS test was shown to be preferable to the but-for test because it is better matched to the philosophical account of what it means to be a cause. In straightforward cases the NESS test does not complicate the causal inquiry, and in more complex cases it is able to resolve causal problems that the but-for test cannot. It was also shown that when applying the NESS test it is necessary to clearly identify the damage forming the gist of the action from the outset because the causal problem will vary depending on whether the damage is 'divisible' or 'indivisible'.

Applying the NESS test, twinned with a clear understanding of damage, it was possible to clarify the scope and meaning of the *Wardlaw* test of 'material contribution to harm'. This analysis showed that in cases of divisible damage where there is more than one source of the harmful agent the *Wardlaw* test equates to an application of the but-for test to a portion of the total damage suffered by the claimant. In cases of indivisible damage the *Wardlaw* test may constitute an exception to the

but-for test. Crucially, however, it does not constitute an exception to the requirement of causation; it merely compensates for the conceptual inadequacies of the
but-for test. The NESS test operates in a simpler way to overcome the same conceptual inadequacies

Having defined clearly the role of causation, and the conceptual requirements
for a test of causation, the book then turned to evidential problems relating to
proof of causation. Chapter three addressed proof of causation in general and
sought to reconcile legal and scientific approaches in order that fuller use can be
made of the available evidence before resorting to exceptional tests of causation.
It emphasised the value of the qualitative nature of the balance of probabilities
standard of proof which requires courts to evaluate the reliability of evidence
rather than reducing it to a rigid quantitative tool. Epidemiological evidence was
studied in order to observe some wider points about the relationship between
legal and scientific standards, as well as to highlight the value of epidemiology in
proof of causation. Epidemiological evidence has become closely associated with
the 'doubles the risk' test for causation, and it was argued that while the 'doubles
the risk' test is flawed this should not mislead us into dismissing the value of epidemiological evidence since a doubling of risk is not taken as indicative of a causal
relationship in epidemiology which is a much richer discipline than the focus on
relative risk implies.

Chapter four considered the issue of loss of a chance in medical negligence cases.
This argument was raised in *Hotson* and in *Gregg* by claimants who were unable to
prove that the defendant doctor's negligent delay in diagnosis of their illness had
caused them to suffer physical harm. Instead they sought proportionate recovery
of the physical harm by reformulating the damage as the loss of a chance of avoiding physical harm. Drawing on the understanding of the interrelationship of the
doctrines of damage, causation and quantification previously set out in chapter
one, it was argued that the House of Lords was right to reject their claims because
a patient in these circumstances does not have an objective chance of being cured.
This means that if proportionate recovery were allowed it would effectively award
damages for the physical harm but apply a discount to reflect the degree of doubt
surrounding proof of causation. However, this chapter proposed a more limited
role for 'loss of opportunity' as an independent form of damage leading to limited
recovery in some medical negligence scenarios. It was argued that although an
epistemological chance should not normally be considered to constitute damage,
negligent misdiagnosis leading to a reduction in epistemological chance entails
damage to the patient's autonomy interest because she is prevented from making
informed choices relating to treatment with her initial prospects of cure. Interference with the patient's autonomy interest ought to be recognised as damage in this
specific context because of the issues of interpersonal responsibility between the
doctor and patient in the diagnosis of existing illness.

Chapter five turned to the issue of the evidentiary gap that first arose in *McGhee*
and subsequently in *Fairchild* and, drawing on the wider understanding of negligence and causation developed in the previous chapters, asked how to achieve

a coherent solution to this problem. The problem of the evidentiary gap relates to the scientific understanding of the aetiology of the disease, so the NESS test is unable to resolve the problem but it does enable us to pinpoint the precise nature of the causal problem facing the claimant. This highlighted that it is not possible to define a 'sufficient set' of conditions to cause the disease, so it is not possible to draw a meaningful inference of causation. The *McGhee/Fairchild* test of 'material increase in the risk of harm' clearly therefore constitutes a relaxation of the causation requirement, so it makes a departure from principles of corrective justice.

This chapter evaluated Lord Hoffmann's attempt to rationalise the *Fairchild* test in *Barker* by reconceptualising the gist of the action as the 'risk of harm' and apportioning liability according to the extent of the defendant's negligent contribution to the total risk. It was shown that this solution is not consistent with corrective justice, because it conflates the notions of damage and breach by making 'risk exposure' central to both.

Both the *Fairchild* test and the *Barker* apportionment principle were shown to be inconsistent with principles of corrective justice and motivated instead by considerations of distributive justice such as the desire to compensate the victims of mesothelioma in *Fairchild*, and the desire to achieve a 'fair' balance between the burdens placed on each party in *Barker*. As shown at the outset of this book, distributive goals cannot provide a coherent foundation for negligence law; the bipolar structure of negligence liability imposes an artificial limit on the attainment of distributive goals, and they are mutually truncating. This results in indeterminacy and incoherence in the law. Where the *Fairchild* principle applies it is preferable that it should apply in conjunction with the *Barker* apportionment principle in order to balance the competing interests of claimants and defendants, but this rests on little more than the author's personal preference as, inevitably, any solution premised on distributive principles must. It is therefore important that the application of the *Fairchild* test should be limited to claims for mesothelioma. It is also important that the courts continue to follow advances in medical science and that they revert to orthodox principles of causation as and when the evidentiary gap is closed.

BIBLIOGRAPHY

Aagard TS, 'Identifying and Valuing the Injury in Lost Chance Cases' (1998) 96 *Mich L Rev* 1335

Amirthalingam, K, 'The Changing Face of the Gist of Negligence' in J Neyers, E Chamberlain and S Pitel (eds), *Emerging Issues in Tort Law* (Hart Publishing, 2007)

—— 'Causation and the Medical Duty to Refer' (2012) 128 *LQR* 208

Anderson GM, 'Disease Causation and the Extent of Material Contribution' (2006) 15 *SLT* 87

Atiyah PS, *The Damages Lottery* (Hart Publishing, 1997)

Bagshaw R, 'Publication Review: Responsibility and Fault' (2000) 116 *LQR* 321

Bailey SH, 'Causation in Negligence: What is a Material Contribution?' (2010) 30 *LS* 167

Barker K and Steele J, 'Drifting Towards Proportionate Liability: Ethics and Pragmatics' (2015) *CLJ* 49

Barnes DW, 'Too Many Probabilities: Statistical Evidence of Tort Causation' (2001) 64 *L & Contemp Problems* 191

Beauchamp TL and Rosenberg A, *Hume and the Problem of Causation* (Oxford University Press, 1981)

—— and Childress JF, *Principles of Biomedical Ethics* (7th edn, Oxford University Press, 2012)

Beever A, 'Cause-in-fact: Two Steps Out of the Mire' (2001) 51 *U Toronto LJ* 327

—— '*Gregg v Scott* and Loss of a Chance' (2005) 24 *U Queensland LJ* 201

—— *Rediscovering the Law of Negligence* (Hart Publishing, 2007)

—— 'Corrective Justice and Personal Responsibility in Tort Law' (2008) 28 *OJLS* 475

—— 'Formalism in Music and Law' (2011) 61 *U Toronto LJ* 213

Bevan N, '*Williams v University of Birmingham*: Personal Injury—Negligence—Asbestos' [2012] *JPI Law* 1

Boon A, 'Causation and the Increase of Risk' (1988) 51 *MLR* 506

Bradford Hill A, 'The Environment and Disease: Association or Causation?' (1965) 58 *Proceedings of the Royal Society of Medicine* 295

Broadbent A, 'Fact and Law in the Causal Inquiry' (2009) 15 *Legal Theory* 173

—— 'Epidemiological Evidence in Proof of Specific Causation' (2011) 17 *Legal Theory* 237

—— *Philosophy of Epidemiology* (Palgrave Macmillan, 2013)

Broadie S and Rowe C, *Aristotle: Nicomachean Ethics: Translation, Introduction and Commentary* (Oxford University Press, 2002)

Brown R, 'Inferring Cause in Fact and the Search for Legal "Truth"' in R Goldberg (ed), *Perspectives on Causation* (Hart Publishing, 2011)

Brown S and Lindsey S, 'Seeing the Wood for the Trees—*Loftus-Brigham* and Apportionment of Damage' (2005) 21 *Const LJ* 431

Burrows A, 'Uncertainty About Uncertainty: Damages for Loss of a Chance' [2008] *JPI Law* 31

Callum C, *The UK Smoking Epidemic: Deaths in 1995* (Health Education Authority, 1998)

Cane P, 'Justice and Justifications for Tort Liability' (1982) 2 *OJLS* 30

—— 'Corrective Justice and Correlativity in Private Law' (1996) 16 *OJLS* 471

—— *The Anatomy of Tort Law* (Hart Publishing, 1997)

—— 'Distributive Justice and Tort Law' [2001] *NZ L Rev* 401

—— 'Responsibility and Fault: a Relational and Functional Approach to Responsibility' in P Cane and J Gardner (eds), *Relating to Responsibility: Essays in Honour of Tony Honoré on his 80th Birthday* (Hart Publishing, 2001)

—— 'Tort Law as Regulation' (2002) 31 *Common Law World Rev* 305

—— Responsibility in Law and Morality (Hart Publishing, 2002)

—— 'The Anatomy of Private Law Theory: A 25th Anniversary Essay' (2005) 25 *OJLS* 203

—— 'Rights in Private Law' in D Nolan and A Robertson (eds), *Rights and Private Law* (Hart Publishing, 2011)

Caun L, 'Multiple Causes of Injury' [2003] *JPI Law* 96

Chapman B, 'Ernie's Three Worlds' (2011) 61 *U Toronto LJ* 179

Chung KC, Swanson JA, Schmitz D, et al, 'Introducing Evidence-based Medicine to Plastic and Reconstructive Surgery' (2009) 123 *Plastic and Reconstructive Surgery* 1385

Clark T and Nolan D, 'A Critique of *Chester v Afshar*' (2014) 34 *OJLS* 659

Coggon D and Taylor AN, 'Causation and Attribution of Disease in Personal Injury Cases: A Scientific Perspective' [2009] *JPI Law* 12

Coleman J, 'Moral Theories of Torts: Their Scope and Limits: Part 1' (1982) 1 *Law and Phil* 371

—— 'Corrective Justice and Wrongful Gain' (1982) 11 *J Legal Stud* 421

—— 'Moral Theories of Torts: Their Scope and Limits: Part 2' (1983) 2 *Law and Phil* 5

—— *Risks and Wrongs* (Oxford University Press, 1992)

—— 'The Mixed Conception of Corrective Justice' (1992) 77 *Iowa L Rev* 427

Davies M, 'The Road From Morocco: *Polemis* Through *Donoghue* to No-Fault' (1982) 45 *MLR* 534

Dawid AP, 'The Role of Scientific and Statistical Evidence in Assessing Causality' in R Goldberg (ed), *Perspectives on Causation* (Hart Publishing, 2011)

Dixon O, 'Science and Judicial Proceedings' in Wionarski (ed), *Jesting Pilate and Other Papers and Addresses by the Right Honourable Sir Owen Dixon* (WS Hein, 1965)

Dore M, 'A Commentary on the Use of Epidemiological Evidence in Demonstrating Cause-in-Fact' (1983) 7 *Harvard Environmental Law Review* 429

Dworkin G, *The Theory and Practice of Autonomy* (Cambridge University Press, 1988)

Edmond G and Mercer D, 'Rebels without a Cause?: Judges, Medical and Scientific Evidence and the Uses of Causation' in I Freckleton and D Mendelson, *Causation in Law and Medicine* (Ashgate, 2002)

Elliott T, 'A Break with the Past? Or More of the Same? *Montgomery v Lanarkshire Health Board*' (2015) 31 *PN* 190

Englard I, *Corrective and Distributive Justice: From Aristotle to Modern Times* (Oxford University Press, 2009)

Feldschreiber P, L Mulcahy and S Day, 'Biostatistics and Causation in Medicinal Product Liability Suits' in R Goldberg (ed), *Perspectives on Causation* (Hart Publishing, 2011)

Finkelstein C, 'Is Risk a Harm?' (2003) 151 *U Pa L Rev* 963

Fischer DA, 'Tort Recovery for Loss of a Chance' (2001) 36 *Wake Forest L Rev* 605

—— 'Insufficient Causes' (2006) *94 Ky LJ* 277

Fletcher GP, 'Law and Morality: A Kantian Perspective' (1987) 87 *Colum L Rev* 533

Foster C, *Choosing Life, Choosing Death: The Tyranny of Autonomy in Medical Ethics and Law* (Hart Publishing, 2009)

French, R, 'Science and Judicial Proceedings: Seventy-Six Years On' (2010) 84 *Australia LJ* 244

Fulham-McQuillan S, 'Judicial Belief in Statistics as Fact: Loss of Chance in Ireland and England' (2014) 30 *PN* 9

Fumerton R and Kress K, 'Causation and the Law: Preemption, Lawful Sufficiency, and Causal Sufficiency' (2001) 64 *L & Contemp Problems* 83

Gardner J, 'What is Tort Law For? Part 1: The Place of Corrective Justice' (2011) 30 *Law & Phil* 1

Geistfeld M, 'Scientific Uncertainty and Causation in Tort Law' (2001) 54 *Vanderbilt L Rev* 1011

Gold S, 'Causation in Toxic Torts: Burdens of Proof, Standards of Persuasion, and Statistical Evidence' (1986) 96 *Yale LJ* 376

Goldberg R, *Causation and Risk in the Law of Torts: Scientific Evidence and Medicinal Product Liability* (Hart Publishing, 1999)

—— 'Causation, Idiopathic Conditions and the Limits of Epidemiology' (2009) 13 *Edin LR* 282

—— 'Using Scientific Evidence to Resolve Causation Problems in Product Liability: UK, US and French Experiences' in R Goldberg (ed), *Perspectives on Causation* (Hart Publishing, 2011)

Gordley J, 'Tort Law in the Aristotelian Tradition' in D Owen (ed), *Philosophical Foundations of Tort Law* (Clarendon Press, 1995)

Green L, 'The Causal Relation Issue in Negligence Law' (1962) 60 *Mich L Rev* 543

Green S, 'Winner Takes All' (2004) 120 *LQR* 566

—— 'The Risk Pricing Principle: A Pragmatic Approach to Causation and Apportionment of Damages' (2005) 4 *Law, Probability & Risk* 159

—— 'Coherence of Medical Negligence Cases: A Game of Doctors and Purses' (2006) 14 *Med LR* 1

—— 'Risk Exposure and Negligence' (2006) 122 *LQR* 386

—— 'Contributing to the Risk of Confusion? Causation in the Court of Appeal' (2009) 125 *LQR* 44

—— *Causation in Negligence* (Hart Publishing, 2015)

Greenberg P, 'The Cause of Disease and Illness: Medical Views and Uncertainties' in I Freckleton and D Mendelson, *Causation in Law and Medicine* (Ashgate, 2002)

Greenland S, 'Relation of Probability of Causation to Relative Risk and Doubling Dose: a Methodologic Error that has Become a Social Problem' (1999) 89 *American Journal of Public Health* 1166

—— and Robins, J, 'Epidemiology, Justice, and the Probability of Causation' (2000) 40 *Jurimetrics* 321

Grubb A, 'Causation and Medical Negligence' [1988] 47 *CLJ* 350

Gullifer L, 'One Cause after Another' (2001) 117 *LQR* 403

Haack S, *Evidence Matters: Science, Proof, and Truth in the Law* (Cambridge University Press, 2014)

Hamer D, '"Chance Would be a Fine Thing": Proof of Causation and Quantum in an Unpredictable World' (1999) 23 *Melb U L Rev* 557

Hart HLA and Honoré T, *Causation in the Law* (2nd edn, Clarendon Press, 1985)

Hill T, 'A Lost Chance for Compensation in the Tort of Negligence by the House of Lords' (1991) 54 *MLR* 511

Hoffmann L, 'Causation' (2005) 121 *LQR* 592

—— 'Causation' in R Goldberg (ed), *Perspectives on Causation* (Hart Publishing, 2011)

—— 'Fairchild and after' in A Burrows, D Johnston and R Zimmerman (eds), *Judge and Jurist: Essays in Memory of Lord Rodger of Earlsferry* (Oxford University Press, 2013)

Hollingsworth K, 'Theorising Children's Rights in Youth Justice: The Significance of Autonomy and Foundational Rights' (2013) 76 *MLR* 1046

Hogg M, 'Re-establishing Orthodoxy in the Realm of Causation' (2007) 11 *Edin LR* 8

—— 'Causation and Apportionment of Damages in Cases of Divisible Injury' (2008) 12 *Edin LR* 99

—— 'Duties of Care, Causation, and the Implications of *Chester v Afshar*' (2005) 9 *Edin LR* 156

—— 'Developing Causal Doctrine' in R Goldberg (ed), *Perspectives on Causation* (Hart Publishing, 2011)

Honoré T, 'The Morality of Tort Law—Questions and Answers' in D Owen (ed), *Philosophical Foundations of Tort Law* (Oxford University Press, 1995)

—— 'Necessary and Sufficient Conditions in Tort Law' in D Owen (ed), *Philosophical Foundations of Tort Law* (Oxford University Press, 1995)

—— 'Medical Non-Disclosure, Causation and Risk: *Chappel v Hart*' (1999) 7 *Torts LJ* 1

—— *Responsibility and Fault* (Hart Publishing, 1999)

Howarth D, 'Three Forms of Responsibility: On the Relationship Between Tort Law and the Welfare State' (2001) 60 *CLJ* 553

—— 'Many Duties of Care—Or a Duty of Care? Notes from the Underground' (2006) 26 *OJLS* 449

Hume D, *An Abstract of a Treatise of Human Nature*, ed. JM Keynes and P Sraffa (Cambridge University Press, 1938) 11f.

Jansen N, 'The Idea of a Lost Chance' (1999) 19 *OJLS* 271

—— 'Duties and Rights in Negligence: A Comparative and Historical Perspective on the European Law of Extracontractual Liability' (2004) 24 *OJLS* 443

Jones MA, 'Proving Causation—Beyond the "But For" Test' (2006) 22 *PN* 251

—— 'Causation and Psychiatric Damage' (2008) 24 *PN* 255

Judicial College, *Guidelines for the Assessment of General Damages in Personal Injury Cases* (11th edn, Oxford University Press, 2012)

Kant I, *Foundations of the Metaphysics of Morals*, (trans. Lewis White Beck) (Bobbs-Merrill Education Publishing, 1969)

—— *The Metaphysics of Morals* (trans Mary Gregor) (Cambridge University Press, 1991)

Keeler J, 'Thinking Through the Unthinkable: Collective Responsibilities in Personal Injury Law' (2001) 30 *Common Law World Rev* 349

Kelley PJ, 'Causation and Justice: A Comment' (1978) 56 *Wash U L Q* 635

Khoury L, *Uncertain Causation in Medical Liability* (Hart Publishing, 2006)

—— 'Causation and Risk in the Highest Courts of Canada, England and France' (2008) 124 *LQR* 103

King Jr, JH, 'Causation, Valuation, and Chance in Personal Injury Torts Involving Preexisting Conditions and Future Consequences' (1981) 90 *Yale LJ* 1353

Kinsky C, 'SAAMCo 10 Years on: Causation and Scope of Duty in Professional Negligence Cases' (2006) 22 *PN* 86

Klimchuk D, 'On the Autonomy of Corrective Justice' (2003) 23 *OJLS* 49

Knutsen ES, 'Clarifying Causation in Tort' (2010) 33 *Dalhousie LJ* 153

Kobyasheva A, 'Using Epidemiological Evidence in Tort Law: a Practical Guide' (2014) 30 *PN* 125

Kramer A, 'Smoothing the Rough Justice of the *Fairchild* Principle' (2006) 122 *LQR* 547

Kress K, 'Formalism, Corrective Justice and Tort Law' (1991) 77 *Iowa L Rev* i

—— 'Coherence and Formalism' (1993) 16 *Harvard Journal of Law & Public Policy* 639

Laleng P, '*Sienkiewicz v Greif (UK) Ltd* and *Willmore v Knowsley Metropolitan Borough Council*: A Material Contribution to Uncertainty?' (2011) 74 *MLR* 767

Lee J, 'Causation in Negligence: Another Fine Mess' (2008) 24 *PN* 194

Lewis D, 'Causation' (1973) 70 *J Phil* 556

Lord Hope of Craighead, 'James McGhee—A Second Mrs Donoghue?' (2003) 62 *CLJ* 587

Lord Neuberger of Abbotsbury, 'Loss of a Chance and Causation' (2008) 24 *PN* 206

Lunney M, 'What Price a Chance?' (1995) 15 *LS* 1

—— 'Causation, Science and Sir Owen Dixon' (2004) 9 *Australian Journal of Legal History* 205

MacCormick N, 'Taking Responsibility Seriously' (2005) 9 *Edin LR* 168

Mackie JL, *The Cement of the Universe: A Study of Causation* (Clarendon Press, 1980)

Maclean A, *Autonomy, Informed Consent and Medical Law* (Cambridge University Press, 2009)

Magnusson E, 'Statistical Proof of Causation' in I Freckleton and D Mendelson, *Causation in Law and Medicine* (Ashgate, 2002)

Martin R, 'Categories of Negligence and Duties of Care: *Caparo* in the House of Lords' (1990) 53 *MLR* 824

Maskrey S and Edis W, '*Chester v Afshar* and *Gregg v Scott*: Mixed Messages for Lawyers' [2005] *JPI Law* 205

Mason K and Brodie D, 'Bolam, Bolam—Wherefore Are Thou Bolam?' (2005) *Edin LR* 298

McBride N, 'Duties of Care—Do They Really Exist?' (2004) 24 *OJLS* 417

McGregor H, 'Loss of Chance: Where Has it Come From and Where is it Going?' (2008) 24 *PN* 2

McIvor C, *Third Party Liability in Tort* (Hart Publishing, 2006)

—— 'Debunking some Judicial Myths about Epidemiology and its Relevance to UK Tort Law' (2013) 21 *Med LR* 553

—— 'The "Doubles the Risk" Test for Causation and Other Related Judicial Misconceptions about Epidemiology' in S Pitel, J Neyers and E Chamberlain (eds), *Tort Law: Challenging Orthodoxy* (Hart Publishing, 2013)

—— 'The Use of Epidemiological Evidence in UK Tort Law' in S Loue (ed), *Global Perspectives in Forensic Epidemiology* (Springer-Verlag, 2013)

McLean S, *A Patient's Right to Know: Information Disclosure, the Doctor and the Law* (Dartmouth Publishing, 1995)

—— *Autonomy, Consent and the Law* (Routledge Cavendish, 2010)

Miller C, 'Coal Dust, Causation and Common Sense' (2000) 63 *MLR* 763

—— 'Judicial Approaches to Contested Causation: Fairchild v. Glenhaven Funeral Services in Context' (2002) 1 *Law, Probability & Risk* 119

—— '*Gregg v Scott*: Loss of Chance Revisited' (2005) 4 *Law, Probability & Risk* 227

—— 'Causation in Personal Injury: Legal or Epidemiological Common Sense?' (2006) 26 *LS* 544

—— 'Loss of Chance in Personal Injury: a Review of Recent Developments' (2006) 5 *Law, Probability & Risk* 63

—— 'Liability for Negligently Increased Risk: the Repercussions of *Barker v Corus (UK) Plc*' (2009) 8 *Law, Probability & Risk* 39

—— 'NESS for Beginners' in Richard Goldberg (ed), *Perspectives on Causation* (Hart Publishing, 2011)

—— 'Causation in Personal Injury after (and before) *Sienkiewicz*' (2012) 32 *LS* 396

—— 'Causation in Personal Injury Law: The Case for a Probabilistic Approach' (2014) 33 *Topoi* 385

Miola J, 'Autonomy Rued, Ok?' (2006) 14 *Med LR* 108

Moore MS, *Causation and Responsibility: An Essay in Law, Morals, and Metaphysics* (Oxford University Press, 2009)

Morgan J, 'Lost Causes in the House of Lords: *Fairchild v Glenhaven Funeral Services*' (2003) 66 *MLR* 277

—— 'Tort, Insurance and Incoherence' (2004) 67 *MLR* 384

—— 'The Rise and Fall of the General Duty of Care' (2006) 22 *PN* 206

—— 'Policy Reasoning in Tort Law: the Courts, the Law Commission and Critics (2009) 125 *LQR* 215

Mullany NJ, 'Common Sense Causation—An Australian View' (1992) 12 *OJLS* 431

Mullender R, 'Negligence Law, the Welfare State, and "Our Moral Life"' (2009) 25 *PN* 187

National Children's Bureau, *Guidelines for Research* (NCB, 2003)

Neyers JW, 'The Inconsistencies of Aristotle's Theory of Corrective Justice' (1998) 11 *Canadian J L & Jurisprudence* 311

Noah L, 'An Inventory of Mathematical Blunders in Applying the Loss-of-a-Chance Doctrine' (2005) 24 *Rev Litig* 369

Nolan D, 'New Forms of Damage in Negligence' (2007) 70 *MLR* 59

—— 'Causation and the Goals of Tort Law' in A Robertson and Tang Hang Wu (eds), *The Goals of Private Law* (Hart Publishing, 2009)

—— 'Deconstructing the Duty of Care' (2013) 129 *LQR* 559

—— 'Damage in the English Law of Negligence' (2013) 4 *J Euro Tort L* 259

Oppenheim R, 'The "Mosaic" of Tort Law: the Duty of Care Question' [2003] *JPI Law* 151

Ost S, 'Balancing Autonomy Rights and Protection: Children's Involvement in a Child Safety Online Project' (2013) 27 *Children and Society* 208

Owen DG, 'Why Philosophy Matters to Tort Law' in DG Owen (ed), *Philosophical Foundations of Tort Law* (Clarendon Press, 1995)

Peel E, 'Lost Chances and Proportionate Recovery: *Barker v Corus*' [2006] *LMCLQ* 289

Perry SR, 'The Moral Foundations of Tort Law' (1992) 77 *Iowa L Rev* 449

—— 'Protected Interests and Undertakings in the Law of Negligence' (1992), 42 *U Toronto LJ* 247

—— 'Professor Weinrib's Formalism: The Not-So-Empty Sepulchre' (1993) 16 *Harv J L & Pub Pol'y* 597

—— 'Risk, Harm, and Responsibility' in DG Owen (ed), *Philosophical Foundations of Tort Law* (Oxford University Press, 1995)

—— 'Honoré on Responsibility for Outcomes' in P Cane and J Gardner (eds), *Relating to Responsibility: Essays in Honour of Tony Honoré on his 80th Birthday* (Hart Publishing, 2001)

—— 'Responsibility for Outcomes, Risk, and the Law of Torts' in GJ Postema (ed), *Philosophy and the Law of Torts* (Cambridge University Press, 2001)

—— 'The Role of Duty of Care in a Rights-Based Theory of Negligence Law' in A Robertson and Tang Hang Wu (eds), *The Goals of Private Law* (Hart Publishing, 2009)

Plowden S and Volpe H, '*Fairchild* and *Barker* in MRSA Cases: Do *Fairchild* and *Barker* Provide an Argument for a Relaxation of Causation Principles in Claims for Hospital Acquired MRSA?' [2006] *JPI Law* 259

Porat A and Stein A, *Tort Liability under Uncertainty* (Oxford University Press, 2001)

—— 'Indeterminate Causation and Apportionment of Damages: An Essay on *Holtby, Allen, and Fairchild*' (2003) 23 *OJLS* 667

Posner RA, 'The Concept of Corrective Justice in Recent Theories of Tort Law' (1981) 10 *JLS* 187

Priaulx N, 'Joy to the World! A (Healthy) Child is Born! Reconceptualising "Harm" in Wrongful Conception' (2004) 13 *Social & Legal Studies* 5

—— 'Injuries That Matter: Manufacturing Damage in Negligence' ExpressO Available at: http://works.bepress.com/nicolette_priaulx/2

Price DPT, 'Causation: The Lords' Lost Chance?' (1989) 38 *ICLQ* 735

Raz J, *The Morality of Freedom* (Clarendon Press, 1986)

Reece H, 'Losses of Chances in the Law' (1996) 59 *MLR* 188

Ripstein A and Zipursky BC, 'Corrective Justice in an Age of Mass Torts' in GJ Postema (ed), *Philosophy and the Law of Torts* (Cambridge University Press, 2001)

Robertson A, 'Constraints on Policy-Based Reasoning in Private Law' in A Robertson and Tang Hang Wu (eds), *The Goals of Private Law* (Hart Publishing, 2009)

—— 'Justice, Community Welfare and the Duty of Care' (2011) 127 *LQR* 370

—— 'Rights, Pluralism, and the Duty of Care' in D Nolan and A Robertson (eds), *Rights and Private Law* (Hart Publishing, 2011)

—— 'On the Function of the Law of Negligence' (unpublished conference paper, Obligations VI: Challenging Orthodoxy conference, Canada, 18–20 July 2012)

Robertson DW, 'Causation in the Restatement (Third) of Torts: Three Arguable Mistakes' (2009) 33 *Wake Forest L Rev* 1007

Robinson GO, 'Probabilistic Causation and Compensation for Tortious Risk' (1985) 14 *J Legal Stud* 779

Rothman KJ, *Epidemiology: An Introduction* (Oxford University Press, 2002)

——, S Greenland and T Lash, *Modern Epidemiology* (3rd edn, Wolters Kluwer, 2008)

Scherpe J, 'A New Gist?' (2006) 65 *CLJ* 487

Schroeder CH, 'Corrective Justice and Liability for Increasing Risks' (1989) 37 *UCLA L Rev* 439

—— 'Causation, Compensation, and Moral Responsibility' in DG Owen (ed), *Philosophical Foundations of Tort Law* (Clarendon Press, 1995)

Scott W, 'Causation in Medico-Legal Practice: A Doctor's Approach to the 'Lost Opportunity' Cases' (1992) 55 *MLR* 521

Sheinman H, 'Tort Law and Corrective Justice' (2003) 22 *Law & Phil* 21

Smith J, 'Causation—the Search for Principle' [2009] *JPI Law* 101

Smith SA, 'Publication Review: Idea of Private Law' (1996) 112 *LQR* 363

—— *Contract Theory* (Clarendon Press, 2004)

Stanton K, 'Professional Negligence: Duty of Care Methodology in the Twenty First Century' (2006) 22 *PN* 134

Stapleton J, 'The Gist of Negligence: Part 1 Minimal Actionable Damage' (1988) 104 *LQR* 213

—— 'The Gist of Negligence: Part 2 The Relationship Between "Damage" and Causation' (1988) 104 *LQR* 389

—— 'Duty of Care and Economic Loss: A Wider Agenda' (1991) 107 *LQR* 249

—— 'Tort, Insurance and Ideology' (1995) 58 *MLR* 820

—— 'Negligent Valuers and Falls in the Property Market' (1997) 113 *LQR* 1

—— 'Duty of Care Factors: a Selection from the Judicial Menus' in P Cane and J Stapleton (eds), *The Law of Obligations: Essays in Celebration of John Fleming* (Oxford University Press, 1998)

—— 'Publication Review—Causation and Risk in the Law of Torts: Scientific Evidence and Medicinal Product Liability' (2000) 116 *LQR* 506

—— 'Unpacking "Causation"' in P Cane and J Gardner (eds), *Relating to Responsibility: Essays in Honour of Tony Honoré on his 80th Birthday* (Hart Publishing, 2001)

—— 'Lords a'leaping Evidentiary Gaps' (2002) 10 *Torts LJ* 276

—— 'Cause in Fact and the Scope of Liability for Consequences' (2003) 119 *LQR* 388

—— 'The Golden Thread as the Heart of Tort Law: Protection of the Vulnerable' (2003) 24 *Aust Bar Rev* 135

—— 'Loss of the Chance of Cure from Cancer' (2005) 68 *MLR* 996

—— 'Two Causal Fictions at the Heart of U.S. Asbestos Doctrine' (2006) 122 *LQR* 189

—— 'Occam's Razor Reveals an Orthodox Basis for *Chester v Afshar*' (2006) 122 *LQR* 426

—— 'Choosing What We Mean by "Causation" in the Law' (2008) 73 *MLR* 433

—— 'Factual Causation and Asbestos Cancers' (2010) 126 *LQR* 351

—— 'Reflections on Common Sense Causation in Australia' in S Degeling, J Edelman and J Goudkamp (eds), *Torts in Commercial Law* (Thomson Reuters Australia, 2011)

—— 'The *Fairchild* Doctrine: Arguments on Breach and Materiality' (2012) 71 *CLJ* 32

—— 'Factual Causation, Mesothelioma and Statistical Validity' (2012) 128 *LQR* 221

—— 'Unnecessary Causes' (2013) 129 *LQR* 39

—— 'An "Extended But-For" Test for the Causal Relation' [2015] 35 *OJLS* 697

Stauch M, 'Causation, Risk, and Loss of Chance in Medical Negligence' (1997) 17 *OJLS* 205

—— 'Taking the Consequences for Failure to Warn of Medical Risks' (2000) 63 *MLR* 261

—— 'Risk and Remoteness of Damage in Negligence' (2001) 64 *MLR* 191

—— The Law of Medical Negligence in England and Germany (Hart Publishing, 2007)

—— '"Material Contribution" as a Response to Causal Uncertainty: Time for a Rethink' (2009) 68 *CLJ* 27

Steel S, 'Uncertainty Over Causal Uncertainty: Karen Sienkiewicz (Administratrix of the Estate of Enid Costello Deceased) v Greif (UK) Ltd' (2010) 73 *MLR* 646

—— 'On When *Fairchild* Applies' (2015) 131 *LQR* 363

—— and Ibbetson D, 'More Grief on Uncertain Causation in Tort' (2011) 70 *CLJ* 451

Steele J, *Risks and Legal Theory* (Hart Publishing, 2004)

—— *Tort Law: Texts, Cases and Materials* (2nd edn, Oxford University Press, 2011)

Stevens R, *Torts and Rights* (Oxford University Press, 2007)

—— 'Rights and Other Things' in D Nolan and A Robertson (eds), *Rights and Private Law* (Hart Publishing, 2012)

Stiggelbout M, 'The Case of 'Losses in Any Event': a Question of Duty, Cause or Damages?' (2010) 30 *Legal Stud* 558

Thomson J, 'The Raising of Lazarus: The Resurrection of *McGhee v National Coal Board*' (2003) 7 *Edin LR* 80

—— '*Barker v Corus: Fairchild* Chickens Come Home to Roost' (2006) 10 *Edin LR* 421

Tribe LH, 'Trial by Mathematics: Precision and Ritual in the Legal Process' (1971) 84 *Harvard Law Review* 1329

Tse MH, 'Tests for Factual Causation: Unravelling the Mystery of Material Contribution, Contribution to Risk, the Robust and Pragmatic Approach and the Inference of Causation' (2008) 16 *Torts LJ* 249

Uberoi M, 'Does the Law of Tort Still Recognise The Concept of Individual Responsibility?' (2003) 7 *EMIS Personal Injury Service* 1

Voyiakis E, 'The Great Illusion: Tort Law and Exposure to Danger of Physical Harm' (2009) 72 *MLR* 909

Waldron J, 'Moments of Carelessness and Massive Loss' in DG Owen (ed), *Philosophical Foundations of Tort Law* (Oxford University Press, 1995)

Walker VR, 'Uncertainties in Tort Liability for Uncertainty' (2002) 1 *Law, Probability & Risk* 175

Weekes R, 'Not Seeing the Wood for the Trees—Risk Analysis as an Alternative to Factual Causation in *Fairchild*' (2003) 12 *Nott LJ* 18

Weir T, 'The Maddening Effect of Consecutive Torts' (2001) 60 *CLJ* 237

Weinrib EJ, 'A Step Forward in Factual Causation' (1975) 38 *MLR* 518

—— 'Toward a Moral Theory of Negligence Law' (1983) 2 *Law & Phil* 37

—— 'The Insurance Justification and Private Law' (1985) 14 *JLS* 681

—— 'Law as a Kantian Idea of Reason' (1987) 87 *Colum L Rev* 472

—— 'Causation and Wrongdoing' (1987) 63 *Chicago-Kent Law Review* 407

——'Legal Formalism: On the Immanent Rationality of Law' (1988) 97 *Yale LJ* 949

—— 'The Special Morality of Tort Law' (1989) 34 *McGill LJ* 403

—— 'Corrective Justice' (1992) 77 *Iowa L Rev* 403

—— 'The Jurisprudence of Legal Formalism' (1993) 16 *Harv J L & Pub Pol'y* 583

——'The Gains and Losses of Corrective Justice' (1994) 44 *Duke LJ* 277

—— *The Idea of Private Law* (Harvard University Press, 1995)

—— 'Corrective Justice in a Nutshell' (2002) 52 *U Toronto LJ* 349

—— 'The Disintegration of Duty' in Stuart Madden (ed), *Exploring Tort Law* (Cambridge University Press, 2005)

—— *Corrective Justice* (Oxford University Press, 2012)

——'Causal Uncertainty' *OJLS* (forthcoming)

Wellington K, 'Beyond Single Causative Agents: The Scope of the *Fairchild* Exception post-*Sienkiewicz*' (2013) 20 *Torts LJ* 208

Wheat K, 'Progress of the Prudent Patient: Consent after *Chester v Afshar*' (2005) 60 *Anaesthesia* 217

Wicks E, *Human Rights and Healthcare* (Hart Publishing, 2007)

Williams G, 'Causation in the Law' (1961) 19 *CLJ* 62

Witting C, 'Duty of Care: An Analytical Approach' (2005) 25 *OJLS* 33

—— 'The House That Dr Beever Built: Corrective Justice, Principle and the Law of Negligence' (2008) 71 *MLR* 621

Wright R, 'Causation in Tort Law' (1985) 73 *Cal L Rev* 1735

—— 'Actual Causation vs. Probabilistic Linkage: The Bane of Economic Analysis' (1985) 14 *J Legal Stud* 435

—— 'The Efficiency Theory of Causation and Responsibility: Unscientific Formalism and False Semantics' (1987) 63 *Chi-Kent L Rev* 553

—— 'Causation, Responsibility, Risk, Probability, Naked Statistics, and Proof: Pruning the Bramble Bush by Clarifying the Concepts' (1988) 73 *Iowa L Rev* 1001

—— 'Substantive Corrective Justice' (1992) 77 *Iowa L Rev* 625

—— 'Right, Justice, and Tort Law' in DG Owen (ed), *Philosophical Foundations of Tort Law* (Clarendon Press, 1995)

—— 'Once More into the Bramble Bush: Duty, Causal Contribution, and the Extent of Legal Responsibility' (2001) 54 *Vanderbilt L Rev* 1071

—— 'The Grounds and Extent of Legal Responsibility' (2003) 40 *San Diego L Rev* 1425

—— 'Acts and Omissions as Positive and Negative Causes' in J Neyers, E Chamberlain and S Pitel (eds), *Emerging Issues in Tort Law* (Hart Publishing, 2007)

—— 'Liability for Possible Wrongs: Causation, Statistical Probability, and the Burden of Proof' (2008) 41 *Loy L A L Rev* 1295

—— 'Proving Causation: Probability versus Belief' in R Goldberg (ed), *Perspectives on Causation* (Hart Publishing, 2011)

—— 'The NESS Account of Natural Causation: A Response to Criticisms' in R Goldberg (ed), *Perspectives on Causation* (Hart Publishing, 2011)

INDEX

UNIVERSITY OF WINCHESTER
LIBRARY